REDUCING INEQUALITY

ADDRESSING THE WICKED PROBLEMS ACROSS PROFESSIONS AND DISCIPLINES

BRUCE S. JANSSON

cognella® | ACADEMIC PUBLISHING

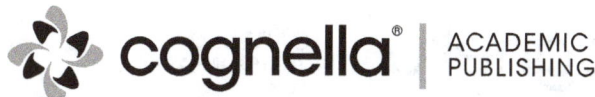

Bassim Hamadeh, CEO and Publisher
Claire Benson, Project Editor
Karen Wiley, Production Editor
Jess Estrella, Senior Graphic Designer
Alexa Lucido, Senior Licensing Specialist
Joyce Lue, Interior Designer
Natalie Piccotti, Director of Marketing
Kassie Graves, Vice President of Editorial
Jamie Giganti, Director of Academic Publishing

Copyright © 2019 by Bruce S. Jansson. All rights reserved. No part of this publication may be reprinted, reproduced, transmitted, or utilized in any form or by any electronic, mechanical, or other means, now known or hereafter invented, including photocopying, microfilming, and recording, or in any information retrieval system without the written permission of Cognella, Inc. For inquiries regarding permissions, translations, foreign rights, audio rights, and any other forms of reproduction, please contact the Cognella Licensing Department at rights@cognella.com.

Trademark Notice: Product or corporate names may be trademarks or registered trademarks, and are used only for identification and explanation without intent to infringe.

Copyright © 2013 by iStockphoto LP/kr7ysztof.

Printed in the United States of America.

ISBN: 978-1-5165-2002-2 (pbk) / 978-1-5165-2003-9 (br) / 978-1-5165-4637-4 (al)

CONTENTS

ABOUT THE AUTHOR — IV

INTRODUCTION — V

CHAPTER 1
REDUCING INCOME INEQUALITY BY ATTACKING ITS TEN CAUSES — 1

CHAPTER 2
THE FIRST TWO STOPS OF THE EQUALITY ROLLER COASTER FROM 1750 TO 1830 AND FROM 1865 THROUGH THE 1920s — 39

CHAPTER 3
THE THIRD AND FOURTH STOPS OF THE EQUALITY ROLLER COASTER FROM 1933 TO 1981 AND FROM 1982 TO THE PRESENT — 76

CHAPTER 4
WHAT WE CAN LEARN FROM HISTORY: WHAT CAUSES THE EQUALITY ROLLER COASTER TO MOVE UPWARD AND DOWNWARD? — 135

CHAPTER 5
IUOPS THAT MIGHT REDUCE INCOME INEQUALITY IN THE UNITED STATES FROM THE BOTTOM-UP — 162

CHAPTER 6
IUOPS THAT MIGHT INCREASE UPWARD MOBILITY, HOPE, ACCESS TO OPPORTUNITIES, AND ACCESS TO HEALTHCARE—AND TO REDUCE DISCRIMINATION — 176

CHAPTER 7
CONCEPTUALIZING IUOPS: FROM WORKING PAPERS TO POLICY BRIEFS — 206

CHAPTER 8
FINDING RESOURCES TO UPLIFT ORDINARY PEOPLE (RUOPS) — 226

CHAPTER 9
MOVING TOWARD GREATER INCOME EQUALITY IN THE POLITICAL ARENA — 247

INDEX — 271

ABOUT THE AUTHOR

Bruce Jansson earned an MA at Harvard University in American history and his Ph.D. at the University of Chicago at the School of Social Service Administration. He is the Margaret W. Driscoll/Louise M. Clevenger Professor of Social Policy and Social Administration at the Suzanne Dworak-Peck School of Social Work at the University of Southern California. He has authored numerous books on social policy including three widely used text books: *Becoming an Effective Policy Advocate*, *The Reluctant Welfare State*, and *Social Welfare Policy and Advocacy: Advancing Social Justice through 8 Policy Sectors*. He has written a critical analysis of national priorities titled *The Sixteen Trillion Dollar Mistake: How the United States Bungled Its National Priorities from the New Deal to the Present*. He has been featured on media platforms such as National Public Radio, and was awarded a major grant from the Patient-Centered Outcomes Research Institute in 2011.

INTRODUCTION

This book evolved from a doctoral class that I teach at the Suzanne-Dworak School of Social Work at the University of Southern California. Each of my students developed promising solutions. I hope that my strategies might also be effective with students in 16 other professions and disciplines that I list below. Here are my pedagogical strategies:

- Ground the subject in 16 marginalized populations that they encounter in their professional work to make clear that extreme income inequality pervades the lives of (at least) half of the American population—and therefore the persons they see on a daily basis in their professional work
- Provide international data to demonstrate the United States possesses greater income inequality than 20 other industrialized nations. Have students explore promising innovations in another nation that are related to ones they develop in the United States
- Ground the subject in the history of the United States by drawing on the work of economic historians to demonstrate that the United States has had extended periods of relative equality and relative inequality. Contend that extreme income inequality is not inevitable by referring to the recent period of relative equality from the mid-1930s through the 1970s as contrasted with the current period of extreme income inequality that began in the 1980s
- Use non-technical language and visuals that I define in this book to make the subject accessible to non-economists including Initiatives to Uplift Ordinary People (IUOPs), Resources to Uplift Ordinary People (RUOPs), Fair Exchanges (that combine IUOPs and RUOPs) and Equality Roller Coaster (that describes the pendulum swings between equality and inequality)
- Provide many examples of IUOPs placed under each of the ten hypothesized causes of extreme income inequality—and discuss how to design them
- Provide many examples of RUOPs and Fair Exchanges
- Discuss the politics of inequality. Candidly analyze contemporary barriers while identifying promising strategies

This book can be used by students in each of 16 disciplines and professions, with assignment of additional readings that are specific to each of them. They include:

- Social workers help marginalized populations surmount poverty, addictions, and homelessness
- Public policy professionals identify policies and regulations that can reduce income inequality
- Public health professionals identify health impediments to employment in different populations and communities
- Physicians/nurses/occupational therapists/physical therapists help patients surmount chronic health conditions that keep them from the workforce or that unnecessarily shorten their lives
- Lawyers help marginalized populations deal with legal problems that deprive them of resources, civil rights, and incarceration
- Journalists cover income inequality in the mass media
- Engineers develop ways to help vulnerable populations reach employment sites rather than commuting long distances
- Architects develop innovative and affordable houses for low income persons, as well as units in existing housing
- City planners develop new or redesigned communities that provide supportive environments for persons in the lower economic echelon
- Psychologists critically analyze whether a "culture of poverty" exists, as well as the unique perspectives that low-income people bring to their interventions
- Sociologists analyze how behaviors of low-income persons differ from affluent persons in the context of different levels of income, different kinds of neighborhoods, and different job possibilities
- Historians trace the evolution of inequality in the context of specific cultural, economic, and political factors
- Political scientists analyze the politics of redistribution of income
- Economists analyze strategies for increasing the wages of low-income workers as well as alternative strategies for policies to reduce inequality
- Accountants can identify tax policies that can promote income equality
- Business professionals can identify strategies to raise incomes of marginalized groups within businesses and by developing new business run by members of these groups

I use the term "Equality Enhancing Programs" (EEPs) to describe institutions of higher education that provide courses in one or more of these disciplines and professions to redress extreme income inequality. Some of them are identified at the end of Chapter 9, but many more will be added to this list in coming years.

A web site, uplifting ordinary people.org, will be developed to augment this text. The site will include additional promising policies/readings for redressing extreme income inequality contributed by users of this book.

REDUCING INCOME INEQUALITY BY ATTACKING ITS TEN CAUSES

The United States has an extreme level of income inequality that is higher than twenty other industrialized nations (Wilkinson & Pickett, 2009). This high level of income inequality has, I hypothesize (at least) ten causes that include: exposure to extreme income inequality; large populations immersed in poverty and near poverty; low levels of upward mobility; low levels of hope among persons in lower economic strata; high levels of discrimination against persons in lower economic strata; lack of access to opportunities of persons in lower economic strata due to low funding of social, economical housing, and educational investments including entitlements like Social Security, as well as lack of access to credit from banking institutions; poor access to mental health and health systems with resulting poor health; inadequate government resources to fund social, economic, and educational investments stemming from low levels of taxation and government waste; failure to place limits on the income and wealth of economic elites; and a political system structured to discriminate against voters and interests that favor greater economic equality. I hypothesize that these ten causes of income inequality, singly and together, contribute to disproportionate levels of income inequality by specific persons and populations who fall into (at least) sixteen at-risk populations that I discuss subsequently.

Consider these ten causes to be ten hypotheses that require more data to prove their effects in causing extreme income inequality in the United States. These hypotheses partly stem from data in contemporary America—a period of extreme income inequality (Piketty, 2014). They stem, as well, from laboratory findings that simulate effects on subjects as they occupy positions of power and income. They stem from data about the sheer incidence of poverty and inequality in the United States. They stem from data about low levels of social, educational, and economic investments in the United States as compared to many other industrialized nations. They stem from low rankings of the United States with respect to high levels of discrimination as compared to other nations. They also stem from the disproportionate levels of discrimination and income inequality among 16 vulnerable populations.

I use historical materials, moreover, that provide contextual information that sheds light on why the United States has moved between extended periods of income equality and income inequality, More research is needed to examine why the nation moved between four major eras of income equality and income inequality from the colonial period to the present.

The ten causes are:

Cause 1: Exposure to extreme income inequality in the United States by members of all social classes. This extreme income inequality rivals levels last seen in the Gilded Age of the 1880s when millions of impoverished immigrants co-existed with economic elites headed by billionaires like John D. Rockefeller and Andrew Carnegie. The top 20% owns more than 84% of the wealth and the bottom 40% owns 0.3% (Fritz, 2015). As comedian Chris Rock recently told reporter Frank Rich, "Oh, people don't even know. If poor people knew how rich (the) rich people are, there would be riots in the street." *Most Americans believe the richest fifth owns 59% of the wealth and the bottom 40% owns 9%* (Fritz, 2015).

Exposure to extreme income inequality has toxic effects on persons and populations. Americans who struggle to meet their basic needs are economically, socially, and politically marginalized in a society with extreme disparities of wealth. While wealthy people send their children to well-funded private schools, charter schools, and public schools, low-income families send their children to poorly funded inner city and rural schools. Social psychologists and epidemiologists have measured the toxic effects of extreme inequality in laboratory settings and discovered that persons given advantages in laboratory games are more likely to feel entitled, believe they deserve to win, and resort to bullying more often than participants who are not given advantages (Miller, 2012). Later, I will discuss research findings that demonstrate that persons who live in nations with extreme income inequality are more likely to develop an array of social problems than counterparts in nations with less economic inequality.

Cause 2: Large populations immersed in poverty and near poverty. Scores of researchers have demonstrated that poverty causes an array of social problems as we discuss subsequently (Barr, 2008; Grusky & Kanbur, 2006). People who live in poverty and near-poverty not only feel marginalized and stigmatized in a nation that values upward mobility and wealth, but they also live their lives mostly absorbed by meeting their survival needs. They often experience economic shortages that deprive them of food, shelter, and healthcare. Roughly forty-five million Americans, or 14.5% of the American population, live under the federal poverty levels of $11,770 for individuals and $20,090 for families of three. Even Americans in the bottom 50% of income with average pre-tax income of just over $16,000 for single persons, are often a paycheck away from eviction, foreclosure, and inability to afford basic necessities. Roughly 50% of seniors have no savings or assets—and often have credit card debt—when they retire, forcing them to rely on Social Security pensions of less than $20,000.

Cause 3: Exposure to low levels of upward mobility. Five research studies have documented that Americans have lower levels of upward mobility than Canadians and many Europeans. Forty-two percent of American males raised in the bottom fifth of the economy fail to rise above this level as compared to only 25% in Denmark and 30% in Great Britain (DeParle, 2012). In contrast, 62% of persons raised in the top 20% remained in the top 20% (DeParle, 2012). While many exceptions exist, African American and Latino youth in high schools with drop out rates of more than 50% are unlikely to move upward in the economic order (Maushard, 2014).

We can only move toward greater equality if many people in the lower economic echelons, drawn disproportionately from numerous at-risk populations, become upwardly mobile. If large numbers remain in their low economic position *and* if large numbers of affluent people retain their high economic position, levels of income equality will remain relatively unchanged. It is important not only to know what levels of upward mobility exist, but whether specific individuals in the lower economic strata believe they can achieve it.

Cause 4: Low levels of hope among people in the lower economic echelons. Tanguy et al., (2014) provide cross-national data that suggest that a person's level of hope powerfully shapes the extent to which they *can* be upwardly mobile. Esther Duflo, MIT Professor and an author of the book titled *Poor Economics* found that in developing nations "a profound lack of hope" created and sustained "a poverty trap." Even small increments of additional resources gave poor people "mental space" to explore new lines of work (*Economist*, 2012). Bolland (2003), Bolland et al., (2005), and Goetz (2003) discuss the high incidence of hopelessness in poverty-stricken populations. A randomized trial of 21,000 persons in six nations that tested the impact of relatively small gifts discovered that persons who received a single cow or goat as a gift worked more hours, took more odd jobs, and increased their savings (Kristof, 2015). The researchers reasoned that people who are impoverished need hope because "poverty causes stress and depression and lack of hope, and stress and depression and lack of hope, in turn, cause poverty" (Quote from Esther Duflo cited by Kristof, 2015). Another study reported that low-income Ethiopians randomly assigned to watch an hour-long inspirational video ended up saving more and spending more on their children's education … forward-leaning behaviors (that) persisted in a six-month follow-up (Tanguy et al., 2014). Some African American youth who attend high schools where more than 50% of their peers fail to graduate come to believe that they are likely to follow the same path (Balfanz et al., 2014). Some low-income members of the White working-class in Appalachia and other areas resort to abusing opiates and alcohol partly because they experience lonely poverty and often have deaths of despair (Chen, 2016). The Organization for Economic Co-operation and Development (OECD) reports that young people who are not employed or in education or training programs have lower levels of happiness, feel disenfranchised, and have low levels of trust, compared to other youth (OECD, 2016).

Cause 5: Exposure to high levels of discrimination by people in the lower economic echelons. Millions of Americans encounter discrimination in places of work, healthcare, housing, law enforcement, criminal justice and juvenile justice systems, and schools (Badawi, 2012). They understand that their fundamental rights are diminished when they are treated unfairly and are marginalized by these experiences. Uber drivers often decline to accept African American customers (White, 2016). Airbnb hosts often do not respond to persons with names associated with African Americans (Clarke, 2016). Employers often don't return the calls of job seekers with these names (Francis, 2016). Existing civil rights laws and regulations are often not enforced, such as prohibitions in the Americans with Disabilities Act that make it illegal to discriminate in workplaces against persons with mental and physical disabilities. The unemployment rate for disabled persons was 10.7% in 2015, or roughly twice the rate of persons with no disability. The 2016 Social Progress Index, published by the Social Progress Imperative, gives the United States a low ranking on tolerance and inclusion as compared to many other industrialized nations (Social Progress Index, 2016, accessed at socialprogressimperative.org on 3/28/17).

Discrimination contributes to both poverty and inequality in the United States. Recall that the United States has a rich history of discrimination against persons of color, including African Americans, Latinos, Asian Americans, Native Americans, LGBTQ, immigrant, women, White trash, low-income persons, persons who have been incarcerated, disabled persons, and others (I discuss these populations subsequently in this chapter as well as in Jansson, 2015.) While considerable progress has been made in decreasing discrimination, such as the passage of many civil rights measures, these at-risk populations still experience it. Discrimination contributes to income inequality to the extent that it blocks members of these groups from economic opportunities, such as hiring and promotion practices in the employment system (Badawi, 2012; Kastanis, 2016). Many economists contend that in developing countries, untapped resources of women, due to discrimination, could raise national incomes greatly (Sacks, 2008). This logic extends to many groups in the United States that suffer from discrimination, which harms the morale and confidence of members of these groups. Unarmed men from racial minorities have been killed by police for no or minor infractions.

Cause 6: Low levels of exposure to adequate opportunities, resources, and services by people in the lower economic strata—as well as resources from entitlements like Social Security that provide American seniors with far smaller pensions than most European seniors. Affluent people have sufficient resources to self-fund childcare, purchases of real estate, transportation, and other necessities. They can purchase education from private schools, or supplement the education of their children with tutors, educational travels, and other resources. Low-income people can't fund these opportunities, resources, and services. They confront relatively meager or underfunded opportunities, resources, and services because they have to rely on those funded by federal, local and, state governments. If affluent persons often receive these advantages from their "social capital," such as access to well-financed schools, educational amenities in their homes, educational trips, stable housing, and quality healthcare, non-affluent persons often lack these amenities. They are dependent on social, educational, and economic resources provided to them and their families by government, such as subsidized childcare, benefits from safety-net programs, subsidized healthcare, publicly funded preschool programs, government subsidies to their schools, pensions from Social Security, unemployment insurance, and entitlements like the Earned Income Tax Credit. These resources often are poorly funded, not available in specific locations, or difficult to access. They often provide smaller benefits to low- and moderate-income Americans than to their counterparts in many industrialized nations. Persons in the lower economic echelons often cannot purchase houses due to lack of access to credit from banks and other financial institutions. They often pay 50% or more of their income on rent.

Cause 7 Poor access to health and poor health. Poor access to health and poor health contribute to extreme economic inequality in several ways. They take millions of Americans from the labor force when they have chronic and other diseases that poorly treated or managed. They prevent millions of Americans from gaining access to healthcare due to lack of universal insurance, excessive deductibles, and excessive copayments. Medical bankruptcy is the leading cause of bankruptcy in the United States because 50 million Americans are uninsured or underinsured so that 1 in 3 Americans have difficulty paying their medical bills. American healthcare is far more expensive than healthcare in Europe or Canada for many reasons including marketing costs and administrative costs of private insurance companies that insure more than 80% of the population, higher costs of medications, and higher salaries of medical specialists (Kane, 2012). "Spending down" their assets to gain access to the means-tested Medicaid Program often impoverishes senior citizens. The American health system insufficiently funds preventive care. It is hardly surprising, then, that the United States ranks behind most other industrial nations in many health measures such as longevity, infant mortality, and days lost from work (Jones, 2012). Indeed, I hypothesize that the American health system contributes to extreme economic inequality unlike most other industrialized nations that give residents better coverage at lower costs with better health outcomes.

Cause 8: Low levels of government resources available to fund strategies to reduce extreme income equality. Even though it is the most affluent nation in the world, the United States lacks sufficient tax revenues to fund strategies that can reduce extreme income inequality. It taxes working and middle classes at lower levels than many European nations (Kleinbard, 2015). It taxes affluent Americans at far lower rates than European nations and Canada (Kleinbard, 2015). Its tax system is riddled with loopholes for affluent taxpayers, including many tax exemptions and tax deductions. It depletes its tax revenues with a wasteful healthcare system that consumes nearly 20% of the nation's GDP as compared to many industrialized nations that spend only about 10% of their GDP on healthcare but with better health outcomes (Brill, 2015). The United States also spends more on its military forces and weapons than the next seven or eight nations combined. This dearth of federal resources means that empirically validated initiatives to address the causes of inequality are not funded sufficiently to reduce income inequality. Chapter 3 discusses the miniscule portion of the federal budget that has been devoted to social and educational investments from the New Deal of the 1930s to the present. I discuss in further detail why the United States has insufficient revenues to fund programs needed to address extreme income inequality in Chapter 8.

Cause 9: Failure to place limits on the income and wealth of affluent people. The juxtaposition of persons in or near poverty with an upper class with extraordinary wealth not only contributes to extreme income inequality, but makes it difficult to correct the problem. Those low income people who view themselves as mired in a nation with rigid economic classes are less likely to believe they can be upwardly mobile. Super-affluent people are more likely to mobilize political pressure to keep their taxes low as compared to economic elites in nations with less income inequality (Kleinbard, 2015). I discuss the higher marginal tax rates on affluent persons in Europe, Canada, Australia, and New Zealand subsequently in Chapter 8.

Cause 10: A political system that discriminates against voters and interests that favor policy changes that would reduce extreme income inequality. Extreme inequality is both caused by and contributes to disparities of political power. While wealthy elites fund political candidates and pay lobbyists to promote tax concessions that help them to preserve their own wealth, many low-income people, often neglected by public officials, do not even vote. When the power of trade unions was markedly reduced in the United States during the last five decades, workers lost bargaining rights in many places of work—as well as a source of pressure on the political system to promote higher wages and workers' rights. A majority of the members of Congress were millionaires for the first time in 2014 when, at the same time, 50% of Americans reported they could not spend $5,000 if an emergency occurred (Rosier, 2014). The U.S. Constitution gives power to smaller and more conservative states, such as Wyoming and South Carolina, and takes power from larger and more liberal states, such as New York State and California, by allocating two Senators to each state regardless of their size. The constitutional founders also made it difficult to enact equality-enhancing policies by creating a balance of powers that gives opponents many ways to block them as compared to parliamentary governments with only a single legislative chamber and a prime minister from the political party with the most members in the parliament.

Cumulative Toxic Effects

Cumulative toxic effects are caused by interactions between the ten causes of income inequality as illustrated by a simple example. If Frank is exposed to extreme income inequality, he will have increased odds of developing specific social problems (toxic effect #1) as compared to someone who is not exposed to extreme income inequality (Wilkerson & Pickett, 2009a and 2009b). If he is also exposed to poverty, he is likely to see himself not only as marginalized by his low economic position, but to toxic effects from daily struggles to meet survival needs (toxic effect #2), including the constant fear that he can't meet those needs, won't meet them in the future, will be evicted when he can't pay rent, and lacks access to healthcare when he has serious health problems. Now, expose Frank to the reality that he has almost no chance of upward mobility (toxic effect #3) because he failed to graduate from high school and has serious medical and mental problems. This realization makes him aware that he will be circumscribed by poverty for years to come—and that he may never be able to enjoy luxuries that he views daily on his television and cell phone, such as expensive (or any) cars. This realization, in turn, robs him of hope (toxic effect #4). Absent hope of upward mobility or a better life, Frank has higher odds of developing mental problems like depression or even suicide, as often occurs in so-called deaths of despair that have been recently been identified among low-income, blue-collar, White males in rural America (Case & Deaton, 2017). His lack of hope may lead him to forego upgrading his education and skills. Next, expose Frank to persistent discrimination based upon his age, race, disability, prior criminal convictions, or any other personal characteristic (toxic effect #5). Persistent discrimination may increase his sense of hopelessness, induce him to believe even more strongly that he can't achieve upward mobility, and may exacerbate his sense that the rules of the game are not fair. We can hypothesize that the odds that Frank will move upward in the economic system decrease as he experiences toxic effects from each or many of these sources. Lastly, expose Frank to the toxic effects he experiences from chronic exposure to lack of health, educational, housing, and recreational amenities throughout his life because he (or his family) lacks resources to purchase them—and because his government fails to invest sufficient resources to provide access to them (toxic effect #6). He may also lack health insurance and access to healthcare so that he does not receive timely or sufficient assistance for chronic diseases (toxic effect #7).

We can also hypothesize that the ten causes are related to one another. If we want to decrease extreme income inequality in the United States, we need to increase resources and opportunities for people in poverty and near poverty (cause 2), increase upward mobility so that fewer people reside in the lowest economic strata (cause 3), increase hope of persons in the lowest economic strata so that they are buoyed by high levels of confidence that they can move upward (cause 4), and decrease the extent to which they experience discrimination (cause 5). We also need to increase public expenditures to increase social, economical housing, educational amenities for persons who lack resources to purchase them and who fail to receive sufficient levels of them to help them to surmount the toxic effects of causes 2 through 5 (cause 6). We need to increase access to health systems (cause 7). We need to fund social, educational, job-training and other programs sufficiently that will decrease poverty and enhance upward mobility (cause 8). Both to enhance government revenues to fund strategies to reduce extreme income inequality and to reduce toxic effects of extreme income inequality, we need to place greater limits on income of affluent people through changes in the tax code as well as other reforms (cause 9). We need to find ways to reform the political system so that advocates can move policy reforms through it, such as limiting the size of contributions by affluent interests to politicians and restoring some of the power of trade unions (cause 10).

Our discussion suggests that an *ecology of extreme income inequality* exists. This multi-faceted ecology suggests that many strategies and policies are needed to redress extreme income inequality. Reformers have to work on many fronts. They also have to target their reforms to members of (at least) sixteen at-risk populations that disproportionately experience high levels of toxic effects that derive from each of the ten causes of extreme income inequality, as well as combinations of them. The sixteen at-risk populations include African Americans, Latinos, Asian Americans, Native Americans, women, persons who have been felons or imprisoned, millennial persons, LGBTQ persons, disabled persons, immigrants, senior citizens, persons who have low levels of education, children and youth, low-income persons including segments of the middle class, homeless people, and White blue-collar persons who live in rural areas or distressed urban areas.

This book discusses how equality advocates can develop three products that may decrease economic inequality. Initiatives to Uplift Ordinary Persons (IUOPs) are policy proposals to reduce extreme income inequality by addressing its first seven causes. Resources to Uplift Ordinary People (RUOPs) are policy proposals to increase public resources that can fund IUOPs such as by increasing taxes or cutting government waste. Political Strategies to Uplift Ordinary Persons (PSUOPs) are policy proposals and political strategies to make government more responsive to equality advocates who seek IUOPs and RUOPs. PSUOPs include working with grassroots campaigns like Reverend William Barber's interracial coalition agains poverty and participating with campaigns to elect equality advocates (Cobb, 2018). It is unlikely that major reductions in extreme income inequality can be achieved without a combination of IUOPs, RUOPs, and PSUOPs. I discuss IUOPs in chapters 5, 6, and 7. I discuss RUOPs in chapter 8. I discuss PRUOPs in chapter 9.

America's Extreme Income Inequality

The United States faces a daunting challenge: it has the highest level of economic inequality of 21 industrialized nations despite its affluence. It ranks just above Portugal when the ratio of the income of the top 20% of its residents is compared to the income of the bottom 20%. The American ratio is roughly nine as compared to the ratios of 3.3 for Japan, roughly 4 times for Scandinavian nations, roughly 5.6 times for Germany and France, roughly 5.9 times for Canada, and roughly 8 times for Portugal (Wilkinson & Pickett, 2009).

To be clear, even the economic holdings of persons in the lower 50% of the American economic order are so low that many of them struggle to meet survival needs. Take data released in late 2016 by economists Emmanuel Saez, Thomas Piketty and Gabriel Zucman (as reported in Ashkenas, 2016). The average pre-tax income of individuals in the bottom 50% of the population was roughly $16,500 in 2016—and only increased to $25,045 when the monetary value of benefits from the Supplemental Nutrition Program (SNAP, or Food Stamps), Medicaid, Medicare, the Earned Income Tax Credit, and other safety-net programs was added. The share of the American economy owned by the lower 50% of the economic distribution and the top 1% of the economic distribution drastically shifted in the United States from 1974 to 2016. While the lower 50% and the top 1% respectively owned 20% and 10.5% of the economy, in 1974, these figures were almost exactly reversed by 2016, when the lower 50% and the top 1% respectively possessed 13% and 20% of the economy (Ashkenas, 2016).

Income inequality has received relatively little public attention in the United States despite its high level. The last seven American presidents, including Democrats Bill Clinton and Barack Obama, rarely uttered the words, income inequality. Hillary Clinton hardly mentioned this phrase, or even the word poverty during her 2016 presidential campaign. Nor did President Trump discuss inequality and poverty much, if at all, in his presidential campaign and during the first months of his presidency—even as he championed low income Whites in rural areas. It is hard to believe that a War on Poverty was waged in the United States in the 1960s, even if it was a poorly funded one. Former president Barack Obama identified income inequality as one of the top four issues facing the nation in his final speech as president.

Many Americans were shocked when French economist Thomas Piketty (2014) documented that income inequality in the United States currently rivals levels last seen in the Gilded Age in the 1880s, when titans of industry at the top, such as Andrew Carnegie and John D. Rockefeller, coexisted with millions of penniless immigrants at the bottom from Europe, Eastern Europe, Russia, Mexico, and Asia. Senator Bernie Sanders (D., VT.) made reducing inequality the centerpiece of his quest to win the Democratic presidential nomination during 2016 Democratic Presidential primaries, even winning 26 states in his competition with Hillary Clinton. In his farewell news conference in early 2017, Barack Obama finally cited income inequality as one of the four major challenges confronting the United States, viewing the current misdistribution of income as unsustainable and even dangerous to American democracy (White, 2017).

Extreme income inequality can be criticized on ethical grounds with use of words like equity, fairness, or social justice. It is appropriate to ask why the top 1% own roughly 20% of the American economy. True, those of them that did not inherit their wealth worked hard to gain their income and wealth, but so also did tens of millions of Americans such as single mothers who worked two or three jobs just to support their children. Even though wealthy Americans, as a group, pay a large share of total American tax revenues, they retain huge resources that could be additionally taxed while still leaving them with extraordinary resources. As Piketty (2014) documents, the current class of highly wealthy persons mostly became ultra-wealthy not from inherited wealth, but from salaries and stock options as top CEOs of large companies, as well as entrepreneurs of new companies. It is fair to suggest they should share their wealth because they rely upon the American educational system, American infrastructure, the American banking system, and American foreign policy to sustain their extraordinary wealth. Many of them ascended the economic order because of lucky breaks.

Yet America's affluent class pays lower income taxes than the top 1%, 5%, and 10% of populations of many other industrialized nations, for several reasons. Their top marginal tax rate was 39.6% in 2014, as compared to top marginal tax rates in Denmark (60.2%), Sweden (56.6%), Belgium (53.7%), Spain (52%), Netherlands (52%), France (50.7%), Austria (50%), Japan (50%), Greece (49%), Finland (49%), Portugal (49%), Canada (48%), Ireland (45%), Israel (48%), Australia (47.5%), and Iceland (46.2%) (Eaton, 2014). By increasing the top marginal rate to 40% and taxing wages, interest, dividends, employer contributions to health plans, overseas earnings, and growth in retirement accounts, the United States would gain $157 billion in tax revenues in the first year. It would gain even more ($276 billion in the first year) if the top marginal rate was increased to 45% which would still allow this group to take home at least $1 million per year (Cohen, 2015). Nor would raising tax rates harm the super-rich since the top 0.1% of American families, who all have assets worth more than $29 million, own more than 20% of all the household wealth in the nation, compared to the 1970s when it controlled only 7% (Cohen, 2015). Let's recall, as well, that affluent Americans paid top marginal tax rates that exceeded 70% from 1933 through 1979 as I discuss in Chapter 3 when the United States had far lower income inequality than in the current period.

The low top marginal rates paid on the top dollars in their taxable income is only part of the story because affluent people have become adept at figuring out ways to shift earnings that would normally be taxed at the top 39.6% rate on ordinary income into capital gains that is taxed only at a maximum of 23.8% (Gabriel Zucman, cited in Cohen, 2015). *Many of these shifting strategies do not exist for wealthy people in Europe, Canada. Australia, New Zealand, and Japan.* Shifting earnings from one tax category to another allows even the top 0.1% (to) pay on average no more than a quarter of their income in federal individual income taxes—despite that top tax bracket of 39.6% (Gabriel Zucman, cited in Cohen, 2015). By eliminating preferential rates on capital gains and dividends, the United States would gain $1.34 trillion over the next 10 years; $644 billion by ending reduced capital gains taxes on inherited assets, and $900 billion by ending the deferral on corporate profits kept overseas (Cohen, 2015). The combined resources achieved by raising top marginal rates and eliminating these tax concessions would allow remarkable increases in the funding of schools, job training, housing subsidies, repair of infrastructure, medical care for low-income persons, mental health services, and safety-net programs such as the Supplemental Nutrition Assistance Program (SNAP, or food stamps). It would allow the United States to fund free tuition at the nation's four-year public colleges and universities, estimated to cost $47 billion; a $2,500 child tax credit proposed by Senator Marco Rubio; and $176 billion needed to improve major urban highways. It would end this year's federal deficit of $426 billion (Cohen, 2015).

Extreme income inequality can also be criticized for its toxic effects. Wilkinson and Pickett (2009) examined correlations between levels of income inequality of 21 industrialized nations and their scores on an Index of Social Problems (see Figure 1.1). They compared the ratio of the income of the top

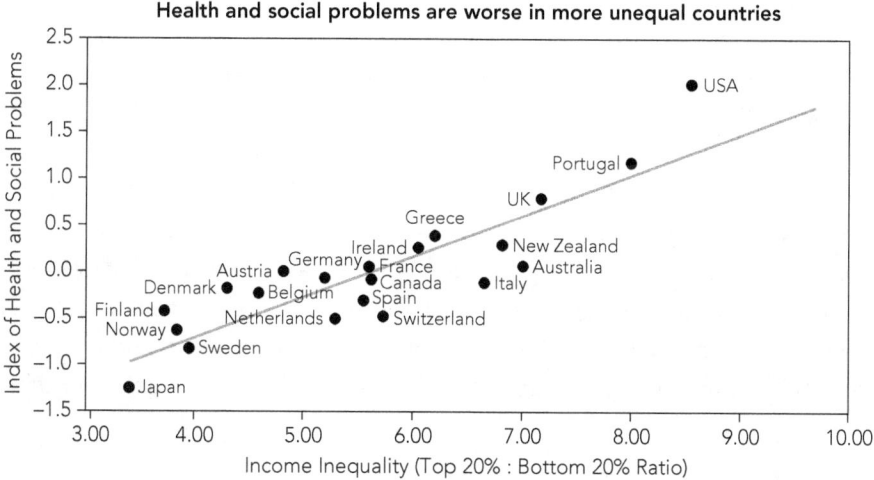

Figure 1.1 Rankings of 21 Industrialized Nations by Inequality and Social Problems

20% of citizens in these nations to the income of the bottom 20% of citizens to measure extent of income inequality in each nation. They measured nations' scores on the Index of Social Problems to compute the relative incidence of 10 social problems in each nation: lack of trust, low life expectancy, high infant mortality, high rates of obesity, poor educational performance, high rates of teenage births, high rates of homicides, high rates of imprisonment, high levels of mental health problems, and low rates of social mobility. The results are presented in Figure 1.1. Scores on the X (or horizontal) axis measure levels of income inequality in the 21 nations and scores on the Y (or vertical) axis measure the relative incidence of the 10 problems as measured by the nations' Index of Social Problems. The rankings of the nations are displayed on the diagonal continuum. The United States had the highest score on the Index of Social Problems with a score of roughly two as compared to the top possible score of 2.5 and the lowest possible score of -1.5. The United States also had the greatest income inequality with a ratio of the income of the top 20% to the bottom 20% of nine to one—a ratio that greatly exceeded those of other nations, with the exception of Portugal. Even Greece, with its massive economic and banking problems, had a far lower ratio than the United States.

Some critics, such as Hillary Clinton in her debates with Bernie Sanders in the 2016 Democratic presidential primary contest these findings, pointing out that none of the nations in Figure 1.1 have populations as large as the United States. Clinton contended that small nations, like Denmark, achieve income equality far more easily than the United States. She neglected to note, however, that nations with relatively large populations, such as Germany and France, with populations of 81 million and 67 million respectively, have far higher levels of equality than the United States. Some critics contend, as well, that many European nations have higher levels of equality because they are socialist, but, in fact, none of the nations in Figure 1.1 are socialist. None of their governments own the means of production. All of them have market economies. All of them have stock markets. All of them depend heavily upon trade with other nations.

To further test the causal link between income inequality and scores on their Index of Social Problems, Wilkinson & Pickett (2009) tested the relationship between income inequality and scores on the Index of Social Problems in American states and counties. They discovered that counties and states with high income inequality also scored higher on the Index of Social Problems. These states and counties vary in their populations, their politics, and their policies, their culture and levels of economic growth. These findings strengthen the conclusion of Wilkinson & Pickett (2009) that exposure to extreme income inequality has toxic effects on people who experience it.

Researchers have sought to explain why income inequality has toxic effects. For example, scientists have identified toxic effects among animals when some of them are subjected to inequality in laboratory settings. The animals develop many physical maladies and high levels of mental distress (Sapolsky, 2004; Sapolsky, 2005). Other studies have demonstrated that people who are exposed to bullying in laboratory experiments, such as taunting behaviors of others, experience short-term mental distress (Piff, 2013; Wilkinson & Pickett, 2014). These experiments indicate that human beings are aware of disparities of power in social settings—a finding that suggests they are aware of disparities of income in nations and their subdivisions. In nations with extreme inequality, like the United States, they may believe that they are destined to remain relatively poor. Five separate research reports have recently documented that persons in the lower class in the United States are less likely to move upward to the middle class than persons in many European nations and Canada (DeParle, 2012; Morin, 2012; Tavernise, 2012)

Further multivariate research is needed to examine to what extent other variables explain why living in nations with high levels of inequality leads to development of many social issues listed in the Index of Health and Social Problems. With respect to the United States, for example, Hacker & Pierson (2016) found that persons living in states with relatively lower levels of investments in social and educational programs had higher levels of various social problems than those living in states with relatively high investments. Poverty may cause more toxic effects in the United States than in European nations and Canada because poverty may be more stigmatized in the United States, with its relatively harsh safety-net programs. With lower odds of achieving upward mobility, psychological orientations of low-income persons, such as hope, may be less positive in the United States than in Europe and Canada. Levels of social capital, as measured by levels of education, familial support, and other support networks, may be lower among American poverty-stricken persons than their counterparts in Europe who have access to better schools, medical systems, and social programs. This may be due to significant numbers of youth in low-income families and among racial minorities who do not graduate from high school and do not have access to quality vocational programs that are relatively widespread in Europe (DeParle, 2012). As suggested by inspections of cities in these nations, persons in poverty in the United States often live in more blighted and dangerous neighborhoods than their European counterparts. Low income Americans may also be more socially isolated than low income Europeans because they are less likely to be members of trade unions and have lower levels of civic participation as measured by their disinclination to vote (Khullar, 2016). The Social Progress Index of 2016, published by an NGO named the Social Progress Imperative, compares nations with respect to their performance on various measures of social and environmental indicators of social progress. This index ranks the United States 19th in the world, with low scores for health and wellness and for tolerance and inclusion (Social Progress Index 2016 Appendix B accessed @ socialprogressimperative.org on 3/28/17), while giving it higher scores on other measures.

Researchers may discover that Wilkinson & Pickett (2009) attribute excessive importance to income inequality as a causal agent. It is possible that other hypothesized causes of extreme income inequality that I discussed earlier in this chapter may cause some of the social problems discussed by Wikinson & Pickett including poverty, discrimination, lack of upward mobility, lack of hope, poor access to health and mental health systems, as well as low levels of social, educational, and economic supports for persons in the lower economic distribution. International data sets, such as comparative data from the Organization of Economic Co-operation and Development (OECD), demonstrate that the United States funds social and economic investments at lower levels than many European nations and Canada, including unemployment insurance, retirement pensions, childcare, parental leave programs, and housing programs (Jansson, 2015, pp. 534–537 for a comparison of Canada and the United States on numerous dimensions). Canada and many European nations often recruit quality teachers by offering higher salaries than America offers its secondary-school teachers. Most of those countries provide universal health care, unlike the United States, which mostly relies on private insurance.

Americans who live in red states have less access to public amenities because they spend far less on them than blue states (Hacker & Pierson, 2016).

The United States can't generate the revenues needed to fund programs that reduce extreme income inequality without increasing taxes on wealthy Americans, who are under-taxed compared to the wealthy in many other industrialized nations, and without reducing wasteful expenditures, as I discuss at more length in Chapter 8. The United States might also consider a federal tax on luxury goods to raise revenues.

Wilkinson and Pickett (2009) wondered if the social problems in these various nations were caused not by income inequality, but by their level of poverty. So they analyzed *absolute* levels of income in each nation, i.e., a nation's relative purchasing power, as compared to *relative* income, which is measured by comparing the ratio of the incomes of the top 20% versus the bottom 20%.

They wanted to know, for example, whether the high incidence of social problems in the United States, Portugal, and the United Kingdom (UK) stemmed not from income inequality but poverty. Might the United States score high on Wilkinson's and Pickett's (2009) Index of Health and Social Problems because the lowest economic strata lacks resources to purchase healthcare, food, housing, and other essentials, as compared to the other nations? They knew that many researchers had discovered that low-income people in the United States and elsewhere had disproportionate levels of many social problems, including those examined by Wilkinson and Pickett (Grusky & Kanbur, eds., 2006). When they discovered that the absolute purchasing power of residents in the lowest economic strata only weakly predicted scores on the Index, they concluded that exposure to high levels of income inequality caused higher scores on the Index of Health and Social problems rather than poverty.

Their conclusions may be premature because many researchers have assembled evidence that poverty has toxic effects in the United States. Persons in poverty may have more social problems than persons in poverty in many other industrialized nations because they have access to fewer services and resources. Studies report that persons living in poverty in the United States, such as in the bottom tenth or fifth of the economic distribution, experience disproportionate levels of adverse health conditions, shortened longevity, incarceration, unemployment, disability, and poor performance in schools (Grusky & Kanbur, eds., 2006). To use the words of Senator Bernie Sanders, "poverty is a death sentence ... 15 neighborhoods in Baltimore have lower life expectancies than North Korea—and two of them have a higher infant mortality rate than in the West Bank" (Bernie Sanders, 2016). Nor is it surprising that poverty has toxic effects. Impoverished people have difficulty purchasing necessities. They are less likely to have health insurance in the United States. They experience stress from the economic uncertainties they experience. They are more likely to be evicted from rental units. They die earlier. They are more likely to abuse substances.

The massive amount of research that identifies toxic effects of poverty in the United States suggests that poverty cannot be discounted as a co-partner with income inequality in causing the problems measured by Wilkinson's and Pickett's Index of Health and Social Problems (Wilkinson & Pickett, 2009). Consider, as well, the effects on persons of poverty in the United States as compared to persons of poverty of Canada and many European nations. These other nations have far more robust safety-net programs. They have universal health insurance. They subsidize the housing of low-income people at far higher levels than the United States. Their pensions for seniors are far higher than in the United States. They subsidize unemployed people at higher levels than the United States. Some of them offer universal childcare. They subsidize schools at higher levels than the United States. They provide free tuition to college. They have far more effective vocational education programs for youth who are not admitted to college. Some of them, like Denmark, offer sabbaticals to all workers including sanitation workers. In other words, persons in poverty in the United States have fewer public supports than those in Canada and many European nations. They are less likely to benefit from safety-net programs due to stricter eligibility requirements. They receive lower levels of benefits, such as shorter periods of unemployment insurance and lower Social Security pensions. They are less likely to belong to trade unions. They vote at far lower levels than low-income persons in many European nations and Canada.

The Dearth of Government Resources

Extreme inequality in the United States has another practical effect: it limits resources that can be used to fund public goods, such as social programs, healthcare, mental health programs, infrastructure improvements, and public education at all levels. Extreme income inequality is caused both by high levels of poverty at the bottom of the economic spectrum as well as by extreme wealth at the top of economic systems where the top 1% possess as much income as the bottom 50%. They possess this income partly because they are taxed at substantially lower levels than affluent people in most other industrialized nations, whether through income taxes, inheritance taxes, or taxes on financial transactions. As a consequence, the United States lacks sufficient public resources to fund adequate educational and social investments needed to lift Americans from poverty or near-poverty.

Epic amounts of national resources are wasted annually on unnecessary expenditures. When analyzing military expenditures from 1950 to 2000, consulting with scores of experts and expert analyses (Jansson, 2001) revealed that as a conservative estimate, the United States wasted roughly $5.47 trillion in 1992 dollars on military costs (or roughly $8 trillion in 2017 dollars). This included an ill-advised failed expansion of the Korean War into China by General Douglas McArthur, a failed Vietnam War, an excessive military build-up by President Ronald Reagan, an excessive level of nuclear forces and general purpose forces during the Cold War, and wasteful procurement policies. No reviewer, including Paul Warnke, the former attorney for the

Defense Department and the Strategic Arms Limitation Treaty (SALT) negotiator for Bill Clinton, questioned these estimates (Jansson, 2001). Since the year 2,000, the nation wasted roughly $3 trillion on an ill-advised war in Iraq, according to estimates by Nobel Prize winning economist Joseph Stiglitz (Stiglitz, 2008). Adding my own data to Stieglitz's estimate, we come up with waste of $11 trillion since 1950 just on military expenditures. Chapter 8 discusses huge loopholes in the tax code that benefit affluent Americans particularly. In addition, enormous amounts of resources are wasted annually on the nation's reliance on private insurance companies to manage payments of health expenditures of roughly 85% of the nation's population. Moving the nation toward Medicare for all, would have saved trillions of dollars between 1950 and the present in 2017 dollars.

At-Risk Subpopulations

Members of at least 16 subpopulations in the United States are most at risk of experiencing toxic effects from the ten causes of extreme income inequality that we have already discussed. In order to help them avoid these toxic effects, equality advocates have to develop policies targeted at them. Next, we discuss the sheer number of people and subgroups who experience them.

- African Americans are two times as likely as Whites to be unemployed. Households headed by Black persons earn roughly one-half, on average what White households earn. White households are roughly 13 times wealthier than their Black counterparts. While more than a third of Whites in age bracket 25+ have bachelor degrees, only 23% of African Americans have them (Pew Research Center, Demographic trends and economic well-being, June 27, 2016, accessed @pewsocialtrends.org.). African Americans experience discriminatory treatment from lending institutions, employers, realtors, and educational institutions despite civil rights laws. It has been estimated that it would take 400 years for African Americans to approach levels of wealth of White Americans because they were often denied bank mortgages and loans from the end of the Civil War until (at least) the 1960s. As they lacked homes and real estate for these many years, Whites had property that appreciated over many decades.
- The Hispanic population was 56.6 million in 2015 or 17.6% of the total population of the United States—making this group the largest ethnic or

racial minority, though its rate of growth has slowed markedly since 2007 even as it accounted for 54% of total U.S. population growth from 2000 to 2014 (Krogstad, 2014). Nearly all Latinos lived in half of the nation's 3000 counties in 2014—and more than half of them lived in 15 metropolitan areas (Krogstad, 2014). The median net worth for Hispanic households was $13,700 in 2013 as compared to $141,900 for White households. The Hispanic poverty rate was 21.4% in 2015 as compared to 9.1% for Non-Hispanic Whites (Krogstad, 2014).

- Native Americans have the highest rate of poverty, at 14.7%, of any racial group in the country (Wilson, 2014). The median household income is $38,530 as compared to $55,775 for the nation. While 9.4 % of the nation lacks health insurance, 20.7% of Native Americans have no health insurance (American Indians by the Numbers, U.S. Census Bureau data accessed from infoplease@infoplease.com). 37% of Native American children live in poverty as compared to 22% of children in the nation (Wilson, 2014).
- Women experience discrimination by employers as illustrated by the infamous glass ceiling metaphor. They often fail to receive work accommodations when they have children. Employers often will not hire women if they believe they will have children or if they are pregnant. Police and public officials have only slowly responded to violence and sexual attacks on women in their households and places of work. Single mothers experience discrimination in places of work where wages are often so low they must work multiple jobs. Single mothers face discrimination by those landlords who will not rent units to persons with young children. (Law Office of Cohen & Jaffe, 2017). According to the U.S. Census, 10.6 million adults with no partner present in the home live with children under age 18 (Marital Status Employment Discrimination Against Single Moms, Law Office of Cohen & Jaffe, accessed at cohenjaffe.com on 2/6/2017).
- Subgroups of the Asian American citizen population fare relatively well in the economy, such as Japanese, Indian, and Filipino citizens that have poverty rates of 7.9%, 7.7%, and 7.3%, respectively. Even members of relatively affluent Asian citizen subgroups experience racial discrimination in employment and education, such as reverse discrimination when significant numbers they achieve significant numbers in specific organizations and occupations or colleges. Hmong, Bangladeshi, and Cambodian citizens, respectively, have poverty rates of 25.6%, 24.6%, and 19.9%—and Chinese, Korean, Pakistani, Taiwanese, Thai, and Vietnam-

ese citizens have poverty rates falling between 13.6% and 19.1% (Valerie Wilson, 2013 ACS Shows Depth of Native American Poverty and Different Degrees of Economic Well-Being for Asian Ethnic Groups, Economic Policy Institute, 9/18/2014, accessed on 2/6/17). According to Michael Luo, Asian Americans experience discrimination in schoolyards, on the street, and in grocery stores (Michael Luo, An Open Letter to the Woman Who Told My Family to Go Back to China, *New York Times*, October 9, 2016). A long history of discrimination against Asian Americans began in the 19th century when many Chinese and Japanese immigrants were not allowed to vote, lived in segregated communities, could not purchase land, and were relegated to poverty as they worked as miners, agricultural laborers, and building railroads. Many Japanese immigrants were sent to internment camps during World War II. Asian Americans were often excluded from many professions and management positions in corporations.

- Persons released from criminal justice and juvenile justice systems. The Brennan Center for Justice estimates that as many Americans have criminal records during their lifetime as college diplomas; such as the 70 million persons arrested and fingerprinted by local, state, or federal agencies (Friedman, 2016). Although far fewer are actually convicted, a past criminal conviction reduces the likelihood of a job offer by 50%. Ex-felons are disproportionately persons of color with low levels of education. Failure to hire and retain ex-felons may cost the U.S. economy as much as $65 billion dollars because they draw up public safety-net programs, do not pay taxes, and are more likely to return to jail (Prison Legal News, Study Shows Ex-offenders Have Greatly Reduced Employment Rates, accessed @ prisonlegalnews.org, 12/15/2011). Only 7 states had adopted ban-the-box laws in 2012 that prevented private employers from asking about conviction histories on job applications—and President Obama signed an executive order to remove questions about criminal convictions from federal job applications. No federal law protects felons from discrimination in employment, housing, or services, but many states forbid employers from discriminating against job applicants solely because they have a criminal conviction unless their offense is directly relevant to the job (Simon & Sparks, 2012).
- Roughly one-half of elderly persons retire with no assets like a house, savings, stocks, or a 501-C-3 private pensions plan that many Americans receive from their places of work (Jansson, 2016). Many have considerable credit card debt. Much of the elderly population rely on Social Security

benefits that averaged $15,528 in 2014 for single persons and $25,332 for retired couples, when poverty levels were $11,173 for single persons and $14,095 for couples (Jansson, 2016). Millions of them spend down their assets and income to become eligible for Medicaid to pay for chronic health problems when they have exhausted their Medicare coverage. Women who spent their lifetimes in the lower 20% of the economy live about 12 years shorter lives than women who spent their lifetimes in the top 10% (Tavernise, 2016).

- Many immigrants fall beneath poverty levels. About 11.2 million unauthorized immigrants live in the U.S. or about 5% of the nation's workforce (Pew Hispanic Center, 2016). The average median household income for unauthorized immigrants was $36,000 in 2007, which was below the median household income of U.S. citizens of $50,000. They constitute 4% of the nation's population and 5.4% of its workforce (Pew Research Center, Hispanic Trends, April 14, 2009, accessed at pewhispanic.org on 2/6/17). Adults are disproportionately poorly educated with 47% not possessing a high school degree although roughly one-half of them, ages 18–24, are in college or have attended college. One-third of their children live in poverty compared with 10% of adults born in the United States. Undocumented immigrant farm workers earn considerably less than documented immigrant farm workers, have less job security, and less schooling (Nisbet, E. & Rogers, W. M., 2013).
- Americans have used the words, White trash, to describe low-income White people in the 19th century and up to the present (Isenberg, 2016). Roughly 20 million White blue-collar people reside in rural areas and dying cities in the United States. Between 1960 and the present day, tens of thousand of manufacturers migrated to developing nations, greatly decreasing job opportunities, and particularly, well-paying jobs. The health of blue-collar White males, particularly ones that have lost work, such as when coal mines closed or when manufacturing plants departed, has deteriorated in many ways, including shorter life spans, addiction to opioids, and high rates of suicide. Many of these men have felony convictions. Many watch television for most of the day. Many do not participate in household activities or civic affairs. Yet this population is mostly invisible because no data had been collected about them; they were outside the employment system and often lived in rural or semi-rural areas (Eberstadt, 2017). During the 20th century, White blue-collar persons have suffered discrimination in employment, housing, schools, and the criminal justice system—and became sufficiently angry at the

insensitivity of the Democratic Party to their needs that they helped elect Donald Trump to the presidency in 2016 (Vance, 2016).
- Disabled persons include those with physical and mental disabilities. According to the U.S. Census Bureau, about 56.7 million people (or roughly 19% of the population) had a disability in 2010, with more than half of them characterizing their disability as severe. They are disproportionately unemployed or underemployed. They earn on average 37% less than persons without disabilities; $6,505 less for persons with high school degrees and $21,000 less on average for those with post-college degrees. These earning disparities are huge despite protections for disabled persons from the Americans with Disabilities Act, civil rights laws, and rehabilitation acts. These income differentials deprive state and federal governments of $31.5 billion in tax revenue and $141 billion in losses to the American economy due to their use of safety-net programs and their payment of lower tax revenues than if they had higher wages (Those with disabilities, 2014).
- Persons with low levels of education have greatly lower earnings and higher rates of unemployment, as evidenced by those who do not complete high school and high school graduates without a higher degree. Roughly 10% of youth dropped out of high school in 2014 with highest rates for Hispanics and lowest rates for Whites (National Center for Education Statistics @nces.ed.gov). High school dropouts earned $19,000 per year in 2013 as compared to $28,000 per year for high school graduates. Non-graduates disproportionately come from poverty-level families, African American families, and Latino families. Dropouts are far more likely to be incarcerated, to become homeless, to engage in violence, and to have substance abuse. Students from low-income families graduate from high school at a rate 15 percentage points behind more affluent students. Students with disabilities graduate at rates 20 points behind the national average (GradNation@gradnation.americaspromise.org). Unemployment rates of youth between ages 16 and 24 not enrolled in school was over 60% in 2015, compared with 30% for high school graduates, 21% for youth with less than a bachelor's degree, and 12% for youth with bachelor's degree or higher. Youth who do not complete high school are more likely to be incarcerated and to live under poverty levels (Data Bank Indicators @childtrends.org, accessed 2/7/17).
- Roughly 564,708 persons were homeless in the United States on a single night in January 2015. This included roughly 206,286 persons with their families and 358,422 individuals; 83,170 of the individuals had been

chronically homeless for an extended time period; 13,105 members of families had been chronically homeless for an extended time period; and 47,725 veterans were chronically homeless (National Alliance to End Homelessness, Snapshot of Homelessness, accessed on 2/17/17 @www.endhomelessness.org). These people became homeless for a variety of reasons, including financial crises, medical emergencies, mental illness, substance abuse, trauma from military service, and unemployment. Many of them are evicted from their housing because they can't afford their rent (Desmond, 2016). Homeless people overwhelmingly live under federal poverty levels. They are subject to discrimination via laws that exclude them from certain areas of cities and that expose them to arrest. Many of them are subject to assaults and theft.

- We are on the verge of obtaining more accurate data from the federal Bureau of Justice Statistics and the National Institutes of Health about the sheer size of the LGBTQ population. A 2011 study estimated that about 9 million Americans, or 3.5% of the population, reported that they were lesbian, gay, or bisexual (Gary Gates, How Many People are Lesbian, Gay, Bisexual and Transgender? Williams Institute at the UCLA School of Law). The U.S. Census Bureau does not yet gather data about sexual orientation or gender identity, but may eventually do so (Kathy Steinmetz, Inside the efforts to finally identify the size of the nation's LGBQ population, *Time*, 5/18/2016). Ian Meyer of the Williams Institute at the UCLA School of Law estimated that 2.4 million LGBT adults over age 50 live in the United States in August 2016 (LGBT Aging: A Review of Research Findings, Needs, and Policy Implications, 8/16). She and other authors estimated that sexual minorities were incarcerated at disproportionately high rates in February 2017 (Meyer et al., Incarceration Rate of Lesbian, Gay, Bisexual People Three Times the General Population Rate, Williams Institute at the UCLA Law School accessed at williamsinstitute.law.ucla.edu.) Gay and lesbian people are subject to many kinds of discrimination, including lack of employment protections, inability of transgender persons to use rest rooms consonant with their gender, discrimination in health programs, and bullying in schools and other settings. Researchers at the Williams Institute contend that LGBT persons are particularly subjected to discrimination in those Mountain, Midwest, and Southern states that rank high on an index that measures discriminatory attitudes about LGBT persons—the areas where LGBT persons are also most likely to fall beneath poverty levels (The LGBT

Divide in California, The Williams Institute at the UCLA Law School, 2015 accessed at williamsinstitute.law.ucla.edu).

- Children and youth beneath age 18. Children and youth in poverty-stricken families, as well as in the lower class and the lower middle class, are at higher risk of developing an array of social problems. Fifteen million children live in poverty—or 21% of all children. Yet research shows that families need an income of about twice that level to cover their basic expenses—meaning that 43% of children live in families that lack resources needed to meet their basic needs (Child Poverty, 2017). If 45% of children under 3 years live in low-income families, 42% of children ages 3 through 17 years live in them. If 33% of white infants and toddlers live in low income families, 69% of black infants and toddler live in them as compared with 63% of Hispanic infants and toddler and 29% of Asian infants and toddlers. These infants and toddler are most likely to live in a low-income family if parents have less than a high school degree or only have a high school degree. Families of single mothers with infants and toddlers are far more likely to live in low-income families than infants and toddlers in families with two parents (Lian, Y., Granja, M., & Koball, H., 2017).
- Low Income Persons including persons in poverty, lowest income persons, the lower middle class and some members of the middle class. We have already discussed the sheer number of Americans who live under federal poverty levels and the hardships they encounter. Now we take a broader perspective that includes lowest income persons, the lower middle class, the middle class, the upper middle class, and the highest class using a typology of the Pew Research Center (Pew Research Center, "The American Middle Class is Losing Ground," December 9, 2015, accessed @assets.pewresearch.org on 9/5/17). The lowest income persons include families of three that have less than half the nation's median income—or less than $31,000. This group includes persons under the federal poverty level. The lower middle class includes families of three with half to less than two-thirds of the median income or from $31,000 to $42,000. The middle class includes families of three with annual household income that is two-thirds to double the national median, i.e., about $42,000 to $126,000 annually for a household of three. The upper middle class households include persons with more than twice the overall median and up to three times the median income or $126,000 top $188,000. The highest-income household lived on more than $188,000 for a family of three. Persons who live in poverty or near poverty, who comprise the lowest income

tier, have increased from 16% of the population in 1971 to 20% in 2015. Persons in the lower middle class have stayed constant in their numbers at 9% of the population from 1971 to the present. The middle class has decreased in size from 61% of the population in 1971 to 50% of the population in 2015. The upper middle class has grown from 10% of the population in 1971 to 12% of the population in 2015. The highest class has grown from 10% to 12% of the population from 1971 to 2015. While all income tiers experienced income gains from 1970 to 2014, lower-income households and middle-class households lagged behind the gains of upper-income households. If upper-income households gained 47% from $118,617 to $174,625 in their median income, middle-income persons gained only 34% from $54,682 to $73,292 in their median income. Lower-income households' income increased only by 28% over this period from $18,799 to $24,074. While we have focused on persons under the Federal Poverty Level earlier in this chapter, these data suggest that inequality extends to many people beyond this group, including people in near poverty and to people in the lower middle class and the middle class. As one example, many people in the lower middle and middle classes lost their homes in the Great Recession of 2007 to 2009—unlike persons in the upper middle and highest class. The middle class is, moreover, "hollowing out" as compared to the lowest class, the upper middle class, and the highest class. We can now describe many members of the lower middle class and even some members of the middle class as "vulnerable populations." More data is needed to determine to what extent members of the lower middle class experience the array of social problems identified by Wilkinson and Pickett (2009). Americans have deemphasized the importance of social class from the colonial period to the present, partly because many believed that any *individual* who worked hard could achieve upward mobility. This mythology has been disproven by scores of social scientists and historians who have documented the importance of social class in the United States (Isenberg, 2016). Social class impacts whether and what diseases people develop, their longevity, their educational achievement, and the odds persons will move upward in the social order (Jansson, 2015). People in the lower class often face discrimination in schools, employment, juvenile and criminal justice systems, and elsewhere. Americans in the lower class have lower odds of upward mobility than their counterparts in many European nations and Canada (DeParle, 2012).

- Millennial persons should consider themselves members of a vulnerable population. Born between 1980 and 2000, they are distinctively different from prior generations. They numbered roughly 75.4 million persons in 2016 (Fry, 2016). Many have college education, but find it difficult to secure jobs since many jobs now require even higher levels of education. They have higher levels of debt, poverty and unemployment, and lower levels of wealth and personal income than the two predecessor generations, Gen Xers and Boomers, had at the same stage of their life cycles (Pew Research Center, Social & Demographic Trends, Millennials in Adulthood, March 7, 2014). Roughly two-thirds of them had average college debt of roughly $27,000 in 2014 compared to an average debt of $15,000 for only half of graduates two decades ago. Many of them suffered unemployment and underemployment in the Great Recession of 2007 through 2009—and considerable numbers of their generation experienced long-term unemployment lasting more than a year. Considerable numbers of young adults in this generation live with their parents, partly to avoid having to pay rent. Those not in the cohort with college degrees (roughly two-thirds of them) suffer low wages and high unemployment at higher rates than their counterparts in the prior two generations.

It is not surprising that the 16 at-risk populations just discussed are disproportionately likely to experience one or more causes of income inequality when we examine the course of American history. It includes slavery and its legacy, failure to honor the rights of immigrants, genocidal policies against Native Americans, barbaric treatment of persons with mental illness, law enforcement and policies of the criminal justice system that discriminate against persons of color, use of words like White trash to describe low-income White people, harsh treatment of persons in the lower class, and willingness to allow vast populations of homeless people to remain on the streets. It includes underfunded social and educational programs, compared to funding in most other industrialized nations.

Yet American history is filled with positive examples of timely assistance to people, such as civil rights legislations, social movements on behalf of persons of color and women, and social programs. Many members of these at-risk groups are highly successful. They empower themselves through collective action, participation in the political process, ownership of business, and participation in civic affairs. Some life experiences immunize people from the toxic effects of extreme inequality, poverty, lack of upward mobility, lack of hope, and discrimination. Persons with elevated levels of social capital, such as degrees from junior colleges, may be protected from toxic effects of extreme inequality, even when they continue to reside in regions with high levels of inequality. Considerable numbers of African Americans with college degrees and professional credentials are voluntarily returning to geographic areas peopled by relatively low-income African Americans because they can find friendly networks in them, but not in the largely White suburbs where they had lived. We can hypothesize that these networks, as well as their economic success, protect them from toxic effects of inequality and racism in the broader society.

Nomenclature Used in This Book

I was unable to find nomenclature that described the policy products needed by equality advocates who seek to reduce extreme income inequality, so I invented the following vocabulary, discussed in more detail in succeeding chapters:

- *Equality Roller Coaster* depicts pendulum swings of income equality during American history drawing on economic data produced by economic historians (discussed in chapters 2, 3, and 4). Establishing a national goal of lowering the Equality Roller Coaster from its present level to its level in 1978 (discussed in Chapter 4)
- *Initiatives to Uplift Ordinary People* (IUOPs) describe proposals to increase income of persons in the lower economic echelons (discussed in Chapters 5 and 6)
- Niche vs. Population-Wide IUOPs (discussed in Chapters 5 and 6)
- Extended working papers and policy briefs (discussed in Chapter 7)
- *Resources to Uplift Ordinary People* (RUOPs) raise revenues to fund IUOPs by (a) eliminating or reducing specific tax expenditures, increasing specific tax rates, and reducing the amount of income hidden in offshore accounts, (b) raising top marginal tax rates of affluent people, and (c) cutting specific kinds of wasteful government spending (see Chapter 8)
- *Fair Exchanges* couple specific IUOPs with specific RUOPs so the net cost to government is zero or greatly reduced (discussed in Chapter 8)
- Stockpiling revenues from RUOPs to fund IUOPs so that these increased revenues are prioritized to fund IUOPs (discussed in Chapter 7) in an Opportunity Trust Fund

- *An Opportunity Trust Fund* that holds portfolios of IUOPs, and RUOPs, (discussed in Chapter 8)
- *Equality-Enhancing Programs* (EEPs) in 16 academic disciplins and professions in institutions of higher education including colleges, universities, graduate programs, and professional schools.

How This Book Advances Understanding of Extreme Economic Inequality

The remarkable work of economic and other historians has greatly advanced our knowledge of economic (i.e., income) inequality in general and with respect to the United States in particular. We know that the United States is an outlier in its sheer level of its economic inequality. We also know that the United States has had extended periods of relative economic equality that lasted for decades—especially from the early 1930s through the 1970s.

This book uniquely identifies an ecology of extreme income inequality by identifying ten of its possible causes. It makes clear that inequality is woven into the fabric of American society. No magic bullets exist. Combinations of new policies have to be identified, tested, and implemented in a political system that has been gridlocked at least from 1984 between the two major parties and between liberals, moderates, and conservatives.

This book uniquely identifies 16 at-risk populations that disproportionately have unequal incomes than others, not just in present-day America, but often during extended period American history. This list is not meant to be comprehensive, but does include an array of them that bear a particular burden of income inequality.

Other Uses of This Book

This book focuses on income (economic) inequality. It can serve as background to the 12 Grand Challenges identified by the American Academy of Social Policy and Social Welfare. (American Academy of Social Policy and Social Welfare accessed @aaswsw.org on September 14, 2017). These 12 Grand Challenges include:

- Ensure health development for all youth,
- Close the health gap,

- Stop family violence,
- Advance long and productive lives,
- Eradicate social isolation,
- End homelessness,
- Create social responses to a changing environment,
- Harness technology for the social good,
- promote smart decarceration,
- Reduce extreme economic inequality,
- Build financial capability for all,
- Achieve equal opportunity and justice.

This book can be used to provide a backdrop for each of the other 12 Grand Challenges. I hypothesize, for example, that each of the twelve Grand Challenges is linked to many of the ten causes that I hypothesize cause extreme economic inequality. Poverty (cause 1) is linked to each of them. We can't close "the health gap," for example without addressing poverty because research has demonstrated that persons' longevity is powerfully linked to their social class (Tavernise, 2016). We can't "stop family violence" without decreasing poverty even though it occurs, as well, among non-poor families (Hines, Malley-Morrison, & Dutton, 2012). "Smart decarceration" must find ways to help reduce recidivism of low-income persons of color who are disproportionately incarcerated. We can't increase "long and productive lives" without reducing poverty because low income persons live shorter lives than more affluent persons (Tavernise, 2016). We can't eradicate "social isolation" without helping many White low-income males obtain jobs since many of them withdraw into social isolation when they lose them (Eberstadt, 2017).

Homeless people are often evicted from their housing because they can't afford the rent due to their low incomes (Desmond, 2016). We can't achieve "equal opportunity and justice" without reducing extreme income inequality (Piketty, 2014).

Even these few examples suggest that this book suggests that portions of the ecology of extreme income inequality apply to other Grand Challenges. The historical background of Extreme Economic Inequality that is discussed in chapters 2, 3, and 4 of this book may usefully provide the context of other Grand Challenges because all of the Grand Challenges emerged from an historical context. We can ask, for example, about the evolution of specific Grand Challenges through time as I have done in this book with respect to Extreme Income Inequality. Chapters 5 and 6 of this book provide a strategy for identifying possible solutions to specific Grand Challenges—an array of solutions needed not just for Extreme Economic Inequality, but for the other Grand Challenges.

Persons who address *any* of the Grand Challenges need to develop working papers and policy briefs as I discuss in Chapter 7 of this book with respect to Extreme Economic Inequality. They will also face the challenge of funding their proposed policy remedies as I discuss in Chapter 8 of this book with respect to Extreme Economic Inequality. They will also have to navigate their proposed policy solutions to their Grand Challenges through the political system as I discuss in Chapter 9 with respect to Extreme Economic Inequality.

Some of the terms that I have invented in this book with respect to strategies to reduce extreme economic inequality may be appropriate for many other Grand Challenges. All of us want, for example, to develop "Initiatives to Uplift Ordinary People (IUOPs)" as well as other terms described in preceding pages under the title, "Nomenclature Used in this Book."

In other words, policy advocates who address each of the 12 Grand Challenges encounter similar challenges, even as each of them presents its own challenges.

I hypothesize, too, that many or all of the 16 vulnerable populations that I identify in this book disproportionately experience extreme income inequality also disproportionately experience many of the Grand Challenges.

Organization of this Book

Chapters 2 and 3 provide an historical evolution of inequality in the United States, from the colonial period to the present, to analyze cycles in equality and inequality that occurred during that period. Its evolution in the United States resembles an equality roller coaster that declines during periods of relative equality, such as between 1750–1800 and 1933–1979, and rises during periods of relative inequality, such as between the late 1860s through the 1920s and from the early 1980s through (at least) 2018. This historical overview demonstrates that inequality in the United States, as depicted in Figure 1.1, is not inevitable as witnessed by relative equality from the early 1930s through the 1970s. Yet the historical overview, drawing on findings of economic historians, documents long periods of income inequality from the Gilded Age through the 1920s (roughly five decades) and from the early 1980s to (at least) 2017 (four decades and counting).

I discuss why the equality roller coaster transitioned from periods of relative equality to periods of relative inequality and vice versa in Chapter 4. No simple answers exist, but we can identify possible political and economic strategies for moving the nation from its current inequality toward more equality by examining these transitions.

Chapters 5 and 6 identify many strategies for reducing income inequality. The list is not complete: indeed, I urge readers to identify new ones. The length of my list illustrates the need to develop multiple strategies to redress extreme income inequality in the United States.

Chapter 7 discusses how students and advocates can develop working papers that lead to policy briefs that succinctly define evidence-based policy proposals aimed at reducing income inequality of a specific population or place.

In Chapter 8, along with co-author Anthony Orlando, I discuss strategies for funding policy briefs. Recall that many policy briefs have been rejected in recent American history because public officials contended they lacked resources. Also realize that income inequality has a zero-sum aspect: those in the lower economic echelons need more resources, which must partly come from increasing taxes on affluent Americans and corporations, expanding the national debt, or both. This statement is not hostile to persons with great wealth in the United States. Affluent Americans pay substantially lower income and inheritance taxes than their counterparts in most industrialized nations even as they benefit from many amenities in the United States, such as the banking system, infrastructure, national security expenditures, the Federal Reserve banking system, and social investments that help them obtain educated employees. It does not imply socialist intentions—none of the industrialized nations depicted in Figure 1.1 are socialist. Nor do increased taxes on affluent Americans need to be draconian. Their affluent peers in the 1950s through the 1970s led comfortable lives, complete with mansions and yachts, even when their top marginal tax rates were far higher than their counterparts in 2018, i.e., ranged between roughly 70% to 85% versus the current rate of 39.6% for single filers earning more than $415,050 and for married joint filers earning between $231,450 and $413,350. Government can also augment revenues that fund social investments to decrease inequality by cutting wasteful spending, as I discuss in Chapter 8. Surely the United States can find ways to cut health spending that nears 20% of GDP at a time when many other industrial nations spend less than 12% of GDP *and* have healthier and longer-living populations. Surely that United States can find ways to cut military spending that currently exceeds the combined military spending by the seven nations with the next highest spending.

Chapter 9 discuses how social work students and other students and graduates of institutions of higher education can stimulate national interest in inequality. They can develop IUOPs, RUOPs, and Fair Exchanges; transmit policy products to public officials via policy briefs; enhance curriculum and research about inequality; and pressure public officials in national elections in 2018, 2020, and beyond to support new policies. All professions and disciplines should contribute IUOPs and RUOPs to the quest to reduce income inequality by redressing its many likely causes.

Appendix to Chapter 1: Some Orienting Concepts

The income of persons comes from two sources: labor income and wealth income. Labor income consists of wages, salaries, work-related benefits, and benefits from social programs; wealth income consists primarily of dividends and capital gains net debt. Inequality is measured by comparing combinations of labor income and wealth income of specific deciles or percentiles of the population, such as the total income of the top 10% versus the bottom 90% (deciles) or the top 1% versus the bottom 99% (percentiles).

We can compare, for example, the total income of Scandinavian nations in 2007 with that of the United States in 2010 by examining tax and probate records, as illustrated in Table 1.1 (Piketty, 2014, p. 249). Data in Table 1.1 show dramatically different levels of inequality between the Scandinavian nations and the United States since considerably higher shares of income are held by the top brackets in the United States than in Scandinavia, while greatly higher shares of income are held by the two lowest brackets in the Scandinavian nations, compared to the United States.

Table 1.1: Inequality of total income (labor and capital)

Levels of Inequality Share of different groups in total income	Low (Scandinavia) 1970s–1980s	High (U.S.) (2010)
Top 1%	7%	20%
Next 9%	18%	30%
Top 10%	25%	50%
Middle 40%	45%	30%
Bottom 50%	30%	20%

The relative mix of income and wealth differs markedly between the top 10% and the lower 90%. The category, wealth, is relatively more important for the top 10% than to the bottom 90% because highly affluent people are more likely to possess stocks, real estate, bonds, and investments, as well as to receive substantial inheritances than others. The bottom 90% relies more heavily on income from work and government income substitutes, such as SNAP, subsidized housing, Medicaid, and subsidized health insurance under the Affordable Care Act. Particularly from the 1950s onward, considerable numbers of people in the bottom 90% purchased houses, both in European nations and in the United States, with the assistance of mortgages that were often insured by national governments.

Persons in the middle 40% and the bottom 50% of the United States have greatly reduced options compared with their Scandinavian counterparts, because they possess a lower share of their nation's income and wealth. United States residents pay lower taxes, but they incur higher expenditures of many kinds. They are less likely to take time off from work when relatives are sick or when their children are born. They are less likely to have vacations. They are more likely to incur debt to pay for higher education. They are less likely to be able to live in congregate living places when they are elderly. They have lower pensions when they retire. They do not receive state-subsidized sabbaticals. They are more likely to experience bankruptcy when family members need medical care. They are more likely to self-fund childcare and preschool education. They have higher out-of-pocket expenditures for health care, including deductibles, exclusions, and co-insurance—and have higher out-of-pocket expenditures for some other social programs. They are less likely to participate in civic activities such as voting. As suggested by data in Figure 1.1, they have higher odds of developing many kinds of social problems.

References

Ashkenas, J. (2016; December 16). Findings about inequality in the United States. *New York Times*.

al Badawi, A.M. (2012). Discrimination in the workplace. *Proceedings of American Society of Business and Behavioral Sciences, 19*(1) 5–11.

Balfanz, R., Bridgeland, J., Fox, J., DePaoli, R., & Ingram, E., (2014). *Building a Grad Nation: Progress and Challenge in Ending the High School Dropout Epidemic.* Retrieved from civicenterprises.net.

Balfanz, R., Building a GradNation; Progress and Challenge in Ending the High School Dropout Epidemic (2016) Retrieved from https://gradnation.americaspromise.org.

Bilmes, L.J. & Stiglitz, J. E. (2008). *The three trillion dollar war: The true cost of the Iraq conflict.* New York: W.W. Norton and Co.

Bolland, J.M. (2003). Hopelessness and risk behavior among adolescent living in high-poverty inner-city neighborhoods. *Journal of Adolescence, 26,* 145–158.

Bolland, J.M., Lian, B.E., & Formichella, C.M. (2005). The origins of hopelessness among inner-city African-American adolescents. *American Journal of Community Psychology, 36*(3–4), 293–305.

Brill, S. (2015). *America's bitter pill: Money, politics, backroom deals and the fight to fix our broken healthcare system.* New York: Random House.

Case, A. & Deaton, A. (2017). Mortality and morbidity in the 21st century. *Brookings Papers on Economic Activity,* Spring 2017, 1–63. Retrieved from https://www.brookings.edu.

Chen, V. (2016, January 16). All hollowed out: The lonely poverty of America's White working class. *The Atlantic.* @https://www,theatlantic.com/business/archive/2016.01/white-working

Child Poverty (2017). National Center for Children in Poverty accessed on 9/5/17@ www.nccp.org/topics/childpoverty.html).

Choi, S.K., & Meyer, I. H. (2016). *LGBT aging: A review of research findings, needs, and policy implications.* Retrieved from williamsinstitute.law.ucla.edu.

Clarke, K. (2016, August 23). Does Airbnb enable racism? *New York Times.* accessed @ https://www.nytimes.com/2016/08

Cobb, J. (2018; May 14). "The Southern strategist: The Reverend William Barber's effort to build a populist interracial coalition against poverty." The New Yorker, pp. 68-75)

Cohen, P. (2015, October 16). What could raising taxes on the 1% do? Surprising amounts. *New York Times.* @ https://www.nytimes.com/2015

Data Bank Indicators. (2016). Retrieved from childtrends.org.

DeParle, J. (2012, January 4). Harder for Americans to rise from lower rungs. *New York Times.*@newyorktimes.com/2012/01

Desmond, M. (2016). *Evicted: Poverty and Profit in the American City* (New York: Penguin Random House).

Eaton, G. (2014, January 26). Which countries have the highest tax rates? *NewStatesman.* Retrieved from http://www.newstatesman.com/politics/2014/01/which-countries-have-highest-top-tax-rates

Eberstadt, N.N. (2017, February 21). Our miserable 21st century, *Commentary.* Retrieved from https://aei.org/publication/our-miserable-21st-century

Francis, D. (2017; March 13). Employers replies to racial names. *National Bureau of Economic Research.* Retrieved from http://www.nber.org/digest/sep03/w9873.html.

Friedman, M. (2015). *Just facts: as many Americans have criminal records as college diplomas.* Retrieved from https://www.brennancenter.org.

Fritz, N. (2015, March 31). Economic inequality: It's far worse than you think. Retrieved from http://www.nber.org/digest/sep03/w9873.html.

Fry, R. (2016. April 25), *Millennials overtake baby boomers as America's largest generation.* Retrieved from http://www.pewresearch.org/

Fry, R. (2016, April 25). Millennials overtake Baby Boomers as America's largest generation, Fact Tank, Pew Research Organization.

Gates, G. (2011). *How many people are lesbian, gay, bisexual and transgender?* Retrieved from https://williamsinstitute.law.ucla.edu/research/census-lgbt-demographics-studies/how-many-people-are-lesbian-gay-bisexual-and-transgender/

Goetz, E.G. (2003). *Clearing the way: Deconcentrating the poor in urban America.* Google books.

Grusky, D. B. & Kanbur, R. (Eds.). (2006). *Poverty and inequality.* Stanford, CA: Stanford University Press.

Hacker, J. S. & Pierson, P. (2016, July 30). The path to prosperity is blue. *New York Times.* Retrieved from https/www.nytimes.com.

Incarceration rates of LGB people three times the general population. (2016). Retrieved from williamsinstitute.law.ucla.edu.

Isenberg N. (2016). *White trash: The 400-year untold history of class in America.* New York: Viking.

Jansson, B. S. (2015). *The reluctant welfare state, 8th ed.* San Francisco: Cengage.

Jansson, B. S. (2001). *The sixteen-trillion-dollar mistake.* New York: Columbia University Press.

Jansson, B. S. (2016). *Social welfare policy and advocacy: Advancing social justice from 8 policy sectors.* Thousand Oaks, CA: SAGE Publications.

Kane, J. (2012; October 22). Health costs: How the U.S. compares with other nations. National Public Radio, PBS Newshour. Linked in by author D. Leonhardt (2017; September 11), Five questions about single-payer health care. *New York Times.* Retrieved from https//nytimes.com.

Kastanis, A. (2016, January).*The LGBT divide in California: A look at the socioeconomic well-being of LGBT people in California.* Retrieved from https://williamsinstitute.law.ucla.edu.

Khullar, D. (2016, December 22). How social isolation is killing us. *New York Times.* Retrieved from https://nytimes.com.

Kleinbard, E. D. (2015). *We are better than this: How government should spend our money.* New York: Oxford University Press.

Kristof, N. (2015, May 21). The power of hope is real. *New York Times,* retrieved from https://nytimes.com.

Krogstad, J. M. (2016; September 8). *Key facts about how the U.S. Hispanic population is changing.* Retrieved from www.pewresearch.org.

Law Office of Cohen & Jaffe. (2017). *Discrimination against single mothers at work.* Retrieved from https://www.cohenjaffe.com

Jian, Y., Granja, M. & Koball, H., "Basic Facts about Low Income Children," National Center for Children in Poverty, January, 2017 accessed @ nccp,org on 9/5/17.

Luo, M. (2016, October 9). An open letter to the woman who told my family to go back to China, *New York Times.* Retrieved from http://www.nytimes.

Migration Policy Institute. (2011). *Frequently requested statistics on immigrants and immigration to the United States.* Migration Information Source. Retrieved from http://www.migrationinformation.org/feature/displaycfm?ID=818

Miller, L. (2012; July 1). The money-empathy gap. *New York Magazine* accessed @ nymag.com/news/features/money-brain-2012-7/.

Morin, R. (2012, January 11). *Rising share of Americans see conflict between rich and poor.* Retrieved from www.pewresearch.org.

National Alliance to End Homelessness. *State of Homelessness Report,* Retrieved from www.endhomelessness.org. on September 14, 2017

National Center for Education Statistics (2014), Digest of education statistics. Retrieved from nces.ed.gov/pubs2014/2014015.pdf

Nisbet, E. & Rodgers, W. M., The State University of New Jersey and the National Poverty Center. (2013, June). Earnings gap between undocumented and documented U.S. farm workers: 1990 to 2008. *National Poverty Center Working Paper Series.* Retrieved from npc.umich.edu @http.npc.umich.edu/publications/u/2013-07-npc-working-paper.pdf

Organization of Economic Co-Operation and Development (OECD). (2016, October 5). *Society at a Glance: OECD Social Indicators.* Retrieved from http://www.oecd.org/social/society-at-a-glance-19991290.htm.

Passel J. S., & Cohn, D. (2016, September 20). *Overall number of U.S. unauthorized immigrants holds steady since 2009.* Retrieved from www.pewhispanic.org.

Pew Research Center. (2014, March 7). *Millennials in adulthood.* Retrieved from www.pewsocialtrends.org.

Pew Research Center. (2016, June 27). Demographic trends and economic wellbeing. In *On views of race and inequality, Blacks and Whites are worlds apart.* (pp. 18–29). Retrieved from www.pewsocialtrends.org.

Pew Research Center. (2009, April 14), A portrait of unauthorized immigrants in the United States, Retrieved from www.pewhispanic.org/2009/…/14/a-portrait-of-unauthorized-immigrants-in-the-united-states.

Piff, P. K. (2014). Wealth and the inflated self: Class, entitlement, and narcissim. *Personality and Social Psychology Bulletin, 40*(1), pp. 34–43.

Piketty T. (2014). *Capital in the Twenty-first Century (A. Golhammer, Trans.).* Cambridge, MA: Harvard University Press.

Poverty is a death sentence. (2016, April 23). Retrieved from https:/berniesanders.com/poverty-death-sentence/

Rosier, S., & the Congress team (2014; July 24). *Changes in the net worth of U.S. Senators and Representatives.* Retrieved from https://ballotpedia.org/Changes_in_Net_Worth_of_U.S._Senators_and_Representatives_(Personal_Gain_Index)

Sacks, J. D. (2006). *The end of poverty: Economic possibilities for our time.* New York: Penguin Books

Sapolsky, R. M. (2004). Social status and health in humans and other animals. *Annual Review of Anthropology, 33,* 393–418.

Sapolsky, R. (2005). Sick of poverty. *Scientific American, 293,* 92–99.

Simon, J & Sparks, R. (2012). Sage Handbook of Punishment and Society (Thousand Oaks, CA).

Steinmetz, K. (2016, May 18). How many Americans are Gay? Inside the efforts to finally identify the size of the nation's LGBQ population. *Time Magazine.* Retrieved from http://time.com/lgbt-stats/

Tanguy, B., Dercon, S., Orkin, K., & Taffese, A. S. (2014). The future in mind: Aspirations and forward-looking behaviors in rural Ethiopia. *Centre for the Study of African Economies Series.* Retrieved from *https://www.economics.ox.ac.uk/Centre-for-the-Study-of-African-Economies-Series/the-future-in-mind-aspirations-and-forward-looking-behaviour-in-rural-ethiopia.*

Tavernise, S. (2012, January 11). Survey finds rising perception of class tension. *New York Times,* Retrieved from https://nytimes.com.

Tavernise, S. (2016, February 12). Disparity in life spans of the rich and the poor is growing, *New York Times,* Retrieved from https://nytimes.com.

Those with disabilities earn 37% less on average [Newsletter]. (2014, December 14). Retrieved from http://www.air.org.

U.S. Census Bureau (2016). American Indians: Census Facts-Infoplease. Retrieved from American Indians by the numbers U.S. Census Bureau.

Vance, J. D. (2016). *Hillbilly Elegy.* New York: Harper.

White, G. B. (2017; January 11). Obama frames his economic legacy. *The Atlantic* accessed on September 14, 2017 @ https://www.theatlantic.com/business/archive/2017/01/obama … economy/512804/

White, G. B. (2016; October 31). Uber and Lyft are failing black riders. *The Atlantic* accessed on Septemger 14, 2017@https://www.theatlantic.com/business/archive/2016/10/uber-lyft … rides/506000/

Wilkinson. R. G. & Pickett, K. E. (2009a). Income inequality and social dysfunction. *Annual Review of Sociology, 35,* 493–511.

Wilkinson, R. G. & Pickett, K. E. (2009b). *The Spirit level: Why more equal societies almost always do better.* London: Allen Lane.

Wilkinson, R. G. & Pickett, K. E. (2014, February 2). How inequality hollows out the soul. *New York Times.* Retrieved from http://nytimes.com.

Williams Institute (2015). The LGBT divide in California, Accessed @ williamsinstitute.law.ucla.edu.

Wilson, V. (2014, September 18), *2013 ACS shows depth of Native American poverty and different degrees of economic well-being for Asian ethnic groups,* Retrieved on September 14, 2017 @ from www.epi.org/blog/2013-acs-shows-depth-native-american-poverty/

Credits

Fig. 1.1: Richard G. Wilkinson and Kate Pickett, "Rankings of 21 Industrialized Nations by Inequality and Social Problems," The Spirit Level: Why More Equal Societies Almost Always Do Better. Published by Penguin Random House UK, 2009.

Table 1.1: Thomas Piketty, "Inequality of Total Income (Labor and Capital)," Capital in the Twenty-First Century, pp. 249. Published by Harvard University Press, 2014. Reprinted with permission.

2

THE FIRST TWO STOPS OF THE EQUALITY ROLLER COASTER FROM 1750 TO 1830 AND FROM 1865 THROUGH THE 1920s

Chapters 2 and 3 discuss the historical evolution of inequality in the United States from the colonial period to the present using an *Income Equality Roller Coaster* that moved downward (toward more equality) and upward (toward more inequality) through the nation's history as an analogy. These were not sudden gyrations, but took place over decades.

Some readers may wonder why it is helpful to analyze the historical evolution of extreme income inequality in the United States. I suggest several reasons. The historical record demonstrates that extreme income inequality is a man-made phenomenon because colonial and early America, as well as the period extending from the Great Depression, through the 1970s, were far more egalitarian than the period extending from the Civil War to 1933 and the period extending from the early 1980s to the present. The dramatic shift from relative equality to extreme inequality in the 1980s was partly caused by social and economic policies enacted by the Congress and signed by the president—but we can't identify them without analyzing history. We can also use the historical record to refute contemporary arguments that the United States cannot move toward greater equality because its population is larger and more diverse than smaller nations that are far more egalitarian than the United States, such as Scandinavian ones. The historical record suggests otherwise. The United States was relatively egalitarian from the Great Depression through the New Deal when it had a large and diverse population—much as Germany and France are far more egalitarian than the United States today even with large and increasingly diverse populations. We can learn about political, economic and cultural factors that hinder and promote greater equality by comparing periods of relative equality and periods of relative inequality in the United States. We can examine points of transition in the United States between periods of relative inequality and relative equality to identify triggering mechanisms that might help public officials and citizens to develop strategy to move the nation toward greater equality today. I identify many research topics in specific historical periods in Chapters 2 and 3 that need to be addressed to yield more information about why pendulum swings occurred in American history between extended periods of relative equality and inequality.

Relatively few Americans realize that the emerging nation in the colonial period was possibly the most income egalitarian of any capitalist economy in world history, with the Equality Roller Coaster in a low position from roughly 1750 to 1820. It rose toward greater income inequality by 1870 in the so-called Gilded Age that was bookmarked by tycoons like Andrew Carnegie and John D. Rockefeller at one extreme and millions of impoverished immigrants at the other extreme. It remained in this upward position from the 1870s through the 1920s for roughly seven decades, and descended rapidly in the early 1930s as the nation battled the Great Depression, only to remain in this low position through the 1970s for roughly five decades. It rose rapidly again in the 1980s, during the presidency of Ronald Reagan, and remained in this high position for almost four decades, until (at least) 2018, with levels of inequality similar to those in the Gilded Age.

These gyrations of the Income Equality Roller Coaster over a period of roughly 250 years make clear that extreme income inequality, a feature of contemporary America, is not inevitable. Reformers pushed it downward toward greater income equality for nearly four decades, beginning in the early 1930s.

Further research is needed to explore to what extent the ten (hypothesized) causes of extreme income inequality actually moved the Income Equality Roller Coaster upward and downward—or sustained it in low or high positions up to the present. Because the United States was only in its formative stages during the colonial period and through the 1920s, this research should give priority to its two most-recent gyrations: its movement downward in the period from 1933 through the 1970s and its movement upward from the early 1980s to the present.

The First Stop: Relative Income Equality in the Colonial Period Coupled with Extreme Poverty and Extensive Discrimination

The colonial period set in motion an ethos of income equality that found expression in words of the nation's founding fathers, the American Revolution, the Constitution, and the Bill of Rights. The founding fathers sought to make the new Republic a beacon to the world marked by income equality. Unfortunately, however, they also helped create a nation marred by slavery, oppression of Native Americans, and subjugation of women.

The colonial period ranked well, then, on two of the ten possible causes of income inequality if we just consider the White population. It had relative income equality and low levels of poverty for White settlers. But it had high levels of discrimination with respect to slaves and women, as well as Native Americans. The federal government was a primitive one when it was established in 1789, lacking even the power to collect a federal income tax. The words *social policy* don't even exist in the federal Constitution since founders believed social programs should be funded and operated by local and state governments.

Why a Beacon on the hill? Most settlers to the colonies and the new nation were refugees—whether from religious persecution, poverty, or limited opportunities in England and other European nations. These refugees included members of the numerous Protestant sects that were viewed as infidels by European state churches, such as Catholic or Anglican churches. The refugees often experienced persecution, ranging from executions to infringements on the ability to attend schools, vote, own property, and hold public office. Vast urban populations in England lived in extreme poverty after they had migrated from feudal rural areas to cities when large estates were divided into pastures to raise sheep and cattle, in a movement known as *enclosures*. Their poverty was increased, as well, by rapid population growth (Foner, 1955).

Large numbers of people made the extraordinary choice to cross the ocean to a wilderness only occupied by indigenous tribes of Native Americans. The fleeing refugees included those who were destitute and those escaping religious persecution. The earliest settlers struggled to survive in the New World among challenges including harsh winters, native peoples unhappy that their lands were invaded, and lack of survival skills. Desperation impelled additional waves of settlers who mostly sought one commodity: land on which they could eke out a bare existence.

The settlers were resilient people. They were mostly members of myriad persecuted Protestant sects. They were hard-working people who sought to control pride, greed, lust, and laziness by working hard. They mostly believed God wanted them to obtain plots of land to farm. They often believed that God wanted land to be farmed rather than occupied by nomadic hunters and gatherers—a belief that often led them into conflict with indigenous people, who they also distrusted because they were not Christians (Katz, 1983).

Small numbers of persons settled in the New Land in the 17th century, and larger numbers immigrated in the first five decades of the 18th century, creating a sizeable population several decades before the Declaration of Independence was written in 1776. Some settlers bought land from others who had large land grants from the English Crown. Others received it directly from the Crown or inherited it from relatives. Still others *squatted* on unoccupied land, hoping to find ways to legalize their possession of it.

This dispersion of the population into frontier settlements in a distant land allowed settlers to escape the controls and hierarchy of European nations. They developed local governments that assumed a variety of functions including making roads and bridges, developing primitive police forces, defending them from Native Americans, developing transportation systems, such as early canals, and developing simple systems of taxation. They organized economies with a mixture of bartering among themselves and the selling goods between themselves, local merchants, and with exporters who sent agricultural produce to Europe. They created a capitalist system not only by growing and selling agricultural products, but also by developing small-scale businesses on their farms and in their small towns (Woods, 1992).

Many settlers experienced or knew about unrest in England and Europe that threatened royalty, state churches, and social hierarchy. Ideas of Locke and other writers during the so-called English Enlightenment deeply influenced the work of the colonists organizing government and economies. These writers fervently questioned monarchical and religious authorities. The colonists were also influenced by writers such as Adam Smith, who questioned excessive governmental intrusion into private matters, and Voltaire, who opposed state religions, during the Scottish and Continental Enlightenment of the 18th century. Many merchants hoped to reduce government taxes and regulations. They had witnessed the development of a Parliament in England whose members won local elections and shared decision-making powers with the English monarch even before 1700. Many of them came to the New World, then, infused with views that made them increasingly restive under the British Governors of the different emerging states along the Eastern seaboard (Commager, 1977).

It was inevitable that frictions developed between these settlers and European powers. Settlers wanted the British to send larger military forces to protect them from Native Americans who understandably wanted to keep their ancestral lands. The colonists resented taxes that were imposed upon them by England as the Crown sought resources to fund its military forces in the New World. They resented policy decisions by British Governors who were placed in charge of specific geographic regions. They sometimes resented the competition between France, Britain, and Spain for control of specific regions in the New World, including areas where the settlers resided or might reside. They came to oppose the royal governors appointed by the crown who, they believed, sought to advance the trade and financial interests of the monarchy by exploiting them. This exploitation took multiple forms: taxing them; demanding exportation of their agricultural products to England, even at the risk of domestic food shortages; forbidding them from manufacturing goods that would compete with English goods; and demanding that only English ships could carry goods to and from England (Wood, 1992).

Despite these economic and intellectual developments, many Americans were not ready to contemplate independence. Most English-speaking Americans remained loyal to the English monarchy. Many colonies declared the Anglican Church as their official religion despite numerous protestant settlers. Many colonies required parents to pass their land on to their oldest son or their children rather than selling it (Wood, 1992).

Although the early towns were small, the sizable numbers of unskilled and semiskilled persons who came to reside in them were subject to the numerous recessions that bedeviled the fragile American economy. In a credit-hungry economy, many Americans became overextended, could not pay debts, and were imprisoned as a result. Produce was often plentiful, but grain exports to Europe were sometimes so great that shortages occurred in American cities. Consumer goods were often scarce in a nation that imported most of its manufactured goods.

Riots were common in both England and the American colonies. Sometimes they were provoked by frustration at the slow workings of cumbersome bureaucracies. Periodic food shortages or rising prices of food prompted riots in local jurisdictions, even in the colonies. American squatters—people who inhabited land without having obtained legal title—often rioted to persuade local officials to give them titles or to allow them to purchase their land at reasonable fees. A series of nine major rebellions, each lasting a year or more, erupted in rural areas in the 17th and 18th centuries. These rebellions were waged by persons with a homestead ethic who believed that their land titles had been unfairly seized by trading companies or that their land was excessively taxed by legislatures (Brown, 1977; Countryman, 1976). American colonists had not developed a distinctive culture or set of political institutions by 1750. They often thought of themselves as Europeans rather than as constituting an independent status in the New World. English émigrés primarily read literature from England, conversed about English politics, and often intended to return to England once they had obtained sufficient funds.

Patterns of change. A dramatically new society was created between 1750 and 1800. Access to land was the most powerful transforming factor in the New World. Whereas two-thirds of colonists owned land in 1750, only one-fifth of English citizens owned land. As they obtained property, many Americans came to perceive themselves not as common laborers, but as stakeholders in an emerging society. Male settlers increasingly demanded to participate in local and colonial politics, and as landholders, were often able to vote. They placed greater emphasis on work and initiative than landless people in England because they realized that their personal economic fate hinged on their ability to produce and sell crops and other commodities, such as candles or garments. If London and other British cities had large, landless, and destitute populations by 1750, this new society was mostly a *landed* one composed of persons with holdings of between 90 and 160 acres (Wood, 1992). As indentured servants finished their terms of service, they often moved onto small plots of land on the frontier, where new immigrants from Europe joined them. As land became scarcer on the Eastern seaboard, they moved to new areas. In a relatively brief period, huge areas of what later became Pennsylvania, New York State, and the Carolinas were flooded with immigrants. The dynamic and changing nature of this new society was fostered not only by mobility but also by population growth owing to the relatively high birthrate and continuing immigration. The White population in the colonies practically doubled every 20 years, increasing from 1 to 2 million between 1750 and 1770. The colonies were largely rural in 1750, with only 5 percent of the population living in cities. The semi-feudal norms and traditions of the early colonies had quickly eroded. Many observers noted that frontier people were a raucous lot. They were often violent, lacked government institutions, and possessed fierce individualism.

As members of the various religious sects became representatives in local and colonial government, they urged separation of church and state. They opposed the requirement in a number of colonies that citizens pay taxes to support the state church. Separation of church and state, which was made explicit in the Constitution, was inevitable in a country with so many religious sects.

Although England was the birthplace of capitalism and its attendant class of merchants, many English people, especially the landed aristocrats, still viewed capitalism with suspicion. Americans came to embrace it with fervor unknown to the English. Most Americans were small capitalists on their farms, where they labored to produce crops and commodities for export to Europe. Many farmers supplemented their income by producing a wide array of goods, including hats, candles, clothing, and tools, in their homes and barns (Wood, 1992).

According to historian Gordon Wood, the American Revolution was the catalyst that moved Americans to define their differences from the Old World and to forge a distinctive set of institutions (Wood, 1992, pp. 169–172). Colonial leaders issued the Declaration of Independence of 1776 after they had become infuriated with King George because he imposed new taxes on many goods to offset costs of protecting the colonies from Native Americans.

The demand for independence and the associated attack on the monarchy drew a wide and favorable response from large numbers of colonists. When viewed narrowly, the American Revolution was a rebellion against an overreaching Crown that insisted on its right to impose taxes without consulting the colonies' elected assemblies. When viewed more broadly, however, the Revolution was the catalyst for colonists to define their new society in terms markedly different from the customs of the Old World (Wood, p. 229). The war of independence lasted seven years after the issuance of the Declaration of Independence in 1776. By the time the American Revolution had ended, about one-tenth of White males had joined the militia. The sheer length of the conflict dramatized the formal separation from England and encouraged widespread acceptance of a new ideology of republicanism that deemphasized hierarchy, lauded individualism, favored the toil of ordinary people, and sought democracy. The battle against the Crown was supplemented, moreover, by intensive conflict *within* the colonies. Many Loyalists (or Tories), often drawn from the ranks of the owners of large parcels of land and the aristocratic class, did not participate in or support the Revolution, with some of them moving to Canada.

The achievement of independence enhanced the self-image of the colonists, who had managed to outwit and outduel a major world power. They confidently believed they could create a utopia of yeoman farmers by embracing capitalism and democratic institutions. Europeans such as Locke, by contrast, knew that their ideas could be only partially realized in societies encumbered by centuries of tradition, and by classes and institutions that resisted change. While Europeans imagined the Enlightenment, Americans created it (Commager, 1997). As most Americans possessed land, no large class of landless and urbanized people existed who wanted to dramatically overthrow government as in the French Revolution. These American revolutionaries fought both for independence and to establish a society grounded on individualism and freedom, but not to effect dramatic changes in the social structure of the colonies.

The importance that colonial leaders attached to land ownership is illustrated by a portion of a letter that Thomas Jefferson wrote to James Madison in 1785, during a visit to France. Jefferson contrasted social conditions in France with conditions in the colonies in a letter where he wrote: "the small landowners are the most precious part of a state (Peterson, 1974, pp. 396–397).

All was not well in this emerging Republic. A host of research strongly suggests that the American Revolution, though accompanied by a surge in idealism and sacrifice, had relatively limited effects on social reform. It did not help to obtain legal parity for women, provide just treatment for Native Americans, end slavery, or reduce the marked inequality between social classes (Green, 1987).

Did the founders make it difficult to address the ten causes? The founders succeeded in producing the U.S. Constitution, but may have included provisions that would later make it difficult to address the ten causes of income inequality. The federal government might have decreased the growing income inequality prior to the Civil War but could not for multiple reasons. The nation's founders had intentionally created a relatively weak federal government because they feared that the president or a majority of the people might obtain despotic power. They developed a division of power between presidential, legislative, and legal branches. They limited the federal government to specific enumerated powers such as regulating interstate commerce, printing currency, and managing foreign policy and a militia. They also included in the Constitution provisions such as improving the general welfare, that might eventually augment the power of the federal government, but it was unclear whether, and how, these powers might be used. They also provided a mechanism for amending the Constitution.

In addition, the relative impotence of the federal government was manifested by the founders' failure to add two additional powers: the power to enact social legislation and the power to levy an income tax. They assumed state and local governments would handle social problems like poverty, unemployment, and old-age pensions. They believed local property and sales taxes, coupled with federal excise taxes and tariffs, would suffice.

The framers wanted to put strict limits on the power of the federal government, but they did not agree about how limited the new government would be. During the two terms of President George Washington, a heated battle developed between two factions led, respectively, by Alexander Hamilton, Washington's secretary of the treasury, and Thomas Jefferson, his secretary of state. A self-made man with aristocratic inclinations, Hamilton wanted a relatively strong central government that would pursue mercantilist policies akin to the Crown. He wanted the federal government to invest resources in roads, canals, and bridges; to establish a national bank to oversee the economy; to fund promising new economic projects; to impose considerable taxes to fund these projects and pay off debts that remained from fighting the Revolutionary War; and to develop a strong navy and militia. Hamilton favored a relatively loose interpretation of the Constitution. While acknowledging that the Constitution mentioned only certain powers, Hamilton believed that it implied other powers, such as the power to establish a National Bank. In contrast, Jefferson favored a limited federal government; he supported *strict constructionism*, according to which the government would be limited to the powers enumerated in the Constitution. He wanted the American economy to center upon agriculture; opposed a National Bank on the grounds that it was not mentioned in the Constitution; opposed mercantilist policies; wanted low federal taxes; and opposed a standing army (Smith, 1993). George Washington often sided with Hamilton against Jefferson—even personally heading militia to Pennsylvania to put down a local rebellion against a federal Whiskey Tax to offset costs of the Revolutionary War.

Jefferson won this battle, however, when he was elected president in 1800. With few exceptions, all of the presidents of the 19th century subscribed to Jefferson's views of limited government. Even in 1854, when reformer Dorothea Dix succeeded in persuading the Congress to authorize the use of some monies from federal land sales to fund mental institutions in the states, President Franklin Pierce vetoed it with a message that expressed the philosophy of virtually all of the presidents of the 19th century: "I cannot find any authority in the Constitution for making the Federal Government the great almoner of public charity throughout the United States" (Axinn and Levin, 1982).

When taken together, then, various provisions of the Constitution, as well as Jefferson's philosophy came to limit the ability of the federal government to reduce income inequality—even several centuries later. Modern-day conservatives held many of Jefferson's views. The division of power in the Constitution made it difficult to legislation through the federal government. Yet another feature of the Constitution was to make reforms difficult: the allocation of two Senators to *each* state. Consider the current situation when relatively liberal and large states, like California and New York State, only have four senators between them, whereas relatively small and conservative states in the South and Mountain States, have as many as 20 U.S. Senators between them. We can't blame the founders for this provision because they could not have predicted that California would even exist or that California and New York State would have such huge populations, but it greatly decreases the ability of modern-day liberals to obtain legislation that could greatly decrease income inequality.

State governments matched the powerlessness of the federal government. They levied negligible taxes. With only a tiny bureaucracy and no police, a localized judiciary system that rarely met more than fifteen to thirty days in any given year, and legislators that in peacetime were rarely in session for more than a month in any given year, state government was small, intermittent, and inexpensive. State legislatures often met only for several weeks a year or every other year. Local governments maintained jails and poorhouses, but mostly concerned themselves with maintenance of local roads.

Why the Equality Roller Coaster was at a low level. It is not surprising that the Equality Roller Coaster was at a low level during the colonial period (see Figure 1.1). Traditional European agrarian societies, such as in France and England, were highly unequal because many generations of landed gentry had built fortunes from their vast amounts of land accumulated over centuries. They relied upon feudal serfs to farm their lands. Small towns dotted the countryside. American colonists, by contrast, were immigrants with scant resources, who managed to obtain small landholdings at relatively low prices, given the sheer quantity of unoccupied land. They lived in a preindustrial era, producing small amounts of agricultural product and timber that they mostly sold in local markets. Most colonists—and then most Americans—obtained their income from relatively small plots of land. The new Republic had a primitive transportation system and only three million residents in 1776. They exported timber and grain to Europe with use of sailing ships. Life was harsh for these American farmers, who had to contend with droughts, hail stones, or insects that ruined their crops (Wood, 1992).

Roughly 800,000 slaves, unable to earn or save money, lived on plantations, mostly in the South. Their economic future was bleak because no early end to slavery was possible. Many of the framers of the Constitution eyed slavery uneasily because they feared that social turmoil from slave rebellions would allow England to conquer the South (for its cotton), or might require the federal government to commit troops to restore tranquility. (These pragmatic fears were more prevalent than moral outrage.) Northerners also feared that Southerners would bolt the Constitutional Convention—and the new nation—if they mentioned abolition, but they did not want slavery transplanted to the frontier. They also did not want Southerners to capture control of the Congress by adding large numbers of slave-favoring congressmen in new states that entered the union from frontier areas (Appleby, 1984).

This conflict between Northerners and Southerners became the most contentious division during the Constitutional Convention in 1787 and led to a series of compromises. The Northerners obtained exclusion of slavery from the frontier north of the Ohio River in the Northwest Ordinance of 1787 and were allowed to place a tax on imported slaves. But Southerners won most of the concessions: slavery was not limited to those states where it existed; slaves were counted as though they were three-fifths of a person for purposes of apportioning congressional representatives; and Congress was not permitted to interfere with the importation of slaves until 1807. (Legislation to prohibit importation was finally enacted in 1808.) Slavery was legitimized by the Constitution, which referred to it in many places.

Both Southerners and Northerners miscalculated during the Constitutional Convention. Southerners assumed that no additional interference with the institution of slavery would develop as they gained control the Congress, as new slave states were added to the Union, and as the population of Southern states increased. Northerners assumed that slavery would disappear as the economy grew and as farmers populated new states in the Midwest. Neither side realized that both regions would obtain new states on the frontier and that a political stalemate would culminate in a civil war.

Appleby (1978) argues persuasively that the framers left war as the only means of abolishing slavery when they legitimated it in the Constitution. Once legitimated, slavery could not be abolished without passage of a constitutional amendment, but the necessary two-thirds vote of both houses of Congress or ratification by three fourths of state legislatures would have been unattainable once the many Southern states became part of the Union. Had the framers *not* mentioned slavery in the Constitution, it could have been eliminated by a simple majority vote in Congress, in a manner akin to its abolition by a majority vote in the British Parliament (Appleby, 1978).

Native Americans also mostly lived outside the market system. Tens of thousands of Native Americans were pushed Westward out of their lands, and many as 90% of them eventually died from diseases transmitted to them by the colonists, for which they lacked biological immunity, such as cholera, diphtheria, whooping cough, and scarlet fever. Settlers believed God wanted them to obtain plots of land and to farm them. They often believed God wanted them to take land from Native Americans because they often were nomadic hunters and gatherers rather than farmers and because they were not Christians.

Indentured servants and farm laborers were extremely poor. Indentured servants could, at least, escape their status as household laborers when their terms of servitude ended, often five to seven years after they began their service. Women had few rights in this emerging nation, often not allowed to earn or inherit money. They could not vote. They could not enter professions. They were often denied education.

Assessing the Colonial Period with Regard to the Ten Causes

Recall that we identified ten causes to an egalitarian society: exposure to extreme income inequality; high levels of poverty, low levels of upward mobility, low levels of hope, high levels of discrimination, low levels of social and educational investments by government, poor health and access to healthcare, inadequate government resources to fund social investment due to low levels of taxation and high levels of government waste; failure to tax affluent elites sufficiently, and a political system structured to discriminate against voters and interests that favor greater economic equality. It is difficult to assess to what extent these ten causes enabled the Equality Roller Coaster to sustain a downward position from roughly 1750 and into the early part of the 19th century. We have empirical data that shows that it was in a low position.

Cause 1. Lindert & Williamson (2013) contend that incomes were more equally distributed in the colonies than in other places like England and Wales just before and after the American Revolution. The richest 1% in the colonies had only 7.1% of total income compared to roughly 20% in contemporary America. Incomes of most colonists clustered together, with very few of them either in poverty or earning substantially more than other colonists. This income equality derived from the sheer number of small farms as well as merchants and artisans in villages, towns, and small urban areas. Income distribution in England was more unequal, with owners of large estates and of large enterprises, like factories and mines, at the top of the distribution. As we discuss subsequently, slaves and Native Americans lived outside of the market economy, prohibited from owning land producing crops, which were the major economic commodity.

Cause 2. Nor was poverty a large threat in colonial America in the White population because most White people lived on small land holdings where they could grow food and barter with neighbors. They experienced hardships in years when droughts, hailstorms, and other hazards ruined their crops. They had to store food through the winter without the modern convenience of refrigeration. They were subject to many diseases and epidemics absent modern medications and technology.

Cause 3. Data about upward mobility in colonial society does not exist to our knowledge. We can hypothesize that upward mobility was substantial due to relatively easy access to land through auctions, purchase, or squatting.

Cause 4. Aside from slaves, women, and Native Americans, it is likely that most people believed that they could obtain land, so levels of hope were probably high in the White population.

Cause 5. The colonists fared far worse with respect to discrimination. Slaves and Native Americans lived outside the market economy. Slaves were given subsistence food and lodging, but had little or no income. Owners treated them in an oppressive way as mere chattel. They were subject to whippings and other punitive measures. They were mostly denied access to education. They could be sold at any time. They lacked virtually any basic civil rights. Slaves that attempted to escape their bondage by fleeing from plantations were often shown no mercy and were slain, mutilated, or otherwise punished. The legality of slavery was upheld in the U.S. Constitution, even allowing Southern states to count individual slaves as two-thirds of a person when establishing the number of representatives they could elect to the U.S. House of Representatives (See Jansson, 2015 for further discussion of slaves, pp. 86–87).

From Christopher Columbus's first encounter with Native Americans through the 18th century, Native Americans were subjected to harsh interactions with White settlers, who pushed them westward off their lands as settlers claimed land for their farms. They died in massive numbers from diseases brought to the New World to which they had no immunity, including cholera, malaria, smallpox, diphtheria, whooping cough, scarlet fever, and influenza. Native Americans faced a tragic dilemma. If they resisted efforts by White settlers to take their lands, they were accused of violent behavior, which led to violent reprisals by White settlers. If they acceded to the Westward movement of the settlers by signing treaties that ceded lands to them in exchange for lands further inland or for superficial gifts, they lost the very lands that allowed them to survive. (See Jansson, 2015, for further discussion of Native Americans, pp. 83–86.)

Women were widely viewed as "weaker vessels," who were inferior to men in their intellect and morally. They could not vote. They were not mentioned in the Declaration of Independence or the Constitution. They often could not inherit property when their husbands died. They could not hold major roles in Church governance. They could work prior to marriage but were generally expected only to engage in household work after marriage. Absent birth control, many women had large numbers of children, but as many as one in every five women died during childbirth. (See Jansson, 2015, for further discussion of colonial women, pp. 81–83.)

Cause 5 did not move the Equality Roller Coaster upward partly because slaves, Native Americans, and women were excluded from data that measured income of White men and White people. Slaves and Native Americans were outside the normal or recognized economy.

Cause 6. Social and educational investments hardly existed in a rural, landholding economy. The concept of universal public education did not yet exist. Social programs hardly existed aside from a few poorhouses, where poverty stricken people, those with mental illness, and impoverished older persons were placed under relatively punitive conditions. They collected sufficient taxes to build roads and bridges, but not much else. The U.S. Constitution did not give the federal government the power to levy income taxes, so the colonies and the early Republic had to mostly rely on property taxes of local jurisdictions as well as excise taxes and tariffs. Social and educational investments did not decrease inequality in the White population because education was relatively unimportant in a pre-industrial agricultural economy.

Cause 7. Access to healthcare was not a major factor in colonial society partly because medical care was primitive and not based on science. It was provided by an assortment of providers. The medical profession did not exist in the modern sense.

Causes 8, 9, and 10. These causes, too, were irrelevant to the agricultural society of the colonial period. Colonists did not collect revenues other than to perform minimal government functions mostly at the local level. They didn't tax affluent people substantially. Many Constitutional provisions would make it difficult to get equality-enhancing policies enacted a century later, but not until the nation had urbanized and industrialized as discussed in the next chapter.

The Rise of the Equality Roller Coaster from 1800 to 1860

The Equality Roller Coaster moved toward a higher position from 1800 to 1860 for a number of reasons that included changes in the agrarian economy, an initial influx of low-income immigrants, and the growth of social problems that presaged a more complex society. The nation only possessed primitive social policies.

Changes in the agrarian economy. Inequities grew within rural areas as some people acquired greater amounts of land. It was difficult to farm in areas where land had to be cleared and when settlers dealt with thick sod that was difficult to plow. They faced droughts, invasion by grasshoppers, hail- stones, and floods. They lacked motorized farm equipment, relying on horses, mules and oxen. In a normal process of bankruptcy of some farmers, and acquisitions by successful ones, disparities in acreage appeared (Pessen, 1978).

The federal government held land auctions in territories on the frontier, but the auctions often favored people who had scouted the lands to locate particularly rich river bottom soil (Sosin, 1967; Rohrbaugh, 1969). Federal auction officials often took bribes to give preferred access to these lands. Boom-and-bust cycles in the prices of agricultural produce contributed to the cycle of bankruptcies and land acquisition. It was difficult to move agricultural produce to small cities and ports where it could be exported to Europe, despite the use of rivers supplemented by canals in Eastern and Midwestern states.

Gradual Growth of Industry and Cities. American society was predominantly an agricultural nation prior to the Civil War. In 1830, 91% of Americans lived in towns of fewer than 2,500 persons. Eastern cities remained small by modern standards. Although Philadelphia had a population of 40,000 people in 1785, by 1830 it grown to a population of only 120,000. Many rural Americans were only distantly aware that a growing population of poor persons lived in urban settings.

Early American cities were rough places. Speculators hurriedly constructed shantytowns and tenements in the absence of housing codes. Abundant public health hazards, including open sewers and poor sanitation, gave rise to epidemics. Prostitution, gambling, street begging, and drinking were rampant. Widespread unemployment accompanied the major recessions in 1819, 1833, 1837, and 1857, when as many as one-fifth of the entire populations of New York and other large cities received welfare benefits in almshouses or from outdoor soup kitchens maintained by public and private agencies (Mohl, 1971; Sellers, 1991). When discussing the hardships of the Panic of 1819, historian Charles Sellers notes:

> Distress was most acute in the cities … In Philadelphia, three out of four workers were reported idle … philanthropic groups distributed soup to the starving … the 8,000 public paupers who alarmed other New Yorkers in 1819 swelled in a year to nearly 13,000 … even the

> smaller towns faced the prospect of families naked—children freezing in the winter's storm ... and everywhere the cities and towns lost population as the destitute fled back to kin in the countryside for subsistence. (Sellers, 1991, p. 137)

Those most susceptible to economic straits during recessions were unskilled laborers, such as cartmen, chimney sweeps, woodcutters, and stevedores, who constituted the largest group in the labor force (Foner, 1955). When American industry was still in its infancy, employees of shoe, textile, and other enterprises often worked in groups of as many as 12 employees or in larger groups in the nation's few factories. Working conditions were generally oppressive. A working week of six 12-hour days was typical; income was at subsistence levels; and rates of job-related injury were high. A wave of strikes occurred in the 1820s and 1830s in Eastern cities. Between 1833 and 1836, there were 172 strikes in New England; strikers demanded a ten-hour day and mobilized a brief "general strike" of 20,000 workers in Philadelphia. Unions maintained a precarious existence, however, because of the newness of American industry, court rulings that were adverse to unions, frequent recessions, and company owners' strong-arm tactics against union organizers (Foner, 1955).

Less information exists about the extent and nature of poverty in agricultural and frontier communities, but a large class of low-paid agricultural laborers helped landowners clear the land and prepare the soil for cultivation. Work on the frontier was often brutally hard; settlers used hand tools and oxen to clear wooded areas. Immigrants were often conscripted to work for labor-contract companies that skimmed profits from their subsistence wages and intimidated them from seeking private employment (Pessen, 1978).

The extraordinary migration of Americans across the landscape, both on the Western frontiers and to Eastern cities from the countryside caused social problems. Prostitution arose to accommodate the imbalanced sex ratios on the frontier and the trend to delay marriage. As people tried to eke out an existence on the frontier or in the growing cities, some responded to economic uncertainty with suicide and alcoholism. In the absence of governmental institutions, churches, and local leaders, unlawful behavior was widespread in many frontier communities (Sellers, 1991).

American cities increasingly became repositories for immigrants from Ireland and Germany. Between 1814 and 1845, nearly 1 million impoverished Irish citizens entered the United States. They were mostly Catholic peasants from southern Ireland, and they replaced the predominant immigrant group of the 18th century, the so-called Scotch-Irish from Ulster, who were Protestant.

Another 1.2 million Irish immigrants followed these in a scant seven years during and after the disastrous potato famine of 1845–1849, which decimated Ireland's population (Sellers, 1991). Irish immigrants encountered extraordinary prejudice. The dominant protestant population disliked Catholics, who they viewed as lacking moral virtue, imbibing alcohol excessively, and spreading disease (Woodham-Smith, 1962).

Growth of Unaddressed Social Problems. A youth crisis developed in the 1840s, when many teenagers, finding themselves without work opportunities at the end of apprenticeship programs, roamed the streets and countryside. However, the crisis eased by the end of the century with the rise of high school education and increasing numbers of jobs in industry. As we shall see, Americans built large numbers of orphanages to house youth who left their homes before the age of 16, or those whose parents voluntarily committed them for lack of personal resources to care for them (Boyer, 1978).

Where social institutions existed to address economic and social needs, they were often poorly maintained. Touring America in the 1840s, Charles Dickens, the noted English author, found American prisons and almshouses to be scandalous, even when compared with the inhumane English institutions of that period. Almshouses, which represented the major social strategy to deal with social problems, were typically crowded, unsanitary, and poorly staffed. In these institutions, orphans mingled with those who had been categorized, rightly or wrongly, as mentally ill, delinquent, or senile (Berthoff, 1971).

Americans were obsessed with "blaming victims." In the first half of the 19th century, America had a potpourri of Protestant sects, some Catholic strongholds in Eastern cities, and a small number of Jewish settlers. Local clergy assumed major social and political roles in promulgating social norms, inveighing against such sins as drinking and swearing, and in urging citizens to be industrious.

Partly because of this religious backdrop, social problems were generally seen in moral terms. Many persons believed that bankruptcy was caused by profligate spending, crime by drinking or lack of deference to social superiors, and insanity by lust. Problems were commonly perceived to be interrelated; thus, persons who ceased to attend church might be expected to become alcoholics and then delinquent or insane (Boyer, 1978).

Social theorists, politicians, and citizens believed that alcoholism, crime, insanity, gambling, prostitution, and vagrancy were caused solely by individual and moral defects—or by immoral special interests such as the liquor industry. They stereotyped paupers as the progeny of families with intergenerational poverty, and they equated common social problems with immigrant populations, whose numbers expanded sharply in the last half of the century. This preoccupation with morality blinded Americans to alternative explanations of social problems, such as lack of employment, an undisciplined economy that led to frequent recessions, discrimination against immigrants, and lack of adequate social institutions for urban residents. These moral conceptions of social problems led Americans to embrace equally simplistic solutions, which tended to combine moral, religious, educational, disciplinary, and deterrent policies that included poor houses (sometimes called almshouses), temperance movements, and the Sunday School Movement to evangelize poor persons (Katz, 1983).

Emerging Tycoons. The Equality Roller Coaster can only move upward when a large low-income population emerges in concert with a population of affluent persons. Even prior to the Civil War, an emerging class of wealthy entrepreneurs had begun to surface. The nation had to develop internal improvements to allow them to transport goods to markets in the U.S. and abroad. The nation had developed a large system of canals in the East and Midwest prior to the Civil War. Useful as this system was, it began to be supplanted, even before the Civil War, by the emergence of trains that came to cross the Continent by 1869. The scant public resources of the debt-ridden nation were largely devoted to internal improvements that would allow transportation within, and settlement of, this frontier empire—not to mention the donation of vast tracts of land to railroads by the federal government.

The California Gold Rush of the late 1840s and 1850s signaled a new source of income for speculators that eventually led to vast fortunes in such minerals as copper and iron ore, as well as coal in such states as Pennsylvania and West Virginia, and oil in Pennsylvania and eventually in many Western states.

Assessing the Period from 1800 to 1865 with Regard to the Ten Causes

Cause 1. The signs were clear; the nation was rapidly heading toward income inequality from 1800 to 1865 in contrast to Jefferson's nation of small landowners (for White people). Income inequality was increasing as more people left farms for cities and as low-income immigrants, such as the Irish, came to the United States. The early signs of industrializing were appearing. Major fortunes were beginning to materialize in mining and manufacturing. With the influx of immigrants and the emergence of agricultural, professional, industrial, merchant, and banking elites, economic inequality increased in the cities of New England between the 1820s, when 1 percent of the population held one-fourth of the wealth, and the 1850s, when 1 percent of the population held one-half the wealth (Pessen, 1978). The Gini coefficient is a measure of statistical dispersion that is widely used by economists to gauge the extent of inequality. A Gini coefficient of zero indicates that everyone has the same income whereas a Gini coefficient of 1 expresses maximal inequality. It rose greatly from 0.40 to 0.53 between 1774 and 1860. In the South, it rose from 0.46 to 0.60, higher than any other country in the world, according to Lindert and Williamson (2013).

Cause 2. Poverty was also increasing, as evidenced by strikes, recessions, and human misery among immigrants and people migrating from rural areas to growing urban areas. With wealth at the top increasing and poverty at the bottom beginning to soar, it was inevitable that the Income Inequality Roller Coaster was about to soar to historic levels. Subject to the vicissitudes of world markets and to frequent recessions, farmers, merchants, and bankers often could not repay loans from local or foreign creditors; many local laws allowed imprisonment of debtors even when small sums were involved. (Local courts often practiced leniency.) There was widespread agitation against imprisonment for debt, as well as against local banks and speculators who charged excessive rates of interest or profiteered in land speculation prior to the Civil War (Pessen, 1978). The nation engaged in rapid building of poor houses.

Cause 3. Data does not exist about rates of upward mobility to my knowledge.

Cause 4. Data does not exist about levels of hope among low-income persons, but we can hypothesize that it declined among some groups in the population from the sheer number of strikes and disturbances in this period, as well as homelessness, vagabonds, and children living on the streets.

Cause 5. Rampant discrimination existed in the period leading up to the Civil War. If slavery had been located mostly in the old South (i.e., the Carolinas, Alabama, and Georgia), it spread westward into Mississippi and Texas where cotton and tobacco were king. As mere property of their masters and not having support from church, government and legal institutions, slaves were at mercy of their masters. Indeed, slave owners hoped to dominate the economy and governments of frontier areas that would become the states of Missouri, Kansas, and Nebraska. Rivalry and conflict grew between slave owners and persons who sought land in these areas for farms. While the Congress staved off war by enacting the Missouri and Kansas Compromises of 1820 and 1850, respectively, it was just a matter of time before armed conflict broke out. The election of Abraham Lincoln as president in 1860 led Southerners to fire the first shot in what became the bloodiest conflict in world history to that point. The fate of slaves hung in the balance: Would slavery be eliminated and the slaves finally emancipated? Would the institution of slavery spread beyond the South, border states, and Texas or be contained within those areas? While slaves *were* emancipated, they endured further hardships, as most of them, given no land or other resources, struggled to survive as sharecroppers who were beholden to White landowners (for further discussion, see Jansson, 2015, pp. 131–137).

Native Americans also suffered a harsh fate. Mostly pushed into lands West of the Mississippi by the end of the Civil War, former Civil War generals launched an assault on the remnant tribes. They were forced onto reservations, mostly in marginal lands in various Western territories and states (for further discussion, see Jansson, 2015, pp. 124–128).

Single White women often worked in various trades, as domestics, and at emerging factories for low wages and long hours. Married women were still mostly confined to child rearing. Remarkable women, such as Elizabeth Cady Stanton, convened a conference in Seneca Falls, New York, where they developed a Declaration of Sentiments that declared, that all men and women are created equal. They demanded suffrage, access to professional jobs, and legal rights. Many women had joined the abolitionist cause prior to and during the Civil War, only to find that they were not mentioned in the 13th Amendment to the Constitution that freed slaves, but left them without rights (for further information, see Jansson, 2015, pp. 118–122).

As settlers moved West of the Mississippi, they encountered a substantial population of persons with Mexican heritage. They found territory suitable for ranching and growing cotton in the 1820s and 1830s. They conquered the indigenous population and established a territorial government that became Texas in 1845. When Mexico refused to recognize this state, the United States conquered Mexico. Over the objections of Abraham Lincoln, its military forces invaded Mexico City and demanded territory that is now California, Nevada, New Mexico, Utah, and parts of Colorado, Wyoming and Arizona. They signed the Treaty of Guadalupe Hidalgo that finalized the exchange of land and required the United States to honor the civil liberties and rights of the indigenous and Spanish-speaking populations. These requirements were not honored in succeeding decades. American settlers refused to honor the land titles that existed under Mexican law. Lacking land and resources and denied civil rights, the large indigenous population became workers on American ranches, in mines, and in agriculture, with minimal wages and without regulations that safeguarded their working conditions. (For additional discussion, see Jansson, 2015, pp. 127–129.)

Asian immigration to American began in the 1840s with Chinese immigrants who came to find gold, to do manual labor building railroads, and working in agriculture and mining. They, too, were denied civil rights: they could not vote, own land, own mines, and in California, could not testify against Whites in court. The Chinese Exclusion Act of 1882 prohibited entry of additional Chinese immigrants to the United States.

Japanese immigrants entered the United States after the Civil War and soon outnumbered Chinese immigrants. They worked as manual laborers in agriculture and some had their own farms and small businesses. They too, found their civil rights violated. The so-called Gentlemen's Agreement of 1907 required Japan halt further emigration of Japanese settlers to the United States, except for family members of existing residents. The California legislature enacted laws to prevent Japanese immigrants from owning land; the U.S. Supreme Court ruled in 1922 that they could not become American citizens because 1790 federal legislation had required that American citizens be Caucasian (for further discussion, see Jansson, 2015, pp. 128–130).

Cause 6. The nation also failed to obtain a high score with respect to funding social and economic investments, even as millions of impoverished immigrants from Asia, Europe, and Russia were about to descend on the nation. The federal government still lacked the power to establish an income tax system even though one was used, temporarily, to fund the government debt incurred during the Civil War. The United States was the first nation to establish compulsory public education, which required considerable expenditures from local governments. The nation built a network of canals and began to invest in railroads with land grants from the federal government.

Cause 7. The nation lacked a formal health system. Mostly untrained practitioners gave persons medical care that included herbs and use of leeches. Medical science was it its infancy. People purchased their health care because no national system of health insurance existed.

Causes 8, 9, and 10. These causes were largely irrelevant to the United States prior to the Civil War. The nation lacked federal income taxes, lacked ways to tax affluent Americans, and had a primitive political system that could not have developed or implemented major social programs to reduce the growing income inequality.

The Equality Roller Coaster's Rapid Ascent From 1865 to 1929

The Equality Roller Coaster had already moved considerably upward prior to the Civil War, but its upward movement accelerated in the wake of the war. Emancipated during the Civil War, freed slaves were mostly mired in isolated rural areas where they could not emulate the White immigrants' economic development. Lacking assets such as land and small businesses, the freed slaves could not develop capital or borrow funds from banks. Mostly illiterate, they often lacked access to the public schools that could prepare them to compete in the capitalist order. Separated from the industrial centers that dominated the American economy by 1900, they could not find an economic niche in manufacturing that might bring a measure of security to them and their children. Trapped in a sharecropping system, African Americans could not save funds, and so they had no resources—much less land or businesses—to pass on to their children when they died. Dispersed in remote areas with poor communication, they could not easily organize associations akin to the self-help groups formed by the Irish and Italians. Once the repressive codes were in place and they had been denied suffrage, they could not develop political machines that would distribute jobs and resources to African Americans. Freed slaves, then, were subjected not just to personal discrimination, but to structural discrimination that made it likely that they would fall behind White immigrants in the North—not because African Americans lacked the work ethic or supportive families, but because they were denied access to the assets, economic opportunities, and associations enjoyed by their Northern White counterparts.

The speed with which America transitioned from an agricultural to an industrial society was unprecedented in world history; only the pace of Japanese and Russian industrialization in the mid-20th century rivals it. No more than 20 percent of Americans lived in cities in 1860, and the nation ranked fourth in the world in the value of its manufactured products. In 1920, however, more than 50 percent of Americans lived in cities, and the nation ranked first in industrial output. The total population of urban areas grew from 5 million in 1860 to 25 million in 1900.

Dramatic acceleration of industrialization occurred during the Gilded Age, from the end of the Civil War to 1900. Further expansion of the railroads opened up new markets and supplied agricultural produce and raw materials to the growing urban areas. Funds to build factories and purchase machinery were obtained from foreign sources, as well as from a rapidly expanding American banking system.

Massive immigration provided a cheap and plentiful labor supply. From 1860 to 1890, nearly 10 million northern European immigrants came to American cities including 3 million Germans, 2 million English, Scottish, and Welsh, and 1.5 million Irish who joined the 4 million who had immigrated in the 1840s and 1850s. A subsequent wave of immigrants from southern and eastern Europe dwarfed prior immigration; nearly 18 million people arrived between 1890 and 1920. Hungry for cheap labor, industrialists actively resisted any effort to stem this immigration.

Americans obtained a competitive advantage over Europeans because their new plants were able to incorporate rapidly developing technology. Moreover, the American business environment—high tariffs, minimal safety regulations, and low taxes—was very favorable to entrepreneurs. Finally, between 1885 and 1900, the Supreme Court restricted the right of government to regulate corporations by ruling, for example, that manufacturing did not fall under the jurisdiction of the federal government because it was not "commerce," and that government could only gingerly regulate corporations because their rights were protected by the due process clause of the Fourteenth Amendment, which had originally been enacted to safeguard the rights of freed slaves. Courts applied the Sherman antitrust legislation, which was enacted in 1890 to restrict corporate monopolies, to union monopolies! Even the power of the federal government to collect income taxes was declared unconstitutional in a Supreme Court ruling in 1895. It is not surprising that industrialization proceeded rapidly in this context (Cochran, 1961).

Cities expanded at phenomenal rates. Frontier towns, such as Cleveland, Detroit, Pittsburgh, and Chicago, became major industrial centers with increasing social and economic problems. In some cities, packs of wild dogs roamed the streets and maimed or killed children. Typhoid, cholera, and malaria epidemics were common and sometimes decimated the populations of entire cities. Dangerous work conditions led to scores of injuries and deaths. Immigrants were particularly subjected to wretched housing and industrial exploitation. The prewar pattern of periodic and devastating recessions continued unabated after the war. Major recessions caused unemployment rates that often exceeded 25 percent in major cities; indeed, 10 percent of the population of New York City received welfare after the recession of 1873. Recessions sometimes lasted for many years including the so-called Long Recession that lasted from 1873 until 1878. Many people were evicted when they could not pay their rent. Unable to find work in the industrial order and lacking the security of family farms, large numbers of Americans became vagabonds and roamed the countryside. Ten to 20 percent of Americans in the late 19th century lived in families where someone had "tramped." As they fell on hard times, citizens frequently came into contact with orphanages, workhouses, and police departments (Boyer, 1978).

American society was characterized by extreme economic inequality. Two classes predominated, the laboring and entrepreneurial classes. Because most people were poor, the middle class was small—no more than 16 percent of wage earners. Factory owners characteristically hired labor on a daily basis at factory gates and retained workers for only brief periods, often turning over their workers each year. Workers had to remain mobile to find jobs in an uncertain economy (Katz, 1982).

Reformers obtained some policy victories during the Gilded Age, including the establishment of limits on the working hours of federal employees, local housing regulations, and some local regulations on working conditions for women and children, establishment of the Interstate Commerce Commission, and passage of the Sherman antitrust legislation. The scope of these policies did not, however, begin to match the magnitude of social needs such as widespread poverty, poor housing, epidemics, and unemployment. Many jurisdictions did not enact regulations on industry, housing, public health, or employers' labor practices. Unemployment insurance, workmen's compensation, and pensions for the elderly were hardly discussed. The Interstate Commerce Commission was not able to regulate railroads because it was not given formal powers or sufficient resources to accomplish its tasks (Skowronek, 1982). The ineffectiveness of the Sherman Antitrust Act, passed in 1890, enabled accelerated development of cartels after its passage.

Intolerance of poor persons increased after the disastrous depression of 1873. As the frontier closed and cities swelled with poor immigrants, many Americans feared that this growing class of landless persons could disrupt existing institutions. Thus, they supported the repression of unions and strikes, as well as the suppression of "foreign radicals." At the same time, there was a surge in punitive policies toward Native Americans and freed slaves, who many Americans believed to be unreceptive to educational and moral uplift projects (Gutman, 1975).

The nation seemed to be returning to the mercantile policies of the colonial period except that those policies now benefited corporations. Land subsidies to railroads, high tariffs to discourage imports, subsidies to shipping industries and telegraph lines, and public funding for river and harbor improvements were motivated by a desire to build America's economy. Colonial mercantilism had been a top-down policy, in which top officials and royalty engineered tariffs and subsidies to help the national economy and unemployed citizens. Political pressures from corporations, which made flagrant use of bribes and lobbying to advance their economic interests, prompted the bottom-up mercantilism of the Gilded Age.

Although no nation had yet developed advanced policies to assist industrial workers, to upgrade cities, and to help persons who experienced unemployment, European societies were beginning to fashion social policies to mitigate the social and economic hardships that accompanied industrialization. The English Parliament, for example, enacted factory regulations in 1833, 1844, 1847, 1853, 1867, 1874, and 1878, as well as many public health measures. Germany enacted old age pensions and unemployment insurance in the 1880s. The United States, which had pioneered suffrage, land distribution, and public education, lagged behind other nations in enacting social reforms (Fraser, 1973). The federal budget itself was so meager that the nation devoted only 5.5 percent of its GNP to public spending (at all levels of government) in 1920, as compared to 25.5 percent for France and 19.1 percent for Great Britain (Webber & Wildavsky, 1986).

Corporations and financiers took advantage of a power and policy vacuum after the Civil War. When the nation began to industrialize rapidly, agricultural interests were placed on the defensive and were fragmented. Unions would have been a logical countervailing force to business, but they were extraordinarily weak and focused on crafts and skilled trades rather than on unskilled workers in factories. Unions were organized by geographic locality and sought a basic wage for all skilled workers in that particular locality. The modest organizing successes of unions in various cities in the 1830s were shattered by the recession of 1833, which led many employers to violate agreements, to fire union members, and to hire nonunion members. There were a number of strikes and riots by factory workers in specific locations, but few unions larger than specific work sites developed. American courts, which began a pattern of rulings that severely limited the ability of unions to organize, often declared unions to represent unlawful conspiracies or to violate the rights of workers by coercing them to enlist. Many American economists believed as well that the "unnatural" wage increases obtained by unions decreased economic growth by absorbing funds from the pool of investment capital (Fine, 1956).

Economists' theories hardly deterred workers from striking: Between 1881 and 1905, 7 million workers participated in 37,000 strikes. Some Americans began to fear that the nation was headed toward class war. After the Civil War, unions of unskilled workers were ruthlessly suppressed. Armed guards beat up strikers or intimidated union organizers. Owners of some Colorado mines forcibly placed strike leaders on a train to Arizona and told them not to come back. Industrialists found powerful allies in government and courts. Local politicians frequently used police and local militia to break strikes, and federal officials, who used the National Guard and federal troops, soon joined them. In 1877, President Hayes mobilized federal troops to break a national strike against the railroads in which nearly 100 people died as rioters torched railroad facilities. Other sensational strikes punctuated the 1880s and 1890s. In the 1886 Haymarket Square riot in Chicago, for example, policemen and strikers were killed. In the Pullman Strike of 1894, federal troops quelled a strike against the railroads, but only after 700 freight cars were burned and 13 people died.

Recessions and immigration frustrated the work of union organizers by breaking their momentum. Waves of immigrants provided industrialists with an inexhaustible source of cheap labor, which they used to break strikes and to depress wages. The weakness of unions in the late 19th century is illustrated by the strange saga of the Knights of Labor, a national organization that organized district assemblies of skilled and unskilled workers from many trades. The Knights engaged in secret rituals, often opposed unions and strikes on the grounds that brotherhood would solve industrial problems, and supported the development of self-employment and cooperative schemes. Although the Knights often supported progressive social legislation, their ideology precluded the development of effective pressure on industrialists (Fink, 1983).

Corporate interests became major contributors to the Democratic and Republican parties at local and national levels and used campaign contributions to obtain antiunion legislation, defeat adverse regulations, obtain tax concessions, and get government contracts. The weakness of governmental institutions and the lack of competing groups, such as unions and agriculture, allowed corporate and banking interests to dominate the political field and to secure favorable policies.

Social reform was also impeded by changes in popular culture. Prior to the Civil War, many Americans had believed that the primary purpose in life was to lead a virtuous existence, which might lead to social mobility. Most persons, it was widely believed, were destined to remain in relatively humble positions. Americans continued to emphasize moral virtues after the Civil War, but they placed far more emphasis on social mobility. Although pauperism had always been reviled, many Americans came to believe after the Civil War that poverty was itself an indication of personal failing. Increasingly, affluent persons were honored as models of success that inspired Americans of humbler origins to redouble their efforts. The Calvinist ambivalence about wealth, which was both revered as a sign from God of His pleasure and feared as a corrupter of moral virtue, was increasingly transformed into unambiguous worship of wealth (Kaestle, 1983).

This shift in culture was reflected in the stature of Herbert Spencer, an English writer who popularized and applied to society the theories of the English naturalist Charles Darwin. Darwin had fashioned a theory of the evolution of animal and plant forms to explain how different species emerged (Jansson, 2015). He maintained that genetic mutations can provide some individuals within a species with a competitive edge, which allows them to survive—and breed—more effectively than other members of the species. As these new characteristics are perpetuated from generation to generation through natural selection, adaptive mutations thus lead to modification of the species. Spencer theorized that genes also influence how persons fare in society. He argued that persons who excel in business or other endeavors, much like animals or plants that survive in nature, possess superior genetic characteristics. His logic led him to conservative political conclusions: If affluent classes possess superior genes, he asked, should not society allow their numbers to increase, while adopting policies to bring reductions in the numbers of low-income persons? By propping up ne'er-do-wells, in Spencer's view, governments and social agencies were artificially and wrongly interfering with natural selection within the social order (Hofstadter, 1955).

Spencer's use of Darwinian theory represented a sloppy and misguided application of biological theories to society. Poverty and other social ills are caused by innumerable factors, including environmental and societal conditions, as is illustrated by the plight of people of color in the United States in the 19th century. No evidence has been found by contemporary scientists to suggest that groups—whether social classes or ethnic groups—possess genetic characteristics that predispose them to inferior educational and economic performance.

Why the Equality Roller Coaster Remained Upward Even During a Reform Movement From 1901 to 1917

The depression of 1893, which lingered through 1896, brought widespread disenchantment with corporate tycoons; these heroes of virtue, hard work, and success had not been able to usher in unlimited prosperity, as the script of the Gilded Age had dictated. Their willingness to fire workers, to shut down plants, and to use violent means of suppressing labor strikes during the depression tarnished their reputations. Many Americans read in the newspapers about industrialists' blatant efforts to garner special treatment for themselves and their corporations by bribing public officials or by threatening to relocate to other jurisdictions that promised more favorable tax concessions. Outlandish efforts to bribe politicians and to finance their campaigns were publicized. The flamboyant lifestyles of corporate executives—once considered a just reward for hard work—came to be resented when more than 25 percent of adult males were unemployed in many areas (Thelen in Mann, 1975).

Reformers took hope when an unlikely politician emerged in 1901. Vice-President Theodore Roosevelt became president in the wake of the assassination of President William McKinley. Unlike his predecessors, Roosevelt chose to confront the large corporations that had come to dominate the nation's economy and politics rather than to be beholden to them. He enunciated a "Square Deal" that was defined by "three C's: control of corporations, consumer protection, and conservation." (Jansson, 2015). Numerous confrontations had taken place in the prior decades between corporations and unions, with presidents and the federal government usually siding with corporations. There were 37,000 strikes between 1881 and 1905 involving 7 million workers, but unions were ruthlessly suppressed or intimidated. Corporate leaders found allies in local police and the federal government who broke strikes by arresting their leaders. In the Pullman strike of 1894, for example, federal troops put down a strike against railroads, but only after 700 freight cars were burned and 13 people died (Jansson, 2015). Corporations often fired dissidents and replaced them with the endless streams of penniless immigrants. Nor were corporate interests timid: they bribed public officials at local, state, and federal levels to ward off pro-union legislation as well as legislation that would help workers. Both Democrats and Republicans used campaign contributions to obtain policies that they favored.

President Teddy Roosevelt made it clear whose side he favored. When 140,000 coal miners went on strike in Pennsylvania and sought a 20% pay increase and a nine-hour workday, Roosevelt intervened, eventually threatening to use a "big stick" to take over the mines and use federal troops to run them. Only then did owners of the mines relent. Then he focused on corporate monopolies, particularly ones that were corrupt. After he brought a lawsuit against Northern Securities Company in 1902, a huge company that controlled most railroads in the northwestern part of the United States, the U.S. Supreme Court ordered that it be broken up. He persuaded Congress to pass laws that empowered the Interstate Commerce Commission to regulate large companies. He enacted regulations of pharmaceutical companies and slaughterhouses with the Meat Inspection Act and the Federal Food and Drug Act of 1906.

By the turn of the 20th century, many Americans believed that environmental factors, such as overcrowding, tenement housing, and poor working conditions, thwarted the healthy development of city dwellers. Many progressives also feared that political machines, large corporations, and widespread corruption threatened democratic institutions. An environmental focus was critical to the development of a reform movement. When the public's attention was drawn to various environmental conditions that were believed to cause social ills, support for social reform to modify those conditions increased.

Social workers like Jane Addams and philosophers like John Dewey believed that people were intrinsically cooperative and became competitive only when they were exposed to environmental cues and models—including an American culture that emphasized winning at all costs. Addams extolled a "cooperative ideal" when she contended that government should try to instill a spirit of cooperation in its citizens, whether through example (by developing social programs, for instance) or through education (Addams, 1902). She argued that regulations and social programs represented expressions of altruism rather than unwarranted interference in the private affairs of industrialists and citizens (Addams, 1907). Many Americans in the Progressive Era also believed that they were rediscovering their own land. Reformers and journalists engaged in a frenzied search for factual evidence of social problems, such as the number of children and women exposed to dangerous working conditions, the number of children placed in adult prisons, the toxicity of many drugs, high rates of infant mortality among specific groups, and instances of political corruption. The appetite for facts and figures was insatiable; the social worker and reformer Paul Kellogg, for example, initiated an exhaustive six-volume survey of social conditions in Pittsburgh that described occupational hazards, housing, health, and other facets of residents' lives (Hofstadter, 1955).

A major political factor limited progressives' reforms: voting was not based on social class so neither Democratic or Republican Party represented persons in the working class who desperately needed reforms like unemployment insurance, a minimum wage, and other social programs. (Voting patterns were dictated by complicated sectional and ethnic traditions—and it was not until the presidential election of 1932 that a vast majority of working-class people voted for the Democratic Party headed by Franklin Roosevelt—so that neither Democrats nor Republicans focused on the needs of the working class.) Democrats were the dominant party in the South, Republicans had considerable strength in New England, and the two parties divided the votes in the Midwest and West. Various ethnic groups supported one of the two major parties on the basis of local tradition rather than for the party's positions on social issues.

The hallmark of progressives' reforms were myriad regulations that successfully got local and state levels of government to enact, along with some regulations at the federal level of government. Regulations are governmental rules that establish what corporations, social agencies, public officials, professionals, restaurants, pharmaceutical companies, developers, landlords, employers, bars or taverns, banks, and others can and cannot do. Breaking regulations results in penalties, including fines, revoking of business licenses, and even imprisonment.

We take regulations for granted in contemporary society. We assume that employers cannot hire 8-year-old children, that pharmaceutical companies cannot put unauthorized toxic chemicals in drugs, and that landlords must provide fire exits in apartment buildings. The primitive welfare state of the year 1900 lacked even these basic rules to guide people's and corporations' actions. In their absence, corporations could make dangerous or shoddy products, establish inhumane working practices, and subject workers to hazardous conditions. In the absence of public scrutiny, politicians could accept bribes, hire relatives, and tamper with elections. Homer Folks, a progressive reformer in New York State, found that state institutions were rarely audited, that laundry and food concessions were awarded to politicians' friends, and that no system of external monitoring existed. He conducted a tireless campaign to establish audit, licensing, and monitoring programs for public bureaucracies; to place staff positions under the civil service; to oust political appointees; to establish standards of sanitation; and to enforce existing laws that required children and insane persons to be removed from almshouses. Many other reformers undertook similar projects in other states (Chambers, 1971).

Often after bruising political battles, progressives enacted housing codes, planning regulations, workmen's compensation, child labor laws, fire codes, and sanitation regulations. Progressives obtained minimum wage legislation for women in 15 states and the District of Columbia by 1923, and legislation that established maximum hours of daily labor in 41 states by 1921. Reformers believed that they had made a lasting breakthrough in 1916 when they finally obtained passage of national legislation to restrict the use of child labor. Specifically, the legislation prohibited interstate commerce of the products of firms that employed children who were less than 14 years of age, and mines that employed children less than 16 years of age. However, reformers' hopes were dashed when the Supreme Court nullified the legislation in 1918 on the grounds that the law fell outside the province of interstate commerce, which had been widely regarded as the only way that child labor laws could be constitutionally legitimized. Although the ruling did not frontally challenge the right of the federal government to regulate child labor, and the staff of the Children's Bureau was able to obtain measures that prevented federal contractors from using child labor during World War I, the ruling had a chilling effect on social reform at the national level (Costin, 1983). Reformers who sought federal labor laws, such as a minimum wage and maximum hours of work, were told that the Constitution did not give the federal government jurisdiction in social matters.

Virtually no major social reforms were enacted in the 1920s. As a result, when the Great Depression began with the stock market crash of 1929, Americans lacked any social programs that might give them resources in times of need, such as unemployment insurance, health insurance, Social Security, welfare programs, food nutrition programs, or subsidized housing—not to mention laws mandating the civil rights of persons of color, women, or disabled persons. Regulations are important, but they don't significantly redress inequality because they fail to put money, food, and housing in the hands of persons who are not in the top 10% of the economic order.

The enactment of the 16th Amendment to the Constitution in 1913 finally gave the federal government the power to raise income taxes, which paid federal debt caused by the financing of American engagement in World War I. The tax revenue also addressed veterans' post-war medical needs. The income tax was levied exclusively on high incomes in 1919 through 1922 partly to defray war debt, but also because some Americans feared that the nation was becoming class ridden as reflected by the speech by Irving Fisher, an economist and Progressive campaigner, who said, "2% of the population owns more than 50% of wealth" while "two-thirds of the population own almost nothing" (Piketty, 2014).

Why the Equality Roller Coaster Remained High During the 1920s

Many Americans believed that economic activity carried out by private enterprise, left unfettered by government, would bring unlimited prosperity. Three Republican presidents presided over the nation: Warren Harding, Calvin Coolidge, and Herbert Hoover, who trenuously resisted the efforts of a small cadre of social reformers (Leuchtenberg, 1958). Harding stated his philosophy succinctly when he said, "What we want in America is less government in business and more business in government" (Leuchtenberg, 1958).

A second American industrial revolution occurred during the 1920s. Steel, mining, and railroad industries had developed during the first revolution; the second focused on consumer products, such as cars, radios, and refrigerators, and on the electrification of homes and industries. However, enormous consumer needs remained unmet in the United States. For example, only one in ten urban homes was electrified in 1920; only one in one hundred households possessed radios; and only one in three families had a car. The rise of a large advertising industry whetted consumer appetites for new products (Leuchtenberg, 1958).

A trickle-down economic philosophy was dominant. Officials believed that economic assistance to affluent persons and industry stimulated investments that could bring jobs to poor and working-class Americans. The low tariffs of the prewar era were supplanted by protective tariffs for American industry; federal taxes had been increased to pay off the national debt in the wake of World War I, but new tax laws reduced them to one-quarter of their previous level. Many regulations enacted during the Progressive Era were relaxed, not implemented, or struck down by the courts (Leuchtenberg, 1958, p. 98).

Vigorous suppression of organized labor supplemented policies that empowered industry and affluent persons. Companies sought to obtain the goodwill of employees by developing stock-sharing schemes, providing fringe benefits, and starting company unions that ostensibly gave workers a mechanism for negotiating higher benefits and wages. When outside unions tried to organize, their leaders were often intimidated or fired, and strikes led to unabashed use of scabs, local police, the National Guard, and injunctions from courts that were usually favorable to management (Brody, 1980).

Assessing the Ten Causes from 1865 to 1932

While affluent Americans often had extraordinary wealth, such as Andrew Carnegie's estimated wealth of more than $300 billion (in present dollars), millions of workers in the emerging industrial state were impoverished. Figure 3.1 at the start of the next chapter illustrates the high level of income inequality at the start of the 20th century. The nation had virtually no expenditures on social needs, relying on bread lines during recessions and a network of poorhouses. The nation did make high school compulsory later in the 19th century financed mostly by local governments and states.

Cause 1. The United States entered a period of extreme income inequality from 1865 to 1933. It had toxic effects on many citizens as evidenced by the sheer number of strikes and protests, the suppression of trade unions, and the economic chasm between workers and corporate leaders. The millions of immigrants who entered the nation found refuge in urban enclaves organized by their countries of origin, such as Irish, Italian, German, and Scandinavian ones. They were juxtaposed with a wealthy class that included captains of industry, railroads, and mines. I hypothesize that residents' experienced some of the toxic effects of exposure to extreme income inequality identified by Wilkinson & Pickett (2009) in the contemporary period in Figure 1.1.

Cause 2. Poverty was widespread during multiple recessions. Roughly 21 million persons in the American population of 92 million persons were immigrants who had arrived in the U.S. after 1880. They became the major source of workers in the burgeoning American industrial order. Forty percent of the populations of the 12 largest American cities were immigrants—and another 20% were second-generation descendants of immigrants. They came from multiple nations. They established neighborhoods with their own newspapers, churches, and clubs. But they were "dirt poor" as a group. (For further discussion of immigrants, see Jansson, 2015, pp. 162–166.) Workers had virtually no rights to organize. No minimum wage laws existed. While the many regulations that were enacted after the turn of the century were needed, they didn't address the poverty, poor housing, lack of services, and lack of medical care that was experienced by tens of millions of immigrants.

Cause 3. We can hypothesize that low rates of upward mobility existed in a nation with almost no middle class, huge populations of destitute immigrants, and a super-affluent class. I am not aware of data that measures rates of upward mobility in this period.

Cause 4. Data about levels of hope in this period do not exist to my knowledge. We can hypothesize that strikes, riots, and general unrest suggest that levels of hope were relatively low among workers. The violent suppression of strikes and unrest also suggests low levels of hope among workers. The emancipated slaves probably had low levels of hope as they tried to survive as sharecroppers on Southern plantations or as they sought to survive in cities even as they experienced racism in both the North and the South. Many women probably had low levels of hope as they worked in factories with low wages and lack of work-safety regulations.

Cause 4. Absent any civil rights laws, discrimination remained rampant. Freed slaves mostly lived as tenant farmers in the South under Jim Crow laws that prohibited them from voting, serving on juries, and entering public facilities. Black sharecroppers and tenant farmers in the rural South were often in debt to the former owners of plantations. White persons lynched many African Americans in the South, hanging them in public as crowds watched. Some African Americans ventured North and West before, during, and after World War I where some of them worked in meatpacking and steel industries. They were often excluded from skilled trades and professions, and were often used as scabs to break unions. They mostly lived in segregated neighborhoods. Yet they built vibrant communities with churches and clubs. Even as late as 1940, only 1% of African Americans had four or more years of college, and many Southern colleges for African Americans were only equivalent to secondary schools. (For further discussion, see Jansson, 2015, pp. 187–189.)

Asian immigrants and their descendants faced considerable discrimination from w hite Americans who often viewed them as sinister and disease-ridden. Yet they demonstrated remarkable skills in developing farms or in developing laundries and small businesses. Despite restrictive laws, many Japanese immigrants leased or owned farms. (For further discussion, see Jansson, 2015, p. 188.)

Latinos in the American Southwest were able to move back and forth over an unrestricted border because the U.S. Border Patrol was not established until 1924.

As many as 195,000 Latinos migrated North between 1900 and 1920, partly because of the Mexican Revolution of 1910; their population grew to more than two million by 1930. They continued to work on ranches, agricultural farms, and mines, as well as in canning and food-processing plants. They entered the workforce of major cities like Los Angeles. Like African Americans, they were supported by churches—the Catholic Church in their case. Like African Americans and Asian immigrants, Latinos faced intense prejudice from the White population (See Jansson, 2015, for further discussion of this population, pp. 188–189.)

Women achieved a major breakthrough during World War I when President Woodrow Wilson agreed to support suffrage after suffragette leaders threatened to target Democrats in upcoming elections and contended that suffrage for women was necessary for national unity during the War. The Suffrage Movement, including women chaining themselves to public facilities and enduring hunger strikes, finally led to passage of the Nineteenth Amendment to the Constitution in 1920. Women were excluded from many kinds of work that were viewed as "protecting" them from exertion. Many women worked in the garment industry where only 3% of them were unionized, often receiving poverty-level wages and working in unsafe facilities. The so-called Mothers Pension, a forerunner of welfare programs, had relatively punitive eligibility standards and was very small. It was illegal even to discuss birth control in public venues, a restriction that led to multiple prison sentences for Margaret Sanger, who tried to persuade doctors to prescribe it (For further discussion, see Jansson, 2015, pp. 185–187.)

Cause 6. The federal government funded few social and educational investments other than high schools, to uplift ordinary people. While enactment of the 16th Amendment to the Constitution gave the federal government an income tax in 1913, its revenues were mostly used to fund debt from World War I and veterans' benefits. Progressive reforms brought many regulations, but almost no social, economic, or medical programs that we take for granted in contemporary society. The nation had no set of policies that could be characterized as a "welfare state" in its modern sense.

Cause 7. No system of public or private health insurance existed, so millions of Americans had poor access to healthcare. A small system of public hospitals treated low- income persons. We can hypothesize that many Americans had untreated medical conditions that physicians might have been able to cure or stabilize even with the relatively low level of medical science.

Causes 8 and 9. The federal government had the power to tax incomes with enactment of the 16th Amendment to the Constitution in 1913—but hardly used this new power other than to help fund debt left over from World War I. While the federal government taxed affluent Americans to repay this debt, it ended these taxes during the 1920s.

Cause 10. The political system was structured in ways that made it difficult to develop equality-enhancing policies. Most Americans believed social legislation fell within the purview of state and local governments with virtually no role for the federal government. Neither the Democratic or Republican Parties represented the working class. Workers lacked the legal right to engage in collective bargaining. State and federal governments were primitive in their size and their functions. High levels of political corruption existed in this period as titans of industry bribed state and federal officials to receive contracts to electrify cities, build roads, and construct public buildings.

Looking Toward the Next Era

No one predicted that a Great Depression would move the Income Equality Roller Coaster downward for the first time in 100 years and that it would remain in a downward position for more than four decades.

References

Addams, J. (1902). *Democracy and Social Ethics.* Urbana, Ill.: University of Illinois Press.

Addams, J. (2016). *Newer ideals of peace.* New York: Macmillan.

Appleby, J. (1984). *Capitalism and a new social order: The Republican vision of the 1790s.* New York: New York University Press.

Appleby, J. (1992). *Liberalism and Republicanism in the historical imagination.* Cambridge, MA: Harvard University Press.

Ashkanas, J. (2016, December 16). Nine new findings about inequality in the United States. *New York Times,* Retrieved from https://www.nytimes.com/.

Axinn J. & Levin, H. (1982). *Social welfare: A history of the American response to need.* New York: Harper & Row.

Berthoff, R. (1971). *An unsettled people: Social order and disorder in American history.* New York: Harper & Row.

Boyer, P. (1978). *Urban masses and moral order in America, 1820–1920.* (1978). Cambridge, MA: Harvard University Press.

Branko, M., Lindert, P.H., & Williamson, J.G. (2011). Pre-industrial inequality. *Economic Journal 121*(551), 255–272.

Brody, D. (1980). *Workers in industrial America: Essays on the twentieth-century struggle.* New York: Oxford University Press.

Brown, R. M. (1977). Back Country rebellions and the homestead ethic in America: 1740–1799. In Brown R. & Fehrenbacher D. E. (Eds.), *Tradition, Conflict, and Modernization: Perspectives on the American Revolution* (pp. 73–95). Cambridge, MA: Academic Press

Chambers, C. (1971). *Paul U. Kellogg and the survey: Voices for social welfare and social justice.* Minneapolis, MN: University of Minnesota Press.

Commager, H. (1977). *The Empire of reason: How Europe imagined and America realized the enlightenment.* Garden City, NY: Anchor Press.

Costin, L. (1983). *Two sisters for social justice.* Urbana, IL: University of Illinois Press.

Countryman, E. (1976). Out of the bounds of law: Northern land rioters in the eighteenth century. In Young, A.F. (Ed.). *The American Revolution: Explorations in the history of American radicalism* (pp. 37–70). Dekalb, IL: Northern Illinois University Press.

Fink, L. (1985). *Workingmen's democracy: The knights of labor and American politics.* Urbana, IL: University of Illinois Press.

Foner, P.S. (1955). *History of the labor movement in the United States, Vol. 1.* New York: International Publishers.

Foner, E. (1955). *History of the labor movement in the United States, vol. 2.* New York: International Publishers.

Greene, J. P. (1987). The limits of the American Revolution. In Greene, J. (Ed.). *The American Revolution: Its character and limits.* (pp. 8–12). New York: New York University Press.

Gutman, H. (1975). The failure of the movement by the unemployed for public works in 1873. *Political Science Quarterly 80,* 254–277.

Hofstadter, R. (1955). *Age of reform: From Bryan to FDR.* New York: Knopf.

Jansson, B. (2015). *The reluctant welfare state: Engaging history to advance social work practice in contemporary society, 8th edition.* San Francisco: Cengage.

Kaestle, C. (1983). *Pillars of the Republic: Common schools and American society, 1780–1860.* New York: Hill and Wang.

Katz, M. (1983). *Poverty and Policy in American History* (New York: Academic Press, 1983), pp. 134–156.

Katz, M., Doucet, M., & Stern, M. (1982). *The social organization of early industrial capitalism.* Cambridge, MA: Harvard University Press.

Leuchtenberg, W. (1958). *Perils of Prosperity, 1914–1932.* Chicago: University of Chicago Press.

Lindert, P. H., and Williamson, J. G. (in press). American Colonial Incomes, 1650–1774. *Economic History Review.*

Lindert, P. H. & Williamson, J. G. (2013). American incomes before and after the revolution. *Journal of American History,* 73(3), 725–765.

Mohl, R. (1972). *Poverty in New York, 1783–1825)* New York: Oxford University Press.

Peterson, M., ed., (1975). *Portable Thomas Jefferson* (New York: Viking Press, 1975), pp. 396–397.

Pessen, P. (1978). *Jacksonian America: Society, Personality, and politics,* Homewood, IL: Dorsey Press.

Piketty, T. (2014). *Capital in the ewenty-First Century,* cCambridge: Harvard University Press.

Rohrbough, M. (1968). *The Land Office Business: The Settlement and Administration of American Public Lands.* (New York: Oxford University Press, 1968), pp. 200–220.

Sellers C.1991). *The Market revolution: Jacksonian America, 1815–1846.* New York: Oxford University Press.

Skocpol, T. (1995). *Social policy in the United States: future possibilities in historical perspective.*Princeton, NJ: Princeton University Press, 1995.

Skowronek, S. (1982). *Building a new American state: The expansion of National Administrative Capacities, 1877–1920.* Cambridge: Cambridge University Press.

Smith, R. (1993). *Patriarch: George Washington and the new American Nation.* Boston: Houghton Mifflin.

Sosin, (1967). *The Revolutionary frontier, 1763–1783.* New York: Holt, Rinehart & Winston.

Thelen, D. (1975). "Not classes but issues" In Arthur Mann (Ed.). *The Progressive era,* New York: Dryden Press, pp. 40–42.

Webber, C., & Wildavsky, A. (1986). *A history of taxation and expenditure in the Western world.* New York: Simon and Schuster.

Wood, G. (1992). *The radicalism of the American Revolution.* New York: Alfred A. Knopf.

Woodham-Smith, C. (1962). *The great hunger: Ireland 1845–1849.* New York: Signet Books.

3

THE THIRD AND FOURTH STOPS OF THE EQUALITY ROLLER COASTER FROM 1933 TO 1981 AND FROM 1982 TO THE PRESENT

The Equality Roller Coaster moved downward toward greater equality soon after Franklin Roosevelt was elected during the Great Depression and continued its downward trajectory through the 1970s. Why did a period of relative equality emerge in the 1930s and remain intact for roughly four decades? Why was it succeeded by a period of relative inequality that had lasted almost four decades by the time Donald Trump became president? The movements between eras equality and inequality depicted in Figure 3.1 demonstrate that the Income Equality Roller Coaster was at a high point as the nation entered the 20th century, began to descend soon after Franklin Roosevelt assumed office in 1933 toward greater equality, and remained low from the mid 1930s through the 1970s. It was an epic run that lasted until the early 1980s to the present.

Roosevelt's Emergency Assistance to Ordinary Americans

The Great Depression began in 1929 with a devastating stock market crash that was followed by a run on banks (Galbraith, 1957). When unemployment skyrocketed and consumption by consumers plunged, businesses slashed prices, a strategy that lowered their profits and raised unemployment even further. A vicious cycle commenced that created the worst economic depression in

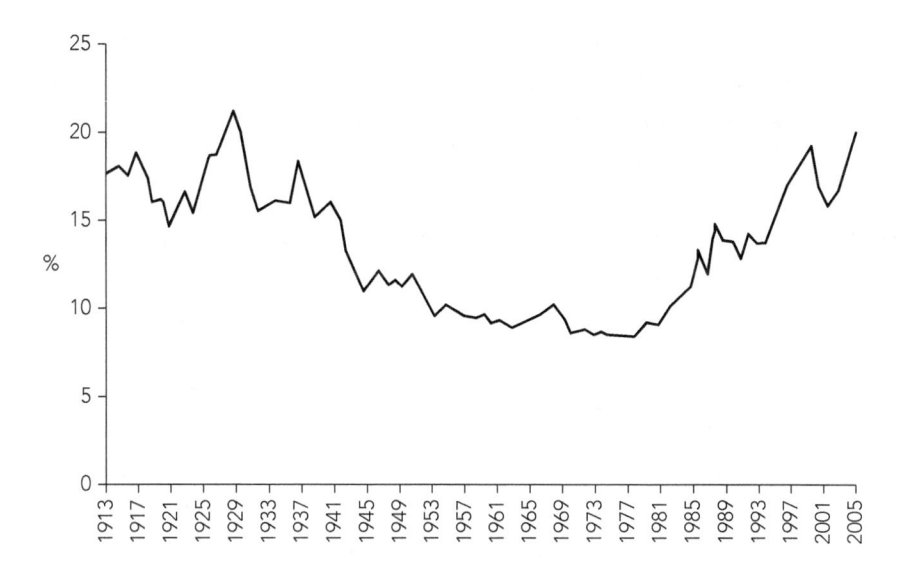

Figure 3.1 Income Share of Highest Income Households, 2011

the nation's history, leading to unemployment that averaged more than 18% from 1931 through 1940, and finally falling to 9.66% in 1941 as war preparations finally cut unemployment rates (Jansson, 2015).

The nation had seen many recessions during the prior 130 years, but none this severe and long-lasting.

An unlikely politician from the upper class emerged to lead the nation during the Great Depression. He contracted polio after serving as the Secretary of Navy in 1921 when he was 39 years old. He was nonetheless elected Governor of New York State in 1928, just one year before the onset of the Great Depression. He observed the devastating impact of the Great Depression on residents of his state and developed a series of programs to help penniless residents. He ran for the presidency on the Democratic ticket in 1932 and won a landslide victory over Republican Herbert Hoover, which gave him commanding Democratic majorities in both chambers of Congress. It was an historic election because, for the first time in American history, most persons in low- and moderate-income groups voted for Democrats while most affluent Americans voted for Republicans. Roosevelt not only had commanding majorities in both the House and the Senate, but led a party that wanted major social reforms to redress the human suffering caused by the Great Depression (Leuchtenberg, 1963). He also obtained almost all the voters of white Southerners who had shifted their allegiance to the Democratic Party from the Republican Party in the wake of the Civil War because they were disenchanted with a Republican Party headed by Republican Abraham Lincoln who had emancipated the slaves.

His hands were tied, however, because the federal government had almost no revenues as compared to the present period. Recall that the federal government was given the power to levy income taxes by the Constitution—an omission that was finally rectified by the enactment of the 16th Amendment to the Constitution in 1916. This federal power to tax incomes was used sparingly, however, since it was levied only on the top economic 5% of the population. The Great Depression cut these Spartan federal revenues in half to a mere $2 billion at a time when the nation had to help tens of millions of Americans who were unemployed (Jansson, 2001). Moreover, states lost most of their revenues from property and sales taxes. Roosevelt hatched a plot in 1932 as he ran for the presidency: Why not use the nation's dwindling income tax, excise tax, and tariffs revenues to balance the regular budget that included the U.S. Post Office and the other minimal functions of the federal government—and why not sell government bonds to investors to finance an "emergency budget" aimed at averting mass starvation and other social ills caused by the Great Depression (Jansson, 2001)? It was a brilliant political strategy. He could argue that he balanced the regular budget with aggressive spending cuts in the regular budget favored by conservative Southern Democrats, who chaired all the major Congressional committees, while financing his many New Deal programs using an emergency budget funded by federal debt, purchased by American and foreign bondholders (Jansson, 2001).

Several factors facilitated this balancing act. Once he took office in early 1933, he received near-unanimous votes from members of Congress to fund many of his New Deal work-relief programs because large numbers of constituents of all members of Congress, including conservative Southern Democrats and Republicans, were unemployed or surviving on low wages. That meant they were often hungry, in need of medical care, lacked housing, and lacked welfare payments in an era before the nation had created Food Stamps, rent subsidies, public or subsidized housing, Medicaid, Medicare, and welfare programs in the 1960s and 1970s. He began his presidency, then, heading a federal government that had no revenues and virtually no welfare state. The nation still relied on so-called (residential) poor houses to deal with destitute people rather than giving them cash relief in their communities.

Even conservatives mostly voted for the programs listed below that moved the Equality Roller Coaster downward (Jansson, 2015; Patterson, 1967).

- The Federal Emergency Relief Administration (FERA) that provided grants to states allowing them to make welfare payments to destitute individuals and families. It required them to establish state commissions

separate from their existing welfare programs with uniform eligibility processes throughout the state, and provisions to discourage discriminatory administration. It began in 1933 and was ended when welfare programs in the Social Security Act were enacted in 1935. It ended so-called poorhouses funded by local governments, where unemployed persons were required to reside under harsh conditions.
- A variety of work-relief programs that gave recipients jobs, including the Civilian Works Administration (CWA) which hired 16 million Americans for 190,000 work projects between November 1933 and January 1934 alone; the Civilian Conservation Corps (CCC), which provided jobs to 2.5 million young men, mostly in rural areas under the administration of the Army and the Department of Interior; and the Public Works Administration (PWA), which built complex projects like airports, dams, and roads throughout the 1930s. Roosevelt replaced the CWA with the Works Progress Administration (WPA) in 1935, which funded hundreds of projects across the nation.
- The Federal Deposit Insurance Corporation (FDIC) and other programs to stabilize banks.
- Programs to combat the aggressive cutting of prices by corporations as they sought to retain sufficient market share to remain afloat during the Depression including the National Recovery Act of 1933 (NRA). It helped industries in specific sectors negotiate set prices, but was declared unconstitutional by the U.S. Supreme Court in 1935.
- Programs to cut foreclosures, such as the National Housing Act of 1934 that established the Federal Home Administration Act (FHA) to help banks refinance home mortgages at lower rates of interest. He averted foreclosures on farmers and homeowners by having the government purchase mortgages and refinance them under the Emergency Farm Mortgage Act and the Farm Relief Act in 1933. He established the Farm Home Administration to insure mortgages and home improvement loans. He established the Wagner-Steagall Housing Act of 1937 to provide low-interest loans to local authorities to build public housing.
- Programs to encourage economic growth in entire regions, such as the Tennessee Valley Authority (TVA) through a network of dams and generating stations to power fertilizer plants and to help fund reforestation and flood control projects.
- The Social Security Act that provided pensions for seniors financed from payroll deductions of employers and employees. It also provided welfare programs funded by matching federal and state funds that included

Aid to Dependent Children (ADC), old age assistance (OAA), and Aid to the Blind (AB); funds for child welfare and public health programs; and unemployment insurance, by appropriating funds to help states administer their unemployment funds in return for agreement by the states to hold fair hearings to avoid discrimination in their distribution of unemployment benefits.
- The Fair Labor Standards Act of 1938 that established fair working conditions and minimum wages.
- The Wagner Act of 1935 that allowed workers to decide whether they wanted to unionize in elections monitored by the National Labor Relations Board (NLRB).
- A variety of programs that addressed nutritional, health, dental and other needs of impoverished persons through various programs that included partnerships between the federal government, states, and not-for-profit organizations.
- The Agricultural Adjustment Agency in 1933 that convened producers of specific crops to reduce crop surpluses that had driven their prices so low that many farmers were bankrupted—and other legislation that protected sharecroppers.

Make no mistake: when taken together, these programs helped persons in the lower economic echelons in ways that were unprecedented in the United States. They increased their resources, wages, food, housing, and employment. They increased their morale during an unprecedented decade of mass unemployment. They kept families together. They averted disease and starvation. They cut homelessness. Consider these policies, in tandem, to be revolutionary in a nation where no strong tradition of federal welfare existed.

It was unknown whether the Supreme Court would declare these federal initiatives to be unconstitutional because the federal government had not been given the power to establish social programs by the Constitution (Steamer, 1971). Roosevelt took steps to avert a showdown with the Supreme Court, such as dividing the Social Security Act in 1935 into many titles so an adverse ruling against a specific title by the Court would not jeopardize the entire Act. The U.S. Supreme Court issued 12 rulings against portions of the New Deal between January of 1935 and June of 1936, but finally blinked by refraining from declaring major social-policy enactments unconstitutional when Roosevelt, using his constitutional power to add justices, proposed to pack it with more liberal justices in 1937. Roosevelt invented the modern federal government by vesting it with unprecedented social and economic roles (Leuchtenberg, 1963).

We should not overstate the extent these programs uplifted the financial status of ordinary Americans. Recall that many of FDR's New Deal programs were not fully operative during the 1930s. The minimum wage was not enacted until 1938. While the Wagner Act was enacted in 1935, trade unions hardly grew in the 1930s despite some noteworthy strikes. Pensions from the Social Security Act of 1935 remained small but grew sufficiently to fund pensions of seniors in the 1940s and subsequent decades. The New Deal's work programs gave only modest wages or payments to its millions of enrollees, but reached only a small percentage of unemployed persons. The benefits of the welfare programs called ADC (Aid the Dependent Children), OAA (Old Age Assistance), and AB (Aid to the Blind) programs were extremely low by contemporary standards. ADC only gave subsidies to the children of single mothers, not to their mothers (Jansson, 2001).

While the New Deal had unprecedented reach and magnitude in the 1930s, it was relatively small compared to contemporary programs partly because Roosevelt had to fund it from his emergency budget that was funded by the sale of bonds, lest he create politically unacceptable budget deficits. Federal income taxes were only sufficient to cover the small military, post office, and other departments of government because they were only collected on affluent persons in the top 5% of the economic distribution. Federal income taxes amounted to only 0.7% of Gross Domestic Product (GDP) in 1934 as compared to 5.8% in 1950, 7.9% in 1960, and 9% in 1970. GDP of $61.1 billion in 1934 was hardly taxed by later standards (Jansson, 2001). Roosevelt also realized that he had to keep his emergency budget within limits because conservative Southern Democrats would not accept massive increases in deficits so soon after the nation had finally retired debt from World War I.

The growth of domestic discretionary spending that financed Roosevelt's work programs was nonetheless remarkable in a nation that had had a very weak central government since the inception of the Republic. With scant military spending and with Social Security still in its infancy, domestic discretionary spending became the dominant feature of the federal budget for the only time in American history. (See Figure 3.2.) Domestic discretionary spending, allocated by the federal government annually to social and other programs, was eclipsed in subsequent decades up to the present by the combined spending of two kinds of spending. First, spending on so-called entitlements that are funded annually to the level of claimed benefits including Food Stamps, Medicare, Medicaid, Social Security, and Unemployment Insurance. Second, spending on the military became a dominant part of the budget during World War II, the Korean War, the Vietnam War, the Cold War, and Wars

[Figure: Area chart showing Federal Budget composition from 1932-1937 with four categories A, B, C, D]

A. "other" spending for miscellaneous items
B. discretionary spending for welfare, social, and work-relief programs
C. interest on the national debt
D. military spending and veterans benefits

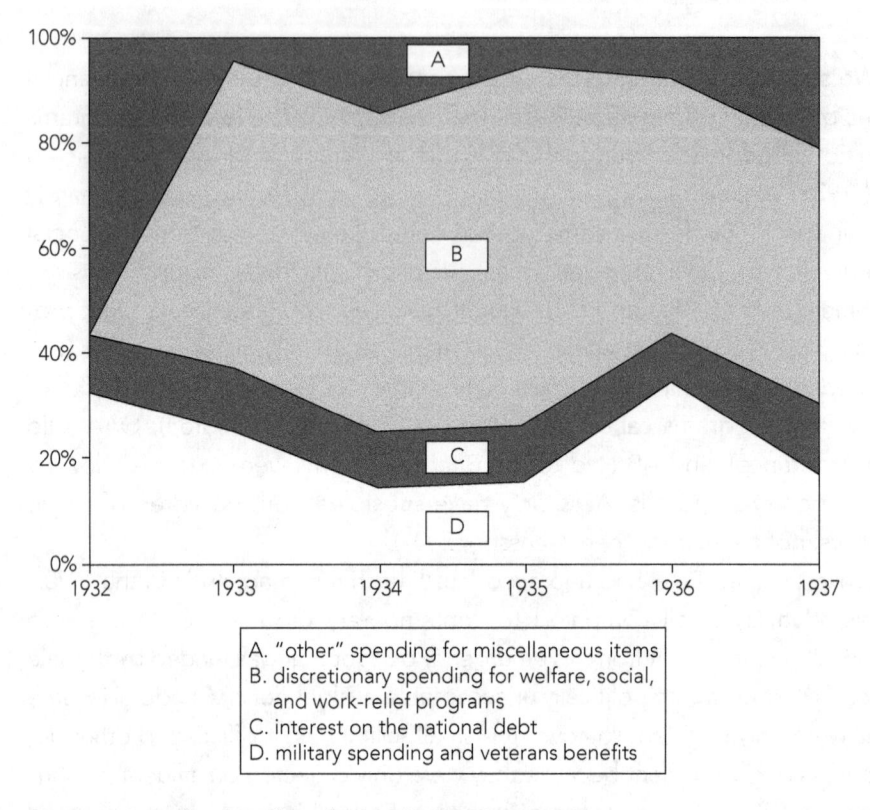

Figure 3.2 Federal Budget from 1932–1937

in the Middle East from 1942 to the present. As our charts later in this chapter reveal, spending on social and educational program became a very small part of the federal government from the 1940s to 2018. Moreover, spending on the national debt has also become a major part of modern federal budgets.

Why Loss of Income and Wealth of the Top 5% Was A Primary Reason the Equality Roller Coaster Moved Downward in the 1930s

Most historical attention has been devoted to discussing the misery of impoverished persons during the Great Depression, but the top 5% also encountered extraordinary hardships. It obliterated or severely reduced their income and wealth as stocks plummeted, banks became insolvent, and companies were bankrupted (Piketty, 2014). Many affluent persons leapt to their deaths from office buildings.

Very affluent Americans lost an estimated 60% of their wealth from 1929 to 1932 and often failed to recover much of this lost wealth in succeeding years, even far beyond the 1930s (Piketty, 2014). They could not recover it in the 1930s because the economy had tanked. Nor did most of them regain their wealth during World War II, due to wage and price controls imposed in 1941 after Pearl Harbor, strict rationing of domestic consumption, and top marginal tax rates that sometimes exceeded 90% and remained high, by historical standards through the 1970s until President Ronald Reagan cut taxes on rich people from top marginal rates of 70% to less than 30%—cutting resources of the federal government by trillions of dollars.

FDR was sometimes unsympathetic to the lost wealth of the top 5% even though he belonged to this group. He knew many of them had opposed his New Deal and viewed him as dictatorial (Patterson, 1967). He knew that the Republican Party, which used to contain relatively liberal politicians like Teddy Roosevelt, had swung in a conservative direction with mostly conservative members he called "economic Royalists."

Desperate for funds to balance the regular budget and knowing he could not levy federal income taxes on the bulk of the population due to the Great Depression, he raised top marginal rates from 24% to 63% in 1932, and continued to raise them steadily higher in the Great Depression with Revenue Acts of 1935, 1936, and 1937. The effective (overall) tax rate of the top 1% roughly doubled from 1932 to 1937, to 15.7%, even if its redistributive effect was somewhat offset by various regressive excise taxes during the Great Depression (accessed 8/5/2015: Four Things Everyone Should Know About New Deal Taxation: www.taxhistory.org). Roosevelt also enacted a tax on undistributed corporate profits that was strongly opposed by business interests and was eventually rescinded by a coalition of Republicans, conservative Democrats, and business leaders in 1938. Even with these tax hikes, the government lacked resources to fund a robust domestic agenda and had to rely on borrowing from bondholders to finance his New Deal programs (Leff, 1984).

Highly affluent persons lost income not only from fallen investments, but also from compensation in the automobile, banking, and manufacturing sectors. Recall that a second industrial revolution had taken place in the 1920s, when the nation manufactured automobiles, appliances, fertilizer, and many other products that greatly increased the wealth of affluent persons. During the Great Depression, many affluent persons were laid off and demoted from corporations that made these products, and suffered cuts in their compensation.

Highly affluent persons also lost much of their political clout that they had possessed in the 1920s because many Americans blamed their speculative practices for causing the Great Depression. They lost power, as well, in the wake of the presidential election of 1932 that had catapulted FDR into the presidency with a landslide victory (Mulder, 1979). If persons in the lower 50% of the economic hierarchy, and even many in the next highest 20% had split their votes between the two parties in prior elections, they moved decisively toward the Democratic Party in 1932. So affluent Americans now belonged to a conservative Republican Party that was out of step with the relatively liberal FDR and Democratic Party.

Roosevelt provided some assistance even to very wealth people as their economic fortunes declined. He restored confidence in the banks by declaring a bank holiday to stop a run on them. He enacted the Federal Deposit Insurance Corporation in 1933 to provide federal insurance to cover banks that became insolvent. He established the Securities and Exchange Commission in 1934 to end excessive speculation by investors and stockbrokers. He tried to interrupt the vicious circle of price-cutting and increased unemployment by establishing the National Recovery Administration in 1933, which convened business leaders to agree on prices, establish common wage levels, and establish production quotas for specific companies. He established the Agricultural Adjustment Agency to stop the vicious circle of price cuts and increased production by farmers (Jansson, 2015).

Assessing the Ten Causes of Inequality in the 1930s

Income inequality markedly decreased during the Great Depression. The income and wealth of the top 1%, top 5% and top 10% declined in the worst economic downturn in the nation's history. They lost huge portions of their investments, whether stocks or real estate. If their parents died in this decade, they lost some or all of their money they would otherwise have inherited. They lost income from their jobs, such as doctors, who found that their patient loads precipitously dropped because patients couldn't afford healthcare in an era when almost no one had health insurance. Poverty is the flip coin of income inequality and, to say the least, tens of millions of Americans became poor overnight. The work relief programs gave them only subsistence wages and episodic relief at best. Social Security pensions had barely begun so they weren't very helpful to seniors.

Cause 1. The Equality Roller Coaster moved downward primarily, I hypothesize, because American affluent persons lost even more income and wealth than persons in the lower economic echelon. Remember that affluent people came into the Great Depression with extraordinary resources that included vast inherited wealth. So they had far more to lose in the Great Depression than persons in the lower economic echelons who mostly worked for low wages in an era when trade unions and minimum-wage regulations did not exist, even though they, too, were hard hit.

Cause 2. The Great Depression thrust into extreme poverty many of the at-risk populations we discussed in Chapter 1. Roughly one-half of African Americans were unemployed in 1932—and vast numbers were unemployed throughout the decade. Many employers fired African Americans to make room for white employees. Many Latinos worked in the fields in the Southwest with minimal wages, long hours, and unsafe working conditions. While some women obtained jobs in the New Deal programs, many remained unemployed for long periods in the New Deal due to the widespread belief that men should receive priority in employment. The toxic effects of extreme poverty may have been somewhat reduced by people's awareness that almost everyone had suffered loss of resources. In other words, everyone was in the same boat. Even many affluent people lost almost everything—and some committed suicide. Roosevelt's optimism and willingness to experiment with new programs possibly decreased the angst of ordinary people.

Cause 3. Upward mobility decreased markedly in the New Deal because it was eclipsed by downward mobility caused by the Great Depression. This included not only many low-wage workers, but also members of the upper class and middle classes. But don't forget that upward mobility had probably been stifled by the extreme economic inequality that had preceded the Great Depression for decades—so its relative absence in the 1930s may not have seemed as ominous as otherwise.

Cause 4. We don't know if the level of hope of low-income persons declined in the New Deal. While many were reduced to survival levels, they knew that the entire population encountered the ordeal of the economic collapse. Their level of hope may have improved when they witnessed the heroic work of Franklin Roosevelt and the people who staffed his many work-relief programs.

Cause 5. Discrimination remained at high levels for persons of color and women in the New Deal. Failure to attack discrimination was the New Deal's most egregious failing. Roosevelt's work relief programs provided some, but insufficient assistance to African Americans, partly because southern democrats resented work programs that paid higher wages than from working in the fields. Lynching increased during the 1930s, partly due to stepped-up activities of the Ku Klux Klan. African Americans were often denied membership in trade unions. African Americans in the South remained subject to Jim Crow laws that disallowed them from voting and using desegregated public facilities. Roosevelt refused to support anti-lynching legislation for fear of causing white Southern members of Congress to oppose passage of his legislation. (For further discussion of African Americans, see Jansson, 2015, pp. 239–240.) Yet many African Americans came to be avid supporters of Franklin Roosevelt—and moved from the Republican Party to the Democratic Party. They knew that Roosevelt had allowed many of them to join New Deal work programs even if some of these programs were segregated. They knew they were eligible for Social Security and Unemployment Insurance, as well as AFDC and other welfare programs. They knew that Roosevelt had some African American advisors and had given some African Americans administrative roles. They knew that Roosevelt was not a friend of the Ku Klux Klan. They knew that Roosevelt tried to help sharecroppers improve their economic condition.

Latino farm workers were not covered in the Wagner Act of 1935, which exempted them from collective bargaining rights. Often working and living in remote areas, they had little help from attorneys when their civil rights were violated, nor were they covered by Social Security or unemployment insurance when the Social Security Act was passed in 1935. Local welfare offices denied them assistance on grounds they should be forced to return to Mexico. Forced evacuation of 400,000 Latinos took place in the 1930s when they were often placed on trains that took them to Mexico. They lived in segregated neighborhoods in cities and towns in the Southwest and were often denied access to public swimming pools and other facilities. (For more discussion of Latinos, see Jansson, 2015.)

Japanese Americans were subject to flagrant violations of their civil rights during World War II. The Japanese airborne attack on Pearl Harbor in late 1941 reawakened a long-held fear of many Americans that Japan might attack the United States. Isolated and afraid, Japanese Americans soon heard that General John DeWitt would head an effort to place them in "internment camps" with the concurrence of Franklin Roosevelt. Executive Order 9066 allowed the U.S. Army to round up about 120,000 Japanese Americans, all of whom were citizens and long-term residents of the United States, and send them to camps in remote areas of the West and Southwest. Allowed only to take what they could carry, most had to sell homes and belongings within days. Even so, about 33,000 Japanese Americans served in segregated Army divisions in World War II.

Women benefited from the advocacy of Eleanor Roosevelt, who insisted that they be allowed to participate in many work-relief programs of the New Deal and to assume high administrative positions in them. However, about 20% of women lost their jobs in the 1930s, often when priority was given to male employees. While many middle class married women now used birth control from their physicians, many low-income women lacked it because birth control clinics were illegal in many areas, due to long-standing obscenity laws. Millions of women obtained jobs in the war effort, including the famous "Rosie the Riveter," but many lost these jobs when the men returned from the war effort because employers prioritized male employees. (See Jansson, 2015, pp. 237–239 for more discussion of women in the New Deal.)

Cause 6. The federal government funded an array of social programs through the domestic discretionary budget for the first time in American history. Recall, however, that this discretionary budget was funded from the sale of bonds rather than current revenues of the federal government. Moreover, Roosevelt envisioned the work relief programs as temporary programs that would end when the Great Depression ended. It is not surprising, then, that conservatives succeeded in ending all of the work relief programs when full employment returned during World War II. As we shall see, social and educational investments of the federal government virtually disappeared from 1942 until 1964, leaving only entitlements funded either by trust funds financed by workers' and employers' contributions (i.e., Social Security and Unemployment Insurance) and welfare programs such as ADC. Local governments funded the nation's public secondary schools while states funded public colleges and universities.

It is important to realize, however, that even low levels of spending by the federal government *seemed* large because it *was* large when compared to paltry domestic spending in the prior century when almost no federal social spending existed.

Cause 7. Roosevelt had wanted to place national health insurance in the Social Security Act, but had refrained because he feared conservatives might scuttle the entire Act. Absent medical insurance, many Americans went without medical care in the 1930s. A remarkable growth of private health insurance took place during World War II, the 1950s and the early 1960s, spurred by a decision in 1948 to give corporations the ability to deduct the cost of employees' private health insurance from corporate income.

Cause 8. We present charts and data in this chapter to demonstrate how the nation had extraordinarily low taxes—mostly collected only on the top 5% in the economic distribution. We discussed how Roosevelt financed New Deal programs not from the regular budget but from the sale of bonds. He funded Social Security and Unemployment Insurance from payments of employers and employers into Trust Funds maintained by the federal government.

Cause 9. We discussed how Roosevelt imposed substantial taxes on affluent Americans throughout his terms in office, even raising their top marginal rates above 95% in portions of World War II.

Cause 10. Roosevelt realized that many of his New Deal work programs would be in peril if the economy righted itself. Roosevelt got his policies through the complex American governance system for several reasons. He won a landslide victory in 1932 and secured large Democratic majorities in both chambers of the Congress. The Democratic Party got large majorities of votes from the working class as well as votes of Southern Democrats. Southern Senators and Congressmen mostly controlled the Chairmanships of Congressional Committees due to their seniority.

Roosevelt obtained near-unanimous votes from the Congress, even from conservative Republicans because politicians' constituents were severely impacted by the Great Depression. Roosevelt's personal popularity enhanced his legislative successes. When the Great Depression ended during World War II and when Roosevelt turned his attention to the war effort, conservatives rescinded all of his work programs. Indeed, Roosevelt made little effort to keep them as his attention was diverted to winning the war.

Why the Equality Roller Coaster Remained Low from Pearl Harbor to 1960

Continuing downward pressure on economic elites. FDR realized in 1940 that he had to raise taxes far higher because federal deficits took off with the extraordinary costs of rearmament. Even in 1940, before Pearl Harbor, he sent a proposal to Congress to increase aircraft construction by 50,000 per year. His top Admiral asked for a 70% increase in the navy to allow for sufficient forces in both the Atlantic and Pacific. In secret planning in 1941, even before Pearl Harbor in December if that year, when the federal budget was only roughly $12 billion with a deficit of $9.2 billion, an economist in the Office of Production Management urged Roosevelt to spend $120 billion to maintain a standing army of 8.5 million men, to produce 60,000 aircraft, 45,000 tanks and 6 million tons of ships (Reston, 1941).

Desperate for revenues, FDR raised top marginal rates to 91% in 1944 and 1945. He also increased the base of the federal income tax by extending it from the highest 5% in the economic distribution to the bulk of the working population albeit at much lower rates. Presidents Harry Truman and Dwight Eisenhower continued these high top marginal rates. Truman inherited debt created by Roosevelt's failure to persuade Congress to raise taxes to far higher levels in World War II. While military spending increased to nearly to 45% of GDP by 1942, federal tax revenues had increased only to 10% of GDP. He engaged in a war with Congress over taxes as the nation's deficits and debt took off. At this point, the debt had risen from $41.1 billion in 1939 to $136.7 billion in 1943, and eventually $270 billion in 1946, a debt so high that Harry Truman had to devote 25% of the entire federal budget to paying interest on it when he succeeded FDR. When Congress whittled a tax bill down to one that produced a mere $2 billion in additional revenues in early 1944, or less than one-fifth that he wanted, FDR vetoed it calling it "not a tax bill but a tax relief bill

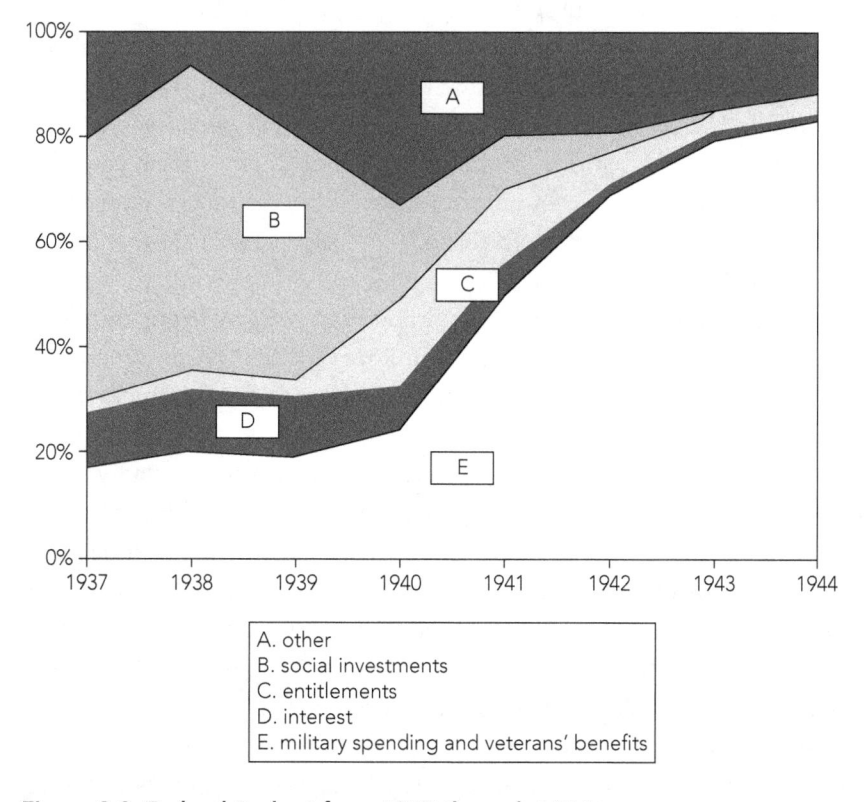

A. other
B. social investments
C. entitlements
D. interest
E. military spending and veterans' benefits

Figure 3.3 Federal Budget from 1937 through 1944

not for the needy but the greedy" (Jansson, 2001). Remarkably, 15 state legislatures approved a resolution to repeal the 16th amendment to the Constitution that allowed the federal government to raise income taxes (Witte, 1985). Conservatives went along with high marginal rates from 1942 through the 1950s because of the massive cost of World War II.

Economic pressure on the top 5% of the economic distribution did not ease in the 1950s when President Eisenhower not only inherited unpaid debt from World War II, but new debt created by the Korean War in the early 1950s. Even more debt was created when the United States entered a new kind of war: the Cold War, which lasted from 1953 through the 1980s. The inception of the ongoing militarization of the United States added a new wrinkle to the nation's economy. If prior wars had been temporary in nature, the nation now entered an indefinite Cold War (Sherry, 1977). Many Americans had viewed the Soviet Union as an emerging menace even in World War II, but their fears grew with three developments: the invasion and conquering of Eastern European nations by the Soviets in the immediate aftermath of World War II, the Korean War, and the development of atomic and hydrogen bombs by the Soviet Union. Stalin eagerly turned Eastern European nations into puppet states in the wake of World War II, even contending that Roosevelt had assented to these actions at Yalta to reward himself for fighting the Nazis on the Eastern Front.

Korea had been divided at the 38th parallel into two sections after the end of World War II, with the U.S., and with the Soviet Union respectively occupying the Southern and Northern portions. When the U.S. and the Soviet Union could not agree on an initiative to hold free elections in the entire Korean nation in 1947, the pro-U.S. and pro-Soviet governments consolidated their holds on the Southern and Northern portions, respectively. When the Northern (communist) government invaded South Korea in 1950, many Americans, including Truman himself, believed that the Soviet Union had precipitated this invasion as a plot to entice the U.S. to commit troops to a war in Korea, which would expose a Soviet invasion to Europe. Truman increased military spending not only to fight the Korean War, but also to prepare itself for a possible war with the Soviet Union (Leffler, 1992). Truman hiked military spending, which had markedly fallen in the wake of World War II, to consume 80% of the total budget by 1953. President Eisenhower continued Truman's massive military budget even after the end of the Korean War in 1954, with military spending composing roughly 65% of the federal budget in 1960.

When fully rolled out by the late 1950s, American military power reached epic levels, even as many experts questioned the actual military power of the Soviet Union. By 1953 the U.S. had roughly 1,600 bombers that could deliver atomic or hydrogen bombs. It had developed myriad missiles and nuclear bombs, and was producing 7,000 nuclear devices per year. These weapons could have destroyed the Soviet Union many times over when the Soviets lacked long-range, nuclear capable bombers until 1956—and even these were targeted at Europe, not the U.S. The Soviets had 300 strategic warheads in 1959, while the U.S. had manufactured 2,200 of them. The U.S. was engaged in an arms race against itself during the 1950s, as theorists and politicians imagined that Soviet military power was greater that that of the United States (Leffler, 1992).

This massive military expansion was also stimulated by the Pentagon's clever placing of military installations and contracts in the districts of virtually every member of Congress who came to lobby Congressional committees to reward their districts. The navy, army, and air force competed for planes, submarines, ships, land-based missiles, guidance systems, intermediate range and intercontinental ballistic missiles, and firing mechanisms in a "baroque arsenal never put to the ultimate test" (Kaldor, 1981). The Defense Department uses this strategy even in 2017.

Faced with the staggering cost of the Korean War and the Cold War, even conservative legislators and President Eisenhower favored retention of high marginal tax rates on the very rich (Witte, 1985). While affluent people benefited into the 1950s from the rebuilding of the domestic economy after World War II, they were still relatively poor compared to their counterparts in the Gilded Age and the 1920's with many of them still not recouping their losses from the Great Depression.

Economic Uplifting of the Lower 50% during World War II and the 1950s

While unemployment during the Great Depression often hovered near 25% of the workforce, it disappeared during World War II when Roosevelt decided that the allies could defeat the Axis powers by out-producing them in tanks, planes, and guns. Production relied on the existing manufacturing capabilities of the nation, particularly in the automobile sector (O'Neill, 1993). Automobile plants were completely converted to produce of tanks, jeeps, and airplanes, as illustrated by the fact that Chrysler Corporation produced only 150 automobiles during the War. The economic condition of the civilian population was greatly improved even with stringent wage controls imposed to prevent runaway inflation, which would have greatly have increased the cost of the rearmament. Vast numbers of men were drafted for military service, joined by considerable numbers of women who worked in non-combat roles. Without these jobs, those people might have been unemployed for substantial periods in the 1930s.

The top 10% of the economic distribution benefited from the opening of many management positions in rearmament industries, as Roosevelt abandoned his virulent attacks on "economic royalists" and relied on private industry to out-produce the Nazi and Japanese armament industries. The income of these leaders was curbed by regulations against excess profits, salary caps in businesses that had contracts with the federal government, and regulations of the National War Labor Board that froze or cut wages of managers, only allowing wage increases for low-paid workers.

Congressional conservatives opportunistically used the distraction of Roosevelt and congressional Democrats by the war, the huge deficits, and debt to attack New Deal work programs, arguing they were no longer needed since unemployment had been eradicated. They terminated all of them except for Social Security, the minimum wage, and the Wagner Act. Confessing he had changed from "Dr. New Deal" to "Dr. Win the War," Roosevelt conceded victory to conservatives on the domestic front to the consternation of congressional liberals.

The domestic discretionary budget, which had often exceeded $5 *billion* a year during the New Deal, was reduced to $140 *million* by 1944, when the total budget exceeded $45 billion. Roosevelt also failed to campaign during the war, even as conservative Republicans gained many seats. So-called "social investments" (or domestic discretionary spending) that funded FDR's work programs absorbed almost 50% of the federal budget from 1933 to 1939, as compared to less than 20% on military spending and veterans' spending, roughly 10% on interest on the federal debt, less than 2% on entitlements like Social Security, and about 20% on other expenditures. By 1942, these social investments composed about 2% of the federal budget, and never again rose above 4% of the federal budget during the remainder of the 20th century and into the 21st century (Jansson, 2001). The devastation of social investments funded by the domestic discretionary spending portion of the federal budget, was accompanied by military spending that came to dominate the federal budget, as would be true in subsequent decades with the Korean War, the Vietnam War, and the Cold War. Leading economists contended in 2016 that the United States will require vast increases in social investments to uplift people in the lowest economic echelons, in sharp contrast to minimal federal expenditures from World War II to the present (Ashkenas, 2016).

At least for the duration of the war, however, the near-eradication of domestic discretionary spending did not markedly harm the well-being of ordinary people because millions were employed by the military or worked in war industries. Roosevelt also enacted two key pieces of legislation during the war that were to have huge positive impacts on ordinary people in the wake of the war, in the late 1940s and well into the 1950s. He coaxed Congress to enact the Servicemen's Readjustment Act of 1944, informally known as the G.I. Bill, that eventually gave 7.8 million veterans educational and training benefits, readjustment subsidies, low-interest and down payments on home loans to 10 million veterans; and vocational education to millions of veterans prior to 1955.

The United States also broadened the base of the federal income tax by expanding it beyond the top 5% of the economic distribution to most citizens. Needing funds to pay for the most expensive war in world history, Roosevelt increased revenues to 21% of GDP by 1945 even if the Congress vetoed his effort to expand them even further.

Why the Equality Roller Coaster Remained Low During the Truman and Eisenhower Presidencies

Harry Truman, who became Roosevelt's surprise Vice-President in 1944, became president after FDR's death in 1945, was reelected in 1948 and served until 1953 when he retired. In addition to the G.I. Bill, the bottom 90% of the economic distribution benefited from a remarkable post-war resurgence of the U.S. economy that defied predictions of many experts, who had assumed another depression would occur. Americans had lots of cash because they could sell the war bonds they had patriotically purchased during the war. They indulged themselves with automobiles and appliances once wartime rationing had ended. They purchased homes from the newly revived housing industry, armed with FHA loans and insurance, as well as cheap mortgages. They increasingly moved to suburban areas. Spending on infrastructure by local, state, and federal governments in these suburban areas expanded with the nation's economic growth (Halberstam, 1993).

The American economy benefited, as well, due to the United States becoming the only economic superpower in the postwar period. European and Asian manufacturing facilities, as well as a significant portion of their workforces, had been devastated during a War that was not waged in the United States. Very affluent persons were still traumatized by their lost wealth during the Great

Depression and high marginal tax rates during World War II. The top marginal rate of 91% was retained through 1951, raised to 92% in 1952 and 1953, and only cut to 91% in the period from 1954 to 1963 to fund debt incurred during World War II, the Korean War, and the Cold War. An ethic of relatively low pay for top managers continued from the Great Depression and World War II, with their pay only 20 times higher than the average pay of workers, compared to a ratio of 240 times the average pay of workers in 2013.

The same economic trends of the immediate post-war era continued during the two terms of the Eisenhower Administration from 1953 to 1960. Ordinary people benefited from jobs constructing suburbs and the highways funded by Interstate Highway Act of 1956, houses in expanding suburbs, and well as airports, water systems, and manufacturing facilities. Persons of moderate income saw their wealth greatly augmented in the wake of World War II, due to expanded ownership of real estate, often financed by mortgages provided by the Federal Housing Administration.

The huge expansion of military spending in the Cold War benefited a wide range of Americans. Millions of workers received well paying, unionized jobs in corporations that manufactured munitions, rockets, ships and tanks. Many other people enlisted in military service. Highly paid engineers and scientists held high-level jobs in the military-industrial complex. So great was the expansion of military forces and manufacturing of munitions, that President Eisenhower warned about the dangers of the military-industrial complex in his farewell speech. During classified discussions with military and budget officials, he frantically sought cuts in military spending (Ambrose, 1984).

Unions vastly increased their numbers during World War II as they organized munitions industries. Their size increased in post-war years in industries that produced housing, automobiles, and appliances, leading to substantial increases in workers' wages and fringe benefits. Roughly 34% of American workers were organized in the early 1950s, compared to roughly 12% in 2009 (History.com, "Labor Movement," accessed on 1/13/2017 at http://history.com/topics/labor). The role of labor in pressuring corporations to increase wages and fringe benefits was huge because unions conditioned non-use of strikes upon positive outcomes of annual collective bargaining. They also pressured the federal government to raise the federal minimum wage and fund social programs.

Danger was on the horizon, however, for American workers. William Ruggles, an editorial writer in Texas, coined the slogan, "right to work" because he believed the labor movement meant to force all workers into unions. Arkansas became the first of 10 states to enact right-to-work laws that allowed trade union members not to pay union dues, partly because they viewed unions as communists in the Red Scare of the 1940s. Over Truman's veto, Congress enacted the Taft-Hartley Act, which undercut the Wagner Act and placed numerous restrictions on unions, including a clause granting states the power to enact right-to-work laws. With the assistance of Fred Koch, the father of David and Charles Koch, who funded the campaigns of many Republicans in the 21st century, Kansas enacted right-to-work legislation in 1958. A total of 19 states had enacted this legislation by 1963 to be joined by six more states by 2015. When trade union membership markedly declined in the late 1960s through the 1980s, wages became and remained stagnant, as the federal government failed to significantly increase the federal minimum wage. Even as late as 2016, it mandated only $7.25 per hour, even though some localities and states had somewhat higher minimum wages.

As can be seen from Figure 3.4, military spending (the white area) consumed between 80% and 90% of the entire federal budget between 1953 to 1960 as the nation funded debt from World War II, the Korean War, and the Cold War. It dominated the federal budget so markedly that all other budget expenses were reduced to small slivers including one representing domestic

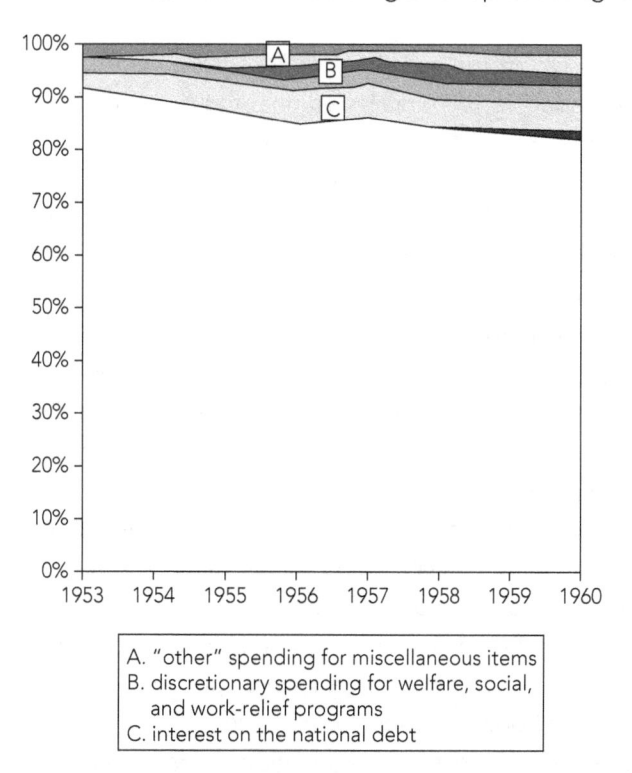

A. "other" spending for miscellaneous items
B. discretionary spending for welfare, social, and work-relief programs
C. interest on the national debt

Figure 3.4 Seven Types of Expenditures as Percentages of Total Outlays, 1953–1960

social programs, including education, training, employment, and social services (the fourth sliver from the top) and another representing Social Security and general government (the top sliver). The minimal domestic expenditures make clear that the relatively high equality in the 1950s stemmed not from domestic spending, but from from jobs created by vast military spending, the building of the interstate highway system, the building of suburbs outside cities, the rise in wages partly due to the growth of trade unions, the expansion of medical care funded by private health insurance and other factors not related to domestic federal expenditures. This relative equality may also have been caused by relatively high taxes on the top 5% with marginal rates far exceeding 70% and relatively low salaries of top officials in business, as well as the continuing inability of wealthy persons to rebuild fortunes that they had lost during the Great Depression.

Why the Equality Roller Coaster Stayed Low in the Kennedy and Johnson Administrations

The big winner on the social investment front was Social Security, because it was expanded far beyond its original focus in the 1950s on pensions for seniors. It became a family program that provided benefits to people with disabilities and their wives, to widows, dependent children, and to survivors of the men who were its initial beneficiaries. Other entitlements were enacted in the 1960s and 1970s that helped keep the Equality Roller Coaster low, including Medicare, Medicaid, and the Earned Income Tax Credit.

When Presidents John Kennedy and Lyndon Johnson came to power, respectively in 1961 and 1963, they realized that funds for social investments hardly existed in the federal discretionary budget (see Figure 3.4). Kennedy proposed increasing social investments, as well civil rights legislation, but had no luck because of his tense relationship with Congress. When Johnson became president after Kennedy's assassination in November 1963, he endorsed Kennedy's pending legislation and added measures of his own. Advocates of social investments took hope.

Few people understood Johnson's ultimate goals (Jansson, 2001). He wanted to best Franklin Roosevelt on both domestic and foreign policy levels, which were lofty goals considering FDR's remarkable successes. He wanted to link liberals and conservatives behind his agenda. Johnson accurately assessed the politics of the Congress when he took office. He could gain support for his social legislation from congressional conservatives by immediately supporting a huge tax cut for virtually all persons, except the top 1% of the economic distribution and by promising not to increase budget deficits even with this tax cut. He could gain liberals' support by endorsing major civil rights legislation and a war on poverty. He could gain hawks' support by gradually increasing advisors in South Vietnam while hinting he might enter the fray big-time. These maneuvers, he believed, would give him control of Congress by gaining a landslide victory in the presidential election of 1964. He wanted it all and he appeared to receive it when he walloped Republican Senator Barry Goldwater in 1964 and gained strong majorities in both Houses of Congress (Califano, 1991).

He gave many benefits to the lower 90%, as well as the bottom 50% of the economic distribution in the scores of legislative measures that came to compose the "Great Society." These included:

- Exempting millions of low-income Americans from paying federal income taxes, and raising exemptions and deductions for many others;
- Enacting the Civil Rights Acts of 1964 and 1965 that protected voting rights of African Americans, desegregated public facilities and transportation, prohibited hiring discrimination in federal contracts, gave the U.S. Attorney General the right to file suits to desegregate schools,—and gave rights to women through Title VII of the Civil Rights Act of 1964;
- Enacting the so-called War on Poverty that came to include the Job Corps, Head Start, the Neighborhood Youth Corps, legal aid centers, and health clinics, and a community action program;
- Enacting Medicare and Medicaid, with the former providing healthcare for seniors and the latter provided means-tested medical benefits for low-income persons;
- Establishing the Department of Housing and Urban Development (HUD) and enacting or expanding various public housing and affordable housing programs;
- Enacting the Older Americans Act, which supports Meals on Wheels and other programs;
- Enacting the Elementary and Secondary Education Act (ESEA) that provided federal funds primarily to schools with large numbers of low-income children.

Yet the Great Society was not as uplifting for ordinary people as the sheer number of its enactments might suggest. Johnson found his resources circumscribed by his massive tax cut in 1964 and his decision to enter the Vietnam War when his nation's budget was already depleted by Cold War military expenditures. He substantially reduced taxes on the very rich, cutting their top marginal rate from 91% to 77% in 1964, and then to 70% from 1965 through 1981. Those cuts suggested that future presidents might one day dramatically reduce them far further. His Cold War military budget was enormous even prior to his commitment of roughly 600,000 troops to Vietnam by 1967. Although the Soviets had greatly increased their nuclear forces, the U.S. had a sizeable lead in weaponry over the USSR, including 6,000 American strategic warheads compared to 2,000 for Russian; advanced submarine technology about to allow the firing of missiles from underwater subs, compared to conventional subs possessed by the Soviets; and 7,200 nuclear warheads in Western Europe, compared to relatively few Soviet nuclear warheads in Eastern Europe. The Soviets had an advantage in conventional forces, but their troops were poorly equipped and poorly armed. While military and veterans' spending rose from $269 billion to $376 billion from 1964 to 1968 (or by $87 billion in 1992 constant dollars), spending on education, training, employment, and social services rose only $22.3 billion, or by $79.3 billion in 1992 constant dollars even when augmented by entitlements. Military spending and veterans' programs consumed 80% of discretionary spending in the Great Society (Jansson, 2001). Levels of funding for social programs, and particularly ones funded by domestic discretionary spending, hardly merit the term, "Great Society." After he left the presidency, Johnson called his tax cut of 1964 the worst mistake of his presidency because it depleted tax revenues needed for social programs, and because congressional conservatives conditioned their support for the tax cuts on his promise not to increase social spending to levels that would cause deficits (Jansson, 2001).

The Equality Roller Coaster remained in a stable and low position during the Great Society, then, for possibly two major reasons. The income and wealth of the top economic echelons was held in check because Johnson kept the top marginal tax rates on the top 5% of the income distribution at roughly 70%, compensation of top executives remained relatively low or roughly 20 times the wages of workers, and estate taxes remained relatively high. The income and wealth of persons in the lower economic echelons benefited from the power of trade unions, beginning benefits of entitlements like Medicare and Medicaid, other programs of the Great Society, employment by the military-industrial complex, and positive economic growth. For the first time, the American federal budget contained growing entitlement spending and (finally) some modest social investments, even as it remained dominated by military and veterans' spending (see Figure 3.5).

[Chart: Federal Budget composition 1964–1969, stacked area showing A. other, B. social investments, C. entitlements, D. interest, E. military spending and veterans' benefits]

A. other
B. social investments
C. entitlements
D. interest
E. military spending and veterans' benefits

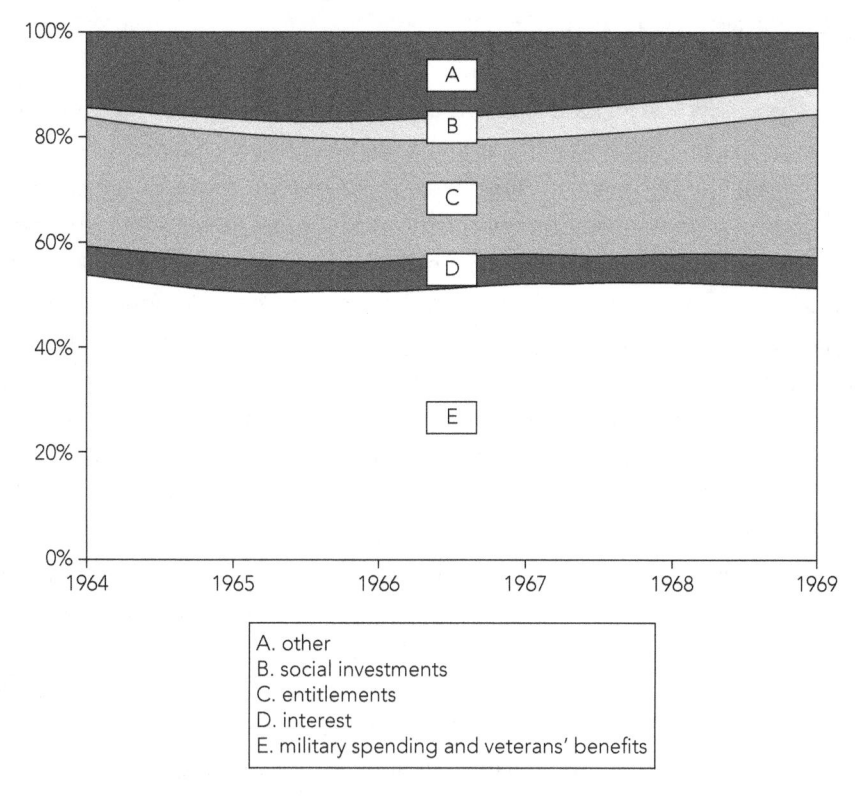

Figure 3.5 Federal Budget from 1964–1969

LBJ made two decisions that eventually undercut the Democratic Party. To his credit, he supported federal Civil Rights legislation that had been mostly framed by President Kennedy (Brauer, 1967). Johnson astutely predicted that southern democrats would eventually exit the Democratic Party in retaliation, rejoining the Republican Party that they exited when Abraham Lincoln, a Republican, freed the slaves roughly a century earlier. Almost all southerners became Republicans over a period of several decades. LBJ's decision to commit 600,000 troops to Vietnam by 1967 split the Democratic Party (Bernstein, 1996). It alienated the liberal base of his party. It attracted the ire of Martin Luther King because it used funds that might otherwise have funded social investments and because African Americans and Latinos were disproportionately conscripted. It enraged many White blue-collar Democratic voters in the North who disliked the civil rights legislation, LBJs' failure to commit even more troops to the Vietnam conflict, and his advocacy of school bussing in northern cities. He opened the door for Richard Nixon to promise he would end the Vietnam War on "honorable terms" and to lure southern democrats and white blue-collar northerners into the Republican Party (Jansson, 2001.)

Richard Nixon's Surprise

No one guessed that Richard Nixon, elected to succeed Johnson in 1968, might have kept the Equality Roller Coaster at a relatively low level by enacting social investments that, when taken together, would exceed those enacted by the Great Society. He had been a conservative during his tenure as Eisenhower's Vice-President and during his losing run for the presidency against JFK in 1960. In 1968 when he ran against LBJ's Vice-President, Hubert Humphrey, he used language geared to arouse racism among Whites in the North and the South, calling them the "silent majority of law abiding citizens" who had rightly attacked school bussing of Black children into White schools and had rightly opposed affirmative action which was, he contended, "reverse discrimination." (Edsall, 1991, p. 111). He was viewed as a hawk that wanted to pursue the Vietnam War aggressively even as he promised an honorable peace (Reichley, 1981).

Nixon's surprise was a robust set of domestic reforms. Sar Levitan, a noted policy commentator, wrote that "the greatest extensions of the modern welfare system were enacted under the conservative presidency of Richard Nixon with bipartisan congressional support, dwarfing in size and scope the initiatives of Lyndon Johnson's Great Society" (Levitan & Johnson, 1984, p. 2). These reforms partly stemmed from Nixon's sympathies for working people, derived from his working-class origins and his Quaker upbringing, but also from his political calculations. Even more important, however, was Nixon's driving ambition to end the Democrats' dominance of the U.S. Congress, which had been in place for the 1950s and 1960s, and to gain revenge for JFK's decisive victory over him in 1960. Why not, he decided, take the social reform card from the Democrats by developing his own reforms? Why not sometimes support Democrats' proposed reforms, but outbid them by making them even larger? Why not simultaneously play some conservative cards with the hope of wresting the South from the Democrats for the first time since the Civil War, and by eating into Democrats' support from relatively conservative White Catholic northern voters? Even when he turned hard right in the presidential election of 1972, when he faced the liberal George McGovern, he still aligned with some liberals and moderates of both parties, while turning to a budget-cutting, conservative mode (Wicker, 1991).

Working with the Democratic Congress, he enacted myriad social reforms that included (Jansson, 2015):

- Indexing Social Security benefits to inflation to assure regular increases;
- Enacting the Supplementary Security Income Program (SSI) to provide means-tested benefits to seniors and persons with disabilities;

- Enacting of the Income Tax Credit of 1975 to give working persons in families tax credits if they earned less than a specified income;
- Expanding the Food Stamps Program by federalizing it and increasing its benefits;
- Enacting the Housing and Community Development Act of 1974 that established rental subsidies for low- and moderate-income persons;
- Establishing the Occupational Safety and Health Administration (OSHA) of 1970 to regulate and improve working conditions;
- Enacting Title XX of the Social Security Act to fund the social service programs of states;
- Enacting the Comprehensive Employment and Training Act (CETA) to train workers and provide them with jobs in public and not-for-profit agencies, with an emphasis on long-term unemployed persons, fund summer jobs for high school students ull time jobs were provided for 12 to 24 months with the goal of providing marketable skills;
- Passing the Rehabilitation Act of 1973 that prohibited discrimination on the basis of disability in programs conducted by federal agencies, programs receiving federal financial assistance, in federal employment, and by federal contractors;
- Enacting the Education for All Handicapped Children Act of 1975 that required all public schools that accept federal funding to provide equal access to education and one free meal a day for all children with physical and mental disabilities;
- Establishing the federal Department of Education;
- Approving affirmative action in the wake of the Supreme Court's decision in *Regents of the University of California v. Bakke*.

When taken together, enactments of the Great Society and policy enactments of the 1970s transformed the American welfare state. Nondefense spending went from 8.1% of the gross national product in 1961 to 11.3% in 1971 and 15.6% in 1981 (Jansson, 2001). About two-thirds of this domestic budget consisted of social insurance and means-tested social programs. Total federal social spending rose from $67 billion in 1960 to $158 billion in 1970 (in 1980 dollars) and to $314 billion in 1980. Many social programs grew tremendously in their total cost during the 1970s. Federal spending on Food Stamps rose from $2 billion to $10 billion: on Medicaid from $5.8 billion to $25.4 billion; on Medicare from $15.2 billion to $38.3 billion; on Social Security from $68.2 billion to $134.8 billion; and on SSI from $4.1 billion to $8.6 billion. Lesser increases occurred for job programs including from $2.4 billion to $3.6 billion for CETA and from $2.8 billion to $4.9 billion on housing assistance. Because of relatively high rates of unemployment insurance, its benefits rose from $2.7 billion to $18.5 billion. Total spending on these programs rose from $109.2 billion to $258 billion, making social spending a major part of the American welfare state for persons who lacked resources, whether because they were old, unemployed, ill, or poor (Jansson, 2015). Many persons used only a single program. A man who became unemployed during the recession of 1976 might use only unemployment benefits because he considered use of the former Food Stamp Program or Medicaid programs to be unnecessary or stigmatizing. Or he may have decided his net income made him ineligible for them. Other families used only the Food Stamps Program, and still others only received Medicaid. Other families qualified for Section 8 housing assistance. The wide range of cash transfer, in-kind, and service programs allowed families to select specific programs that improved their quality of life at a specific point in time. Other consumers used combinations of programs. A single woman with several preschool or school age children might receive AFDC, Food Stamps, health services reimbursed by Medicaid, and live in publicly subsidized housing. An elderly family might use Medicare, SSI, and Social Security benefits. A young adult who had received a kidney transplant could receive SSI as well as medical services from Medicare. An unemployed person could receive unemployment insurance, job training from CETA, Food Stamps, and Medicaid. The availability of combinations of programs was crucial to many individuals and families, and especially to large families, whose members needed a range of services and resources. Many people used such programs as unemployment insurance, Food Stamps, and Medicaid for brief periods of unemployment, illness, or poverty; others needed assistance for longer periods. Of all the recipients of the nation's welfare programs, about 50% used them for less than three years; about 33% used them for three to seven years; and about 12% used them for eight or more years (Smeeding, 1984). These programs dwarfed Franklin Roosevelt's New Deal even though they, too, were a startling innovation.

Ominously, however, disaffected Democrats, such as the White Catholic working class in the North, who disliked the liberal wing of the Democratic Party, and Whites in the South who disliked Johnson's civil rights measures, would provide the votes to elect conservative Republicans Ronald Reagan in 1980, George H. W. Bush in 1988 and George W. Bush in 2000, not to mention Donald Trump in 2016.

The Equality Roller Coaster maintained its low level not only during the presidency of Richard Nixon, but the gridlocked presidency of Republican

Gerald Ford, who served the final two years of Nixon's term from 1975 to 1976 when he resigned from office in the wake of the Watergate scandal. It also remained low during the relatively conservative presidency of Democrat Jimmy Carter. Neither president cut social spending; spending from Medicare, Medicaid, and the Earned Income Tax Credit continued its remarkable ascent throughout the 1970s. Compensation for CEOs to workers remained relatively low at a ratio of 29.9 to 1, compared to a ratio of 376 to 1 in 2000 (Mishel & Davis, 2015). High marginal tax rates remained in place at roughly 70%.

Assessing the Ten Causes of Inequality from 1950 to 1979

As can be seen in Figure 3.1, the United States retained levels of income equality that developed during the 1930s through the 1970s. It took decades for some of the wealthy elite to rebuild the fortunes they had prior to the Great Depression, and decades for a new elite to emerge after 1982 that contained highly paid CEOs of major companies and highly paid professionals. (The Equality Roller Coaster began its steep rise in the early and mid 1980s as we discuss subsequently.) All presidents from 1933 through the 1970s maintained top marginal tax rates of more than 70%, meaning that very affluent people were taxed at far higher rates than in 2018 and following years.

The considerable growth of the American welfare state, including discretionary spending and entitlements like Social Security, Medicare, Medicaid, Food Stamps, and the Earned Income Tax Credit, increased income of persons in the lower 50% and 20% of the economic distribution, Wages of workers rose steadily up to the mid 1970s. Many workers were members of trade unions that pressured corporations to raise wages and to fund health benefits. Workers benefited from rebuilding of infrastructure after World War II, and from the domination of American corporations over Asian and European economies, after those regions were devastated by bombing and warfare during World War II.

More research is needed to describe the extent these policy developments, or other policies and economic factors, kept the Equality Roller Coaster at low levels.

Cause 1. We can hypothesize that the continuing relative equality of the United States meant that many Americans did not experience toxic effects from extreme economic inequality that Wilkerson and Pickett (2009) identified. More research is needed to test this assertion, however.

Cause 2. The poverty rate in the United States was roughly 23%, with 40 million Americans living in poverty in 1959, which is a huge number and a high percentage. (For an historical chart extending from the late 1950s through 2015, as well as reservations about the accuracy of some measures of poverty, see *Poverty in the United States at en.wikipedia.org*, accessed on 3/6/17). This high level of poverty partly reflected poverty of African Americans who left the deep South for other states. Unfortunately, they encountered poverty and discrimination in states other than the deep South including high levels of discrimination by employers, discrimination by bankers that made it difficult to purchase property, and discrimination by realtors that forced them to live in segregated areas. They often lacked access to quality education in inner city schools.

High levels of poverty also reflected widespread discrimination against women in the workplace, who were mostly excluded from male-dominated professions and high-level administrative positions. Millions of Latinos continued to work in low-paid agricultural settings.

The poverty rate declined substantially in the 1960s and through most of the 1970s partly due to the enactment of scores of federal safety-net programs and Medicaid as we discussed in this chapter. More research is needed to identify what factors caused this decrease in poverty, and to what degree each factor contributed.

Cause 3. Data about rates of upward mobility do not exist over an extended period to my knowledge. I hypothesize that the rate of upward mobility was relatively high for Whites due to the power of trade unions and the massive investments in infrastructure and housing in the 1950s and 1960s.

Cause 4. Longitudinal data about levels of hope do not exist for this time period to my knowledge. I hypothesize that levels of hope were relatively high in the White population because of factors discussed in Cause 3. Descendants of White immigrants, often in the second and third generations, often moved out of urban enclaves to suburbs as they became more affluent.

Cause 5. Historic civil rights legislation was enacted in the 1960s and 1970s, including the Civil Rights Acts of 1964 and 1965, discussed earlier in this chapter. The U.S. Supreme Court made major rulings that advanced desegregation of schools, such as *Brown v. Board of Education* in 1954 even if huge numbers of African American students remained in segregated schools. Specific social programs advanced civil rights as well. Southern hospitals were desegregated in the wake of enactment of Medicare in 1965, which forbade Medicare reimbursements in segregated hospitals. Once African Americans had advanced their civil rights through federal legislation, leaders of other at-risk populations pushed to apply these measures to their own groups, as well as to enact additional civil rights legislation. Women obtained a ban on gender-based discrimination with Title VII of the Civil Rights Act of 1964, as well as enactment of Title IX of the Education Amendments Act of 1972 that forbade exclusion of women from the benefits of any education program or activity funded by the Federal government. Supreme Court rulings expanded the civil rights of women, such as the 1965 decision in *Griswold v. Connecticut*, which forbade laws that declared the use of contraceptives to be a crime, and *Roe v. Wade, which* prevented states from outlawing abortions in the first trimester of pregnancy.

Other groups received expansion of their civil rights as well. The Rehabilitation Act of 1973 prohibited discrimination against disabled people. The Age Discrimination Act of 1967 prohibited discrimination by employers against seniors. The Supreme Court ruled in *O'Connor v. Donaldson* that persons in mental institutions have a right to treatment rather than warehousing them. Civil rights legislation, statutes, and regulations are only effective, however, if they are monitored and enforced, and many jurisdictions tried to evade or circumvent them. For example, the Hyde Amendment in 1976, forbade use of Medicaid funds for abortions—and employers continued to fire persons in their 50s and 60s up to the present day.

Cause 6. I have provided figures in this chapter that document that spending on social investments constituted a relatively small but growing part of the federal budget—and that entitlements including Social Security, Medicare, and Medicaid came to dominate the federal budget. More research is needed to ascertain to what extent they contributed to relatively high levels of equality in the 1970s. Spending by states and local governments on social investments was limited by their reliance on sales taxes.

Cause 7. The enactment of Medicaid and Medicare finally created insurance and coverage options beyond private health insurance. Even so, many Americans remained uninsured because American companies were not required to provide it and because they did not meet the eligibility requirements of Medicare and Medicaid.

Cause 8. The United States continued to underfund its welfare state due to the many loopholes in its federal tax code, its diversion of resources to military spending, and its use of private health insurance companies to manage and fund its health programs. For example, President Lyndon Johnson underfunded many social programs during his tenure by deciding to invade Vietnam over the objections of many experts. In addition, he enacted a massive tax cut in 1964, just as he was launching his Great Society domestic programs and planning to send (eventually) 600,000 troops into Vietnam. Such programs as the War on Poverty received little funds as did many other programs funded by the discretionary budget.

Cause 9. While the United States taxed affluent people at relatively high levels as measured by their high top marginal rates, affluent Americans made clever use of the many loopholes in the federal tax code, Even so, I hypothesize that the high rates contributed to the low level of the Equality Roller Coaster.

Cause 10. Presidents Lyndon Johnson and Richard Nixon established a much broader welfare state than the one created by President Franklin Roosevelt. If Roosevelt's huge achievement was the Social Security Act, Johnson and Nixon created scores of programs including entitlements like that Earned Income Tax Credit, Medicaid, and the Earned Income Tax Credit. Many Americans used combinations of these programs in ways that markedly increased their income. They were able to accomplish this feat only because Democrats dominated the Congress. Republican Richard Nixon enacted many social programs in liaison with Congressional Democrats because he didn't want Democrats to get the credit for domestic legislation. Equality advocates can get legislation through the federal maze of the different branches and levels of government only if Democrats dominate the Congress. When Republicans gathered strength in the 1980s and beyond, gridlock and polarization made enactment of reforms much more difficult.

Why The Equality Roller Coaster Ascended from 1982 to the Present

Everything changed when Ronald Reagan was elected president in 1980 because he frontally attacked the relatively liberal course of history during the preceding 4.8 decades. His landslide victory over President Carter also gained him a substantial majority in the Senate. While Democrats had a 38-vote majority in the House, Reagan had swept the southern and western parts of the United States, carried the male vote, won the evangelical vote, and wrested many blue-collar voters, who Roosevelt had attracted to the Democratic Party years earlier. Many southern Democrats lost their seats to Republicans.

Reagan's victory emanated from the period of economic discontent and hardship of the 1970s. The stagflation of the 1970s defied existing economic wisdom, which posited that economies were either overheated, which brought inflation as too many dollars chased too few goods, or stagnating, when too few dollars chased to many goods. So called "stagflation" included both inflation and stagnation, and no one knew how to attack them simultaneously. Inflation spiked to 10% in 1974, 1979, 1980, and 1981, whereas inflation had not exceeded 1.6% in a seven-year period prior to 1966. Gasoline soared from 37 cents per gallon in 1970 to $1.60 in 1977, and was rationed by the federal government during part of the 1970s. Interest on bank loans briefly exceeded 20%. Presidents Nixon and Carter resorted to price and wage controls. Those policies hadn't been used since World War II. Yet the annual unemployment rate exceeded 8% in 1975 and almost reached 10% in 1982.

Developments in the 1970s signaled a turn to the political right. Tax revolts took placed in many states in the wake of Howard Jarvis's successful enactment of Proposition 13 in California, which greatly reduced property taxes (Kuttner, 1980; Roberts, 1984). Many conservatives vowed to cut growing federal deficits by cutting spending. President Nixon undermined Democrats' Southern wing when he won five southern states in 1968 and lured White northern Catholics and blue-collar voters in the North and the South, using language and policies based on "White backlash" against affirmative action, civil rights, and termination of the Vietnam War. (Edsall, 1991). The unpopularity of Lyndon Johnson and Jimmy Carter, as well as assassinations of John and Robert Kennedy, also weakened the Democratic Party. In addition, Nixon solicited support from Evangelical Christians who had traditionally viewed politics as un-Christian, but who resonated with Nixon's rhetoric. Reagan inherited and further augmented Nixon's gains in evangelical and blue-collar populations (Jansson, 2015).

While liberals dominated the political dialogue from the New Deal through Johnson's presidency, many conservative thinkers came forward to contest their views in the 1960s and 1970s, such as economist Milton Friedman, who published *Capitalism and Freedom* in 1962, and William Buckley, who hosted the national television show *Firing Line* and founded the conservative journal *The National Review*. Baptist preacher Jerry Falwell became leader of the grassroots pressure group called the Moral Majority, which represented the religious right, and favored abolition of abortion, censorship of pornographic literature, and policies that allowed prayer in schools (Phillips, 1983).

Reagan, who had initially held liberal views, came to detest Franklin Roosevelt, who he viewed as developing heavy-handed government and regulations, as well as excessive welfare and public works programs. He became enamored with supply-side economics as an alternative to Keynesian economics. He accepted the economic theories of Arthur Laffer, who believed that investments from affluent persons power the economy: investments that occur only if the funds of affluent persons are augmented by low marginal rates of taxation on them (Roberts, 1984). Many liberals who called Laffer's theories, "trickle down economics," ridiculed his deification of economic elites. For example, Paul Conrad, the cartoonist for the Los Angeles Times, portrayed a man in a Wall Street suit whose gold coins dropped from his top to his bottom hand. In a departure from Laffer, Reagan also proposed to cut the taxes of low-income, moderate-income, and middle-class persons in 1981, but not as much as the cuts for affluent Americans. He exempted many poor persons from federal taxes. He did not cut entitlements, including Social Security, the Earned Income Tax Credit, and Food Stamps, but did change hospital reimbursement rules for Medicare.

How Reagan Moved the Equality Roller Coaster Sharply Upward by Helping the Top Economic Echelons

President Reagan introduced the Economic Recovery Tax Act in August of 1981, which was the most sweeping overhaul of the American tax system since World War II. It provided for 20% cuts in the income taxes of most Americans, spread over three years, and major cuts in corporate taxes. Reagan slashed top marginal tax rates on affluent Americans from 70% in 1980 to 28% in 1988 (Jansson, 2015). He slashed taxes on capital gains to 20%, the lowest rate since the Hoover administration. Reagan's tax cuts for affluent persons far exceeded those for persons further down the economic hierarchy. Between 1981 and 1985, the combined tax rate for Americans in the lowest 20% of economic strata went from 8.4% to 10.6%, whereas the tax rate of persons in the top 20% declined from 27.3% to 24%. These inequities took place during a decade when the pretax income of poor people declined, as low-paid service jobs steadily replaced unionized industrial jobs (Jansson, 2001).

Piketty (2014) speculates that Reagan created a culture of wealth in the United States that contributed to huge pay increases for top corporate executives that greatly increased their income and wealth. The ratio of the salaries of top managers to other corporate employees had slowly risen over prior decades, to a ratio of roughly 30 to 1 in 1980. The ratio of the salaries of CEOs did not immediately soar in the 1980s, rising only to 58.7 to 1 by 1989, but they zoomed to 376 to 1 in 2000 and to 303 to 1 by 2013 (Michel & Davis, 2015). While highly affluent persons lost favor in the wake of the Great

Depression, the general public now viewed them more favorably, even when they often failed to achieve positive results for the corporations that hired them. As their compensation increased, top executives came to think they deserved it as just reward for their work. They increasingly adopted life styles that required higher incomes to maintain them, such as purchasing Western ranches, condominiums that overlooked Central Park (in New York City), and private airplanes. They increasingly lived in gated communities and joined exclusive clubs. They returned, in short, to the ethos of the Gilded Age, just as the Equality Roller Coaster moved upward to levels comparable to the Gilded Age.

Reagan's cuts in the top marginal tax rates for the people in the top 1% of the nation's economic distribution also encouraged corporations to raise executive compensation. Were the federal government to tax executives' income at 100% over a specific level, such as $50 million, corporations would immediately establish that level as their maximum salary level, because they would realize that compensation over that level would go to government coffers rather than the executives.

How Reagan Cut Resources of the Bottom 50%

Reagan made deep cuts in domestic discretionary spending that funded social programs to help people in the lower economic echelons (Clark, 1981; Jansson, 2001). They included:

- Introducing the Omnibus Budget Reconciliation Act in July 1981, focused on cuts in means-tested programs mostly used by persons in the bottom 15% of the economic strata;
- Eliminating the Comprehensive Employment Training Act (CETA), the public service program for unemployed workers created by President Nixon;
- Cutting the Aid to Families with Dependent Children (AFDC) program by 17.4% by removing 400,000 persons from the rolls, and cutting funding for Food Stamps by 14.3%;
- Cutting the social services block grant, which gave funds to poor people, by 23.5%;
- Cutting low- and moderate-income housing subsidies by 57% by reducing it from $33.5 billion in 1981 to $14 billion in 1987.

Reagan placed downward pressure on domestic discretionary spending and created unprecedented budget scarcity by simultaneously cutting taxes and vastly increasing military spending (Stockman, 1986). He proposed military budget that roughly equaled the expenditures of the United States on the Vietnam War and increased military spending from $142 billion in 1980 to $368 billion in by 1986 (Jansson, 2001). Minus hard data, he insisted that the Soviet Union was preparing to launch missiles against the United States and engage in military operations in developing nations. Again minus hard data, he contended that the Soviets had a 500-ship navy that was vastly superior to the American navy (Pasztor, 1995).

Reagan's runaway deficits alarmed leaders of both parties sufficiently that in 1985 they enacted the Gramm-Rudman-Hollings measure, which contained a procedural gimmick to solve annual budget stalemates between the Republicans and Democrats, as well as between Reagan and the Congress. The measure required across the board budget cuts if Congress could not reduce deficits annually between 1986 and 1991 so that they would incrementally drop to zero. It gave the Congress a big out by allowing Congress to extend the schedule for balancing the budget, but also placed pressure on it by including the military budget in this "sequestration" so that it would suffer cuts if Congress failed to cut deficits. It placed even greater pressure on the discretionary budget by exempting Social Security, Medicaid, Food Stamps, and veterans' benefits from sequestration, meaning the nonmilitary cuts had to come mostly from domestic discretionary spending. Senate hawks amended the Gramm-Rudman-Hollings to establish a firewall between military and discretionary spending so that cuts in domestic accounts could not be extended to the military budget.

Reagan bought into Laffer's insistence that deficits created by increases in military spending and tax cuts would rapidly diminish as the tax cuts stimulated economic growth. No empirical evidence existed for this claim, and many economists were certain that Reagan's policies would lead to huge deficits. David Stockman, Reagan's budget director, vainly argued throughout 1981 that the combined effects of Reagan's legislation would create budget deficits so large that the nation would soon have to spend as much as 25% of the entire budget to fund interest payments to bondholders who financed the annual deficits and the national debt that they caused. That figure matched the percentage of the federal budget that President Truman had to pay to fund debt incurred by World War II (Stockman, 1986).

The historical record vindicates Stockman. The deficit rose to historic peacetime levels. Political gridlock between Democrats and Republicans mostly precluded either domestic budget cuts that were opposed by Democrats, tax increases opposed by Republicans, or cuts in military spending that often had bipartisan opposition during the remainder of the 1980s and throughout the 1990s.

Reagan contributed to stagnating blue-collar wages by attacking trade unions. He had promised the Professional Air Traffic Controllers Organization that he would increase numbers of controllers, leading to its endorsement of him in fall of 1980. When contract negotiations between it and the Federal Aviation Administration had failed eight months later, and its members had voted to strike, violating an oath that federal employees sign, Reagan fired 11,000 air traffic controllers and had them permanently replaced by invoking a provision of the Taft-Hartley legislation. Many of the union's local leaders were imprisoned and former strikers were banned from the Civil Service. After Reagan broke this union, large-scale strikes fell from 145 in 1981 to 11 in 2014. Only 11.3 percent of all American workers and 7 percent of private sector workers belonged to a union in 2013 (Kaufman, 2015). The exodus of many corporations to developing nations also undermined unions, as corporations found cheap and nonunionized workers in Mexico, China, and elsewhere from the late 1960s onward. Reagan's success in weakening the power of trade unions in manufacturing and related industries also reduced pressure on corporations to limit the pay of top executives, because trade unions had often contended that a reasonable balance should be maintained between executive compensation and the compensation of union members.

Reagan's assault on trade unions was coupled with militant opposition to increasing the federal minimum wage on grounds it would lead to higher unemployment. The federal minimum wage had its highest purchasing value in 1968, at $10.88 in 2014 dollars, but was hardly raised for decades so that its purchasing power in 2014 was lower than in 1968, despite a near doubling of productivity ("Economists Hit Back," 2014). Six hundred economists signed a letter in 2014 arguing that elevation of the minimum wage would stimulate the economy as workers spent their increased earnings ("Economists Hit Back," 2014).

Figure 3.6 illustrates how entitlements dominated the federal budget by the end of Reagan's presidency, even greatly exceeding military and veterans' spending, and how social investments funded with discretionary spending remained a relatively small part of the federal budget (Jansson, 2001).

[Figure: stacked area chart showing percentages from 1981 to 1989, with regions labeled A, B, C, D, E]

A. other
B. social investments
C. entitlements
D. interest
E. military spending and veterans' benefits

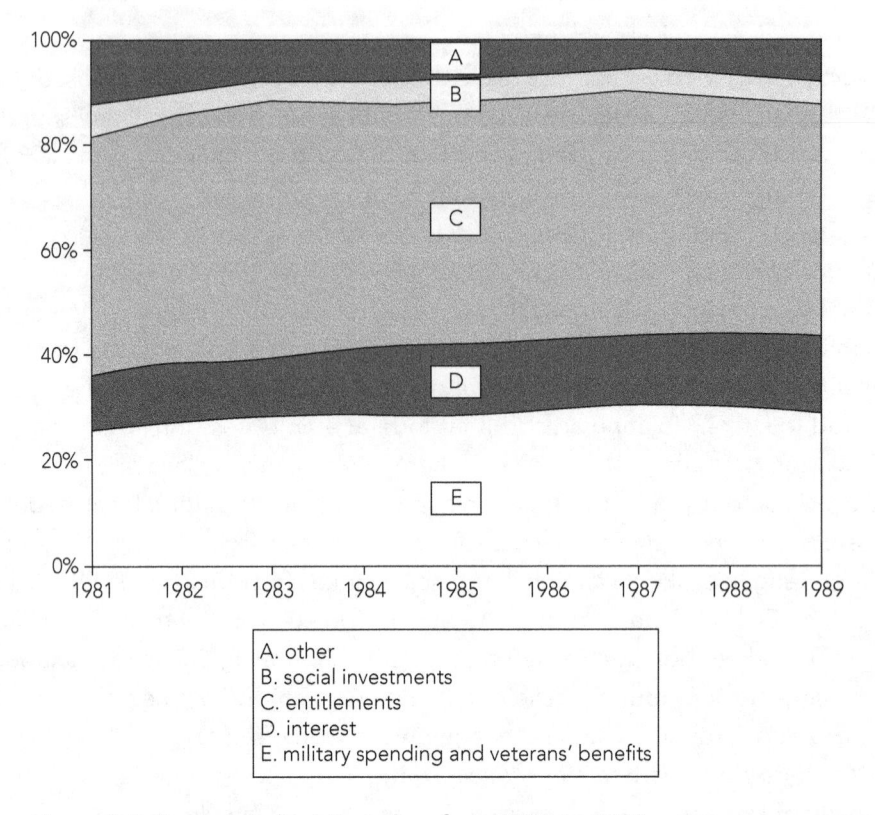

Figure 3.6 Federal Budget Spending from 1981 to 1989

George H. W. Bush's Political Miscue

George H. W. Bush, Sr. had minimal impact upon domestic matters because he had no interest in them. Instead, he focused on foreign policy and the unwinding of the Soviet empire which took place in 1989 through 1992 (Duffy & Goodgame, 1992). He vetoed most domestic measures that Congress sent to him with the notable exception of the Americans with Disabilities Act. Widely viewed by many Republicans as too moderate, he secured his selection as the Republican presidential nominee at the party's 1988 presidential nominating committee by pledging: "Read my lips. No new taxes." In 1990 Congressional Democrats probably ensured his defeat in the presidential race of 1992 by ensnarling him in a budget trap (Darman, 1996). Faced with the huge deficits that Reagan had bequeathed to him with his massive military budget and tax cuts, the Gramm-Rudman legislation of 1985 required across the board cuts in military and other spending if Congress failed to enact a deficit-free budget. Bush wanted no military cuts because he was on the edge of invading Iraq after it had invaded Kuwait, so to avoid sequestration, he assented to some new taxes, including taxes on highly affluent Americans. This decision so alienated the right wing of the Republican Party that its members stayed on the sidelines in the presidential election of 1992, allowing Democrat Bill Clinton to defeat Bush.

George H. W. Bush failed to seize the opportunity to increase domestic spending when the Soviet Union dissolved. While Richard Nixon partly funded social programs with the so called "peace dividend" from the termination of the Vietnam War in 1973, Bush took the advice of Dick Cheney, his Secretary of Defense, to retain the military budget even though the Cold War had ended with the disintegration of the Soviet Union (Faux, 1991).

Why Bill Clinton Did Not Move the Equality Roller Coaster Lower

Bill Clinton had the misfortune to be elected in the aftermath of two conservative presidencies and to inherit huge deficits mostly created by President Reagan. While Democrats' liberal base wanted liberal initiatives after a long drought that made Roosevelt and Johnson distant memories, many Americans from both parties worried about the huge national debt created by Reagan. Angst about it had been fanned by presidential contender Ross Perot in the presidential campaign of 1993 in an election that pitted Clinton against Bush, Sr. and Perot.

Bill Clinton was not a traditional liberal, partly because he came from Arkansas, a conservative Southern state, and partly because he wanted to direct Democrats in a more centrist direction so they could regain their political footing after Reagan's onslaught (Maraniss, 1995). Yet he had strong social reform and populist convictions, recoiling from segregationist policies of Arkansas Governor Orval Faubus and campaigning for the liberal George McGovern in the 1972 presidential contest. He can best be viewed as a chameleon that depended on political consultant Dick Morris from 1980 onward to point him in directions dictated by political polls. He helped found the Democratic Leadership Conference in 1985 to define a political platform that fell between traditional liberal and conservative directions, favoring balanced budgets, national standards in education, free trade, and infrastructure improvements, over redistribution of resources to the poor, affirmative action, and cuts in defense spending.

Clinton easily won the Democratic nomination in 1992. He and Bush, Sr., partly responding to independent candidate Ross Perot's obsession with reducing federal deficits, promised they would cut deficits if they were elected.

Clinton promised to halve it within four years from $237 billion to $118 billion. Yet Clinton also promised major increases in job training and other investments in human capital and infrastructure, partly due to the influence of Brandeis Professor Robert Reich, who feared American workers' wages would further decline if American corporations continued to offshore their operations in developing nations. Clinton won by the narrowest margin since 1968 getting only 43% of the vote as compared to 38% for Bush and 19% for Perot.

President Clinton was caught in a vortex of competing policy decisions (Woodward, 1994). Perot and many newly elected members of Congress wanted to cut the deficit, but liberal Democrats wanted to shorten the recession with social investments and stimulus spending. Clinton decided to seek immediate stimulus spending of $30 billion and social investments of $230 billion over five years, to be funded with revenues from a tax on gas and energy, and major tax increases on the wealthy that would increase their top rate to 36% (Jansson, 2001). He argued that this package would produce revenues of $328 billion from tax increases, combined with savings from spending cuts of $375 billion over five years, which would cut 100,000 federal jobs (Jansson, 2001). These combined measures satisfied conservatives, but angered liberals, who were dismayed by the spending cuts that exceeded the social investments.

The liberals were soon shocked, however, when it became clear that anti-deficit sentiment exceeded social reform sentiment in the Congress. After complex and lengthy maneuvering, a bipartisan coalition refused to enact Clinton's social investments and most of his stimulus plan. He received only $10 billion in social investments, even as Congress greatly cut spending. But he received $429 billion in deficit reduction from his $250 billion in new taxes, and $179 billion in spending cuts, mostly from the domestic discretionary budget. Even as ex-president, Reagan hovered over the Congress by bequeathing his huge budget deficits, causing Congress to focus on cutting deficits rather than enacting new social reforms. Congress added an exclamation point to its anti-reform impetus by failing to enact Clinton's proposal for national health insurance in 1994, which did not even receive a vote in the Senate. Clinton instead settled for enactment of an anti-crime bill in 1994 (Jansson, 2015).

The Emergence of the Hard Right in 1994

Clinton's political challenges had only begun. While Congress had blunted Clinton's reform initiatives, many conservative Republicans concluded they could only complete Reagan's anti-government campaign by capturing control of the Congress in 1994. They were led by Newt Gingrich, who had conducted a kind of guerilla warfare against Democratic leadership in the House that earned him the nickname "Neutron." He built a cadre of loyal Republican candidates over the years, which had won House seats and were schooled in his aggressive tactics. He became chair of a private organization named GOPAC that funded Republican campaigns in 50 House districts with conservative constituencies and candidates. He became House minority leader in 1994. He mobilized and worked with conservative think tanks, foundations, columnists, and talk show hosts, as well as wealthy donors, to take control of the Congress (Balz & Brownstein, 1996)

Conservatives launched a barrage of attacks on Clinton in 1994, accusing him of launching class warfare on the rich through his tax increases, calling him a big spender who didn't care about the deficit, and developing a campaign statement called Contract with America that stated their policy goals, which included a constitutional amendment to require balancing the budget, increasing military spending, and cutting taxes.

In 1994 Republicans gained control of both Houses of Congress for the first time in 40 years, as well as a majority of governorships. They took the offensive in 1995 and demanded that the budget be balanced by 2002 with spending cuts that exceeded $1.5 trillion, primarily by cutting entitlements and delegating some of them to the states, only exempting Social Security from the cuts.

Clinton became a counterpuncher in the ensuing budget battles of 1995 and 1996 (Jansson, 2001). He allowed Republicans to put forward their proposed cuts in entitlements. He enticed them not only to propose these cuts, but to move forward the dates for balancing the budget, requiring them to make even bigger cuts in Medicare and Medicaid. He proposed just enough cuts of his own to show that he wanted to balance the budget, but not enough to satisfy them. He baited them to shut down the federal government to force him to accept their proposals, a tactic that backfired when public opinion swung toward Clinton as citizens recoiled from losing access to government services. Republicans were forced to abandon their extreme demands, paving the way for Clinton's reelection in 1996, even as Republicans kept control of the House and the Senate.

Many liberals were dismayed by Clinton's decision in 1996 to overhaul AFDC, which was the major source of revenue for low-income women (Edelman, 1997). The Personal Responsibility and Work Opportunities Act of 1996 consisted of nine titles, or sets of provisions, that covered welfare, SSI, eligibility of immigrants for public benefits, child-care, child nutrition, and Food Stamps. Its welfare provisions replaced AFDC with the Temporary Assistance for Needy Families Block Grant (TANF), to be funded until the year 2002 at roughly the annual level of federal expenditures for AFDC in the year preceding the enactment of TANF. After 2002, the Congress could fund TANF at any level it desired. Many measures were placed in the legislation to discourage recipients from using TANF and prohibiting immigrants from using many programs. TANF enrollments greatly declined in succeeding years, to the point that many single mothers with children became homeless in succeeding years, particularly during the Great Recession of 2007 to 2009 (Jansson, 2016).

Virtually every spending measure in the federal budget came under attack during Clinton's first term, including domestic discretionary spending, which briefly escaped attention from Republicans when they focused on cutting entitlements in 1995 and 1996. It came under fire when the Balanced Budget Act of 1997 stated that the federal government would balance the federal budget by 2002 with large cuts not only in Medicare and Medicaid, but severe caps on domestic discretionary spending.

The caps on discretionary spending were so severe that spending could not even keep up with inflation through 2002, a policy that boded ill for federal spending on social services, education, training, and employment for the next six years. Future federal funding of these domestic programs was rendered even bleaker because the president and Congress supported substantial increases in military spending in coming years that competed with domestic discretionary spending. Many critics wondered if the military needed huge budgets in a post–Cold War era when the United States primarily had to deal with regional conflicts, such as those in Somalia, Bosnia, and Kosovo (Meeropol, 1998).

With scant resources available in the discretionary budget, Clinton cleverly obtained major educational reforms in 1997 by securing enactment of several tax expenditures (or tax concessions) that together provided $35 billion in benefits. These included HOPE scholarships, which were tax credits (or rebates) of up to $1,500 toward the first two years of postsecondary education for students whose parents had an adjusted gross income of less than $50,000 for a single parent or $100,000 for two parents; Lifetime Learning Credits for students in their last two years of college or in graduate school; and education savings accounts to be formed by annual contributions from parents (not to exceed $500). The principal and interest from those savings accounts could be withdrawn tax free to finance a portion of their children's postsecondary education.

Clinton accelerated the time schedule for balancing the federal budget, achieving a budget surplus in his final year. Clinton hardly changed the federal budget that he inherited from his two Republican predecessors, with 50% of it devoted to entitlements, 20% devoted to military spending, and only 3% devoted to education, training, and social services.

Reagan had, in effect, won the battle over national priorities even so many years after he was in office. By creating massive deficits and animus to social spending, he had induced Clinton to focus on cutting the deficit and social spending while maintaining military spending. Clinton created a budget surplus by cutting interest payments on the national debt from roughly 30% to 10% of the federal budget and cutting spending, but he failed to expand domestic discretionary spending as he had intended at the outset of his presidency (Jansson, 2001).

It is not surprising, then, that the Equality Roller Coaster kept its high position during Clinton's tenure. He did not markedly increase resource allocations to the bottom 90% of earners. He marginally raised tax rates of the top 1% of income earners, but compensation of highly affluent executives continued to rise during his two terms so that the ratio of their income to the income of their workers increased from 122.6 in 1995 to 383.4 in 2000. Clinton raised the top marginal income tax rates to 39.6% for incomes above $250,000 (or roughly $450,000 in 2012), which was still low compared to rates from 1933 through the 1970, which ranged from 70% to 96%.

How President G. W. Bush Kept the Equality Roller Coaster at a High Level

George W. Bush, Jr. had grown up in West Texas. Convinced that the 1960s had corrupted American values with its drug culture, liberalism, and rapid growth of social programs, he followed in his father's footsteps by attending Yale and becoming a Navy pilot in the National Guard. He was groomed for politics by participating in many campaigns under the tutelage of Lee Atwater and Karl Rove (Moore & Slater, 2003). He deeply admired Ronald Reagan, including his supply-side economics. With Rove's assistance, he won the Texas governorship by defeating the incumbent liberal governor, and then won a landslide victory in 1998 as a prelude to running for president in 2000. He presaged his policies as president by enacting a large tax cut in his second term as governor.

Bush won a controversial victory over Al Gore, Clinton's Vice-President, in the 2000 presidential race, which was finally decided by a narrow victory in Florida that was deeply contested by Democrats, but finally upheld by the U.S. Supreme Court. Bush was highly motivated. He wanted to avenge his father's 1992 defeat by Clinton. He wanted to restore traditional and religious values to the United States, downsize the federal government, rebuild the military, and transfer many programs from the federal government to the states. He wanted to achieve the realignment that Reagan had begun by ushering in a Republican era that might last for decades. He wanted to invade Iraq partly to avenge threats by Saddam Hussein, its leader, to assassinate his father.

Even though Bush had received fewer votes than Gore, he acted as if he had a mandate to cut taxes substantially, not just to appease conservatives, but to deplete resources that Democrats would otherwise use during the coming decade to propose domestic reforms. He delighted conservatives by taking a page out of Reagan's book, now proposing a $1.7 trillion tax cut that would wipe out most of the surpluses that Clinton had engineered. He used another $2 trillion in Clinton's surpluses to buttress the Social Security and Medicare Trust Funds. Bush argued that the tax cut would stimulate a lagging economy, but many economists countered that it would have little stimulatory effect—like Reagan's—because about 40 percent of the tax cut's benefits went to the wealthiest 1%, who would likely not spend new resources on consumer goods (Jansson, 2015).

Conservatives were delighted by Bush's proposed tax cut even though Democrats were able to decrease it by $1.35 trillion. It rewarded Republicans' corporate and affluent campaign contributors by slashing corporate income taxes and the taxes of affluent Americans, and pleased conservatives who wanted to downsize the federal government. Bush invested far more political resources in this tax cut than all other domestic measures in the first three years of his presidency. David Frum, Bush's former speechwriter and strong supporter, viewed the tax cut as Bush's greatest, and last, domestic achievement (Frum, 2003).

Many Democrats argued in vain against the tax cut. It would, they feared, plunge the United States back into deficits if economists' 10-year projections about economic growth (and therefore tax revenues) were excessively optimistic. It would increase economic inequality further, exacerbating a trend that had begun in the 1970s. No new federal resources would be available for schools, social services, prescription drug benefits under Medicare, or programs to give health insurance to the uninsured. To their chagrin, sufficient numbers of moderate and conservative Democrats supported the tax cut to allow it to be enacted.

Critics of other Bush initiatives doubted that they would raise the incomes of the least wealthy 90% of Americans. Bush wanted to establish federal student tests that identify low-performing public schools so that parents, armed with $1,500 federal vouchers, could send their children to other schools, including parochial and other religious-based schools. He failed to explain how if they were not given additional resources to hire or retain talented teachers or to reduce their student-to-teacher ratios, this could improve low-performing schools. Nor did he explain whether $1,500 vouchers would be sufficient to entice private schools to accept low-income students. He proposed a partial privatizing of Social Security, which would have workers start individual investment accounts with part of their payroll taxes that they would invest in stocks. Critics feared that this proposal would enrich Wall Street firms that would handle workers' investments, and deplete the Social Security Trust Fund. They also feared that these investments might be devastated during periodic declines of the stock market that occurred with recessions. This turned out to be a prescient prediction, because many investors soon had huge stock losses in the Great Recession of 2007 to 2009 (Gorman, 2001). Bush's only major domestic initiative was an amendment to Medicare in 2003 that allowed it to fund seniors' prescribed medications.

Bush's popularity had sagged during spring and summer 2001, but everything changed with the Islamic terrorists' attack on the World Trade Center in New York City, the Pentagon in Virginia, and other attempted targets on September 11, 2001. Bush declared a war on global terrorism in the immediate aftermath of the attacks. He persuaded Congress to enact a war resolution that gave him the authority to use military force to defeat the Taliban and to attack terrorist forces anywhere in the world as well as nations that harbored them. He issued an ultimatum to the Taliban to turn over bin Laden or face invasion. He assembled a broad coalition of nations to participate in possible military action at a time when world opinion was overwhelmingly supportive of the United States. When the Taliban refused, he ordered a massive bombing campaign in Afghanistan that was quickly followed by the introduction of ground troops. In liaison with forces of some other nations, the United States quickly defeated the Taliban and installed a new regime, but the elusive bin Laden escaped (Jansson 2015).

Bush turned his attention to Iraq in summer 2002 as his popularity declined during a recession. He shifted attention from domestic to international affairs in hopes of winning the upcoming Congressional elections. Administration officials contended that Saddam Hussein not only harbored weapons of mass destruction, but that he had links with Al-Qaeda. Only later was it definitively proven that neither assertion was true, but Bush and his top officials used these assertions to justify an invasion of Iraq (Woodward, 2002). Hussein was ultimately captured and executed, but the United States became enmeshed in military operations in Iraq until President Obama declared the end of American involvement in 2011. Like Reagan, Bush had created a pincer attack on domestic discretionary spending by cutting taxes and increasing military spending (Woodward, 2002). Some experts estimated the short-term cost of the Iraq War at $3 trillion (Stiglitz & Blimes, 2011). Representative Frederica Wilson enumerated what could have been purchased with just the funds expended in Iraq for education, workforce development, shoring up Medicare and Social Security, and repairing infrastructure (Wilson, 2013).

Bush was not finished with tax cuts. He proposed an additional $700 billion multiyear tax cut in early 2003. The centerpiece of the tax legislation was a reduction in the tax on stock dividends, a change that favored affluent Americans who owned stocks. With Democrats and moderate Republicans leading the way, the Senate pared the proposed cuts down to $350 billion and included some revenue-sharing funds for the states, with the conference committee approving a final version amounting to $400 billion. Bush supported these cuts with the dubious argument that they would promote economic growth.

Bush's tax, international, domestic, and counterterrorism policies had radically changed America's national priorities from those that he had inherited from Clinton. He cut taxes by almost $1.7 trillion spread over 10 years. He increased military spending annually from $250 billion to $400 billion, or an increase of more than $1 trillion spread over 10 years. He spent more than $2 trillion on the Iraq War. He devoted $70 billion annually to counterterrorism, or at least $700 billion over 10 years. In other words, as much as $6.4 trillion was taken from the federal budget in the coming decade that might otherwise have been used for domestic programs (Jansson, 2015).

These policies also resulted in huge increases in the federal debt since Bush's policies led to annual federal deficits of $400 billion for years to come; deficits that would further deplete funds for domestic programs. Bush's policies would fiscally tie the hands of his presidential successors, such as Barack Obama, by forcing them to focus on cutting deficits rather than addressing domestic needs, and by giving Republicans the argument that Congress should cut social spending to reduce the deficits and debt that Bush created.

Bush defeated Democrat John Kerry in the 2004 presidential election, while retaining Republicans' strong majority in the House and obtaining a narrow majority in the Senate, partly by supporting a constitutional amendment to ban gay marriage when same-sex marriage bans were winning on many state ballots. Democrats achieved a large majority in the House and a one-vote majority in the Senate in the 2006 Congressional elections, partly because more than 60% of Americans believed the American invasion of Iraq had been a mistake. With gridlock preventing major reforms, the nation awaited the 2008 presidential election that came to pit former First Lady Hillary Clinton against Barack Obama for the Democratic nomination.

The feeding frenzy of top executives continued under Bush as the ratio of CEO-to-worker compensation maintained itself at 351.3 to 1. The top marginal tax rate was 35%. Capital gains taxes were reduced from 20% to 15%, putting more money in the pockets of affluent persons.

It is not surprising, then, that the Equality Roller Coaster remained high during Bush, Jr.'s presidency. He was almost a carbon copy of President Ronald Reagan. He created large budget deficits by cutting taxes and raising military spending, and used these huge deficits, like Reagan, to argue against increased spending on social investments. Unlike Reagan, however, he didn't aggressively seek cuts in social spending, to the chagrin of many conservatives.

Why Barack Obama Didn't Lower the Equality Roller Coaster

Barack Obama became the Democrats' presidential nominee in summer 2008 after he bested Hillary Clinton in the Democratic presidential primaries. Liberals hoped he would enhance domestic spending. Like FDR, he had come to office during a deep downturn of the economy: the Great Recession. Roosevelt had mobilized blue-collar voters, Jews, intellectuals, African Americans, and Southern Democrats. Obama brought together African Americans, Asian Americans, Latinos, women, intellectuals, independents, persons who had not finished high school, persons with college and postgraduate degrees, Jews, persons earning less than $100,000, persons earning more than $200,000, and young voters with a campaign strategy that coupled soaring rhetoric with a sophisticated ground game. The ground game included technology that directed campaign staff and volunteers to millions of potential voters deemed likely to vote for Obama. Like Roosevelt, he won a landslide victory that gave Democrats a large majority in the House and only a narrow margin in the Senate.

Aside from having only a small minority in the Senate, the election looked like a replay of 1932 that could lead to policies that would greatly move the

Equality Roller Coaster downward. This script was interrupted, however, by the emergence of the Great Recession in 2007 even before he took office. Problems emerged with the hedge funds of Bear Stearns in June 2007 and in a large French bank in August. Worry changed to panic when Lehman Brothers filed for bankruptcy on September 15, but decreased when the government helped Bank of America purchase it. Housing prices began to decline in late 2007 as Merrill Lynch declared losses of $5.5 billion in October. When Bear Stearns collapsed in spring 2008, the government hastily helped J. P. Morgan take it over. While not on the same scale as the Great Depression, Americans had lost 30 to 40 percent of their net worth on paper or several trillion dollars by October 2008, just before Obama took office (Alter, 2010). Roughly 700,000 jobs evaporated per month from September 2008 through January 2009 (Alter, 2010). This economic crisis was precipitated by the elimination in the 1980s, 1990s, and into the Bush administration, of many federal banking regulations that had been enacted during the Great Depression and in succeeding decades, which required banks to retain considerable reserves to protect themselves against large numbers of delinquent loans and mortgages that often occur during recessions. Moreover, provisions of the Glass-Steagall Act enacted by Roosevelt that had prohibited banks from engaging in speculative trading of stocks and other investments were overturned during Clinton's presidency, as were other housing regulations that had required consumers to place substantial down payments on homes and to limit the amount of their monthly mortgage payments to a specified percentage of their net income so they would not become financially overextended.

During the Bush years, minus these regulations, many banks and mortgage lenders issued mortgages to consumers who would not have qualified for them a decade earlier, including persons of color and blue-collar Whites. Making little or no down payment, these consumers often believed they could afford these mortgages at low (or "subprime") rates because housing prices continued to rise at historically unprecedented rates. They believed they would merely need to sell their homes and pocket the profits if they could not afford their mortgages, not realizing that housing prices had entered a speculative bubble that would soon burst. This would leave millions of homeowners under water, with homes that were worth far less than the mortgages that had financed them. Houses had lost, on average, more than 25% of their value by December 2011, even exceeding the decline in housing values of the Great Depression. Many consumers, too, had not read the fine print of their mortgages, which said that the mortgage's interest rate would be re-set in coming years to a much higher rate. As the Great Recession took hold in late 2007, foreclosures increased in late 2008 with particularly high numbers in Florida, California, and Nevada, as well as in other states with high unemployment, such as Ohio and Michigan. The foreclosures continued through 2009 and beyond. Indeed, many houses remained under water even in 2017.

The recession was also caused and worsened by bankers' greed. Some banks began bundling mortgages into new financial products called mortgage-backed securities, or derivatives. They sold these products to investors and other banks that assumed their value would rise as the housing markets rose. As more banks foreclosed on consumers mortgages, the value of these products rapidly declined or even became worthless, leaving the banks and investors who had bought them fiscally vulnerable. These grim realities became evident in fall 2008, when Lehman Brothers went bankrupt and when many large banks and investment houses teetered on bankruptcy, including American International Group (AIG), Wells Fargo, Bank of America, J. P. Morgan, Citigroup, Goldman Sachs, and 13 other large banks that held the vast majority of the nation's financial assets. Ben Bernanke, the head of the Federal Reserve Bank, feared the recession could spin out of control into a repeat of the Great Depression (Jansson, 2015).

As in the first year of FDR's tenure, the government launched large remedial measures. During Obama's campaign for the presidency, Henry Paulson, the Secretary of the Treasury, and Ben Bernanke proposed the Emergency Economic Stabilization Act of 2008, which established the Troubled Asset Relief Program (TARP) to restore stability to the financial system by allowing the Treasury Department to buy or insure up to $700 billion of these "troubled assets" from banks, so that the banks could balance their accounting books, avoid further losses, and provide new loans and credit to consumers and businesses.

Since TARP had to be approved by Congress, it soon became caught up in the presidential campaign between Obama and John McCain, the Republican presidential candidate. The two candidates were invited to an economic summit hosted by President Bush and Henry Paulson, to obtain their approval of this legislation and to convince other party leaders to approve it. They knew they were on precarious ground: the TARP plan was developed so hurriedly that it was only three pages long and placed few conditions on the banks that would receive $700 billion of taxpayers' funds. Obama improved his appeal to voters by quickly supporting the legislation. He urged other Democrats to vote for its first tranche of $350 billion in loans, even though some Democrats wanted some of the big banks to be nationalized. McCain harmed his electoral chances by appearing indecisive and out of touch with the economic situation, even admitting he had not read the three-page plan. After an initial defeat of

TARP in the House, Congress enacted the legislation with unanimous support from Democrats and considerable opposition from Republicans. Bush signed the legislation on October 3, 2008 (Alter, 2010).

The federal government took over Fannie Mae and Freddie Mac, huge mortgage-lending agencies, in September 2008 committing $1.9 trillion in direct investments to the agencies, and created a program to purchase their mortgage securities and debt. Because private investors and many banks chose not to purchase mortgages due to the drop in housing prices, by September 2009 the federal government was financing about 9 of every 10 new home loans. When TARP expenditures are added to other business-related expenditures, the total government expenditures included $290 billion in direct investments in banks; $3.2 trillion in short-term loans; guarantees on bank debt and deposit accounts; insurance against the losses for Citigroup and Bank of America; up to $2 trillion in cheap financing for investors to buy troubled mortgage securities and bonds backed by business and consumer loans; $83 billion in loans to GM, Chrysler, and their suppliers; $3 billion for "cash for clunkers" to subsidize consumers' selling of old cars to buy new ones; and $183 billion of direct investments in AIG. We must remember that the federal government eventually received some of this money back from banks, such as the repayment by financial institutions of all but $30 billion of the TARP loans and grants, repayment of most loans and grants given to GM, and income tax payments from tens of thousands of auto and dealership workers who retained or gained employment due to loans and grants to GM and Chrysler (Alter, 2010).

Soon after his election, Obama and his economic advisors realized that they would have to initiate a massive economic stimulus to stop the Great Recession from becoming another Great Depression, since the economy was shrinking by nearly 6 percent annually. Obama pushed congressional Democrats to write and enact the American Recovery and Reinvestment Act (ARRA), which came to be known as the Stimulus Plan when Obama signed the legislation in February 2009 (Grunwald, 2012).

The Stimulus Plan contained $787 billion that surpassed Roosevelt's pump priming during the Great Depression when measured as a percentage of GDP (Grunwald, 2012). Its stated purposes were to preserve and create jobs and promote economic recovery; assist those most impacted by the recession; provide investments needed to increase economic efficiency by spurring technological advances in science and health; invest in transportation, environmental protection, and other infrastructure that will provide long-term economic benefits; and stabilize state and local government budgets to minimize and avoid reductions in essential services and counterproductive state and local tax increases.

The Plan's resources would be staggered over several years for several reasons. Only about $40 billion of "shovel ready" construction and related projects existed, so additional funds could be spent only after the necessary permits were secured. States would need help over a period of several years because the Great Recession had hugely reduced their revenues from property taxes, income taxes, and sales taxes. Many Americans would need help with unemployment insurance for an extended period. As many Americans lost employment, they would have to rely on the Medicaid program that could only handle its increased number of enrollees if the federal government gave resources to states to help fund it. States and localities would need federal resources to keep schools operating, and to fund salaries of public employees. Resources of the Stimulus Plan were first expended in spring 2009 and continued into spring 2011.

Relatively few people realized that the Stimulus Plan also funded $250 million in middle-class tax cuts. It gave moderate-income earners tax cuts, as well as elderly persons and veterans. It allowed middle-income families to escape the so-called Alternative Minimum Tax. It permanently expanded the Earned Income Tax Credit (EITC) with wage supplements of up to $6,000 for the working poor, extended unemployment benefits to 33 weeks, expanded Food Stamps, and gave $50 billion in "stabilization funds" to states and localities that were often running huge deficits. It greatly increased federal funding of Medicaid. It increased AmeriCorps funding, which gave young people jobs working in a large number of public and nonpublic agencies. Had Obama created separate programs for each of these initiatives rather than including them in the stimulus bill, he would have received far greater credit for them, such as Roosevelt and Johnson received for the scores of programs they created. The Stimulus Plan created between 1.2 million and 2.8 million jobs and reduced the unemployment rate by 0.7 to 1.5 percentage points, and, in the process, increased federal income tax revenues (Grunwald, 2010).

Obama did not lower the Equality Roller Coaster in the same fashion as Franklin Roosevelt, however, for at least three reasons. First, he was under constant assault from Republicans. Obama's landslide victory in 2008 was shallower than Roosevelt's victory in 1932. Both were epic victories, but FDR's was deeper and more lasting because the Republican Party of his era had been discredited by the onset of the Great Depression, and by the bumbling policies of President Herbert Hoover from 1929 to 1932. FDR had the support of the entire South due to the near universal movement of Southerners to the

Democratic Party after Abraham Lincoln emancipated slaves roughly 70 years earlier. Armed with their support, the Northern working class, and intellectuals, FDR built a long-lasting coalition and great majorities in both chambers of Congress. Obama narrowly won the Senate in 2008. He faced, moreover, a potent conservative minority that had nearly sabotaged Bill Clinton's presidency and that had elected George W. Bush to two terms. He received additional bad news when the so-called Tea Party of ultra-right Republicans emerged in 2009 and pledged to overturn any legislation that Obama might propose or enact, including the ACA and bank regulations that were enacted in 2010. While Roosevelt followed his 1932 landslide victory with a substantial victory in House and Senate seats in 1934, Obama's party suffered a stunning loss in 2010 after his landslide victory of 2008 (Corn, 2012). While Democrats controlled the Senate, they lost the House by a wide margin, and they suffered similar losses in 2014 after Democrats achieved a significant victory in 2012. While FDR presided over large majorities in both Congressional chambers, Obama's presidency became engulfed in gridlock with endless battles over budgets from 2010 onward that mostly led to cuts in discretionary spending, even if entitlements remained unscathed.

Second, Obama lacked resources to fund large programs that could uplift ordinary citizens in a nation with income inequality at levels of the Gilded Age. He not only inherited huge debt created by President George W. Bush, but experienced catastrophic decreases in federal revenues caused by the Great Recession of 2007 to 2009, a recession he did not create but inherited from Bush. Debt created by the Stimulus Plan added to his inability to make large policy moves to lower the Income Equality Roller Coaster.

Third, Obama focused his attention in his first term on helping the nation recover from the Great Recession and on passage of the Affordable Care Act. While the ACA eventually gave health insurance to more than 20 million people who had lacked it, it wasn't the kind of reform that redistributed resources in a major way to people in lower economic echelons. Obama chose to invest his political capital not in long-term social reforms or in a massive infrastructure program, but in the Affordable Care Act (ACA), over the advice of most of his top advisors who realized that he would have to invest virtually all of his political capital in this venture, given intense opposition from drug companies, private insurance companies, medical device companies, and physicians (Brill, 2015). Partly to offset conservative opposition to the ACA, Obama hardly discussed the remarkable accomplishments of the Stimulus Plan that many conservatives disliked (Grunwald, 2012). He kept it secret because he did not want to rile up conservatives for fear they would oppose the ACA as well as budget deals.

Some of his closest advisors, such as Ed Rendell, the former Governor of Pennsylvania, said, "I'm not Barack Obama, but if you gave me an hour to explain the (Stimulus Plan) to the country, I could've made the case" (Grunwald, 2012).

Not surprisingly then, the Income Equality Roller Coaster remained in its high position during Obama's presidency. Aside from bank regulations and the ACA, long-term reforms were not advocated, much less reforms that would markedly decrease income inequality in the United States. Nor were the words "income inequality" even used by high-level officials, and Obama rarely uttered the word "poverty." Thomas Frank argues that Obama was an "administrative liberal" rather than a "redistributive liberal" in the mold of Senator Bernie Sanders (Frank, 2016). He wanted to make American government more efficient. He wanted to tweak existing programs to make them more effective. He did not contemplate redistributing resources downward in a massive way. Nor did he propose large increases in taxing affluent people, although he did fund the ACA partly with tax increases on the wealthiest 1%. Nor did he, like Hillary Clinton in her run for the presidency, talk about reducing income inequality until Senator Bernie Sanders put the issue on the table in the presidential election of 2016.

The First Year of Donald Trump's Presidency

It is likely that the budget and tax policies of Donald Trump and the Republican Party will elevate the Equality Roller Coaster somewhat. Trump's presidency was an unlikely one that virtually no one predicted, not even Trump himself. He defeated 17 Republican rivals for the Republican presidential nomination and defeated Democrat Hillary Clinton to become president. He cultivated a base composed of White blue-collar voters mostly from rural areas and distressed cities and towns that had often lost manufacturers that had migrated to developing nations, along with a cadre of White voters from more affluent classes.

His campaign rhetoric suggested he might support policies that would uplift his blue-collar base, such as a massive infrastructure program and tax cuts for them, as well as re-negotiating or repeal in trade treaties that gave American companies incentives (he argued) to migrate to other nations. His campaign rhetoric was filled, as well, with attacks on women, Muslems, Latinos and Latino immigrants, and other groups.

It became apparent by summer 2017 that he was more conservative than populist. He focused on banning immigrants from Muslim nations, building a wall to block migration of immigrants from Mexico, and attacking sanctuary cities that refused to help federal officials locate (and deport) undocumented people.

He devoted much of the summer to seeking the repeal and replacement of the Affordable Care Act ("Obamacare"). He supported a House version that would have cast 23 million Americans off health insurance—and a Senate proposal that would have cast almost that many off insurance rolls.

He supported budget and tax policies that were skewed toward affluent people and corporations in fall, 2017. They included cutting corporate tax rates from 35% to 21%, cutting top marginal rates from 39.6% to 37%, drastically cutting inheritance taxes, and retaining many tax loopholes for affluent Americans. While he made some cuts in taxes of middle class and lower-middle-class people, they were overshadowed by larger cuts for affluent Americans and corporations.

Trump was more "conservative" than "populist." His huge tax cuts would, moreover, create roughly $1.5 trillion of additional deficits over 10 years that would not only burden the federal budget with higher interest payments to the bondholders financing these new deficits, but would decrease resources that might have been used to fund social, education, housing, and job training programs.

The Staying Power of the Ten Causes of Inequality from Reagan Through Clinton

It not surprising, then, that the Equality Roller Coaster did not move from the high position that it had held from the early 1980s through 2016. Four Republican presidents (Reagan, George H.W. Bush, George W. Bush, and Donald Trump) were dedicated to retaining high levels of inequality and, with help from one or both chambers of Congress, succeeded in cutting taxes on the rich while not increasing social investments for people in the lower 50% of income earners. Two Democratic presidents (Clinton and Obama) were mostly gridlocked by Republicans even though neither of them placed the reduction of inequality high on their priority list. The Income Equality Roller Coaster tells it all: From the mid-1980s to the present, the United States remained at income inequality levels of the Gilded Age of the 1880s.

Cause 1. We can hypothesize that exposure to extreme economic inequality impacted members of all social classes from the mid 1980s to the present. It made economic elites far more brazen about asserting their views in the public realm. It made them seek ever-higher wages and stock options when they held high corporate positions. It led many of them to purchase huge mansions, expensive cars, and vacation property. Exposure to extreme economic inequality may have had the toxic effects identified by Wilkinson & Pickett (2009) including poor health, higher rates of incarceration, and many other social problems.

Cause 2. Poverty rates declined from roughly 23% of the American population in 1959 to 13.5% in 2015. These rates "flat-lined" from the early 1980s to 2016 with minor undulations. The story is not so positive with respect to the numbers of poor people. While this number declined sharply from 40 million in 1959 to 25 million in1978, it increased to 43.1 million in 2015. While the rate stayed constant at 13.5% from the early 1980s to 2015, but the number grew substantially. This is not a positive picture. It partly reflects growth in the American population, but may be caused, as well, by significant cuts in domestic discretionary spending, changes in the American economy from unskilled jobs to jobs that require advanced skills and education, migration of manufacturing plants abroad, failure to raise the federal minimum wage significantly, and a decline in trade unions. Bear in mind, too, that many researchers contend that the Federal Poverty Line is set too low. Other statistics also describe a large population in or near poverty levels including 46.5 million Americans who used the Supplemental Nutrition Assistance Program (SNAP or Food Stamps) in 2012. Monthly household income cannot exceed 100% of poverty to be eligible for SNAP benefits, which average only $1.44 per person per meal. One in seven households, or 17.2 million persons, were in families deemed by the U.S. Department of Agriculture to have "low food security without hunger" or "food insecurity with hunger," and 3.9 million of these households had children in them. Huge numbers of children qualify for school lunches (31.6 million) and school breakfasts (11.7 million). Another 20 million children qualify for free or reduced-price lunches. A huge network of food banks, pantries, and soup kitchens provide food to hungry people (Jansson, 2016).

Members of the 16 vulnerable populations identified in Chapter 1 have high rates of poverty, including 23.6% of Hispanic persons, 26.2% of African American persons, 28.3% of Native Americans, 20% of millennial persons, 12% to 29% of disabled people, depending on the nature of their disability, and 39.6% of single-mother families.

Cause 3. Data does not exist about rates of upward mobility over an extended period to my knowledge. Chapter 1 discussed five separate research studies that revealed that contemporary American rates of upward mobility fall beneath levels in many European nations and Canada.

Cause 4. Levels of hope have not, to my knowledge, been measured over time. I hypothesize that high levels of low income, low levels of upward mobility, and low graduation rates from secondary school among persons of color decrease the levels of hope among significant groups.

Cause 5. It is difficult to measure levels of discrimination at different points in time because discrimination takes many forms and includes many populations. Important gains were made in the period from 1982 to the present, including at the federal level with respect to the LGBTQ population in the military, equality of marriage, laws that prohibit violence against women, the Americans with Disabilities Act (ADA), and the Family Medical Leave Act. The Immigration Reform and Control Act granted asylum to 3 million undocumented workers in 1986. The U.S. Supreme Court ruled in favor of same-sex marriage in 2015. Many states enacted laws that protected rights of transsexual persons, homeless people, seniors, disabled people, and other at-risk populations. Federal courts outlawed some discriminatory laws against immigrants.

Setbacks took place. The Congress failed to enact immigration legislation in 2007 that would have allowed more than ten million undocumented persons to work toward citizenship. Many states enacted discriminatory laws against immigrants. A conservative U.S. Supreme Court restricted use of affirmative action in higher education. The nation was shocked by the slaying of scores of unarmed African American males, beginning with Trayvon Martin in 2012 that were detected only because they were recorded by mobile phones. Many states enacted laws that allow police to apprehend persons who "looked like" undocumented immigrants, but many were overturned by courts. Many states enacted anti-abortion laws with some overturned by courts. Hate crimes accelerated in some locations against LGBT persons, Jews, and other at-risk populations. The rhetoric of Donald Trump during presidential primaries and the election of 2016 included anti-immigrant, anti-Latino, misogynist, and xenophobic views. Trump started a "birther movement" to try to deny the presidency to Barack Obama on (false) grounds that he was not an American citizen.

We can't reach an accurate view of discrimination in this period without considering whether laws prohibiting discrimination were enforced. Conservatives' anti-regulatory ethos led many conservatives not to fund monitoring and enforcement sufficiently. As one example, the requirement that employers cannot discriminate against disabled persons in Americans with Disabilities Act (ADA) has been poorly monitored and enforced. As another example, only recently have many police forces put in place training programs to decrease excessive use of force—and with uncertain results.

For further discussion of discrimination against various at-risk populations, see the following pages in Jansson, 2015: against women from 1970 through 2015, pp. 326–327, 423–424, 514–516; against African Americans, pp. 424–427,

518–519; against Latinos pp. 518–519; against the LGBT population, pp. 369–370, 429–430, 521–523; against disabled persons, pp. 327–336, 370–371, 519–521; against immigrants, pp. 367–368, 427–428, 516–518; against children, pp. 372, 428–429; against seniors, pp. 372–373, 521; against homeless persons, pp. 373–374; against persons with criminal records, 523–524; and poor people, pp. 511–514.

Cause 6. Domestic discretionary spending by the federal government remains a small percentage of the federal budget as illustrated by spending tables in the Clinton and other presidencies. Low levels of discretionary spending at the federal level curtails funding of an array of housing, job training and social-service programs.

Cause 7. The difficulty that President Obama faced in getting *even* the Affordable Care Act (ACA) through the Congress reveals the extent of conservative opposition to "socialized medicine." The ACA addressed the medical needs of people who lacked private health insurance, as well as millions of persons who failed to qualify for Medicaid because their income placed them just above Medicaid eligibility levels. With the ACA under attack in the Trump presidency, it is likely that millions of Americans will remain uninsured for the indefinite future. Moreover, millions of Americans enter bankruptcy because they cannot afford deductibles and co-insurance of their private plans. We can hypothesize that enactment of a Medicare-for-All medical plan would enhance income inequality not only by covering everyone, but reducing administrative and marketing costs of private insurance companies.

Cause 8. The gridlock between the two political parties over budget issues during all of the presidencies from Reagan through Obama illustrates why the United States often can't fund many of its social programs at sufficient levels. With tax revenues depleted by tax cuts or by loopholes for affluent persons or by waste in expenditures, federal revenues are depleted. Members of both of the major parties engaged in budgetary gridlocak almost every year. While Republicans often wanted to cut deficits, cut taxes, and expand military spending, Democrats wanted to fund domestic programs at higher levels, cut military spending, and not cut taxes. The parties fought so furiously that so-called "continuing resolutions" had to be enacted near the end of many years to keep sufficient funding to keep the government from defaulting on its fiscal obligations. The scarcity of resources available for social and educational investments makes it difficult to fund IUOPs in sufficient size and numbers to reduce the toxic effects of income inequality and poverty. Chapter 8 discusses the fiscal challenges encountered by equality advocates in more detail.

Cause 9. Deep cuts in federal taxes in the presidencies of Reagan, G. W. Bush, and Trump, when combined with huge increases in military spending, contributed to extreme income inequality in Period 4.

Cause 10. A perfect storm took place from the second year of the Reagan presidency to the first year of the Trump presidency. Extreme polarization between the two parties and considerable sharing of power between them led to gridlock. Year after year, Congresses achieved few legislative successes as the popular ratings of Congress plummeted. We discuss in Chapters 4, 8 and 9 why enactment of equality-enhancing policies sufficient to move the Equality Roller Coaster downward will be challenging to enact and fund.

What History Reveals About the Roller Coaster's Trajectory

We analyze factors that appear to have lowered and raised the Equality Roller Coaster from the colonial period to the present in the next chapter, while realizing that many mysteries remain. Technical analysis is needed to ascertain with more precision the factors that lowered or raised the Equality Roller Coaster in different eras. What were the relative effects on moving the Equality Roller Coaster or keeping it in a static position of budget decisions, economic opportunities for persons in the lower 20% of income earners, tax policies, entitlements, domestic discretionary spending, military spending, the rise and decline of wealth through investments in housing, stocks, and bonds, inheritance taxes, the rise and fall of wages, and the impact of trade unions? Piketty (2014) contends that the new economic elites are corporate managers who often earn more than $5 million per year—and often more than $50 million per year—while others also implicate hedge fund managers and entrepreneurs who initiate new businesses. It is difficult to gauge the causes of the movements of the Income Equality Roller Coaster through time because variables change through time. Piketty (2014) contends, for example, that inherited wealth greatly contributed to its rise from the 1880s through the 1920s, while salaries of corporate officials assumed a larger role from the 1980s onward. We should not ignore, however, political factors that are discussed in the next chapter when we place the Income Equality Roller Coaster in the context of history, politics, culture, wars, racism, and prejudice. We ask what it might take to move the Equality Roller downward once again.

References

Alter J. (2010). *The promise*. New York: Simon and Schuster.
Ambrose J. (1984). *Eisenhower: the President*. New York: Simon and Schuster.
Balz D. & Brownstein R. (1996). *Storming the gates: Protest politics and the Republican revival*. Boston: Little, Brown.
Bernstein, I. (1996). *Guns or butter: the presidency of Lyndon Johnson*. New York: Oxford University Press.
Brauer, C. (1967). *John F. Kennedy and the second reconstruction*. New York: Columbia University Press.
Califano, J. (1991). *The triumph and tragedy of Lyndon Johnson*. New York: Simon and Schuster.
Clark, T. (1981, February 14). Want to know where the budget ax will fall? Read Stockman's big black book. *National Journal*, pp. 274–281.
Corn, D. (2012). *Showdown*. New York, William Morrow.
Darman, R. *who's in control? polar politics and the sensible center*. New York: Simon and Schuster.
Duffy M. & Goodgame D. (1992). *Marching in place*. New York: Simon and Schuster.
Edelman, P. (1997, March). The worst thing Bill Clinton has done. *Atlantic Monthly*, pp. 43–50.
Edsall, T. (1991), *Chain reaction: The impact of race, rights, and taxes on American politics*. New York: W.W. Norton.
Faux, J. (1991, September 13). Back to the peace dividend: the budget pact protects a bloated pentagon. *New York Times*, pp. A15.
Frum, D. (2003). *The right man*. New York: Random House.
Galbraith, J. (1957). *The great crash, 1929*. Boston: Houghton Mifflin.
Grunwald, M. (2012). *The new deal, the hidden history of change in the Obama era*. New York, Simon & Schuster.
Gorman, S. (2001, March 31) The makings of a deal. *National Journal* pp. 630–631.
Frank, T. (2016). *Listen liberal*. New York: Metropolitan/Henry Holt.
Halberstam, D. (1993). *The fifties*. New York: Villard.
Jansson, B. S. (2015). *The reluctant welfare state: engaging history to advance social work practice in contemporary society, 8th ed.* San Franciso, CA.
Jansson, B. S. (2001). *The sixteen-trillion-dollar mistake: how the U.S. bungled its national priorities from the New Deal to the present*. New York: Columbia University Press.
Kaldor, M. (1981). *The baroque arsenal*. New York: Hill and Wang.
Kaufman, D. (2015, June 14). Scott Walker and the fate of the union. *New York Times Magazine*
Kuttner, R. (1980). *Revolt of the haves: tax rebellions and hard times*. New York: Simon & Schuster.
Leff, M. (1984). *The limits of symbolic reform: The New Deal and taxation 1933–1939*. Cambridge: Cambridge University Press.
Leffler, M. (1992). *A preponderance of power: national security, the Truman Administration, and the Cold War*. Palo Alto: Stanford University Press.
Leuchtenberg, W. (1963). *Franklin Roosevelt and the New Deal: 1932–1940*. New York: Harper & Row.
Levitan S. & Johnson, C. (1984). *Beyond the safety net: Reviving the promise of opportunity in America*. Cambridge, MA: Ballinger.
Maraniss, D. (1995). *First in his class: A biography of Bill Clinton*. New York: Simon and Schuster.

Meerpol, M. (1998). *Surrender: How the Clinton Administration completed the Reagan revolution*. Ann Arbor, University of Michigan Press.

Mishel L. & Davis, A. (2015, June 31). "Top CEOs make 300 times more than typical workers," Economic Policy Institute, accessed @ epi.org on September 15, 2017.

Moore J. and Slater, W. (2003). *Bush's brain: How Karl Rove made George W. Bush presidential*. Hoboken, NJ: John Wiley & Sons.

Mulder, R. A. (1979). *The insurgent Progressives in the United States Senate and the New Deal*. New York: Garland.

O'Neill, W. (1993). *A democracy at war: America's fight at home and abroad in World War II*. New York: Free Press.

Patterson, J. (1967). *Congressional Conservatism and the New Deal*. Lexington, KY: University of Kentucky Press.

Pasztor, A. (1995). *When the Pentagon was for sale*. New York: Scribner.

Phillips, K. (1983), *Post-Conservative America: People, politics, and ideology in a time of crisis*. New York: Vintage Books.

Piketty, T. (2014). *Capital in the twenty-first century*. Cambridge, MA: Harvard University Press

Reichley, J. (1982). *Conservatives in an age of change: The Nixon and Ford Administrations*. Washington, DC: Brookings Institution.

Roberts, C. (1984). *The Supply-Side revolution: An insider's account of policy-makingin Washington*. Cambridge, MA: Harvard University Press.

Reston, J. (1941, December 5). Put victory plan at $120 billion. *New York Times*, p.1.

Sherry, M. (1977). *Preparing for the next war: America plans for the next war*. New Haven: Yale University Press.

Smeeding, T. (1984). Is the safety net still intact? In Bawden, D. L. (Ed.). *The social contract revisited: aims and outcomes of President Reagan's social welfare policy*. Washington, DC: Urban Institute.

Steamer, R. (1971). *The Supreme Court in crisis: A history of conflict*. Amherst: University of Massachusetts Press.

Stiglitz J. & Blimes L. (2008). *The three trillion dollar war: The true cost of the Iraq conflict*. New York: W. W. Norton.

Stockman, D. (1986). *The triumph of politics: Why the Reagan revolution failed*. New York: Harper and Row.

Wicker, T. (1991). *One of us: Richard Nixon and the American dream*. New York: Random House.

Wilson, F. (2013, March 19). What could we have bought instead of a $3 trillion Iraq War? *Huffington Post*.

Witte, J. (1985). *The politics and development of the federal income tax*. Madison, WI: University of Wisconsin Press.

Woodward, B. (1994). *The agenda: Inside the Clinton White House*. New York: Simon and Schuster.

Woodward B. (2002). *Bush at war*. New York: Simon & Schuster.

Credits

Fig. 3.1: Source: https://eml.berkeley.edu/~saez/saez-UStopincomes-2010.pdf.

Fig. 3.2: Source: US Bureau of the Budget

Fig. 3.3: US Bureau of the Budget

Fig. 3.4: Source: US Bureau of the Budget

Fig. 3.5: Source: US Bureau of the Budget

Fig. 3.6: Source: US Bureau of the Budget

4 WHAT WE CAN LEARN FROM HISTORY: WHAT CAUSES THE EQUALITY ROLLER COASTER TO MOVE UPWARD AND DOWNWARD?

Thanks to the work of economic historians, we can trace the movements of the United States between periods of equality and inequality over roughly 250 years. Many factors influenced its movements, including political and ideological developments including government tax and spending policies; economic developments; presidential leadership; political elites in the dominant political party; wars; levels of corporate salaries; and extent workers are unionized.

Because so many factors shape the movements of the Equality Roller Coaster, it is difficult to determine the influence of different factors and combinations of factors. Inequality is, in short, a wicked problem, yet we have to analyze why it exists, what promotes it, and what decreases it, because it has extraordinary power to in shape the wellbeing of the American people. With roughly 45 million persons currently under federal poverty levels, we must find ways to decrease inequality. We also have to redress discrimination against many at-risk populations. To accomplish these goals, we have to find resources that can fund Initiatives to Uplift Ordinary People (IUOPs) and enact Resources to Uplift Ordinary People (RUOPs) can fund IUOPs and that reduce income of people at the top of the economic distribution.

This chapter discusses four specific periods of relative equality and inequality including:

- Period 1: Relative equality in the colonial period from roughly 1751 to 1825

- Period 2: Relative inequality from roughly 1866 to 1930
- Period 3: Relative equality from roughly 1933 to 1980
- Period 4: Relative inequality from roughly 1981 to (at least) 2018

Let's ask the following questions to orient ourselves to a complex subject:

- Do levels of equality move in tandem with the ten hypothesized causes identified in this book—or vice versa? If so, why?
- What do these four periods tell us about factors that triggered or catalyzed movement into a cycle of equality or inequality?
- What factors may have fostered equality or inequality in each of these periods?
- What factors sustained relative equality or inequality in each of the four periods? Why didn't the U.S. move back and forth between equality and inequality frequently rather than sustaining each of these four periods for many decades?
- If periods of inequality last for many decades, should contemporary equality advocates despair?

Our answers to these questions are often conjectural because of the complexity of the topic, the paucity of data, and linkages between equality and many other factors like culture, social class, politics, social psychology, and economics. These questions are difficult to answer, as well, because American society and governance has markedly changed over time. Only 4 million persons (excluding Native Americans) lived in the largely agrarian United States around 1800, for example, as compared to later periods when more than 300 million people inhabited an industrialized United States. The demographics of the nation greatly changed over time with respect to the number of immigrants in the nation's population, the diversity of its population, and whether the nation was mostly rural or concentrated in urban areas. While the federal government had virtually no tax resources prior to World War II, because only the top 5% of the economic distribution paid federal income taxes, it possessed much greater tax revenues from World War II to the present.

We face another problem: the Income Equality Roller Coaster has shifted between periods of income equality and inequality only four times in the nation's history from 1750 to the present. With only four movements, we don't have sufficient sample size to test hypotheses about possible reasons why it moved downward or upward—or why it remained in an up or down position for many decades during each of the four periods. Moreover, many factors have changed during these time periods. At a minimum, the movements of the Income Roller Coaster tell us that extreme income inequality is not a permanent feature of the United States.

Ascertaining What Causes the Roller Coaster's Movements from Period 3 to Period 4

It may make sense, then, to compare periods 3 and 4 with respect to the 10 hypothesized causes of income inequality because these two periods are relatively proximate in time. We can ask whether levels of poverty, discrimination, low mobility, hope, access to opportunities, and access to medical care were more available or present in the period of relative equality (period 3) as compared to the period of relative inequality (period 4). We can ask whether expenditures for social investments were higher in period 3 than in period 4. We can ask if the federal government invested in social opportunities more heavily in period 3 than in period 4. We can ask if the federal government taxed affluent people more heavily in period 3 than in period 4. We can ask if the American political system did not discriminate against equality advocates as markedly in period 3 than in period 4.

We anticipate ambiguous findings. Take poverty levels as one example (cause 2). Extraordinary poverty existed in the Great Depression in period 3, but almost disappeared in World War II and its immediate aftermath, only to rise during the 1950s. Poverty may not be a causal factor for portions of period 3, but may be a predictor of equality for other portions of period 3, such as when the numbers of poor people declined from roughly 40 million in 1959 to 25 million in 1968 and remained at roughly 25 million through1978. By contrast, the number of poor people rose in Period 4 from 30 million in 1981 to roughly 43 million in 2015. This finding may indicate that levels of poverty have a role in moving the Income Roller Coaster downward (for portions of period 3) and upward for period 4. However, the rate of poverty remained in a relatively tight zone between 10% and 15% from 1960 to the present.

It is difficult to measure levels of discrimination as experienced by persons in vulnerable populations. However, the extent of enactment of civil rights legislation and court rulings that upheld enforcement of civil rights was greatly greater in period 3 than in period 4. Enactment of myriad regulations and civil rights laws in the 1960s and 1970s may have reduced certain types of discrimination against persons of color, women, and seniors. Legislation decreased discrimination against Asian American immigrants. Southern hospitals were desegregated almost overnight after Medicare was enacted because it forbade federal reimbursements to segregated hospitals.

Some civil rights laws were enacted in period 4, such as the Americans with Disabilities Act of 1990, but they were relatively few in number as compared to period 3. It is possible that persons of color, women, and immigrants *believed* the nation wanted to protect their rights in period 3 due to the sheer volume of civil rights and regulations that were enacted.

It is difficult to compare rates of upward mobility in periods 3 and 4. I discussed the five research studies that documented relatively low levels of upward mobility in the United States in the latter part of period 4 in Chapter 1. If data could be found that demonstrated that rates of upward mobility were higher in significant portions of period 3, excluding the Great Depression, we might be able to implicate upward mobility as a factor that moves the Equality Roller Coaster higher.

Levels of public investments in education, job training, mental health, and other many social programs may have had a role in moving the Equality Roller Coaster lower in the portions of period 3, but we presented Figures in Chapter 3 that suggest that social programs were often poorly funded across periods 3 and 4 due to high military spending, tax loopholes and wasted expenditures in the medical programs.

By contrast, relatively few social programs were enacted in period 4. The ability of social programs to increase income equality partly hinges upon their relative levels of funding. Taxation of affluent Americans appears to be an important factor in moving the Roller Coaster downward. High marginal tax rates on affluent people from 1933 through the 1970s may have helped to increase income equality—just as the lowering of these tax rates in the 1980s and subsequent decades may have decreased income equality.

Access to medical care was problematic in both periods 3 and 4 as witnessed by millions of uninsured people even after Medicaid and Medicare were enacted. More than 80% of working Americans received private insurance in both periods once private health insurance took off in the 1950s. When coupled with Medicare and Medicaid, private health insurance may have moved the Equality Roller Coaster downward in period 3, but large numbers of Americans were not medically insured in both periods 3 and 4. The enactment of the Affordable Care Act in 2010 appears not to have moved the Equality Roller Coaster since it gave medical insurance only to a relatively small fraction of the American population.

It is probably not possible to measure levels of hope as a causal factor in moving the Equality Roller Coaster due to lack of historical data. Levels of hope may be important, however, in understanding the entrenched poverty in specific subpopulations in specific time periods such as homeless people, persons who don't graduate from high school, some inner-city persons of color, some released prisoners, and White persons in rural and semi-rural areas that currently lack jobs.

I discuss subsequently that political variables may have assumed a significant role in lowering and raising the equality roller coaster including the power of trade unions and the relative power of Democrats and Republicans in the Congress and Presidency: Democrats in period 3 as compared Republican domination in period 4. Due to the domination of the politics by Democrats in period 3, far more social legislation was enacted in it than in period 4 that was dominated by Republicans.

We need to identify exogenous factors that may have moved the Equality Roller Coaster down or up other than the ten hypothesized causes. Some of them are discussed in Chapter 3 such as the Great Depression that may have taken even more income and wealth from affluent people than from low-income people; the large increases in taxes on affluent Americans in World War II during the 1950s, 1960, and 1970s when the U.S. needed resources to fund the Korean War, the Vietnam War, and the Cold War. We discussed how the building of the suburbs, housing programs of the federal government, and infrastructure in the late 1940s, 1950s, and 1960s may have contributed to the downturn of the Equality Roller Coaster. Possibly the growth of the American military during the Cold War had some role in lowering the Equality Roller Coaster. Compensation policies of corporations shifted radically from period 3 when the ratio of CEO's pay to average workers' pay was relatively low, but that zoomed upward in the 1980s to the present. Wages of working-class persons stagnated for four decades from 1970 to the present while salaries of CEOs and affluent people rose dramatically. Were it not for the huge expenditures of Social Security, Medicare, Medicaid, and many safety-net programs like SNAP and the Earned Income Tax Credit, income inequality might have been considerably greater in period 4.

Different measuring tools used by researchers confirm the broad movements of the Equality Roller Coaster. Wilkinson & Pickett (2009) confirm extreme economic inequality in 2009 when measuring the ratio of the income of the top 20% to the bottom 20%. Emanuel Saez reaches similar results using the income share of highest-income households (Saez, 2009). The Gini Coefficient, a number that ranges from 0 (perfect equality) to 1 (perfect inequality) based on residents' net income yields similar findings as other measures (Gini

Coefficient, Wikipedia). In other words, the movements of the Equality Roller Coaster are real.

The Impact of Politics on Inequality?

Considerable evidence suggests that partisan factors shaped policy priorities in periods 3 and 4. While Democrats dominated Period 3, Republicans dominated Period 4. Democrats controlled the House of Representatives from 1933 to 1981 except for the four years from 1947 to 1949, and from 1955 to 1957. They had majorities that exceeded 60% of House members in all of these 48 years except 10 years, during which Republicans controlled the House for four years. Democrats similarly controlled the Senate for 48 years, from 1933 to 1981, except for four years, with majorities that exceeded 60%, except 10 years (1947 to 1949, 1955 to 1957, and 1951 to 1957). Roosevelt created a coalition of intellectuals, Jews, poor and working-class voters, some middle-class voters, and African Americans. Democratic dominance helped keep the Equality Roller Coaster in a downward position from 1933 to 1981. Democrats were prime movers of the domestic reforms of the New Deal and the Great Society. They induced Richard Nixon to support and help enact many domestic reforms during his administration. Nixon came to believe that Republicans would be unable to contest Democrats' dominance without supporting social programs that helped working-class voters. Domestic spending soared from $158 billion in 1970 to $314 billion in 1980 (all in 1980 dollars), with about two-thirds of that spending consisting of means-tested social-insurance programs. Nondefense spending went from 8.1% of GDP in 1961 to 15.6% of GDP in 1981, so it is possible that domestic programs, i.e., Medicaid, Food Stamps, the Earned Income Tax Credit, AFDC, housing subsidies, SSI, Medicare, unemployment insurance, and CETA considerably increased the resources of the bottom 90% of the economic scale, and specific subpopulations within that 90%. Tens of millions of workers benefited from America's leading manufacturing position in the world, the building of suburbs, and construction of infrastructure in the 1950s and 1960s.

Reagan initiated an era extending through 2016, during which Democrats never controlled 60% of the Senate and even lost it for 12 years (1981 to 1989 and 2003 to 2009). While Democrats had previously controlled the House except temporarily, Republicans controlled it from 1995 through 2016 aside from 2009 to 2013—or for 16 years. I did not include the first year of Trump's presidency in preceding data, but Republicans controlled the presidency and both Houses of Congress in 2017.

Chapter 3 discussed how the politics of the United States changed markedly when Franklin Roosevelt won a landslide presidential victory over Herbert Hoover in 1932. For the first time in American history, Republicans and Democrats were polarized by social class, with working-class Americans consistently voting Democratic and affluent Americans consistently voting Republican. Prior to 1932, the parties were divided between ethnic groups and geographic regions, but they now revolved around social class and ideology. While Roosevelt never liked "radicals" or even ideology, he embraced a philosophy that emphasized development of a "caring" federal government that would come to the assistance of persons in poverty. The New Deal was the expression of this philosophy. Republicans, by contrast, went toward a conservative political philosophy that stressed a limited government, minimal domestic programs, and small numbers of regulations. They hewed to this conservative philosophy throughout the Roosevelt and the Truman presidencies. Republicans had a moderate wing that included Presidents Eisenhower, Richard Nixon, and Gerald Ford, as well as Senators like Jacob Javits and Edward Brooke, but conservatives remained a dominant force that became even stronger during period 4.

Other political developments strengthened the liberal and conservative orientations of the Democratic and Republican parties, respectively.

From Franklin Roosevelt onward, Democrats have been relatively liberal except for the strong contingent of Southern Democrats who left the Republican Party in the wake of the emancipation of slaves. From Richard Nixon onward, these relatively conservative Southern Democrats became Republicans—a departure that made the Democratic Party considerably more liberal. By the same token, the Republican Party from Franklin Roosevelt's administration forward became relatively conservative, a conservatism that was further bolstered by the influx of Southern Democrats in the 1970s and subsequent decades. White working-class people increasingly joined the Republican Party. They had been part of the Democratic Party in the 1930s, but gradually departed for the Republican Party from Nixon onward—a group that Nixon called the "silent majority of law-abiding Americans."(Edsall, 1991). More recently, these White working-class constituents and White Southerners had often not voted until Donald Trump, a billionaire, energized them, allowing the surprise presidential victory of Trump in 2016. Meanwhile, large numbers of millennial voters born between 1980 and 2000 mostly moved into the Democratic Party, as did many persons of color, new citizens drawn from the ranks of immigrants, and Latinos. Trump speeded their movement to the Democratic Party with his negative comments about immigrants, a Latino judge, Muslims, and his role over many years in questioning whether President Obama was an American citizen.

Gerrymandering of electoral districts by members of both parties decreased the likelihood of bipartisan cooperation that often existed in the 1960s and 1970s because neither party's elected officials receive many votes from members of the opposing party. One party dominated 60% of Congressional districts in 2016, meaning that voters in them rarely met and talked with voters from other parties. This polarization was somewhat mitigated by the growing numbers of independent voters who came to decide elections in many jurisdictions by picking either Democratic or Republican candidates.

It is not surprising, then, that the policy priorities in periods 3 and 4 matched the ideologies of their presidents. Relatively liberal Democratic presidents in Period 3 favored greater income equality, policies that could reduce levels of discrimination against specific at-risk populations, and disliked high levels of poverty. Relatively conservative Republican presidents in period 4 often believed that income inequality was a positive development that spurred initiative and punished persons who were were relatively poor. They were more likely than their Democratic counterparts to view poverty as stemming from defects of character than from systemic factors in the economy and the welfare state (Jansson, 2015).

So a strong case can be made that, on balance, Americans are more likely to work to decrease levels of poverty and levels of discrimination in periods of relative equality than in periods of relative inequality. President Roosevelt did develop myriad work-relief programs to help destitute persons during the Great Depression. Presidents Franklin Roosevelt, Johnson, and Nixon did construct the American welfare state in the 1960s and 1970s that did route hundreds of billions of dollars to people at the bottom of the economic system. They did tax wealthy people at relatively high levels with top marginal rates exceeding 70%. Compare these actions with the domestic agendas of Presidents Reagan, George H. W. Bush, George W. Bush and Donald Trump who mostly emphasized cutting domestic programs or not adding to them, during a period of marked income inequality. They cut taxes of affluent Americans. Republican presidents and Congresses in Period 4 mostly failed to enact civil rights legislation. Indeed, President George Bush, Sr. as well as President Reagan opposed the Civil Rights Act of 1964 long before their presidencies (Jansson, 2015). These observations suggest a partisan conclusion, but one that is supported by evidence. Equality advocates are more likely to obtain a period of relative equality by helping to elect Democratic presidents and members of Congress. It follows that period 4 will be extended by years or decades if Republicans win the presidency and the Congress on numerous occasions in coming years. It also follows that many Democrats will embrace an agenda of income equality, reduction of poverty, and lower levels of discrimination if they could inaugurate a Period 5 if history repeats itself when they were the prime movers of civil rights, safety-net programs, and even entitlements.

Even in its early stage in fall of 2017, the presidency of Donald Trump appears to be following this script as Republicans control the presidency and both chambers of Congress. President Trump wants to increase military spending by roughly $50 billion. Republican leaders wanted to gut the Affordable Care Act even when that meant depriving as many as 23 million persons of health insurance. Many of them favored disallowing states to increase eligibility levels of the Medicaid program that the ACA allowed if states chose this option. They have vowed to keep the strict limitations on spending in the discretionary budget that were established in the sequestration agreement between Republicans and President Obama in 2012. They wanted to cut SNAP (food stamps) and housing vochers deeply. President Trump promised to cut one-half of all of federal regulations during his presidency. He has displayed little interest in enacting new civil rights legislation, even resorting to racial, gender-based, and immigration-based attacks during his presidential campaign. He signaled that he might make a deal to work with Democrats to establish the legal right of immigrant youth to remain in the United States after their undocumented parents brought them into the nation as children, but it was unclear in December, 2017 that a deal would be finalized. President Trump cut taxes of affluent Americans and corporations deeply in 2017 and 2018.

Other Factors that May Cause Transitions Between Periods of Equality and Inequality

Our brief history suggests that contextual factors assumed an important role in causing transitions between periods 1 through 4. Each period was preceded by a major disruption, whether the Declaration of Independence and the American Revolution (period 1), the Civil War (period 2), the Great Depression (period 3), or a conservative political revolution combined with a meltdown of the Democratic (period 4). Recall that movements of the Equality Roller Coaster describe transitions between these four periods, whether from high positions toward relative equality (periods 1 and 3) or low positions toward relative inequality (periods 2 and 4) as I now discuss.

The inception of Period 1. The very earliest settlements in the New World were relatively hierarchical in nature, as I discussed in Chapter 2, even as they became less hierarchical as it moved into the early 18th century. The Declaration of Independence and the American Revolution led many Americans to view themselves as Americans rather than as English citizens who hoped to return home once they improved their economic conditions. Contemporary Americans can hardly grasp the impact of going to war as a developing nation with a world super-power: England. Nor can we easily grasp the hardships experienced by Americans from this seven-year war. These epic events led many colonists to increasingly view themselves as members of a new society rather than as members of the nations from which they had emigrated. It led them to conceptualize the United States as a land of equality composed of small landowners who would govern themselves, rather than as English citizens who deferred to a monarch or a landed aristocracy. They were greatly assisted by limitless land occupied only by Native Americans in what became the Eastern and Midwestern parts of the United States. They expected this land would be sold to colonists in relatively small plots to bring to fruition the agrarian democracy that they were establishing. They believed they were making history by creating the first egalitarian agrarian democracy of small landowners. They created a system of governance in the Constitution dedicated to avoiding undue power by mobs or aristocrats or monarchs, and they quickly established democratic institutions in villages and towns across their settled lands. Such leaders as Jefferson eloquently expressed this vision of an agrarian egalitarian utopia.

The inception of Period 2. A long transition took place from roughly 1800 to the end of the Civil War in 1865 as a relatively egalitarian society of small landowners shifted toward a less egalitarian society that included small cities, an influx of low-income immigrants, the start of manufacturing enterprises, and the development of railroads. The Civil War disrupted American society possibly more than any other single event in its history because of its brutality and its length. It accelerated the emergence of an industrial order because the North defeated the South by rapidly creating a munitions industry, a sophisticated system of railroads, and federal taxes and a banking system, all in order to support the war. The North ended the plantation aristocracy by emancipating slaves and defeating the Confederacy. It facilitated development of an industrial democracy that would dominate the world by 1900 and that would be based in the Eastern and Midwestern parts of the North. Jefferson's limited government was replaced by Lincoln's philosophy: elimination of slavery, a national government that protected its manufacturing industries with protective tariffs, a national bank that supported these institutions, and a robust educational system. The victory by the North over the South allowed Lincoln's philosophy to prevail, although the nation had to wait until the 20th century to develop the Federal Reserve System to complete its national banking system.

The Northern victory over the South did not initiate greater equality, which had already declined markedly from the colonial era, even with the emancipation of the slaves. Americans ruthlessly repressed Native Americans, as well as Mexican inhabitants of what came to be the Southwestern part of the United States, after obtaining it by force of arms, culminating in the Treaty of Guadalupe Hidalgo with Mexico in 1848. The national manufacturing system relied on low-wage immigrants in a mostly unregulated capitalist system. Millions of immigrants, as well as migrants from rural America to cities, received virtually no help from local, state, and federal governments during numerous recessions. The nation lacked all of the safety net programs we take for granted in contemporary America. Ultra-rich persons bribed officials at all levels of government to get contracts and special deals during the Gilded Age.

The inception of Period 3. The Great Depression shook the nation to its core. Almost no one was unscathed by its severity and its length. Rich people, middle-class people, and poor people were all caught in its vortex, losing investments, jobs, homes, family businesses, farms, banks, and other assets. They were emotionally shaken by this event that defied solution in an era of primitive government with limited resources and power.

The deification of wealth and inequality of period 2 came under attack. Hadn't rich people caused this catastrophe by excessive speculation? Didn't Hoover, widely seen to represent them, lack compassion for Americans mired in economic uncertainty? They found a compelling leader in Franklin Roosevelt, a pragmatist who avoided ideology even as he uplifted tens of millions of Americans, whether by putting them to work, helping them buy houses, saving their farms, giving them pensions, giving them access to welfare programs, or allowing them to organize trade unions. He created a coalition of working people, intellectuals, and ethnic groups that formed the constituency of the modern Democratic Party and that allowed him to be elected in four consecutive presidential contests. He taxed the top 5% of the economic distribution at relatively high rates—a population that also lost as much as 60% of their income and wealth during the Great Depression (Piketty, 2014).

The inception of Period 4. Much as Roosevelt had ushered in an extended period of equality, Reagan changed the conversation from equality to free markets, helping rich business people through supply-side economics, and military might. Reagan was a conservative with a smile who endeared himself to many Americans with his communication skills (Cannon, 1991). He wanted, however, to turn the clock back to the Gilded Age when he believed

American civilization had achieved its zenith with minimal taxes, reliance on state and local governments, and harsh safety-net programs. He was obsessed with re-building the American military to contest the Soviets, who he falsely portrayed as having vastly greater military forces than the United States (Jansson, 2001). He entered annual budget negotiations demanding no new taxes, deep reductions in domestic spending, and huge increases in military spending, even as top aides like David Stockman, his budget director, predicted runaway deficits. Those deficits appeared as early as his second year in office, continued throughout his presidency and into the presidencies of his immediate successors. When his two terms had expired, the truth came out: his cumulative annual deficits had increased the national debt more than all prior presidents from George Washington onward combined—deficits that led to budget gridlock during the 12 years that followed his presidency (Stockman, 1986). Reagan's ability to initiate a conservative political revolution was increased by the disintegration of the Democratic Party as it lost its Southern base as well as large portions of its blue-collar and Catholic base in the 1970s and subsequently.

Lesson Learned. The shift from the current period of inequality to period of equality may not take place unless a destabilizing event takes place, like another Depression or even stagflation. From early indications, actions and unusual behaviors of President Donald Trump may themselves be a destabilizing force. He failed to expand his constituency beyond rural blue-collar White voters and conservative Republicans. He filled his Cabinet with billionaires and multi-millionaires. He mostly favored conservative policies when he sought to repeal and replace the ACA. Trump was under investigation for possible collusion with the Russians during the presidential election of 2016, as well as possible obstruction of justice in the investigation headed by Robert Mueller, the Director of the FBI. Poll data revealed an erosion of support for Trump by December, 2017 when only 33% of Americans approved of his presidency. (For a fuller discussion of Trump's presidency, see Jansson, 2018, chapter 13). His early budget and tax proposals veered in a conservative direction. All bets are off, so equality advocates have to press hard to get equality on the policy agenda of voters and public officials.

What *Sustained* Periods of Equality and Inequality?

We need to better understand another puzzling phenomenon: Why did Periods 1 through 4 last so long, each for many decades? Indeed, why couldn't

Republican presidents Eisenhower, Nixon, and Ford shorten the relatively liberal period 3 and why couldn't Democratic presidents Clinton and Obama shorten the relatively conservative period 4? Our brief history suggests that a combination of factors, some idiosyncratic to specific periods, possibly contributed to their length.

Period 1. The colonial period of relative equality didn't happen in a vacuum: it depended upon relatively free access to land, coupled with an open system of immigration. The colonists had almost universally experienced hardship in Europe, whether because of their religious beliefs, their social class, their lack of land rights, or their political beliefs. They willingly endured the hardships of crossing the ocean to improve their economic condition and in search of religious toleration. Colonial leaders did not have to worry about deep poverty in cities because large cities did not exist. They came to view themselves and their colonies as markedly different from European nations where class, aristocracy, and the Crown were dominant. Despite their rhetoric that extolled freedom and upward mobility, they created a deeply flawed society where slaves and Native Americans were subjected to violence and subjugation, and where women mostly could not own property.

While conflict existed between founding fathers, including between George Washington, John Adams, and Thomas Jefferson, about the role of government in the emerging nation, these differences were moot because the federal government had virtually none of the tax revenues or domestic powers that came to exist from the New Deal onward.

Period 2. During and after the Civil War, when the nation embarked on an unregulated manufacturing economy with large cities, the Equality Roller Coaster had to move upward probably for a combination of reasons. Industrialists and entrepreneurs vastly increased their wealth in a nation with unregulated capitalism. They could develop large enterprises because growing cities and railroads gave them access to significant numbers of customers. They could grow their enterprises because they had a plentiful supply of low-wage workers,from millions of immigrants that entered the United States (Jansson, 2015). They were virtually untaxed by the federal government with respect to their incomes and their investments, because a federal income tax did not yet exist and because state and local governments had low taxes. They could build their enterprises in a nation that lacked work-safety standards and a minimum wage. They benefited from the near absence of unions, which were brutally suppressed by local and federal governments (Jansson, 2015). They frequently bribed public officials of local and state governments to obtain contracts (Cochran, 1961). Persons in the lower 50% of the economic distribution who experienced poverty, unemployment, or hunger had to rely on poor houses and breadlines outside police stations during periodic recessions. The Equality Roller Coaster moved upward under these circumstances, and maintained this position through the 1920s possibly for a combination of reasons. Aside from a few radical figures, like Eugene Debs who garnered millions of votes as a third-party candidate in the election of 1912, the nation relied on Democratic and Republican parties that were decidedly conservative, with leaders who were often racist. Leaders of the so-called Progressive Movement, which included leaders of the small liberal wings of both major parties, mostly focused on getting regulations enacted by local and state governments, including housing codes, restrictions on production and sale of drugs, and abolition of child labor. They were unable to develop and fund social programs because the federal government had scant revenues until enactment of the 16th Amendment to the Constitution, which allowed it to tax incomes. State and local governments mostly relied on relatively low property taxes. Republicans controlled both the House and the Senate of the federal government from 1865 to 1931, aside from 1875 to 1897 when Democrats mostly controlled the House. Voting for the two major parties was mostly determined by ethnicity rather than by social class (Jansson, 2015).

Period 3. Roosevelt fundamentally altered American politics for decades to come. He aligned the Democratic and Republican Parties by social class. For the first time in American history, working class Americans voted for the Democratic Party (Jansson, 2015). Republicans, by contrast, adhered to the conservative ideology of limited government and limited taxes even as they mostly voted for Roosevelt's work programs, because many of them were unemployed.

Roosevelt created an enduring dominance of the Democratic Party for more than four decades. The Equality Roller Coaster remained in a downward position from 1933 through the 1970s partly because all of the presidents in this era, regardless of party, supported high marginal tax rates on the top 5% of the economic distribution, ranging from 70% to 95%, to help pay for costs incurred by World War II, the Korean War, the Vietnam War, and the Cold War (Piketty, 2014).). In addition, many affluent persons had not yet rebuilt investments that they had lost in the Great Depression, even after several decades.

American political culture may have assumed an important role in keeping the Equality Roller Coaster in a downward position from 1933 through the 1970s. As compared to presidents who governed from 1981 through 2018, who rarely (if at all) even mentioned the word "poverty," many presidents developed programs to assist people in the bottom 20% of the American economy during this period. Roosevelt viewed his New Deal as preventing starvation and destitution. A "War on Poverty" was initially proposed by John Kennedy and enacted and implemented by Lyndon Johnson. Richard Nixon proposed a version of a "guaranteed income" in his welfare legislation even if the Congress did not enact it. Robert Putnam recalls in his book, *Our Kids: the American Dream in Crisis* (2015) that an ethos of equality existed in his youth in the 1950s, unlike in the latter part of the 20th century. American culture supported relatively low salaries for top executives, in contrast with Ronald Reagan's glorification of wealth, his adherence to an economic philosophy based on "trickle-down economics" from the rich to the poor, and deep cuts in taxes on wealthy Americans.

Period 4. The sheer power of decreasing top marginal rates and other taxes of the top 5% of the economic distribution in moving the Equality Roller Coaster upward was illustrated in 1981, when Ronald Reagan cut top marginal rates from 70% to 28% and reduced taxes on capital gains from 28% to 20%, the lowest rate since the Hoover Administration (Piketty, 2014). He also cut other taxes of the super-rich. His spending cuts in social programs had not yet taken effect, nor had salaries of the top 5% of the economic distribution been significantly increased, yet the Equality Roller Coast began moving upward. Further research is needed to determine to what extent Reagan's cuts in social spending contributed to increasing inequality.

We have already described Reagan's political philosophy, which although different from Roosevelt's, also fundamentally changed the politics of the nation. Democrats mostly controlled both Houses of Congress at the time, often with 60% or greater majorities in each of them. This made Republican victories in Congress essential for Republicans' quest to retain Reagan's policies. By controlling at least one chamber of Congress from 1981 to 2016, they could practice the policy of budget gridlock to stymie Democrats' attempts to enact social legislation, raise domestic spending, contain military spending, and impose taxes on the super-rich—policies that would have elevated the Equality Roller Coaster.

Relatively low top marginal rates were retained by Reagan's successors, including Presidents George H. W. Bush, Bill Clinton (who raised them somewhat), George W. Bush, Barack Obama, and Donald Trump, and these policies greatly contributed to keeping the Equality Roller Coaster in its high position. These presidents also retained many other facets of the tax code that enriched the top 5%, and particularly the top 1%.

To a remarkable degree, presidential successors of Ronald Reagan were unable to markedly depart from his policies of low taxes on the rich, periodic cuts in domestic discretionary spending, and failure to enact major new programs. George H. W. Bush, Sr. was Reagan's clone with respect to social spending and high military spending, though probably lost the election of 1992 to Bill Clinton because he deviated from his penchant for low taxes by violating his pledge to support "no new taxes." His son, George W. Bush, Jr., also acted as a Reagan's clone, making further cuts in taxes of the super-rich, greatly increasing military spending, and creating huge deficits—even though he did not veto spending increases for social programs. Like Reagan, he made two large cuts in federal taxes at the same time that he greatly increased military spending to fund wars in Iraq and Afghanistan. These policies, like Reagan's, greatly increased budget deficits. Like Reagan, he cut taxes on wealthy persons more aggressively than he cut taxes on non-wealthy persons, which helped keep the Equality Roller Coaster at a high level. He enacted only a single major domestic program: adding a pharmaceutical benefit to the Medicare program. Donald Trump was also Reagan's clone, cutting taxes mostly of corporations and affluent people and enacting tax reforms in 2017 that would likely increase the national debt by more than $1 trillion within 10 years.

Bill Clinton was determined to break from Reagan's policies, but largely remained ineffective due to militant opposition from Congressional Republicans. He increased marginal tax rates of the top 1% of the economic distribution somewhat, only to find them reduced again by George W. Bush. He sought major increases in domestic discretionary spending only to have it jettisoned by Congress. Congressional Republicans scuttled his national health proposal, only allowing him to enact a crime bill. His major accomplishment was outmaneuvering Republicans in annual budget battles, allowing him to balance the budget in FY 2000. Not able to increase social spending or markedly increase top marginal rates, Clinton was unable to lower the Equality Roller Coaster. It isn't clear that he even wanted that result, particularly as he erased important regulations on Wall Street (and other) banks that had a role in the banking crisis that triggered the Great Recession in 2007.

Nor was Barack Obama able to lower the Equality Roller Coaster even when he confronted the Great Recession at the outset of his presidency. He raised top marginal rates somewhat and even increased taxes of the top 1% of the economic distribution to fund the Affordable Care Act, but this proved insufficient to move the Equality Roller Coaster lower (Jansson, 2015). Working with Ben Bernanke at the Federal Reserve, he skillfully maneuvered the nation through the Great Recession, but had no vision about how to markedly elevate the economic status of the lower 90% of the economic distribution

(Alter, 2010). He displayed remarkable tenacity in getting Congress to enact the Affordable Care Act and Dodd-Frank banking regulations, but neither of these measures addressed the economic needs of the lower 90% head on, even if the ACA provided health insurance to 20 million Americans who had lacked it and if Dodd-Frank possibly saved many Americans from foreclosure caused by deceptive lending practices (Alter, 2010).

Aside from a relatively large but short-lived Stimulus Plan, Obama invested his political capital in the ACA and Dodd-Frank bank regulations in 2010. These measures did not focus on redistribution. Obama faced a series of budget showdowns with Republicans that made it impossible for him to secure large spending increases for social programs, and, indeed, in 2012 he ended up with a sequestration agreement that will lead to $1 trillion in spending cuts by 2023. It is not surprising, then, that Obama was able to raise top marginal rates only modestly to 39.6% or to cut the ratio of managers' salaries to employees' paychecks only modestly (Corn, 2012). Obama belatedly acknowledged in 2017 that extreme income inequality was one of the four top problems of the nation just before he left office.

Commonalities between Periods 3 and 4. Periods 3 and 4 are the two phases of the Equality Roller Coaster that are most relevant to us because they are most proximate to our time. Dominant presidents (Roosevelt and Reagan) placed their stamp on culture and politics at the outset of these two periods in a vivid and powerful way, with landslide presidential victories at the outset in 1932 and 1980, and with immediate enactment of clusters of policies that represented, respectively, liberal and conservative directions. Presidents Truman and Johnson succeeded Roosevelt and sought to advance his agenda. Bush, Sr. and Bush, Jr. followed Reagan and sought to advance his agenda.

Both Roosevelt and Reagan established enduring electoral coalitions that endorsed their liberal and conservative agendas, respectively. Democrats mostly controlled both houses of Congress through the 1950s, 1960s, and 1970s, and Republicans mostly controlled at least one house of Congress from 1980 to the present, with the notable exception in 2008. Democrats were able to obtain a liberal Supreme Court through the 1970s with the appointment of Earl Warren in 1953. Republicans obtained a more conservative Supreme Court with appointments by Nixon, and markedly more so with appointments by Reagan, Bush, Sr., and Bush, Jr., when it became possibly the most conservative court in American history, prior to the naming of Sonia Sotomayor and Elena Kagan by Barack Obama.

The substantial policy victories at the outset of the Roosevelt and Reagan presidencies made it difficult for others to change the directions that they established. It was impossible for Republicans to rescind the Social Security Act, the minimum wage, the Tennessee Valley Authority (TVA), and the Wagner Act because they had huge constituencies that supported them. Democrats found it difficult to turn back many of Reagan's tax cuts and spending cuts, as well as his massive expansion of the military because he had received votes for these policies even from many of their own party.

The power of these two presidents partly derived from culture shifts in the nation. Roosevelt established a culture of helping persons in the lower economic strata, using government as a positive instrument for change and appealing to citizens' altruism. Reagan established a culture of moving power from the federal government to states, cutting taxes, cutting budgets, and slashing funds for means-tested programs. Piketty (2014) speculates that Reagan changed the nation's culture by enacting tax cuts in 1981 that enriched affluent Americans. Unlike Roosevelt who criticized economic elites, except during World War II when he needed their productive might to win the war, Reagan extolled them as leaders who would trigger efforts to emulate them in the broader population. Reagan popularized negative images of low-income persons. He invented the term, "welfare queen" when he invented a woman in Chicago who he castigated for having babies to enlarge her welfare checks. Mitt Romney revived such images in the presidential campaign of 2012 when he talked about "takers" as compared to "makers."

Periods of Transition. Each of the four periods was preceded by a period of transition that may have prepared the way for movement of the Equality Roller Coaster upward or downward.

From 1607 to 1750. The earliest colonies in the New World "fashioned a new society in the wilderness" (Jansson, 2015, p. 65). These small and mostly rural colonies initially resembled the semi-feudal society of England that contributed most of the settlers, where much land was owned by monarchs, economies where strictly regulated from above, goods were bartered in a subsistence economy, and land was held by monarchs or trading companies rather than individuals. Quasi-capitalist and quasi-democratic institutions gradually replaced these arrangements. A market economy gradually supplanted bartering in the early colonies as farmers created agricultural and timber surpluses that they could sell internally or export. Control of the colonies remained in the hands of the British Parliament and the British monarchy, which maintained British Governors in the colonies, and exacted taxes to fund British troops sent to protect colonists from intrusion by foreign powers and to defend from attacks by Native Americans. As the colonies developed their own legislatures and elections, they increasingly chafed at policy controls from abroad, as well as British taxes. While they valued protection from Native Americans by British troops, many of them resented having to fund them. The geographic realities in the New World also worke against control from abroad. The English Parliament and Monarchy could only control the colonies via months-long trips by sailing ships across the Atlantic Ocean. Settlers assertively often claimed land rather than purchasing it through trading companies established by the Monarchy and Parliament. Colonists increasingly wanted self-government. They moved rapidly toward an agrarian economy of small landowners, even in the South where some wealthy plantation owners arose. These realities led Thomas Jefferson to envision a democratic utopia with small landowners, democratic institutions, and independence from the British.

From 1800 to 1865. The seeds of destruction of colonial agrarian society were sown in the transition period of 1800 to 1865. Some settlers accumulated larger plots of land than others in the normal functioning of capitalism. They bought land from settlers in economic distress, or were able to buy larger plots due to their economic success on the frontier, or they acquired wealth by selling profitable farms in non-frontier areas. A class of agricultural laborers developed to help settlers clear their land and plant their crops. In an unregulated capitalist society, recessions often occurred, pushing some people into poverty. Some American settlers were ravaged by alcoholism, which cast many of them into poverty. Settlers often had large families so that some offspring could not inherit farms of their parents, making it difficult for those offspring to accumulate capital. Absent regulation or insured accounts, banks often became insolvent, casting some of their customers into poverty. Some settlers became rich as they mined gold and other minerals in a nation with abundant stocks. When taken together, these developments gradually increased inequality as the nation moved toward the Civil War.

During the 1920s and early 1930s. The roaring 1920s brought a sexual revolution, and also considerable poverty. Policies that empowered industry and affluence were supplemented by vigorous suppression of organized labor. Companies sought to obtain the goodwill of employees by developing stock-sharing schemes, providing fringe benefits, and starting company unions that ostensibly gave workers a mechanism for negotiating higher benefits and wages. When independent unions tried to organize, their leaders were often intimidated or fired, and strikes led to unabashed use of scabs, local police, the National Guard, and injunctions from courts that were usually favorable to management.

Social reformers were on the defensive during the 1920s; some were stigmatized as radicals, communists, or traitors. African Americans continued to live under oppressive Jim Crow laws in the South, encountered race riots and residential segregation in the North, and found it difficult to obtain jobs in the industries that were now producing consumer goods in the second industrial revolution. Latinos and Asian Americans continued to experience rampant prejudice and adverse policies in the West and Southwest. Women experienced new sexual freedoms in the era of the flapper, but found that their voting privileges did not lead to major policy reforms that would give them access to more remunerative work or professional jobs.

Americans were intrigued by social change and often tended to glamorize technology and science, but they were also fearful of new ideas. In the famous Scopes trial in 1925, for example, a schoolteacher was successfully prosecuted for teaching the theory of evolution in a Tennessee school. (The verdict was later overturned on a technicality.) Enacted as the Eighteenth Amendment to the Constitution in 1919, prohibition was supported by many Protestants, who insisted that local and federal officials strictly enforce the legislation. Many Americans supported stringent reductions of immigration, whether on racial grounds or because they believed the nation could no longer absorb immigrants. The Immigration Act of 1924 was blatantly racist. Its goal was to limit of immigration to 150,000 people each year, with quotas for each nationality in proportion to its size in the existing population. This policy was intended to reduce the proportion of immigrants from southern and eastern Europe. A complete prohibition was placed on Japanese immigration (Jansson, 2015).

Surface impressions of prosperity in the 1920s were misleading because unemployment ranged from 5 to 13%, and agriculture was in a state of depression throughout the decade. Although the upper third of the populace conspicuously consumed consumer products, the lower third were often unemployed or lived near or below the poverty level in a society that had virtually no safety net programs.

Extraordinary income and wealth existed in the United States from a second American industrial revolution. Steel, mining, and railroad industries had developed during the first revolution; the second focused on consumer products—such as cars, radios, and refrigerators—and on the electrification of homes and industries. Enormous consumer needs remained unmet in the United States. Only one in 10 urban homes was electrified in 1920; only one in 100 households possessed radios; and only one in three families had cars. Consumer appetites for new products were whetted by the rise of a large advertising industry. Persons who had obtained wealth in the Gilded Age had often passed it on to their children and remained in a moneyed class, which now included high-level officials and owners of companies and plants that produced goods.

A trickle-down economic philosophy, the dominant approach by people in power, held that affluent persons and industrial tycoons stimulated investments that would bring jobs to poor and working-class Americans. A case can be made, then, that the onset of the Great Depression in 1929 led many Americans to question the trickle-down economics espoused by Hoover, as well as his animus toward deficits, as wrong-headed. President Herbert Hoover discredited economic views allowed Roosevelt to defeat him in a landslide election in 1932.

During the 1970s and early 1980s. A cluster of developments in the 1970s gave rise to the so-called Reagan Revolution of the early 1980s that ended nearly five decades of relative equality. These included Watergate, stagflation, the first military defeat of the United States in a foreign land coupled with the taking of American hostages in Iraq, the unraveling of the Democratic Party, and the growing influence of conservative ideology. The resignation of President Nixon just before he would otherwise have been impeached for political crimes led many people to lose confidence in existing political institutions. The odd mixture of rationing, high unemployment, and runaway inflation of the 1970s soiled the reputation of public officials and presidents because they couldn't restore the economy to its normal state. The victory of the Vietcong over the United States after a long war in Vietnam angered citizens of all political persuasions after the United States had invested huge treasure and lost many lives in this ill-fated venture. President Nixon began a process of realigning American politics by converting many Southern Democrats, White blue-collar people, Evangelical Christians, and Catholics to the Republican Party. These events, when taken together, created a perfect political storm that led to the landslide victory by Ronald Reagan in 1980.

When Might Period 5 Begin?

Our discussion of the staying power of the egalitarian era initiated by Roosevelt (for 47 years) and of the period of inequality initiated by Reagan (for 35 years and counting) may be intimidating for equality advocates. Even if they so desired, they can't manufacture crises like the Great Depression that precipitated the downward movement of the Equality Roller Coaster or the mixture of events in the 1970s that greased the rails for the launching of Reagan.

Some developments in the current period from 2007 to 2018 are reminiscent, however, of the 1920s. While persons in the lower 50% of the economic distribution had relatively low income in the 1920s, the lower 50% has had stagnating wages from the late 1970s to (at least) 2018. While anger against affluent elites and banks was high from 1929 into the 1930s because they were widely perceived to have caused the Great Depression, anger against Wall Street arose during the Great Recession from 2007 through 2009, as Americans came to realize that banks' speculative and illegal activities caused the Great Recession. Even though the Great Recession was shorter and shallower than the Great Depression, it created economic havoc in the United States. Banks foreclosed on millions of houses that were "under water," i.e., the size of their mortgages was more than market prices. While the unemployment rate exceeded 10% during the Great Recession, African American and Latino communities experienced far higher rates, particularly among youth whose unemployment exceeded 40%. Obama's Stimulus Plan may have only lasted for several years, but it demonstrated that economic policies that had not been used since the Great Depression could be implemented, including massive improvements of infrastructure, federal assistance to states to augment safety-net programs, and youth work programs. These policies deviated markedly from the free market policies of the Reagan presidency and its aftermath. Stringent bank regulations were also developed that harkened back to some of Roosevelt's banking regulations.

The Great Recession revealed to many Americans the economic fragility of many residents. Roughly half of Americans live from paycheck to paycheck. Banks foreclosed on the mortgages of roughly seven million families and many Americans abandoned their homes when the value of their homes declined beneath the amount owed on their mortgages. Many African Americans lost their homes and jobs. Many single mothers ended up on the streets, partly due to difficulties accessing the Temporary Assistance to Needy Families (TANF), stemming from restrictions enacted in 1996. Some resorted to selling blood, prostitution, doubling up and other measures to survive. These hardships sensitized many Americans to economic hardship and inequality in the United States. Even after the Great Recession, 74 million Americans used SNAP in FY 2015, not to mention 21 million children who benefited from child nutrition programs, 6 million women and infants who used the Special Supplemental Nutrition Program (WIC), and tens of millions of children and youth who used School Breakfast and School Lunch Programs.

The Great Recession created widespread discontent among the roughly 67 million millennial voters born between 1980 and 2000. Many of them were deeply indebted by college loans. Many of them could not find work during the Great Recession, or found it belatedly, often at such low wages that they had to live with their parents.

Many unarmed African American men had been killed by police officers for eons, but these slayings became publicized by video produced by cell phones, and went viral by social media. Slaying of mentally ill people, Latinos, and others were recorded as well. These slayings led to the formation of social movement, *Black Lives Matter*.

Many Americans came to realize, as well, that approximately 20 million White blue-collar Americans encountered serious problems, including a decline in life expectancy due to these economic hardships, high suicide rates, alcoholism, and addiction to pain-killing opioids (e.g., morphine, methadone, Buprenorphine, hydrocodone, and oxycodone). Physicians prescribed these drugs at excessive rates throughout the nation. A black market quickly grew as criminal elements sold them to addicted persons. Many opioid addicts switched to heroin, also an illegal opioid. Many White males who had only high school degrees (or less) found themselves without skills to compete in the American economy. They had high rates of suicide and mental illness, and had short life expectancies in many communities in the South and Midwest. Blue-collar Whites' angst increased because their plight had been largely ignored by the Democratic Party that many of them had joined during the Great Depression, only to be ignored again by the Republican Party when many of them joined it in the 1970s and beyond. They latched onto Republican Donald Trump in sufficient numbers that he defeated Hillary Clinton in the presidential election of 2016 in rust-belt states where manufacturing had greatly declined, partly due to trade treaties.

Anger against bank officials peaked during the Great Recession as a group of protesters mounted a protest movement called *Occupy Wall Street*. They developed a tent city, conducted sit-ins at banks, and demanded bank reforms to curtail unethical practices, such as not disclosing that interest rates would "balloon" on mortgages, or that customers lacked resources to afford specific homes.

Bernie Sanders' made a strong case in the Democratic presidential primaries that wealthy people and special interests had corrupted American political institutions. He eloquently discussed extreme inequality in the United States and put it on the national agenda for the first time in the modern era. He appealed primarily to millennial voters from roughly age 18 to 35 during

Democratic primary debates with Hillary Clinton. Millennial voters resonated with his quest to reduce economic inequality by offering free tuition to all students in public universities, eliminating or markedly reducing the debt of millennial graduates, increasing the national minimum wage to $15, revising prior treaties and rejecting a pending treaty to prevent the migration of American corporations to other nations, and moving beyond the Affordable Care Act to universal coverage of medical care through Medicare. He supported large increases in taxes on affluent persons. Even if he did not describe them in detail, he supported a massive program to repair the nation's infrastructure of roads, bridges, airports, and other public facilities. He won 26 primary contests against Clinton after most experts had initially perceived him to be a fringe candidate.

Donald Trump, a casino and real estate mogul, won the Republican nomination by defeating 17 opponents in the Republican primaries of 2016. A self-described populist, he had strong populist themes in his presidential campaign even as many of his speeches were laden with racism, immigrant bashing, and sexism, not to mention denigration of persons with physical disabilities. He sought support from White blue-collar workers who had lost their jobs in manufacturing centers as their corporations moved abroad and White males in rural areas of swing states, which gave him electoral votes from states that Democrats had taken for granted: Michigan, Wisconsin, Pennsylvania, and North Carolina. Trump proposed $1 trillion program to rebuild America's infrastructure. He promised to revise trade treaties and reward corporations that returned to the United States to provide more jobs for blue-collar workers. He also promised to create new jobs for American citizens by reducing the flow of undocumented immigrants, by building a wall between the United States and Mexico and deporting undocumented immigrants. Many economists contended, however, that he might ignite trade wars with China and other nations if he flouted existing trade treaties, and that immigrants augmented the nation's economic growth rather than taking jobs from American citizens.

Even in the first year of Trump's presidency, it became clear that he would betray the White blue-collar voters he had championed during his campaign. He did not create jobs in their distressed communities. He supported versions of the Affordable Care Act that would deprive more than 20 million Americans of health insurance—many in the Rust Belt and rural areas that he had championed. He supported deep cuts in Medicaid that funded treatment for opioid poisoning disproportionately experienced by White blue-collar males. He supported tax policies that mostly favored affluent Americans and corporations in late 2017 including deep cuts in inheritance taxes, a cut in the top marginal rates from 39.6% to 37%, and a cut in corporate rates from 35% to 21%. He supported a substantial child tax credit at the last minute when Senator Marco Rubio threatened otherwise to vote against the entire tax package in December, 2017. He supported tax cuts to owners of real estate including himself. He packed his Cabinet with multi-millionaires and billionaires. He supported the provision in his tax package that ended the mandate that all Americans not on Medicaid and Medicare must enroll in private insurance plans—estimated by experts to push at least 13 million from insurance rolls. He agreed to tax cuts that would raise budget deficits by at least $1 trillion over 10 years according to the Joint Committee on Taxation of the Congress.

Trump may have became the Herbert Hoover of the modern era whose indifference to the suffering of unemployed people in the early stage of the Great Depression triggered a backlash against Republicans that led to a landslide Democratic victory in 1932. While unemployment rates were low, tens of millions of workers received wages that had stagnated for decades. We will not know if a backlash against Trump grows until the Congressional elections of 2018 and the presidential and Congressional elections of 2020. We only know in late 2017 that his popularity had slipped to 33%—lower than any modern president at this stage in their presidency. We know that considerable independents and suburban voters, as well as women, left Trump's ranks as revealed in pivotal elections in late 2017 in Virginia, New Jersey, and Alabama. Even his sole major legislative victory in 2017—the enactment of a large tax-reform package in December—was supported by only 23% of the population. Only 40% of registered voters believed Trump was "fit for office" on November, 14th in 2017, including 93% of Democrats, 60% of independents, 93% of African Americans, 70% of Hispanics, and 48% of Whites (McCaskill, 2017). Trump's electoral chances may be hindered by deep divisions in the Republican Party between hard-right, centrist, and moderate factions—as well as animus toward him by many Republicans that he had attacked in Tweets and in person. (For a fuller discussion of Trump's presidency, see Jansson, 2018).

As Republican fortunes appear to have decreased in 2017 even with enactment of the tax package, Democrats appear to have improved their fortunes. They showed remarkable solidarity in 2017, unanimously opposing Trump's efforts to repeal and replace the Affordable Care Act, to build a wall on the Southern border, and to ban Muslims from entering the United States. While many experts believed that Democrats would control the House in the wake of 2018 Congressional elections, some experts increased their estimates of the odds that Democrats would take control of the Senate as well. African

Americans voted in remarkable numbers to defeat Roy Moore in the Senatorial race in Alabama in late 2017. Democrats remained popular with tens of millions of millennial voters, women, and Latinos, as well as white voters with college degrees—and growing numbers of suburban voters.

New Policies for a New Era?

New kinds of policies will be needed to move the Equality Roller Coaster lower in the future, because of fundamental changes in the American economy and society (Piketty, Saez & Zucman, 2016). The economic order has dramatically changed during the past 40 years, due to loss of manufacturing jobs, increasing need for technological skills, increasing foreign competition, and other factors. We know that additional threats to the economic well-being of the bottom 50% of the economic distribution exist in occupations where robotic and electronic devices will reduce jobs, like driving trucks and cabs, working in warehouses, janitorial work, flying airplanes, and manufacturing. Electronic tractors guided by drones will plow farms. Robots will care for elderly persons in convalescent and nursing homes. Second, while government spending for safety-net, infrastructure, defense and education programs have elevated incomes of the bottom 50% of the economic distribution, they have done so only modestly. (Piketty, Saez and Zucman, 2016). Recall that budget charts in Chapter 3 illustrated safety-net expenditures and discretionary spending as small slivers compared to entitlements and military spending with no end in sight.

Most of the economic gains of the bottom 50% accrued to elderly persons for their health needs from payments from Medicare, Medicaid, and Social Security—leaving scant resources for other programs. We have already noted that inequality has increased remarkably as "the top 1% and the bottom 50% have swapped relative shares of national income between 1974 and 2016" (Piketty, Saez, and Zucman, 2016).

Based on the discussion of tax policy in Chapter 3, it should not surprise us that taxes are far less progressive in 2016 than in 1974. Tax rates of the top 1% of the economic distribution declined from about 45% in 1944 to 36% in 2016, while tax rates of the bottom 50% rose, from about 15% in 1944 to roughly 24% in 2016.

Finally, the victory of Donald Trump in 2016 turned the political world upside down when Trump won votes that had mostly gone to Democrats in the coalition created by President Franklin Roosevelt, from the bottom 50% of the economic distribution. Equality advocates need to keep inequality in front of the public conscience for the foreseeable future in hopes that a party and candidate can champion their cause in Period 5. We discuss a wide range of options at their disposal in the next chapter.

References

Alter, J. (2010). *The Promise* New York: Simon & Schuster.
Cannon, L. (1991), *President Reagan: The role of a lifetime.* New York: Simon and Schuster.
Cochran, T. (1961). *The age of enterprise: A social history of industrial America.* New York: Harper & Row.
Corn, D. (2012). *Showdown,* New York: William Morrow.
Gini coefficient, Wikipedia, accessed at en.wikipedia.org on September 15, 2017.
Edsall, T. (1991). *Chain Reaction: The impact of race, rights, and taxes on American politics.* New York; W.W. Norton.
Jansson, B.S. *The reluctant welfare state: Engaging history to advance social work practice in contemporary society.* Boston: Cengage Learning: 2018, chapter 13.
Jansson, B.S. (2015). *The Reluctant Welfare State: Engaging History to Advance Social Work Practice in Contemporary Society, 8th ed.* San Francisco, CA.
Jansson, B.S. (2001). *The Sixteen-Trillion-Dollar Mistake: How the U.S. Bungled Its National Priorities from the New Deal to the Present.* New York: Columbia University Press.
Leuchtenberg W. (1963). *Franklin Roosevelt and the New Deal: 1932–1940.* New York: Harper & Row.
Meerpol, M. (1998). *Surrender: How the Clinton Administration Completed the Reagan Revolution.* Ann Arbor: University of Michigan Press.
Nolan McCaskill, "Poll: 40 percent of voters believe Trump is not fit to be president, a new low," *Politico*, November 14, 2017.
Piketty, T. (2014). *Capital in the Twenty-First Century.* Cambridge, MA: Harvard University Press.
Piketty, T., Saez, E., & Zucman, (2016, December 6). Economic growth in the United States: A tale of two countries. Washington Center for Equitable Growth accessed at equitablegrowth.org.
Poverty in the United States. Wikipedia. Accessed at https://en.wikipedia.org/wiki/Poverty_in_the_United_States on September 15, 2017
Putnam, R. (2015). *Our Kids: the American Dream in Crisis.* New York: Simon & Schuster.
Robert Putnam, *Our kids: The American dream in crisis.* New York: Simon & Schuster, 2015.
Saez, E. (2009). Striking it richer: The evolution of top incomes in the United States (update with 2007 estimates) accessed @ http://elsa.berkeley.edu/~saez/saez-US-topincomes-2010.pdf.
Stockman, D. (1986). *The Triumph of Politics.* New York: Harper & Row.

5 IUOPs THAT MIGHT REDUCE INCOME INEQUALITY IN THE UNITED STATES FROM THE BOTTOM-UP

The purpose of Chapter 5 and 6 is to identify an array of policy proposals to reduce income inequality—ones that are placed under each of the ten hypothesized causes of income inequality that I discussed in Chapters 1 through 3. Some of these policy proposals have been empirically tested, while many others have been proposed but not tested. The list of policy proposals in Chapters 5 and 6 should not be considered as exhaustive, but as a stimulus to identify and test additional ones. Additional hypothesized causes of extreme income inequality should also be identified. Ones related to the first two causes (exposure to extreme income inequality and widespread poverty) are discussed in this chapter. Ones related to the third through the seventh causes are discussed in Chapter 6 (low levels of upward mobility, low levels of hope, high levels of discrimination, lack of access to opportunities and resources, and poor access to health and mental health). Ones related to the eight and ninth causes are discussed in Chapter 8 (lack of resources in the public realm and failure to establish sensible limits on the resources of affluent people). Ones related to the tenth cause are discussed in Chapter 9 (lack of accessibility of American political and policy-making institutions to advocates of greater equality).

This chapter provides an overview of IUOPs. It discusses IUOPs that address the first two causes of extreme income inequality while chapter 6 discusses IUOPs that address the third, through seventh causes of extreme income inequality.

An Overview of Initiatives to Uplift Ordinary People

IUOPs come in many forms. They include IUOPs that impact large populations, such as raising the federal minimum wage from its level of $7.25 per hour in 2016 to $15 per hour by 2020. Wage increases would impact tens of million of workers who earn only $7.25 per hour in those states that have chosen not to enact higher minimum wages. They include "niche" IUOPs that impact far smaller populations, such as providing some fraction of the nation's 4 million deaf persons between ages 18 and 64 with job mentors, job trainers, and placement experts.

They include IUOPs that monitor and enforce regulations outlawing employment discrimination against persons with disabilities, such as the Americans with Disability Act (ADA).

Other IUOPs deliverer services to specific populations, such as physical and mental health services, financial counseling, job placement, housing, and case management services for graduates of foster care between ages 18 and 24 to decrease their levels of homelessness and incarceration.

They include increasing eligibility levels and benefits of existing safety-net programs, such as the Supplementary Nutritional Assistance Program (SNAP), that currently provides food stamps to families of three that earn less than 130% of the federal poverty level (FPL), roughly $26,200 per year for a family of three.

Some IUOPs propose place-based IUOPs to improve the economies of neighborhoods, town, cities and regions.

Some IUOPs change the tax codes of local, state, and federal jurisdictions, such as the Earned Income Tax Credit that provides tax rebates to individuals and couples whose income is beneath a specific level. Many states, such as Washington, rely heavily on sales taxes for their revenue, for example, but sales taxes place an excessive burden on low- and moderate-income persons, unlike some state income taxes that have more progressive rate structures.

Some IUOPs seek to prevent specific social problems, such as an IUOP that prevents diabetes—a chronic disease that often removes persons from the labor force. IUOPs to prevent youth from dropping out of high schools decrease the odds that school-dropouts will become homeless, have encounters with the juvenile justice and correctional systems, and experience poverty.

The goal of Chapters 5 and 6 is to encourage readers to construct IUOPs by selecting one or several IUOPs discussed in this chapter—or some other topic—as the basis for developing extended working papers and policy briefs that can be presented to public officials as discussed in Chapter 7.

Many IUOPs can be identified in existing literature. Others can be identified from web sites, like the Center on Budget and Policy Priorities (www.cbpp.org). Some IUOPs have been empirically validated. Others have been implemented in the field but have not been scientifically evaluated, often because they are relatively new approaches or because they are variations of IUOPs that have been tested, perhaps with other populations or places. It is easier to market those that have been empirically validated. Policy advocates can also develop IUOPs that have not been empirically tested, but with a plan to test their effectiveness when they are implemented.

The criteria for evaluating IUOPs include:

- To what extent do specific IUOPs augment income and wealth of persons in lower economic echelons?
- What specific populations will receive income and wealth augmentation?
- To what extent and in what time frame are IUOPs that do not immediately augment the income and wealth of persons likely to achieve these gains in the future?
- Do specific IUOPs have a theoretical underpinning?
- Are specific IUOPs cost effective, i.e., decrease inequality efficiently?
- Can a specific IUOP be enacted?
- Can a specific IUO be implemented?

Criteria for Selecting IUOPs

Equality advocates have to wrestle with a series of questions and issues that often do not have easy answers. Here are some of them:

1. *Which of the first seven causes of extreme income inequality should equality advocates address in their IUOPs? Should IUOPs primarily address income inequality, poverty, upward mobility, lack of hope, lack of access to opportunities, discrimination, and poor access to mental health and health systems?* Some IUOPs redress several of these causes. An IUOP that helps low-income students graduate from high school, junior college, college, professional schools, and graduate schools may cut income inequality by uplifting graduates' likely income; decrease levels of poverty; enhance upward mobility; instill hope; and cut discrimination. Other IUOPs focus on a single or several causes, such as a modification of SNAP that increases its

eligibility level to decrease poverty by expanding access to it to a broader income population.

2. *Should IUOPs prioritize immediate results in reducing any of the seven causes?* It is tempting to want immediate results from specific IUOPs, such as measurable gains in income in a short time span. This will sometimes be possible, such as when IUOPs remove specific barriers to wages, benefits, and eligibility. But many IUOPs identify ways to improve work skills, graduation rates, movements of specific people to places where greater opportunities exist, and other strategies that take years to demonstrate results. Some IUOPs seek to prevent problems from occurring rather than to redress existing ones.

3. *Should IUOPs prioritize people near the bottom echelon of the economy, such as the lower 10%, or also include people in higher echelons, such as below the lower 50%?* It is tempting to develop IUOPs that focus upon the people most in need such as people in the lowest 10% or 20% of the economic order. Remember, however, that people just above or near the bottom 20% can drop down into the bottom 20% with the loss of a job, a paycheck, sickness, or other hardships. With this in mind, it may make sense to focus on a broader population, not only to raise resources of people in the bottom 20% but to decrease the odds that persons in the next tenths will not move downward. The Pew Foundation defined "middle income" as two-thirds to double the national median after adjusting income for household size. The middle class had an income range extending from $42,000 to $125,000 for a family of three in 2014. Significant portions of the middle class earn income barely sufficient to meet their survival needs. Were we to exclude members of the lower middle class from specific IUOPs, we might risk not helping them climb higher into the middle class.

4. *Should IUOPs prioritize people most likely to move upward in the economic strata?* It is tempting to develop IUOPs that give services and resources only to those persons with the highest odds of moving upward in the economic order. Were we to try to decrease rates of dropping out from high school, for example, we could focus services on drop outs with the highest GPAs, lowest rates of truancy, and highest scores on standardized tests. This decision might lead to higher success rates than also accepting youth with poorer records, but it would conflict with the ethical principle that IUOPs should

help everyone succeed. Bill Gates enunciated this principle when he angrily confronted economists who wanted to ration services and resources to those persons most likely to improve their economic status by arguing in the mission statement of the Bill and Melinda Gates Foundation that "We see equal value in all lives ... we are catalysts of human promise everywhere."

5. *Should we prioritize IUOPs that have widespread support?* It is tempting to develop IUOPs that have widespread support from public officials and others. Political realities do need to be considered. Excessive emphasis on political feasibility may skew IUOPs, however, to relatively simple solutions and relatively non-stigmatized populations.

6. *Should we prioritize IUOPs that give money, in-kind resources, or services that help them gain upward mobility?* It is tempting to focus on money and in-kind resources when addressing income inequality. But the odds that people will acquire resources vary widely with their income, education, assets, opportunities, skills, mental health, health, upbringing, civil rights, geographic location, race, inheritances, financial management skills, and other factors. Persons with mental illnesses or physical disabilities, as well as people from poverty households, often need services of many kinds to help them achieve upward mobility. Some persons need place-based IUOPs that create environments where they can thrive. We need IUOPs, then, that help people get resources and opportunities, but that also address these other causes of inequality.

7. *Should IUOPs untangle messy causes of inequality?* Some public figures and academicians identify complex causes of inequality, such as a trade treaty like the North American Free Trade Agreement (NAFTA) that President Donald Trump contends eliminated jobs for American workers. It is difficult to disentangle the effects of trade agreements because goods flow reciprocally across nations' borders with some benefits for each nation. They may stimulate production and investments in participating nations. They help avoid tariff wars where nations adopt protectionist policies that can sometimes decrease economic growth in participating nations. Yet it is important to identify negative impacts of trade treaties, such as excessive incentives for companies to move their operations abroad that raise unemployment even for thousands of workers.

8. *Should advocates insist on definitive evaluative evidence when developing an IUOP?* Some IUOPs have been empirically evaluated and may have greater credibility in the public arena. Others may have merit, however, because they apply an existing IUOP to a new population or because they draw upon credible theory. Some IUOPs were developed prior to being evaluated and proved later to be effective by researchers. It took years, for example, for researchers to demonstrate that the Head Start Program for low-income preschoolers had long-term positive effects, such as increasing high school graduation rates. Some IUOPs may have ethical import that means they should be proposed even if data does not exist. Violence against members of vulnerable populations should not be tolerated no matter whether its reduction brings tangible economic gains to specific populations.

9. *Should advocates attack policy proposals that will increase economic inequality rather than developing ones that decrease it?* We have discussed how equality advocates propose IUOPs to reduce inequality. They also have to be alert to policy proposals that *increase* inequality. Take the example when Congressional Republicans proposed a repeal of the Affordable Care Act. While they seemed to argue that it would ultimately help low-income persons, even cursory examination of it by equality advocates, such as the Center on Budget and Policy Priorities, revealed that it would not only withdraw health insurance from millions of people who had received it from the ACA, but would also raise the costs of healthcare for many low-income people. Indeed, the Congressional Budget Office, which released its official evaluation of the proposal in March 13, 2017, decided it would cause 24 million Americans to *lose* insurance coverage by 2024 such as by ending the so-called Medicaid expansion that had given states the option to raise the Medicaid eligibility levels for millions of Americans. Paradoxically, reviews by other independent analysts suggested that the proposal advanced by House Republicans would harm millions of aging White blue-collar men that had voted for President Trump (Levey, 2017).

10. *Increasing the "Power" of IUOPs.* Equality advocates may want to combine or couple IUOPs to move the Equality Roller Coaster downward toward more equality. Multiple IUOPs can be placed in an omnibus congressional spending package or portfolio much as when welfare for single mothers (ADC), welfare for older persons (OAA), unemployment insurance, social security, and other measures were placed in the Social Security Act of 1935. Combinations of IUOPs can

reduce inequality more rapidly than single IUOPs, enlist support from an array of constituencies that advocate for the different IUOPs, combine regulations, and change the tax code in a single IUOP package. For example, helping single mothers obtain and keep good jobs by giving them free childcare, subsidizing their rent at higher levels, and increasing food stamps (SNAP) benefits could be combined in a single IUOP package. Portfolios of IUOPs can be organized around specific at-risk populations, such as single mothers.

11. Even if they are not placed in omnibus packages, different IUOPs can be developed that target specific populations or geographic areas. Take the case, for example, of a package of IUOPs that increases services to prevent truancy in specific schools, increases mental health services, increases vocational job training programs, funds a corps of tutors for students who need special assistance to reach grade level, and funds mentors for youth with a combination of behavioral, attendance, and course-performance problems.

A Menu of Initiatives to Uplift Ordinary Persons (IUOPs)

This chapter discusses IUOPs that address causes 1 and 2 of extreme income inequality.

Cause 1: IUOPs that seek to decrease extreme income inequality. Single IUOPs lack the power to make the Equality Roller Coaster move downward unless they greatly increase the income of persons in lower economic echelons possibly while also greatly decreasing the income of wealthy persons. (We call the latter initiative an RUOP, i.e., Resources to Uplift Ordinary People.) Assume, for example, that a guaranteed national income (GI) was enacted that guaranteed an income of (hypothetically) $60,000 for a family of three. To move the Equality Roller Coaster, the GI would have to augment the combined income of the families with income lower than $60,000 to move it significantly downward.

A Guaranteed Income could be juxtaposed with major tax increases on affluent Americans to reduce the net income of persons in the top 20% of the economic distribution. (I call this Resources to Uplift Ordinary People or an RUOP in Chapter 8.) If their top marginal rate were increased from its current level of roughly 39% to levels that existed in the United States from 1933 through 1978 at or above 70%, the *combination* of the GI and higher marginal tax rate might move the Equality Roller Coaster lower because it increases income among low-income persons and decreases income of high-income persons. The higher marginal tax rate on persons in the top 1% could have an important secondary effect of reducing the salaries of top executives that currently run in the millions of dollars along with huge stock options and bonuses. Realizing that a considerable portion of high wages would be taxed away by the government with high top marginal tax rates, corporations would reduce wages of top executives to lower levels that were common in the 1950s, 1960s, and 1970s (Leonhardt, 2017). Now assume that eligibility and benefit levels of many safety net programs were raised and increased, even more income would flow to people in the lower economic echelons.

While mathematical calculations are needed, the combination of a guaranteed income, hikes in top marginal tax rates, and significant increases in eligibility and benefit levels of widely used safety net program might move the Equality Roller Coaster lower. Some other nations are considering or experimenting with providing a guaranteed national income. It was tested in experiments in Manitoba (Canada) in the late 1970s and the United States in the 1960s. Canadian researchers found that the well being of residents in Dauphin, Manitoba improved when enrolled in an experiment that distributed monthly checks called "Mincome" that gave thousands of participants a basic income. "Hospitalization rates fell. More teen-agers stayed in school … and work rates … barely dropped at all" (Surowiecki, 2016).

A proposal to implement a guaranteed income in the United States would confront serious political opposition from conservatives, but also among moderates and liberals. It would be costly to fund, particularly if eligibility levels and levels of the GI were relatively high. Yet we should remember that conservative economist Milton Friedman supported GI as compared to traditional welfare programs like Aid to Families with Dependent Children (AFDC), now replaced by the Temporary Assistance to Needy Families program (TANF) (Friedman, 1962). He argued that a guaranteed-income program would not require the large bureaucracy required to implement AFDC—and would cut the cost of other safety-net programs since recipients of a GI would not need to make as extensive use of them. Yet another rationale may gather strength in coming years. The number of persons displaced by technology such as robots, electronic assembly lines, self-driving vehicles, and electronic readers of X-Rays will grow tremendously. Advocates of a guaranteed income will ask: why shouldn't displaced workers obtain a guaranteed income when they cannot find jobs? The ancient prejudice that most persons who can't find work are lazy wasn't true for most poor people in the past—and certainly will not be true for the vast majority of displaced workers who will be victims of technology.

Nor should we forget that high marginal tax rates on affluent Americans at 70% and higher existed in the United States for roughly 45 years from (at least) the early 1930s through 1978. During these years, the ratio of salaries of corporate executives to workers was often 20 to 1 as compared to the current 271-to-1 ratio in 2017. Higher tax rates on affluent people could lead the nation back to an era when a culture of wealth did not exist at the top end, while still paying executives at sufficiently high levels that they can still afford mansions and expensive cars. Leonhardt (2017) contends, "there is no evidence that a modestly higher (tax) rate (on affluent people) would hurt the economy."

Cause 2: IUOPs that decrease poverty and near-poverty. We have already discussed how equality advocates have to decide what income cut-off to use when decreasing poverty and near-poverty. For example, they can chose specific tenths of the income distribution, such as persons in the bottom 10%, 20%, 30%, 40%, and 50%. No science exists to make this selection. Persons in the lowest tenth are more disadvantaged than persons in higher tenths, but it is difficult how to measure "extent disadvantaged" when even people in the 40th to 50th percent of the income distribution often live paycheck to paycheck. Data do show that longevity incrementally increases as persons move up this income ladder (Tavernise, 2016).

It is less expensive to focus on, say, increasing resources of persons in the bottom 10% than persons in the bottom 50%, but this strategy fails to address helping many people whose lives would improve with augmented incomes. So we use the terms "poverty" and "near-poverty" to give equality advocates latitude in deciding who they wish to prioritize in their IUOPs.

Augmenting safety-net programs. Equality advocates can augment incomes of low-income people by increasing eligibility levels of specific safety-net programs, increasing their benefits, or both. Take the case of the Supplemental Nutrition Assistance Program (SNAP or Food Stamps). It has roughly 46 million beneficiaries who receive, on average, roughly $1.50 per person per meal. Recipients' families net monthly income cannot exceed 100% of poverty or less than $2,000 for a family of four. The federal treasury expended $70.9 billion in FY 2016 for SNAP. In-kind programs like SNAP increase families' income by the monetary value of food that they would otherwise have had to purchase. It decreases poverty but also enhances upward mobility because nutritious diets improve peoples' quality of work, reduce lost time on the job, and (possibly) increase their hope. Its benefits extend beyond merely the extent the program augments the nutrition of low-income persons and families. Because benefits of safety-net programs are so widely distributed to low-income people, even minor increases in eligibility and benefit levels have strong redistribution effects. Take a stab at revising the eligibility level by 10% and increasing the per-meal subsidy by 25% to illustrate just how much redistribution even this change would cause.

The federal Earned Income Tax Credit is another example of a safety-net program that can be revised. It is currently the largest anti-poverty program in the United States. It gives married couples with three or more qualified children and income less than $43,272 tax refunds of as much as $5,657 per year when they fill out a W-5 tax form during the year. The EITC lifted 6.5 million persons, including 3.3 million children, from poverty in 2009 (Jansson, 2016).

Eligibility and benefits for other safety-net programs that could be increased include the Temporary Assistance to Needy Families (TANF), the Special Supplemental Nutrition Program for Women, Infants, and Children (WIC), federal School Breakfast and Lunch Programs, Summer Nutrition Programs, Child and Adult Care Programs, Meals on Wheels Programs, the Earned Income Tax Credit, Section 8 Rental Housing Subsidies, Public Housing, and the Job Corps. (See Jansson, 2016, pp. 248–278 for a description of these programs.)

Were eligibility levels and benefit levels raised simultaneously for an array of safety-net programs, omnibus legislation could be developed, possibly named The American Safety-Net Augmentation Act. This Act could place billions of dollars in the hands of low and moderate-income Americans.

Many conservatives, such as Paul Ryan, the Speaker of the House, insist that increasing eligibility and benefit levels of safety-net programs harms the work ethic of recipients. Empirical evidence disputes this claim: most people *want* to work as attested by the fact that most recipients of SNAP and other safety-net programs *do* work. *Not* to increase eligibility and benefit levels punishes tens of millions of workers with low or intermittent wages. Moreover, the replacement of Aid to Families with Dependent Children (AFDC) with the much harsher Temporary Assistance to Needy Families (TANF) did *not* increase incomes of TANF recipients, but actually led to lower incomes for them. According to the Center on Policy and Budget Priorities, TANF did not reduce childhood poverty, reaching a smaller percentage of them than AFDC. Its benefits, established by each state, eroded over time as states failed to fund block grants sufficiently. TANF benefits fell further behind housing costs from 1996 to 2017. States spent little of their TANF funds to increase recipients' employability. Lack of employment and low wages were a result of the economy and poor schooling. Turning funding of welfare over to the states through a block grant mostly funded by states resulted in greater poverty for mothers and children (Schott, 2017). In other words, Paul Ryan's solution—to cut welfare to provide greater incentives to women to work—has been shown by evidence to be simplistic and incorrect. What's needed is a TANF program with higher grants to raise women and children above poverty and a far more robust system to improve mothers' levels of education, housing, training, and work opportunities.

Raising the minimum wage. We discussed how markedly different proposals for increasing the minimum wage were advanced during the presidential primaries and presidential campaign of 2016. While Senator Bernie Sanders wanted to raise federal minimum wage from $7.25 per hour to $15 per hour by 2023, Hillary Clinton opted for $13 per hour and Donald Trump opted for $10 per hour. These contrasting proposals would obviously lead to different results, but predicting their effects would be complex. It would depend on how many employees were let go by employers who believed they could not afford their current roster at the elevated wage level. It would depend on competitors pricing of their products. Would they raise their prices to fund the more expensive workers or find ways to cut their other costs to keep prices at old levels? Would some businesses increase their number of part-time workers to compensate for wage increases? How would competitors respond to each other's price increases? Would some businesses leave the market as wages rose, reducing the number of businesses, and allowing remaining businesses to raise the price of their products? Economists would surely examine the effects of minimum wages in those states, such as California and New York that have already increased their minimum wages to see what effects they've had on decisions of firms.

IUOPs that market safety-net programs. Only roughly 50% of eligible persons actually use safety-net programs for which they are eligible, including SNAP, the Earned Income Tax Credit, Unemployment Insurance, Medicaid, SSI, SSDI, and other safety-net programs. Non-use of these programs by eligible persons reduces the net income of low-income people by tens of billions of dollars per year. An IUOP could propose to send mobile units and outreach workers into communities where roughly 50% of eligible persons do not use such safety-net programs. The outreach program could be bolstered by media advertisements, use of social media, and outreach to churches. Another IUOP could require public agencies to survey their clients to ascertain whether (1) they are eligible for specific safety-net programs, (2) have applied for their benefits or services, (3) have received their benefits or services, and (4) need assistance from agency staff to apply for specific benefits or services.

IUOPs that reform regulations of the federal Department of Labor. An IUOP could propose raising the cutoff for overtime pay, set in 2004 at $23,660, to $47,476 for most salaried workers. This regulation would require employers to pay employees time-and-a-half overtime pay for working over 40 hours per week. Employers would have the option of reducing hours worked to avoid having to pay employees overtime, but many employers prefer paying overtime to hiring more employees.

IUOPs that provide housing with supportive services. Homeless people populate not only large cities, but also middle-sized cities and rural towns. Many homeless people are not only too poor to afford rents in these jurisdictions, but also possess mental health and substance abuse problems. Social workers and policy makers recently believed that they required extensive counseling and preparation to be able to move into a subsidized housing unit with rents paid by Section-8 HUD subsidies or another source of funds. Another solution proposed by some policy makers is to accelerate the process of obtaining subsidized housing so that they were placed in housing almost immediately, and then give them supportive services in their new homes. Evidence-based trials of this new concept, an innovation called Housing First—Pathways to Housing funded by the federal Department of Housing and Urban Development (HUD), discovered that this new approach was more effective than the older approach. Homeless people move rapidly through a "reception stage," shared housing or "training dwelling," regular dwellings with (time-limited) occupation agreements based on special conditions, and (finally) regular self-contained dwellings with a rent contract. This innovative approach led to lower levels of recidivism back to the streets than the traditional approach, cutting homelessness in Utah by 72% overall since the program was initiated in 2005 by the Utah Division of HUD. Incarceration rates were reduced by 76% and substance abuse detoxification increased by 82%. These data allowed HUD to declare the program a "best practice." Experts estimated that implementation of Housing First, if fully funded, would cost about the same amount of money as Americans spend on Christmas decorations and flowers each year, and about one-fourth the cost of tax write-offs for corporate meals and entertainment. Yet the program remained greatly underfunded in 2016 even as it made some gains in many cities.

Housing First can't work, however, if insufficient numbers of new dwellings are produced in specific areas where housing shortages often exist. Some combination of finding new sources of money for them from local, state, and federal government, monies to subsidize far more housing vouchers, rent control, changes in local zoning to allow the construction of more homes including so-called "granny homes" on lots of existing homes, tax incentives to landlords that rent units to low income people, and improvements in employment and training of low-income tenants and homeless persons are needed, in tandem, to decrease homelessness.

IUOPs that increase pensions of low-income people. Employees with 401-K pensions have markedly higher retirement pensions than low- and moderate-income employees, as do employees of public agencies where unions have negotiated pensions. Americans that only have social security pensions averaged $12,530 per year in 2012 as compared to persons with combined social security and private corporate or public pensions that often exceeded $70,000 per year. This is greatly inequitable. Why should low income persons receive such lower pensions even when they mostly have worked as many years as their affluent counterparts? Employees in corporate, university, and other settings often have *both* 401-K pensions that allow them to accrue monies in a pension account without paying federal income taxes on these funds until they are paid as pensions after they retire *and* Social Security pensions. These *combined* pensions often give them pensions that exceed $100,000—and much higher in many settings, The pensions of low-income persons could be funded by lifting the cap of $110,000 for taxable salaries and wages that fund Social Security pensions. This cap means that affluent people who earn more than $110,000 *only* are taxed to that level whereas persons who earn less than that cap must pay taxes on *all* of their income. Low-income people *both* receive lower benefits than affluent people since benefits are partly calculated on wage levels *and* they pay higher taxes than affluent people as a percentage of their income. The proceeds from the higher taxes on affluent persons would fund the higher retirement benefits for low-income persons.

IUOPs that terminate debt of students in public community colleges and public four-year colleges. As discussed in Chapter 1, millennial students are often burdened with considerable debt as are millions of older persons. Senator Bernie Sanders proposed to eliminate all of the debt for all students that received degrees from colleges—and to fund the tuition of students prior to their graduation. At the bidding of Joe Biden, Barack Obama proposed eliminating tuition and debt for students who attend community colleges. Hillary Clinton proposed to cover tuition of students that attend public colleges but only if they come from families with less than $125,000 income. Legislators at the state level are working with the governors to reimburse tuitions of public university students. Advocates of these proposals need to estimate their cost and justify it by analyzing the adverse effects of debt on students. Many other industrialized nations already fund college tuition, tuition of professional schools, tuition of graduate education, and tuition of vocational schools.

Private colleges and universities may try to convince legislators and public officials that their students should also qualify for reimbursement.

IUOPs that restore organizing rights of trade unions. We discussed in Chapter 3 how trade unions have been drastically reduced in number during the past 60 years. Minus trade unions, workers cannot rely on unions to pressure their companies to increase wages—a major reason why wages have stagnated since the 1970s. Most other industrialized nations have far higher rates of union participation than the United States. These IUOPs would create a nation-wide system of regulations and laws that would give workers the same collective bargaining rights they possessed prior to various right-to-work laws and other restrictions were placed on trade unions.

References

Friedman, M. (1962). *Capitalism and Freedom*. Chicago: University of Chicago Press.

Jansson, B. S. (2016). *Social welfare policy and advocacy: Advancing social justice through 8 policy sectors.* Thousand Oaks, CA: SAGE Publications.

Leonhardt, D. (2017, September 5). When the rich said no to getting richer. *New York Times*.

Levey, N. (2017, March 12). Obamacare replacement hits Trump voters hard. *Los Angeles Times*.

Manning, A., & Markovitz, L. (2016, February 29). *White people do more drugs, Black people serve more time.* Retrieved from http://www.vocativ.com/291203/white-people-do-more-drugs-black-people-serve-more-time/

Pew Research Center (2016, May 11) America's shrinking middle class: A close look at changes within metropolitan regions. Retrieved from www.pewsocialtrends.org.

Schott, L. (2017: February 22). Block-granting a safety-net program has significantly reduced its effectiveness. Center on Budget Priorities. Retrieved from CBPP.org on 12/16/17.

Surowiecki, J. (2016, June 20). The case for free money. *New Yorker*.

Tavernise, S. (2016, February 16). Disparity in life spans of the rich and poor is growing. *New York Times*.

Wilkinson R. G., & Pickett, K.E. (2009). Income inequality and social dysfunction. *Annual Review of Sociology, 35,* 493–511.

6

IUOPs THAT MIGHT INCREASE UPWARD MOBILITY, HOPE, ACCESS TO OPPORTUNITIES, AND ACCESS TO HEALTHCARE—AND TO REDUCE DISCRIMINATION

This chapter discusses IUOPs that address causes 3, 4, 5, 6, and 7 including low levels of upward mobility, low levels of hope, high levels of discrimination against vulnerable populations, lack of access to opportunities and resources, and insufficient access to healthcare and poor health. (Causes 8, 9, and 10 are discussed in Chapters 8 and 9.)

My placement of specific IUOPs under these various causes may give the misleading impression that most IUOPs address only one of them. Take the case of the YVLifeSet Program, which is discussed next. While it provides supportive services and some housing to youth who graduate from foster care, it enhances upward mobility and likely increases hope, health, and access to opportunities. Many IUOPs likely similarly address multiple causes of extreme income inequality.

Some IUOPs that Address Cause 3 (Lack of Upward Mobility)

The YVLifeSet Program, formerly the Transitional Living (TL) Program. Many youth endured the trauma of separation from their natural families when child welfare agencies placed them in foster care due to parental neglect or abuse. Those who were not reunified with their natural parents or relatives and not adopted "aged out" at age 18, only to find themselves without support services. Many youth suffered ill effects, such as homelessness, unemployment, lack of food, development of mental health problems, violent relationships, failure to complete high school,or involvement in criminal behavior. Operated by the nonprofit Youth Villages, the YVLifeSet Program gave these emancipated youth clinical services reviewed by clinically licensed staff, linkages with community agencies, and transitional living (TL) specialists, who assessed each youth weekly and helped the youth work on goals. In these interactions, specialists used evidence-based assessments, curricula, motivational interviewing, and cognitive behavioral therapy. They engaged youth in action-oriented activities, like opening bank accounts and visiting colleges. They established a study with 1,300 youth, ages 18 to 24; 534 youth assigned to a control group receiving no TL Services, but with access to community services; and 788 assigned to an experimental group who were offered TL services and access to community agencies. After one year, the experimental group was more likely to finish high school and be employed, and less likely to become homeless, develop mental issues, or have involvement with the criminal justice system. This project enhanced upward mobility among these youth (MDRC, 2015).

IUOPs that revise trade treaties. As many as 70,000 manufacturing plants have left the United States, according to Donald Trump, leading to the loss of millions of jobs over many decades. (Many other estimates exist.) No one disagrees that many jobs were lost, but Trump and others fail to discuss how many companies would have exited the nation even had the North American Free Trade Agreement (NAFTA) not been enacted, thanks to lower wages, reduced benefits, absence of trade unions, and fewer working condition regulations in developing nations. Nor do they discuss sufficiently to what extent renegotiations of trade treaties might lead to retaliatory measures from Mexico and other trading partners of the United States. In other words, renegotiating trade deals can cause mixed effects, which have been insufficiently identified and analyzed. Equality advocates also need to identify penalties that will persuade CEOs and Boards of Directors of companies not to exit the nation, while realizing that companies that choose to stay will sometimes go bankrupt because other companies that chose to migrate to developing nations will sell their products at lower prices. Simple solutions often do not exist, even as most experts acknowledge that trade treaties can and do give corporations incentives to leave the country if exit taxes or other disincentives exist.

We need to understand more fully why the American middle class decreased from 61% in 1971 to 50% in 2015, probably from multiple causes, and not just because many companies migrated to developing nations.

Inadequate training of middle class persons, enhanced education, movement of persons to new occupations, and other remedies should be considered, as well as helping persons migrate to areas where greater employment options exist. Only then can IUOPs and RUOPs be developed to increase the number of middle-class Americans that Piketty (2014) defines as Americans between the 50th and 90th percentiles of the national income distribution.

IUOPs that give persons the option to move to new places. An antipoverty experiment called Moving to Opportunity (MTO) was initially implemented in the 1990s during the presidency of Bill Clinton. Many families with young children were relocated from their low-income neighborhoods in New York City to more affluent neighborhoods, where they received housing subsidies so they could afford to live there. (MTO was also implemented in Baltimore, Boston, Chicago, and Los Angeles.) Initial data obtained several years after the moves suggested that youth who were moved to more affluent neighborhoods fared no better than youth that remained in the low-income neighborhoods, with respect to their adult earnings, college attendance, and sustaining a two-parent household. However, research published in May, 2015, by two Harvard economists (Chetty & Hendron, 2015) discovered that the MTO youth had better outcomes than the youth that remained in their old neighborhoods. They obtained data from the experimental group (the MTO youth who moved) and the control group (youth who remained). The MTO youth had average annual adult earnings of $14,747, compared to $11,270 for the youth who remained in their low-income neighborhoods. Twenty-one percent of the MTO youth attended college, compared to 16.5% of the control group. Thirty-three percent of the MTO youth developed two-parent families, compared to 23% of the non-MTO youth. This was a classic example of a delayed effect of an IUOP that led persons to dismiss its efficacy prematurely (Leonhardt, Cox & Miller, 2015).

When African American children are moved from segregated and lower-income neighborhoods more affluent and white neighborhoods, they are more likely to graduate from high school, community colleges, and colleges. They are likely to attend better schools with higher paid teachers, compared to schools in their original neighborhoods, and experience higher expectations of teachers, as suggested by considerable research that compares mostly White suburban schools with inner-city schools, mostly populated by students of color. They may also have more access to networks that help them get admitted to institutions of higher education and to find jobs. However, some African American students who move to more affluent areas did not fare better.

A possible negative effect of MTO needs to be considered: the ill effects on low-income neighborhoods from moving promising youth to more affluent neighborhoods. It might be offset by targeting schools in low-income neighborhoods with enhanced resources, recruitment of promising teachers with higher pay scales, programs that give enhanced support to students who are truant or who fail classes, and other remedies.

Upgrading and integrating schools. Arnie Duncan, the former head of the U.S. Department of Education, acknowledged in an interview on National Public Radio (NPR) in 2015 that researchers widely agreed that African America children do better in integrated schools than in segregated schools. Recall that the *Brown v. Board of Education* decision in 1954 by the U.S. Supreme Court held that *de jure* segregation was unconstitutional, meaning that states and localities cannot *require* students of color to attend segregated schools, as was common in the South and some Northern states. It did not declare that *de facto* segregation was unconstitutional. This distinction led to an unfortunate result in the eyes of integrationists: segregated schools throughout the nation, stemming partly from the widespread segregation by neighborhoods of millions of African American and Latino youth.

Yet considerable controversy exists. A study of 4,000 African American first graders' reading skills in schools with minority composition of 75 percent or more lagged as compared to Black first graders in integrated schools (DiversityInc Staff, 2014). Using "propensity score matching," the researchers concluded that the reading differences stemmed not from children's background, but from the schools they attended. The segregated schools had higher turnover of teachers, more novice teachers, and fewer resources for high-quality instruction.

So we have a conundrum. We need equalization of resources, teachers, and facilities in schools disproportionately attended by youth of color and youth from low-income backgrounds, as compared to schools disproportionately attended by relatively affluent White youth. This becomes a major priority because lagging performance of students in the former schools may be linked not to their personal characteristics, but to quality of the schools they attend (Lewis-McCoy, 2014). Numerous scholars found that youth of color often fared better in integrated schools than in segregated schools and experienced additional positive benefits (Riley, 2016). Schools with disproportionate numbers of low-income youth also need resources to fund support services for low achieving students because poverty itself is a predictor of lower achievement. For example, many low-income students may start falling behind, have high rates of truancy, and have mental problems even as early as the 6th grade (Balfanz et al., 2015).

Families of color ought to be able to choose whether they want their children to be bussed to schools with more affluent and with more White students. Busing children of color to predominantly White schools has been politically divisive because of White parents' opposition to this strategy, as well as adverse decisions of the U.S. Supreme Court. For example, the Supreme Court declared school busing to be unconstitutional in Seattle in *Community Schools v. Seattle School District No. 1* in 2007. Not only do many White parents oppose the policy, but many removed their children from public schools and sent them to private or charter schools in Seattle.

Equality advocates who want to equalize spending on schools have to contend with political opposition from parents and staff at schools with affluent, White students who may fear that public monies will be diverted to schools with low-income students. Yet the educational and ethical case is clear: low-income students and students of color deserve equal educational opportunity. Yet the state of California has embarked on an ambitious program to direct state funds to schools with high percentages of low-income students. The federal government might give far more funding to the Elementary and Secondary Education Act to allow it to equalize spending in schools with low-income children.

IUOPs that diminish use of part-time workers. Part-time workers (1) often receive no benefits; (2) have difficulty finding full-time work or lack of work credit from potential employers; and (3) receive low wages even when prorated for their part-time status. Part-time workers are covered by the Fair Labor Standards Act, which does not make a distinction between part- and full-time workers, such as the right to $7.25 per hour and break time for nursing mothers. However, some employers fail to fully pay part-time workers, who often fear reprisal if they complain. The percentage of the workforce composed of part-time workers increased from 13.5% of U.S. employees in 1968, peaked at 20.1% in 2010, and declined only slightly, to 18% in 2017 (Kurtzleben, 2017). Part-time workers are often asked to work difficult hours, such as evenings and weekends. Many workers have to find several part-time jobs to meet their basic economic needs. Six million of them want full-time jobs (Kurtzleben, 2017). Employers fill many other jobs that are contract jobs with workers from contract agencies. Many jobs added in the Obama administration were part-time because many employers switched from full-time to part-time workers during and soon after the Great Recession as the profits of their companies decreased (Mislinski, 2017). Yet the number of full-time workers increased by 10 million persons from 2010 through 2016 (Kurtzleben, 2017). Regulations of the Department of Labor might be changed to place limits on employers' use of part-time workers and to increase part-time workers' benefits.

IUOPs that provide employment to low-income youth and long-term unemployed people. The use of public employment was first attempted on a large scale during the Great Depression with a large number of work-relief programs as discussed in Chapter 3. With persons of all races desperately poor, people enthusiastically joined these work-relief programs including the Works Progress Admimistration (WPA), the Public Works Administration (PWA), the Civilian Conservation Corps (CCC), and Neighborhood Youth Administration (NYA). The Comprehensive Employment and Training Act (CETA) enacted by President Nixon in 1973, trained and employed low-income and long-term unemployed adults, and also provided summer jobs to low-income high school students until President Reagan terminated it in 1982. CETA offered full-time jobs in public agencies and nonprofit organizations that lasted from 12 to 24 months, in hopes that its graduates could find unsubsidized jobs. The program employed more than 700,000 persons at its peak. Relatively little research has been conducted on the program. See Norton Grubb 1996 and Larry Orr et al. 1996 for issues related to public work programs. The case for large public employment and training programs needs to be revisited because of the likely loss of millions of jobs due to technology in coming years as I discuss subsequently.

IUOPs that provide construction jobs on a massive scale. Drawing on the examples of President Eisenhower's program to build the Interstate Highway System under the Federal-Aid Highway Act of 1956, President Franklin Roosevelt's Public Works Administration (PWA) in the Great Depression, and infrastructure improvements in President Obama's Stimulus Plan, President Donald Trump announced that he would develop a $1 trillion infrastructure program funded by a combination of private and public funds. Like the PWA, it will, he said, repair a wide spectrum of public facilities including airports, highways, bridges, roads, and water systems. The projects of Presidents Eisenhower and Roosevelt had prodigious accomplishments that still remain key parts of the nation's infrastructure. Any similar programs should address key questions, which may include: who gets priority in obtaining jobs, what degree of job training will be provided, what role unions will have in recruiting and training workers, and whether persons of color, low-income persons, and disabled persons will receive priority? Will workers trained and hired by Trump's program be helped to find jobs in the civilian economy and will inner city and rural residents have access to these jobs? (His infrastructure proposal had not been revealed by May 15, 2018.)

IUOPs that revive climate-control jobs of the Stimulus Program. In the depths of the Great Recession, Congress enacted the American Recovery and Investment Act, popularly known as the Stimulus Program (Jansson, 2015; Grunwald, 2012) in early 2009. Many of its programs provided jobs to low- and moderate-income youth placing insulation in buildings, constructing and installing solar panels, and installing more efficient heating and air conditioning systems. It also funded programs to move the nation away from using fossil fuels, including installing facilities that recharge electric cars and installing heating systems powered by solar panels. It is worth considering whether low-income youth and currently unemployed adults could obtain major roles in these programs and training for new jobs in the environmental field.

IUOPs that develop entrepreneurial strategies to increase unemployment. Entrepreneurs like basketball legend Magic Johnson have greatly increased employment in minority communities by investing in businesses owned by persons of color. Deborah Hoe, a USC doctoral student in gerontology, developed a "social investment proposal in aid of low-income older adults" in 2016 modeled after an existing restaurant in Hong Kong called Gingko House (Hoe, 2016). She proposed establishing a restaurant managed and implemented by older Americans. According to Pynnonen et al., (2012), older adults that participate in such businesses boost their health status and decrease their mortality risk. The most immediate barrier to implementation is the threat of failure. It is well known that startup failure rates are high. Therefore, the proposed approach would follow important principles that must be embraced from the very beginning (Wasserman, 2012). These include assembling the right founding team, outlining the core values of the team without compromise, selecting the right location for the business, and finally, assessing the fit with other investors based on their expected terms and conditions (Gibney & Howery, 2012). Wasserman and Hellmann (2016) also caution startups to spend considerable time thinking about their equity partnership.

The second biggest barrier is financial sustainability (CB Insights, 2014). A lack of marketing research prior to starting up any business could spell disaster in terms of the ability to counter threats and leverage strengths. These shortcomings may result in problems with cash flow and inevitably, liquidity. Without sufficient product differentiation, or a unique value proposition, participation rate in the business from both supplier and consumer standpoints may suffer, adding to cash flow problems. With the assumption that the likelihood of failure is high, the proposed policy options may best be initiated via a pilot project with strict selection criteria.

Other IUOPs that develop entrepreneurial approaches include:

- Help elderly persons, homeless persons, and members of other vulnerable populations develop business enterprises that primarily hire members of their groups, by providing them with start-up capital and technical assistance;
- Vastly expand Individual Development Accounts (IDAs) in local, state, and federal jurisdictions or in the private sector to allow low- and moderate-income persons to obtain assets, such as houses, or to use assets for education of themselves or family members, start businesses, obtain health insurance, or other designated purposes. Professor Michael Sherraden at the George Warren Brown School at Washington University has championed this IUOP where he directs their Center for Social Development (Sherraden, 1991). He has initiated and is testing Child Development Accounts (CDAs) in the United States.

IUOPs that develop strategies for massive loss of jobs due to technology. The American labor force is rapidly changing. Many workers are and will be displaced by technology just as janitors (due to robots that clean offices), truck drivers (due to electronic self-driving trucks), cab drivers (due to electronic self-driving cars), and coal miners (due to machines that render human labor obsolete). Moreover, the economy is on the verge of incredible technological change, which includes robots, self-driving cars, machine learning, and digitization of shopping. Amazon built many huge warehouses in Southern California that in the past might have had many employees, but today use robots instead, to move goods. Farmers increasingly use drones and computer-guided machines to plow fields and harvest crops. Robots are used in senior citizen institutions to care for seniors. Tens of thousands of long-distance drivers of 18-wheelers will be replaced by self-driving trucks (Thompson, 2015).

No one has found answers to dilemmas posed by massive displacement of workers by automation. Some cadre of highly skilled workers will be needed to plan and manage the technology, but millions of workers could lose their employment during the coming decades. Speeding economic growth is an unlikely solution. So here are some ideas for IUOPs.

- Institutionalize work time to 35 hours or less per week so that more workers can find jobs even as nations implement more and more automation. In the Netherlands, for example, a four-day workweek is nearly standard

among working mothers. Some companies in Sweden are moving to a six-hour work day;
- Develop a guaranteed national income to provide income to everyone who cannot find work;
- Shift millions of workers to "soft jobs," like working with students who need tutoring, helping seniors in convalescent hospitals and nursing homes, filling positions currently held by workers in their 50s and 60s like electricians, plumbers, and carpenters;
- Tutor and teach persons who are currently warehoused in prisons, juvenile correction facilities, and mental institutions;
- Hire seniors to tutor students in schools with high drop-out rates;
- Fill back-up roles for teachers, psychologists, and others, such as by visiting clients or students in their homes;
- Place limits on some technology until strategies are developed to find employment for displaced workers, such as delaying by five years the implementation of self-driving 18-wheelers on Interstate Highways;
- Learn from other nations to find evidence-based strategies that they have employed.

Consider this IUOP to be open-ended. No one has yet charted, much less tested, strategies for finding work for displaced workers on a massive scale.

IUOPs that train younger workers to replace aging workers. Some occupations will lack sufficient workers due to aging of their labor forces, including farmers, electricians, and carpenters (Thompson, 2016). Governments need to help displaced younger workers and prepare them for occupations that currently possess large numbers of elderly workers. Employers appear to have "upskilled" during the Great Recession, requiring college education and computer skills for jobs that were relatively unskilled in the past (Thompson, 2016).

IUOPs that link NGOs and public agencies with government job training and placement programs. Insufficient links exist between agencies that serve vulnerable populations and public agencies that provide training and job referrals. Establish IUOPs that:

- Link agencies that serve persons with mental and physical disabilities with job training and placement programs for persons with mental and physical disabilities, as well as chronic diseases like COPD and diabetes;

- Link public job training and placement services with for-profit companies to facilitate movement of their personnel into technical and other positions.

IUOPs that prepare people to succeed in the economy. Most people obtain the bulk of their monetary resources from salaries, wages, and benefits from their employment, whether in private markets or public employment. Establish IUOPs that:

- Link inner city children to junior colleges and colleges from elementary school onward with enriched summer programs and on-campus programs. Facilitate frequent contact with neighborhood youth with students in these institutions. Link them with innovative curriculum year-round with extensive parental involvement programs. Help students apply for community colleges and four-year colleges after they complete high school;
- Subsidize training of employees who work on infrastructure projects by unions, including for trainees who are not members of unions;
- Vastly increase funding for the Carl D. Perkins Career and Technical Education Act, the Trade Adjustment Assistance grants, and the Community College to Career Fund to align classroom teaching and learning with real-world business needs, to strengthen community college programs and workforce partnerships, and to train workers and high school students for high-growth industries;
- Increase high school programs that prepare disadvantaged students to seek training in specific professions, such as nursing and social work;
- Offer subsidies to private employers that provide training, education, and jobs to specific vulnerable populations;
- Develop and fund mentoring and training programs for persons with mental and physical disabilities to help them find and retain jobs in the public, private, and not-for-profit sectors;
- Increase government subsidies for low- and moderate-income students who enter vocational programs in community colleges.

Other IUOPs could include:

- Prepare a new workforce to work with aging boomers whether in their homes, organized daycare programs, or institutions;
- Develop rapid-response housing and relocation services so that people can move and live in areas where critical labor shortages exist or are impending;

- Develop on-the-job training programs for unemployed or underemployed persons to give them on-the-job experience with trades and professions that are currently occupied by persons who will retire in the near future. They can obtain skills needed to "inherit" their jobs, such as plumbers, electricians, carpenters, farmers, and ranchers.

IUOPs that remove disincentives to work. Many people discontinue employment because they encounter disincentives to work, including lack of transportation, lack of childcare, caring for disabled family members, and the need to hold multiple jobs to make ends meet. Some safety-net programs discourage work, such as SSI and SSDI, which place obstacles in the way of enrollees that want to work. IUOPs are needed that:

- Provide single parents with free or subsidized childcare for minor children;
- Provide transportation subsidies to low- and moderate-income persons who must use public transportation to reach places of employment because they cannot afford cars;
- Provide in-home assistance for single parents caring for their parents or family members with disabilities;
- Provide subsidies for persons who have to work multiple jobs to meet their basic needs or to reach a specific economic level such as the Federal Poverty Level.

IUOPs that address barriers to graduation from secondary schools, junior colleges, and colleges. Roughly half of low-income students do not complete secondary school. A majority of students who enter junior colleges withdraw before obtaining degrees, many from low-income families. Many students withdraw from colleges or do not obtain their degrees in a timely manner. I discuss a strategy developed by Professor Robert Balfanz to reduce school dropouts in inner city schools with high percentages of low-income students of color in Chapter 7. He conducted longitudinal research in Philadelphia's public schools that allowed him to predict with considerable accuracy which sixth graders would drop out of high school. If students had problems with attendance, behavioral problems, or failure to complete math or English in the silxth grade, they had considerably higher odds of not completing high school. He developed interventions for these students as well as school-wide reforms that lower these odds considerably (Balfanz, 2011). When President Obama proposed to offer free tuition to all students attending junior colleges, he failed to discuss how he would fund support services for these students to increase their graduation rates. Other IUOPs could include:

- Provide in-home aides to families to relieve school children who care for younger children and disabled children in order to increase the youths' high school graduation rates;
- Provide shelter and assistance to homeless children so they can attend schools and to obtain degrees;
- Require institutions of higher education to accept specific percentages of low- and moderate-income enrollees;
- Subsidize junior colleges and colleges to provide more programs that help members of vulnerable populations who do not progress toward their degrees in a timely manner.

IUOPs that provide geographic access to quality jobs. Millions of workers find it difficult to access and retain employment due to lack of affordable housing proximate to places of employment. Many low- and moderate-income persons travel many hours per day to reach places of employment at a significant financial cost and threats to their health. IUOPs are needed that:

- Construct affordable housing near major job sites with use of eminent domain by local governments, states, and the federal government if necessary. Many states and local jurisdictions have been unwilling or unable to make necessary zoning changes or require developers to reserve sufficient numbers of units for low- and moderate-income persons;
- Develop subsidized public transportation that connects large employment sites with workers who currently commute long distances due to lack of affordable housing near their job sites

IUOPs that rescue people from downward trajectories. Many people lose momentum when seeking degrees or credentials and find themselves in economic straits for a variety of reasons. Timely assistance may allow these persons to regain traction in economic and educational realms.

USC doctoral student Jose Reyes (2015) developed an IUOP to reconnect Latino community youth, age 16–24, who are not working or in school. Many of them drop out of high school and "disappear." Staff from their former high schools often do not reach out to them or even know their addresses. These youths are likely to experience long-term consequences from inability to accumulate human capital in the form of education and work experience, lack of social mobility, and a decrease in future earnings (Jacobs, 2014). Over ten million individuals under age 25 who were school dropouts were unable to obtain full-time employment in 2013 (Maloney, 2010). Roughly one-fourth of them live in poverty, many engage in criminal activities, and many have been institutionalized. Local, state, and federal governments bear a large economic cost from lost tax revenues, the cost of social services, health care, and the criminal justice system. Reyes proposed establishing a Community Youth Reconnecting Initiative that develops a "Youth Engagement and Success Board" that links the community, schools, local government, and business. The young adults would serve as apprentices in businesses and NGOs, and would earn educational and entrepreneur credits. They would be linked to adult volunteers, social workers, or both who serve as mentors. The project would help the youth transition to adulthood by resuming their education, finding stable employment, or both. The total cost for each worker would be $6,960 annually for up to three years. This initiative would link with the federal Workforce Innovation and Opportunity Act of 2014 as well as former President Obama's My Brothers' Keeper initiative and Starbucks' 100,000 Opportunities Initiative that will hire 100,000 Americans, age 16–24, who are not in school or employed. Some research shows that disconnected youth can benefit from comprehensive and integrated models that combine education, occupational skills, and support services.

IUOPs that help people avoid dead-end trajectories: Diverting juveniles from institutions and camps. Millions of persons decrease their chances of upward mobility when they do not have high school, junior college, or college degrees. As an example, many juveniles of color are incarcerated even before age 18 in the United States. Many of these so-called juvenile offenders, once "criminalized," are imprisoned for considerable parts of their lives partly because they have entered the criminal justice system. It is important, then, to divert many of them to community programs.

The Campbell Collaboration conducted a meta-analysis in 2010 to determine whether juvenile offenders fared better if they were incarcerated, such as in juvenile camps or juvenile institutions, or "diverted" from the juvenile-justice system, through supervision in the community. (They defined the former option as "formal system processing" as compared with "diversion.")

The meta-analysis included 7,304 youth, ages 17 and younger, who were subjects in 29 randomized experiments over a 35-year period. The research population included low-level offenders, guilty of offenses of low or moderate severity, including small property crimes and disorderly person violations. They also included youth who committed serious felony offenses.

This project produced important findings (Petrosino, Turpin-Petrosino & Guckenburg, 2012). It discovered that juveniles with low-level offenses who were placed in institutions were more likely to report they had re-offended than youth who were diverted to communities by a small but statistically significant amount. The authors reported that youth who stayed in institutions for long periods, from 3 to 13 months, were no less likely to commit juvenile offenses than youth who stayed in them for shorter periods. They found that community-based supervision of youth was as effective in decreasing rates of antisocial activity as incarceration of youth with serious offenses. We can hypothesize that the longer-term prospects of youths not placed in institutions was better than youths who were placed in them. Moreover, community placements were considerably less costly to implement than institutional placements. According to Governor Terry McAuliffe, the State of Virginia has cut numbers of youth in juvenile institutions by two-thirds with highly successful outcomes (CNN, 2017).

In the political realm, advocates of community placements often encounter objections from persons who believe that, absent deterrence, many juveniles will commit criminal offenses. Special interests, such as unionized correctional officials, may fear loss of jobs if community placements replace institutional placements.

IUOPs that facilitate "Smart Decarceration." Correctional institutions remove persons from employment but they often fail to prepare incarcerated persons for jobs when they are released. Due to the stigma of incarceration, employers are reluctant to hire persons who have been incarcerated. IUOPs need to propose creative ways to engage in "smart decarceration" to help former prisoners join the workforce and refrain from conduct that led them to prison in the first place. We need first to dispel myths: even cutting in half the number of people sent to prison for drug offenses would cut the prison population only by 3% by the end of 2021 according to an interactive "prison population forecaster" of the Urban Institute (Eckholm, 2015). In contrast, *not* incarcerating people for low-level drug offenses and *not* revoking paroles for minor violations could reduce prison admissions for nonviolent crimes by half, and would cut the number of inmates by more than 25% by 2021 in states that adopt these changes. Cutting sentences for violent offenders by 15% would reduce the number of inmates by 7% by 2021—again, not a huge reduction. (About one-half of state prisoners have been convicted of violent crimes.) Equality advocates must understand, then, the dynamics of incarceration to predict what is possible and to decide who to target in their IUOPs. Who should have and who should not have reduced or no sentences? What interventions are effective or not effective with specific kinds of prisoners? According to

Eckholm (2015), the real debate over how to deal with criminals has hardly begun whether at the level of state or federal prisons. Because state prisons house hold 86% of American prisoners or 1.4 million inmates, compared to only 216,000 inmates in federal prisons in 2013, large decreases in inmate populations must take place at the state level. Other IUOPs might aim to increase rights of incarcerated persons or strike records of their incarceration on employment forms so they can more successfully seek employment.

IUOPs that upgrade professions. Preschool teachers usually lack bachelor degrees. They are overwhelmingly female. They earn roughly $23,000 for full-time work. Los Angeles Trade and Technical College (LATTC) is pioneering a program to give thousands of them community college and academic courses toward four-years diplomas on grounds that these degrees will not only upgrade their pay levels, but improve their services to preschool children (accessed Child Development Center, 9/11/17).

IUOPs that upgrade professions IUOPs that place persons with disabilities in jobs. People who experience physical or mental disabilities have high rates of unemployment and poverty partly because their trauma impedes them from entering or succeeding in the workforce and requires accommodations from employers. Employers often fear that their productivity will be decreased because of workers' disabilities—and both employers and fellow employees discriminate against them in their places of work. IUOPs are needed that enforce the prohibition against discrimination in places of work on the basis of disability.

Persons with mental disabilities have particular problems in employment and in higher education. Researchers report most persons with lifetime mental disorders develop them by age 24, and 7.4% of individuals between the ages of 19 and 25 have major depressive disorder (Mendon, 2016). One in three college students report sufficient depression to impair functioning. Suicide is the second leading cause of death among young adults. Many college students with mental health problems find it difficult to protect themselves from discrimination, removal, and disciplinary actions. Courts usually defer to academic institutions when students sue colleges.

USC doctoral student Sapna Mendon developed an IUOP in 2016, called "I am, and I will" (IAIW) to emphasize that college students have to empower themselves rather than let their diagnoses control them. It combines rehabilitation services with treatment to keep students in school, help them return to school after experiencing an emotional disturbance, support them through transitions from community colleges to four-year universities, and to allow them whenever possible to remain in school rather than taking mandated leaves of absence sometimes imposed on them by educational institutions. A multidisciplinary team is placed in the student-counseling center that includes an education/employment support specialist (ES). The ES maintains relationships with the student services center staff, instructors, and academic advisors. After initial psychiatric assessments, this team meets with a student, the student's parents, and the student's academic advisor. The team helps the student identify stressors. The ES works with instructors to educate them about depression and suicidality. The team formulates a plan, such as giving the student a decreased load, beginning classes later in the day, and joining a lab on another day to allow the student not to have a full day. The ES role-plays with the student so that the student can feel at ease in study groups and collaborate with peers. The ES helps the student during downturns and suicide attempts. In the case of one student, the student continued his treatment with the team and the ES, finishing with a degree five years after he began school. The ES helps students who have been helped to graduate to transition to employment or graduate school after they graduate.

This model is closely related to an employment services model (ISP) developed by Drake and Becker (1996), which has been tested in many randomized controlled studies. As described by Bond (1998), the first core principle of ISP focuses on competitive employment. Unlike sheltered employment, the concept relies on reinforcing community integration into adult roles. It has three features, the first of which moves beyond the idea of a counselor or therapist suggesting that a person look for work. The IPS model stresses that IPS specialists focus on a targeted approach with their clients to look for and obtain competitive employment. "Competitive employment" means a job paying at least the Federal minimum wage that is not reserved for people with mental illness. Secondly, a rapid job search leads the patient to obtain a job directly rather than participating in lengthy pre-employment training programs. This challenges the notion commonly held by mental health professionals that patients must be helped through step-wise, gradual training programs to become work-ready prior to attaining employment. Considerable data has shown the step-wise approach is no more effective than a rapid job search. The third core component emphasizes developing an interdisciplinary team whose members are co-located within the mental health agency rather than having some if its members placed in the community. Co-location of its members, including rehabilitation staff, makes coordination less complex and increases positive employment outcomes (Mendon, 2016). On average, the competitive employment rate was 61% for individuals receiving IPS services, compared to 23% for traditional approaches.

The average time to obtain a competitive job (measured by mean days) was 50% faster for individuals receiving IPS services compared to traditional approaches.

Other IUOPs might include:

- Help persons with PTSD, including inner city youth exposed to gang violence and victims of violence, to obtain and retain employment;
- Help persons on the autism spectrum or with other mental disorders to live independently and to find and keep employment after they graduate from high school, including creating and funding independent-living facilities for them;
- Augmenting the "Housing First Program" for homeless persons to help them obtain jobs using evidence-based practices developed for other vulnerable populations;
- Launch a national campaign against addiction to pain drugs, such as opioids, since addiction negatively impacts the employment as well as the health of addicted persons;
- Develop a national campaign against family violence that includes anger management classes, increased penalties against persons who engage in violent behaviors in families, and enhancing migration from violent situations by adult victims.

Place-based IUOPs. IUOPs can take three forms: they can develop and fund investments in entire communities; they can provide social, economic, and health services to citizens in specific geographic areas; or they can combine both of these options (Crane & Manville, 2008). The Model Cities Program that was authorized by the Demonstration Cities and Metropolitan Development Act of 1966, illustrates the first option. Established during the presidency of Lyndon Johnson, it funded more than 150 five-year long experiments in urban areas. It sought to coordinate activities of many federal departments, as well as some at state and local levels, to focus an array of rebuilding, rehabilitation, social service delivery, and citizen participation projects in specific urban areas. It received roughly $3 billion until President Richard Nixon ended it in 1973. Some evaluations suggest that it was not effective (Schechter, 2011). Critics contend it wrongly tried to keep residents from migrating from distressed areas to less distressed areas and didn't focus benefits on specific at-risk persons, such as those with health, addiction, unemployment, and other problems. (Schechter, 2011).

Community policing is another place-based initiative. Take the case of a specific project in Los Angeles in a neighborhood called Harvard Park, which is one of the most violent parts of South Los Angeles, with four shooting deaths in just the last 4 months (Chang, 2017). In an extension of the Los Angeles Police Department's (LAPD) Community Safety Partnership that began in 2011 in the Jordan Downs public housing development, it embedded police in the community where they build deep relationships, become mentors to our young people, and coach sports leagues according to LA Mayor Eric Garcetti. LAPD claims that 81% of homicides were solved in a recent year compared to only 50% years ago because residents were not afraid of gang members and trusted the police. The project "restored public places" for residents. However, some residents of Harvard Park still weren't certain if they wanted to remain in the neighborhood. Many variations of community policing exist.

Some place-based IUOPs contain both community interventions and interventions that help specific people. For example, homeless people can receive support services in a community that also receives community-oriented policing, after-school recreational services, removal of graffiti, and employment services, as well as upgrading of its infrastructure. IUOPs that combine people-based and community interventions are needed to address the lack of employment in rural areas mostly inhabited by White working-class people, such as areas where coal was extensively mined. White males in communities in coal country have high rates of addiction to alcohol, opiates, and cocaine, as well as high rates of suicide (Griswold. 2017). A multi-pronged program could be initiated that upgrades building not in compliance with housing codes, enhances medical and mental health services in the local hospital, provides job training for welding to construct pipes in fracking projects, installation of solar panels and insulation in local buildings, and provides nursing programs to help persons with opioid poisoning and substance abuse.

No one has answers to this problem, but the transformation of Garden City, Kansas may provide clues (Morris, 2017). Like coal mining areas, it lost considerable population: as farms grew larger in the area and the remaining families were smaller, and as residents increasingly shopped online, career opportunities in the town dried up, leading ambitious young adults to move away (Morris, 2017). Observing that many rural cities in Kansas were becoming ghost cities, the elders of Garden City asked themselves what they might do to avoid this fate. They decided to become the meat-packing center of Western Kansas and persuaded large meat packers to move to Garden City. To find sufficient numbers of employees, they invited immigrants to come to the City from Asia, Mexico, Central America, and elsewhere, over the objections of some White residents who were uncomfortable with such diversity. The diversity had a side-benefit because tourists were attracted by the variety of restaurants that immigrants established, with a variety of international menus. The city developed, upgraded, and advertised an array of tourist sites including museums and an indoor waterpark.

Some place-based IUOPs use epidemiological tools to decrease gun and gang violence in specific communities, combined with rapid-response programs where unarmed negotiators meet with gang leaders prior to their engagement in armed conflict with other gangs. Relatively small numbers of persons are violent in specific communities, so if police and local officials identify them, they can focus their efforts on apprehending them and removing them from the streets. Murders in New Orleans greatly decreased when police used "a focused deterrence strategy" to identify those people, usually gang members, that engage in retaliatory gun violence. According to Professor Corsaro, "You concentrate your efforts, from policing, prosecution, probation, parole, federal prosecution, to let the offenders of those groups know that specific activities will be focused on those individuals, if they continue to engage in violence" (Kaste, 2017). This strategy included "call-ins" where dozens of people who engaged in gang violence were told at the courthouse that they would be next if they continued with gun violence. This approach emphasizes the certainty of punishment more than its severity to make offenders refrain from gun violence.

IUOPs that increase job and wage growth. Critics of American capitalism have documented that financial institutions and corporations often do not make productive investments geared toward increasing employment and raising wages, but engage instead, in shielding corporate funds from taxation by moving abroad, investing in financial instruments, funding stock buybacks and dividends, and increasing corporate debt. These trends have been called the "financialization" of the American economy where business has coalesced around the financial sector from the late 1970s onward (Krippner, 2010). These trends have increased inequality in the United States by diverting resources from investments that increase employment and facilitate higher wages (Foroohar, 2016). IUOPs are needed that develop regulations, tax policies, incentives, and penalties that work together to:

- Increase the percentage of capital coming from banks that funds business investments from the current level of roughly 15%;
- Decrease lending against existing assets such as houses, stocks, and bonds, while increasing job-creating investments, i.e., "productive lending;"

- Restrict stock buybacks and high dividends by corporations that reward shareholders as compared to making productive investments;
- Decrease the extent that CEO compensation consists of stock rather than incentives based on creating jobs and raising wages of existing workers;
- Repatriate corporate cash in foreign nations and insist that much of it be used to invest in businesses unlike the tax legislation enacted by the Congress in December 2017 that expatriated corporate cash without requiring a significant fraction be used to raise wages or create new jobs.

IUOPs that decrease loss of jobs to other nations. Many American corporations have devastated the economies of hundreds of communities in the United States since the late 1960s. Lost jobs have decreased the economic wellbeing of millions of blue-collar workers in rural and urban areas, including low- and moderate-income White and African American workers. Many of these blue-collar workers have shortened longevity, engage in substance abuse, and have rising rates of suicide. Preventive measures are needed to decrease the outflow of jobs as well as to entice some corporations to return to the United States. Other measures are needed to target these populations with job training, public-service jobs, health services, and assistance in migrating to places where employment shortages exist. As we discussed earlier, modifications of trade treaties and exit taxes placed on corporations that leave the United States may trigger retaliatory actions by foreign nations, which may increase unemployment in the United States. Possible initiatives might:

- Tax corporations that move abroad on the sum total of their reductions in wages and their reduced taxes in the United States to provide a disincentive to relocation abroad;
- If an employer moves abroad, enroll American workers who lose jobs in intensive job training programs and then finance their migration to jobs they obtain in other locations;
- Develop "exit taxes" on corporations that are considering migrating to other nations, with sharply escalating taxes depending on the number of American employees that will lose their jobs, the magnitude of corporations' profits during a prior time period (e.g., five years), and the magnitude of tax concessions and cash subsidies companies received from local, state, and federal governments during their operations in the United States;

- Provide American corporations with tax incentives and cash subsidies to return to the United States.

IUOPs that remove barriers to trade unions. As discussed in Chapter 3, the percentage of American workers in trade unions markedly plummeted from 1960 to the present. The weakening of American trade unions has adverse consequences for reducing inequality. Unions lose the leverage to place pressure on employers to increase their pay scales, leaving many workers earning only $7.25 per hour, i.e., the federal minimum wage in 2017. Strong unions can pressure employers not to hire so many part-time workers. Strong unions can train workers for infrastructure projects, such as work on highways, repairing bridges, and upgrading water systems. It will be politically difficult, but Taft-Hartley legislation and other anti-union legislation need to be revised.

Other IUOPs to increase upward mobility. Other IUOPs to increase upward mobility could include:

- Development of programs that help avoid bankruptcy during its early stages, such as temporary loans, loan forgiveness, or reduction of interest on loans or mortgages. Establish early warning systems provided by banks or bankruptcy courts;
- Prepare a new workforce to work with people released from detention and prisons, including nurses, social workers, psychologists, teachers, and members of other professions;
- Help seniors find jobs when their income declines with retirement;
- End the pipeline of high school students to the juvenile justice system for non-violent actions, including drug use and truancy. Some school districts, like the Los Angeles Unified School District (LAUSD) have issued directives to principals and their staff to suspend students only under very specific conditions in order not to stigmatize them or place then en route to the so-called "suspension to jail pipeline;"
- Divert non-violent adult offenders from confinement or greatly reduce the length of their sentences in local, state, and federal prisons;
- Convert criminal-justice institutions into job-training programs, both within the institutions and through a system of work-related releases modeled upon these institutions in Norway (Benko, 2015);
- Massively increase programs to reduce homelessness. Use evidence-based practices to move homeless people towards affordable and subsidized housing. Develop niche programs for specific homeless

subgroups, including the growing number of elderly persons, veterans, families with children, and persons with mental illness and substance abuse. Use local, state, and federal powers of eminent domain if needed to find land on which to place housing. Use the power of local, state, and federal governments to establish rent control in those jurisdictions where only affluent people can afford rents. Vastly increase emergency response teams who intervene soon after someone becomes homeless;

- Develop programs that decrease fraud and lack of equity among lenders including retaining and expanding the Consumer Protection Bureau established by the Dodd-Frank Wall Street Reform and Consumer Protection Act of 2010.

IUOPs that Address Cause 4 (Low Levels of Hope)

IUOPs that seek to increase hope. People in at-risk populations need hope when they encounter many barriers to upward mobility (Wilkerson & Pickett, 2014). We can hypothesize that many of the IUOPs discussed in Chapters 5 and 6 increase "hope" by providing opportunities. Homeless people, low-income high school students who are truant and face high odds of not graduating, and single mothers who work three part-time jobs need hope to surmount barriers.

Hope is closely related to other mood states, such as, happiness, optimism, kindness, cheerfulness, confidence, pride, and joy. The World Happiness Report surveyed people from different nations using a Cantril ladder, which asked respondents to evaluate themselves as a rung of a ladder with the top rung indicating for example, the happiest they could possibly be and the bottom rung indicating the least happy they could possibly be (their scores were weighted on six other factors: levels of GDP, life expectancy, generosity, social support, freedom, and corruption). Samples of 2,000 to 3,000 responses over three years were drawn from each nation to estimate the population's mean at a 95 percent confidence interval. The rankings extended from Denmark at 7.526 as most happy, to 5.921 for Japan (Hrala, 2016). The U.S ranked 13th at 7.104. Some adaptation of portions of this report or other validated scales may be useful in measuring hope. I refrain from providing well-established scales that measure depression because I don't want to suggest that persons from at-risk populations are usually afflicted with clinical depression—although some of them have this problem. More broadly, we can hypothesize that many of them lack hope because of the many barriers they encounter as they try to better their lives, including toxic effects of extreme income inequality, poverty, lack of upward mobility, and discrimination (not to mention inadequate funding of IUOPs that could help them improve their condition).

Here are some questions to be considered. To what extent can motivational interviewing and counseling increase hope of persons in at-risk populations? What role can staff who have completed college and become mentors in schools assume in helping students in at-risk populations, such as African Americans and Latinos, increase their hope of graduating? To what extent can mental health services increase hope by alleviating clinical depression among members of at-risk populations? Does involvement in community projects increase hope among members of at-risk populations? Should IUOPs routinely embed strategies to enhance hope in members of at-risk populations who wonder if they can surmount obstacles that they confront?

Research is needed to explore whether persons' level of hope increases as they benefit from IUOPs that address the other hypothesized causes of income inequality in this book. Does level of hope increase, for example, as people move up the economic ladder from the many IUOPs were have discussed in this chapter?

IUOPs that Address Cause 5 (High Levels of Discrimination)

IUOPs that enhance civil rights legislation for disabled people in workplaces. Advocates for the disabled hoped that enactment of the Americans with Disabilities Act (ADA) would finally lead to less discrimination by employers against this at-risk population. The problem was particularly serious for persons with mental health problems because many employers, as well as employees, were prejudiced against a population that sometimes exhibited behaviors that they found troublesome. Moreover, they did not know how to make accommodations for this population in their workloads such as leaves of absence when mental illness surfaced. They feared their work product would be harmed by their disability.

Employees with mental illness are often afraid to discuss it openly for fear they will be stigmatized or fired. Patrick Kennedy, the son of the late Senator Ted Kennedy, had first hand experience with drug addiction, alcoholism, and mental illness (Galanes, 2017). He was diagnosed with bipolar mental illness and tried to hide it for years rather than disclosing it. He found that even his father counseled him not to "come out." When he went to the Mayo Clinic for his addictions, he refrained from going to the ward where they treated mental illness, fearing his condition would leak out. Kennedy stated that the ADA has had limited effect for persons with mental problems because they are often not willing to come out of the shadows. Kennedy views this as the last great frontier in civil rights. Many veterans with PTSD fail to disclose even to family members.

The ADA is coordinated, monitored, and enforced by many federal agencies including the Department of Justice, the Equal Employment Opportunity Commission, the Department of Education, the Department of Labor, and others. Research is needed to better understand the extent of enforcement of the ADA's provisions, and what IUOPs might be proposed to enforce them more effectively.

This remains a frontier in civil rights. How do we help persons with addictions and mental illness disclose their conditions to employers and fellow employees, without fear of stigmatization? Do employers need incentives, monetary or otherwise, to help their employees surmount these problems? How do employers sensitize their employees not to stigmatize fellow employees with these issues?

How do we persuade employers to hire staff with mental health expertise, to provide mentors to employees with mental and physical disabilities, and to make accommodations, similar to those available to college students?

IUOPs that enforce rights of LGBT persons in the military. Katie McNamara (2016) developed an IUOP called "Operation Uplift our Troops: Integration and Equal Rights for LGBT Service Members." She discovered that Sweden was in the vanguard of honoring the rights of LGBT service members (Sundevall & Persson, 2016). Drawing upon Swedish practices, she outlined a step-by-step solution to discrimination against LGBT service personnel in the U.S. military. While she welcomed the decision by the U.S. military during the Obama presidency to discard the "don't ask, don't tell" policy established during Clinton's presidency, she wanted the military to state that the military itself is responsible for changing attitudes, not members of the LGBT population. The military should welcome the establishment of Operation Uplift Our Troops (OUT). They should establish service-wide regulations that clearly state obligations of service personnel. They should establish periodic on-line trainings about this population and nondiscriminatory policies for all military personnel. OUT should partner with women working to decrease marginalization of women. The military should create specific policies for sanctioning military personnel who engage in homophobic activities or use homophobic language. They should seek to decrease early exiting from the military by LGBT service members. They should charge a specific administrator in central headquarters with monitoring the implementation of these policies throughout the military.

Other IUOP ideas are listed below.

- Deprivation of civil rights has contributed to the inequality of members of many vulnerable populations by demoralizing them, depriving them of equal access to jobs and schools, and injuring or killing some residents through police brutality;
- Monitor the emforcement of laws that prohibit discrimination in hiring practices with respect to women, persons over age 50, persons with mental and physical disabilities, LGBTQQ persons, persons of color, and members of other vulnerable populations. Enforce these laws through court action if necessary;
- Improve monitoring of employers to prevent on-the-job discrimination against persons including women, persons of color, disabled persons, aging persons, and others;
- Provide legal resources to persons denied jobs on the basis of race, gender, sexual orientation, age, disability, and other protected populations;
- Decrease police violence against members of vulnerable populations by reforming police practices and hiring. Require police forces to hire significant numbers of police from the communities that they serve. Require police forces to mirror the ethnic and racial mix of the communities that they serve. Augment police forces with unarmed seniors, women, clergy, and others that have strong community ties. Consider hiring former gang members and community members that have reformed their lives after serving sentences in prison. Require the use of video cameras attached to police officers;
- Vigorously enforce voting rights of all citizens, including seniors, disabled persons, and persons of color in those areas where they are not enforced.

IUOPs that Address Cause 6: Access to Opportunities

I argued in Chapter 1 that persons with low social capital, such as income, parents with high levels of education, stable housing, and other amenities often lack access to opportunities that are taken for granted by people with high levels of social capital.

IUOPs that expand educational opportunities for low-income youth by institutions of higher education. Many universities and colleges create programs that expose low-income youth to educational opportunities. They place student interns in local public schools to work with youth around specific assignments. They create weekend programs that engage local youth in research projects. They provide internships in laboratory research. They help youth gain admission at four-year colleges. Examples include programs at the University of Southern California, the University of Pennsylvania, and Earlham College. These programs could be greatly expanded with state and federal resources.

IUOPs that provide support services to low-income students that attend junior colleges and institutions of higher education. Federal funds are needed to expand support services for low-income students in light of their large drop-out rates. For example, President Obama might have coupled his proposal to offer free tuition of low-income students in junior colleges with funds for support services such as mental health staff and mentors (EAB, 2016).

IUOPs that help low-income youth transfer to institutions of higher education from junior colleges and other institutions. Some colleges and universities, such as the University of Southern California, (USC) help low-income students transfer from junior colleges. USC has a large support staff that provides mental health, financial, curriculum, and other supports. It facilitates interactions of the students with other students (Anderson, 2016).

IUOP that restores funding of Head Start. The funding of Head Start was cut in 2013, allowing 57,000 fewer children to enroll until roughly 2020. Since children in Head Start have been shown by researchers to be more likely to graduate from high school and to obtain higher education, these cuts impede upward mobility of many youth (Kleinbard, 2015, p. 181).

IUOPs that improve access to healthcare in rural areas. Rural hospitals are particularly important in rural areas. They attend to urgent health needs like opioid poisoning, malnutrition, substance abuse, chronic health conditions, emergency health care, mental health, and other needs. They bring to rural areas highly trained professionals including physicians, nurses, psychologists, and social workers. Many rural hospitals have a precarious financial footing. They rely heavily on Medicaid resources because many rural areas have a substantial elderly population that needs nursing and convalescent care. These hospitals should be linked to public health agencies and staff to develop preventive services to decrease addictions and chronic health conditions. They need to engage in outreach services to homes and schools. Because they rely so heavily on Medicaid reimbursements to remain solvent, the Medicaid program cannot be cut if they are to thrive as Republican replacements for Obamacare proposed. Indeed rural hospitals need substantial subsidies in light of the elderly nature of their patients, the sheer number of patients that cannot afford their care, and the amount of emergency care they provide (Sable-Smith, 2017).

IUOPs that fund steps toward universal healthcare, such as Medicare-for-All. The American healthcare system has produced public health outcomes decidedly poorer than European nations, Canada, Japan, Australia, and New Zealand. It is also far more costly than health systems of these nations (Kane, 2012). Many experts concur that single payer systems are more efficient and produce better health outcomes than the American system that makes extensive use of private insurance as well as means-tested programs for persons that lack private insurance (Leonhardt, 2017). Equality advocates should propose an IUOP for Medicare-for-All by putting forward Bernie Sanders proposal that was published in September 2017—or alternative versions if they exist. If it is found not to be politically feasible in light of the deep ideological divide, they should immediately push for many routes to move the United States toward single payer (Pollack, 2017). It can require all states to raise eligibility levels for Medicaid so that millions of American just above current Medicaid eligibility levels are insured. It can seek a single payer option in the state exchanges established by the Affordable Care Act (ACA). It can allow Medicare to bargain with drug companies to secure lower prices. It can reimburse by quality of care rather than quantity of care. It can make adults eligible for Medicare at age 55.

IUOPs that expand funding of community-based public health. Develop programs that identify and help families where malnourishment of children occurs. Data shows that malnourishment of children in the first 1,000 days impedes brain function and cuts lifetime earnings by 20%. One percent of American children are malnourished. Restore funding levels of the Supplemental Nutrition Program for Women, Infants, and Children Program (WIC) that was cut during the budget sequestration in President Obama's second term (Kleinbard, 2015, p. 25). The funding of the Children's Health Insurance Program (CHIP) was uncertain in late 2017 when its authorization had expired. It funds healthcare for millions of children who would not otherwise possess it. Its funding needs to be placed on a more secure footing in future years.

Placing IUOPs on Paper

Chapter 7 discusses how to construct IUOPs with traction in the political arenas at local, state, and federal levels of government by developing working papers and policy briefs. Chapter 8 discusses how to construct Resources to Uplift Ordinary People (RUOPs). Chapter 9 discusses Political Strategy to Uplift Ordinary People (PSUOP).

References

Anderson, N. (2016; May 12). "At the University of Southern California, a rare open door for transfer students," accessed at *The Washington Post* on September 19, 2017.

Balfanz, R. & Fox J. (2011, October). *Early warning systems—Foundational research and lessons from the field* [Powerpoint slides]. Lecture presented at National Governors Association, Philadelphia. Retrieved from https://www.nga.org/files/live/sites/NGA/files/pdf/1110EARLYDROPBALFANZ.PDF.

Benko, J. (2015, March 26)."The radical humaneness of Norway's Halden Prison," The New York Times Magazine." Retrieved at newyorktimes.com

Bond, G. R. (1998). Principles of the individual placement and support model: Empirical support. *Psychiatric Rehabilitation Journal, 22*(1), 11.

Camera, L. (2015, September 24). Study finds students underperform in schools with large Black populations. *U.S. News and World Report.* Retrieved from https://www.usnews.com/news/articles/2015/09/24/study-finds-students-underperform-in-schools-with-large-black-populations.

Catalan, J. (2014, August 1). Study: Are Black students in integrated schools getting a better education than segregated students? Retrieved from http://www.diversityinc.com.

CB Insights. (2014, October 8). The top 20 reasons startups fail [Online chart]. Retrieved from https://www.cbinsights.com/blog/startupfailure-reasons-top/.

Crane, R. & Manville, M. (2008, July). People or place: Revisiting the who versus the where of urban development. *Land Lines, Lincoln Institute of Land Policy.*Retrieved from http://www.lincolninst.edu.

Drake, R. E. & Becker, D. R. (1996). The individual placement and support model of supported employment. *Psychiatric Services, 47*(5), 473–475.

EAB, (2016, February 11). "Obama doubles down on free community college in 2017 budget proposal." EAB accessed at eab.com;

Eckholm, E. (2015, August 11). How to cut the prison population (see for yourself). *New York Times.* Retrieved from https://www.nytimes.com

Galanes, P. (2017, March 11). "Glenn Close and Patrick Kennedy on the weight of mental illness." *New York Times.* https://www.nytimes.com

Gibney, B., & Howery, K. (2012, March 9). Four things to get right when starting a company. *Harvard Business Review.* Retrieved from https://hbr.org

Griswold, E. (2017, July 3). "The future of coal county.": *The New Yorker* accessed at www.thenewyorker.com.

Grubb, N. (1996) *Learning to work: The case for reintegrating job training and education.* New York: Russell Sage Foundation.

Grunwald, M. (2012). *The New Deal, the hidden history of change in the Obama era.* New York: Simon & Schuster.

Hoe, D. (2016). Pocket money: A social investment proposal in aid of low-income older adults. SW 733 in doctoral program of the Suzanne Dworak-Peck School of Social Work, University of Southern California.

Hrala, J. (2016, March 17). The world happiness index 2016 just ranked the happiest countries on earth. Science Alert Retrieved from https://www.sciencealert.com/the-world-happiness-index-2016-just-ranked-the-happiest-countries-on-earth.

Jacobs, E. (2014). *Twelve ways to fix the youth unemployment crisis.* Governance Studies, Brookings Institute. Retrieved from: https://www.brookings.edu

Jansson, B. (2015). *The reluctant welfare state: Engaging history to advance social work practice in contemporary society, 8th ed.* San Francisco: Cengage.

Kane, J. (2012; October 22). Health costs: How the U.S. compares with other countries. PBS Newshour.

Kaste, M. (2017, February 23). New Orleans and the hard work of pushing down the murder rate. *New York Times.* https://www.nytimes.com

Kleinbard, E. D. (2015). *We are better than this: How government should spend our money.* Oxford University Press.

Kurtzleben, D. (2017: January 7). What kind of 'Jobs President' has Obama been—in 8 Charts. NPR, Southern California Public Radio, Retrieved from http://www.npr.org

Leonhardt, D., Cox, A., & Miller, C. C. (2015, May 4) *An atlas of upward mobility shows paths out of poverty. New York Times,* https://nytimes.com

Leonhardt, D. (2017; September 11, 2017). 5 questions about single-payer care. *New York Times.*

Lewis-McCoy, R. (2014). *Inequality in the promised land: Race, resources, and suburban schooling.* Palo Alto, CA: Stanford University Press.

MDRC. (2015). Large, vigorous study finds youth villages program increases economic well-being, reduces homelessness among youth aging out of foster care and juvenile justice. at Retrieved from www.ytfg.org.

Mendon, S. (2016).*Creating new opportunities for students with mental illness: The art of re-integration.* Unpublished manuscript, Suzanne Dworak-Peck School of Social Work, University of Southern California, Los Angeles, USA.

Mislinski, J. (2017). The ratio of part-time employed remains high, but improving. Advisor Perspectives, Retrieved from http://advisor perspectives.com.

Morris, F. (2017, February 19). A thriving rural town's winning formula faces new threats under Trump Administration [Radio broadcast]. Weekend Edition, National Public Radio. Retrieved from http://npr.org

Orr, L.L., Bloom, H.S., Bell, S.H., Doolittle, F., & Lin, W. (1996). *Does training for the disadvantaged work? Evidence from the national JTPA study.* Washington, D.C.: Urban Institute Press.

Petrosino, A., Guckenburg, S., & Turpin-Petrosino, C. (2010). *Formal system processing of juveniles: Effects on delinquency.* Campbell Systematic Review. Retrieved from https://www.campbellcollaboration.org

Piketty, T. (2014). *Capitalism in the Twenty-First Century.* Cambridge, MA: Harvard University Press.

Pollack, R. (2017; September 11). Single-payer isn't the only progressive option on health care. Vox

Pynnönen, K., Törmäkangas, T., Heikkinen, R.L., Rantanen, T., & Lyyra, T.M. (2012). Does social activity decrease risk for institutionalization and mortality in older people? *The Journals of Gerontology Series B: Psychological Sciences and Social Sciences, 67*(6), 765–774. doi:10.1093/geronb/gbs076.

Reyes, J. (2015). Policy analysis and advocacy in a comparative social policy context [Unpublished manuscript]. Suzanne Dworak-Peck School of Social Work, University of Southern California, Los Angeles, USA.

Riley, S. (2016: April 13). How Seattle gave up on busing and allowed its public schools to become alarmingly resegregated. *The Stranger*. Retrieved from www.thestranger.com.

Sable-Smith, B. (2017; June 22). Republican's proposed Medicaid cuts would hit rural patients hard. Shots: Health News from NPR. Accessed @ npr.org on September 19, 2017.

Sachs, J., Becchetti, L., & Annett, A. (2016). *World Happiness Report 2016, Special Rome Edition (Vol. II)*. New York: Sustainable Development Solutions Network.

Schechter, J. (2011). *An empirical evaluation of the Model Cities Program* [Unpublished thesis]. University of Michigan, Ann Arbor, MI.

Sherraden, M. (1991). *Assets and the poor: A new American welfare policy*. New York: M. E. Sharpe.

Sundevall, F. & Persson, A. (2016). LGBT in the military: Policy development in Sweden. *Sexuality Research and Social Policy, 13*(2), 119–129.

Thompson, D. (2015: July/August). A world without work. *Atlantic Monthly*. Retrieved from https://www.theatlantic.com/magazine/archive/2015/07/world-without … /395294/

Thompson, D. (2016: October 31). When will robots take all the jobs? *Atlantic Monthly*. Retrieved from https://www.theatlantic.com/business/archive/2016/10/the-robot-paradox/505973/

U.S. Congress Joint Economic Committee. (2010). *Understanding the economy: Unemployment among young workers*. Washington, DC: Government Printing Office. Retrieved from https://www.jec.senate.gov/public

Wasserman, N. (2012). *The founder's dilemmas: Anticipating and avoiding the pitfalls that can sink a startup*: Princeton, NJ: Princeton University Press.

Wasserman, N., & Hellmann, T. (2016). The Very First Mistake Most Startup Founders Make. *Harvard Business Review*. Retrieved from https://hbr.org

Wilkinson R., & Pickett, K. (2014, February 2). How inequality hollows out the soul. *New York Times*. Retrieved from https://www.nytimes.com

7 CONCEPTUALIZING IUOPs: FROM WORKING PAPERS TO POLICY BRIEFS

Equality advocates develop working papers that contain the goals, timelines, implementing mechanisms, and budgets of their Initiatives to Uplift Ordinary Persons (IUOPs). These working papers can range in length from 5 pages to 20 pages. Equality advocates present policy officials, such as legislators, staff in the Executive Branch, leaders in the private sector, and civil servants, with "policy briefs." They *are* brief, and they also "brief" policy officials about their IUOPs in only one to three pages. They have to be short because policy officials lack the time to read longer documents.

Working papers and policy briefs are central to the work of equality advocates. They can and should be modified as equality advocates get feedback from public officials and others.

An Illustration: Increasing High School Graduation Rates By Making Reforms in Middle Schools

To illustrate how the content of an IUOP might develop, I use Professor Robert Balfanz's proposal for a "Civic Marshall Plan to Build a Grad(uation) Nation" as well as additional materials from him and from the Everyone Graduates Center (Balfanz & Fox, 2011; Balfanz, 2009; and Balfanz et al., 2014). We do not present a working paper or policy brief, but use this example to illustrate the analytic process that policy advocates use as they develop them.

Balfanz & Fox (2011) proposed that a coalition of non-profits, government, and school organizations implement a "Civil Marshall Plan" to target 1,746 "dropout factories & feeder elementary and middle schools" with dropout rates of 50%, and target another 3,000 high schools with graduation rates between 61 and 75%. They hoped that the nation could achieve a national graduation rate of 90% by 2020 if the nation expeditiously developed effective initiatives, starting with middle schools. Implementing reforms in 2012–13 to transform or replace "dropout factories" would result in higher graduation rates, allowing 600,000 additional students in the Class of 2020 to earn diplomas.

This IUOP is highly relevant to the goal of decreasing inequality in the United States because considerable research has already revealed that persons without high school diplomas have higher rates of unemployment and lower wages than persons with diplomas. Furthermore, few of them graduate from two-year community colleges, colleges, or receive graduate degrees. College graduates earned $17,500 per year more than employed adults with only a high school diploma (Pew Research Survey, "The rising cost of not going to college," Pew Research Center, February 11, 2014). Balfanz & Fox (2011, p. 31) argued "we are left with a giant engineering challenge of getting the right supports, to the right students, at the right time, at the scale and intensity required." Their optimism was linked to their empirical findings that early warning systems (EWSs) predict as early as the 6th grade which students will drop out of high school. While considerable variation exists across middle schools (grades 6 through 8), students are considerably more likely to drop out of high school if they develop one or more of the following problems in the 6th grade:

- Miss 20 or more days of school (attendance, or A),
- Have two or more behavior infractions in a year, such as suspensions or sustained mild misbehavior (behavior, or B),
- Have final grades of "F" in Math, English, or both in the middle grades (course performance, or C).

Balfanz and Fox (2011) documented that sixth-grade students with one or more of these three indicators (A, B, or C) have only a 15% to 25% chance of graduating from high school. Balfanz and Fox (2011) argued that identifying students with these problems in the 6th grade could allow schools to predict 75% or more of eventual dropouts in high-poverty school districts.

Using this project as an example, we discuss the analytic process by which equality advocates develop working papers and policy briefs. They must:

- Identify a core problem,
- Analyze why the core problem increases inequality,
- Identify the distribution and scope of the problem,
- Identify ethical reasons for addressing this problem,
- Identify causes of the core problem,
- Find empirical evidence for a proposed IUOP,
- Identify and select rationing options,
- Estimate the cost of the IUOP,
- Demonstrate that an IUOP produces positive outcomes,
- Give an IUOP a creative name,
- Make the case that an IUOP will significantly increase equality,
- Determine where it will be positioned in the American governance system,
- Demonstrate the political feasibility of an IUOP,
- Determine how the IUOP will be funded.

Identify a core problem. Equality advocates need to identify a core problem in their working papers and policy brief. Professor Balfanz and colleagues identified high dropout rates from high school as his core problem. While 85% of White student freshman graduated from high school, only 68% of African American and 76% of Latino freshman students graduated from high school in 2012. While 87% of students from non low-income families graduated in 2012, only 72% of students from poverty-level families graduated (Balfanz et al., 2014).

Analyze why the core problem increases inequality. Recall that "inequality" is often manifested by income inequality, poverty, and/or discrimination. With respect to income inequality, a linear relationship exists between the number of education credentials or degrees that people obtain and their annual income. If dropouts from high school earned $19,000 per year in 2013, high school graduates earned $28,000, graduates of community colleges earned $30,000, and graduates of college earned $45,000 (Balfanz et al., 2014; PolitiFact, 2013). Persons with graduate or professional degrees had even higher income. With respect to poverty, persons who fail to complete high school have a poverty rate of 30.8% (Breslow, 2012). As discussed in Chapter 1, poverty causes many other problems, including shorter lives, homelessness, mental illness and substance abuse, incarceration, and engagement in violence. People with these social problems are less likely to have remunerative jobs.

Identify the distribution and scope of the problem. Equality advocates gain support for their IUOP if they demonstrate that their core problem is significant. We have already discussed the huge percentages of students of color and low-income students who drop out of high school. These data demonstrate that dropping out of high school is a major national problem, particularly in low-income schools. The large numbers of people who fail to complete high school greatly increase the nation's inequality. Therefore, this IUOP should be given the highest priority.

Identify ethical reasons for addressing this problem. It is not surprising that many students drawn from some at-risk populations discussed in Chapter 1 disproportionately experience the A, B, and C problems including youth of color, disabled youth, low-income youth, and White youth in many rural and semi-rural areas. Many of their parents did not receive high school diplomas so they lack role models. Many students are distracted by complex family problems like substance abuse and family violence. Many students develop mental problems, such as PTSD, when they are exposed to violence in their neighborhoods. Many students from at-risk populations have inadequate nutrition, unaddressed health problems, and undiagnosed hearing and vision problems. Some of these students are homeless for brief or long periods, making it nearly impossible to do homework and to concentrate on academic success (Breslow, 2012). Many students from these groups receive their education from schools that are under-resourced, compared to schools that affluent and White persons attend (Balfanz et al., 2014). These experiences, singly and in tandem, increase the odds that students from these at-risk populations will develop more A, B, and C problems, compared to more advantaged students. Society has an ethical obligation to help these students because they experience toxic effects of income inequality, poverty, and discrimination through no fault of their own, which relatively affluent youth do not experience.

Identify causes of the core problem. As discussed, youth who fail to graduate from high school disproportionately experience poor nutrition, family violence, poverty, lack of parental support for education, and lack of stable housing (Rumberger, 2013). Many immigrant students lack proficiency in English. Many low-income students lack models of educational success in their households. Many low-income students do not view education as a path to success because many of their peers fail to graduate from high school, and may be unemployed even when they do complete high school. Low-income students often attend secondary schools with poorer teachers than affluent students partly because of pay differentials that lead more talented teachers to migrate from inner city to suburban schools. Some students drop out because they lack mentors who help them stay on track in school. Some need jobs to provide economic assistance to their families (Balfanz et al., 2014, pp. 55–56).

Students who are truant cannot thrive in educational settings. Students beset with behavioral problems are often unable to establish positive relationships with their teachers, administrators, and peers, or unable to concentrate on their academic work. Students that do not complete courses cannot progress through the educational system.

Balfanz et al., 2014, pp. 62–63) also identified institutional problems that frustrate efforts to address the A, B, and C problems in many inner-city schools. School staff often suspend students with behavioral problems, a strategy that often places those students even further behind their peers. They often refer them to juvenile justice authorities, a strategy that often places them in a school-to-prison pipeline. School staff often have low expectations for their students. They often view truancy, low grades, and behavior problems as inevitable because of their sheer number, as well as their inability to address them when their schools have low staff-to-student ratios and lack sufficient support services from social workers, psychologists, and other specialists. The morale of school staff often declines when their schools receive lower aggregate scores on standardized tests than schools with more affluent students.

Find empirical evidence for IUOPs. Balfanz and Fox (2011) conducted longitudinal research in the Philadelphia school system that followed students from the first grade through high school to see if his hypothesized predictors had empirical merit. He discovered that the ABC's predicted whether students would graduate from high school even as early as the 6th grade. He discovered that students who missed more than 10% of classes (problem A), had two or more behavioral problems (problem B), or received failing grades in Math or English classes in the 6th grade (problem C) were far more likely not to graduate from high school than other students. Why not, he decided, see if interventions with these students would increase their odds graduating from high school?

School personnel would benefit, as well, from empirical data regarding the three problems. With respect to Problem A, what interventions would bring truant students back toward regular attendance? Do episodically truant students need different interventions than chronically truant students? Does staff routinely locate truant students in their neighborhoods? What kinds of counseling are effective? Are specific incentives effective? To what extent are parents, relatives or both enlisted in helping truant students return to school? When are juvenile authorities consulted? What kinds of professionals or paraprofessionals can most effectively help truant students? Can community-based agencies assist?

With respect to Problem B, what kinds of behavioral problems do students present, including depression, anxiety, PTSD, fighting, or bullying? What behavioral problems do students on the autism spectrum present? To what extent can group therapy be used? What kinds of professionals can most effectively help students with behavioral problems? What partnerships can be forged with social agencies in the community? What time limits, if any, will be placed on efforts to help students resolve behavioral problems?

With respect to Problem C, what kinds of course performance problems do students present, including low or failing grades, failure to complete homework assignments, or low scores on standardized tests of competency in math, English, or other subjects? To what extent does individual tutoring help and for what time periods? What kinds of professionals can most effectively help students with course performance problems? In what circumstances will students be asked to repeat specific classes? To what extent can after-school classes, summer school classes, or tutoring be used? What partnerships can be forged with community agencies or groups?

School personnel would also benefit from empirical data that analyzes the duration and intensity of interventions needed to help students surmount problems A, B, and C. To what extent can these interventions be mostly limited to students in the 6th grade to increase high school graduation rates substantially? To what extent would these interventions have to extend to 7th and 8th grades for some or many students?

Recall that Balfanz and other researchers identified some institutional factors that they believed would impede the implementation of these interventions, including excessive use of suspensions to discipline students; beliefs by teachers and school administrator that widespread truancy, behavioral problems, and failing grades are inevitable; lack of creativity in school activities; and insufficient numbers of support staff (Balfanz & Fox, 2011; Balfanz et al., 2014).

High school staff would also benefit from empirical research that analyzes the effectiveness of interventions directed to high school students. Is it necessary to continue interventions with A, B, and C problems in 9th grade, in light of Balfanz's assertion that students who enter high school with far lower math and English proficiency than their peers will be less likely to achieve parity with their peers in these subjects than students who "closed the gap" in their prior grades due to tutoring or other interventions (Balfanz & Fox, 2011)? Would many students in the 10th, 11th, and 12th grades also need interventions to help them surmount the A, B, and C problems?

Balfanz and colleagues also had to discover what strategies would induce school administrators, teachers, and support staff to support and participate in school-wide, and even district-wide, campaigns to increase high school graduation rates (Balfanz, 2009; Balfanz & Fox, 2012; Balfanz et al., 2014). They wanted staff to prioritize a system of interventions geared toward increasing graduation rates of high school students. They knew that most teachers and administrators want to increase high school graduation rates, yet schools with a high number of low-income students are already burdened with insufficient numbers of teachers and support staff. Would the schools develop data management systems to identify specific students with A, B, and/or C problems in the 6th grade and ensuing grades? Would administrators assign teachers and support staff to each of these students in a timely manner? Would they track these students through time so that teachers and support staff could be reassigned to students who backtracked with respect to A, B, and/or C problems? Would they surmount shortages of staff and resources that are common in many schools with low-income student populations, even as they receive funds from the federal Elementary and Secondary Education Act (ESEA), that prioritize school districts in low-income areas? Would they partner with community mental health agencies, civic associations, churches, and other non-government agencies (NGOs)?

Balfanz developed some recommendations about the rollout of this intervention in middle schools, including:

a. Phase this strategy into place gradually from a pilot phase "and listen to end users before going too far." "Build and obtain the required capacity to launch and sustain the Early Warning System by engaging stakeholders beyond the school systems (non-profits, corporations, community organizations, etc.)" (Balfanz, 2011, p.15).

b. Develop school-wide interventions that include mission building, professional development coaching, and networking in surrounding communities. The entire school needs to embrace these interventions. The mission should stress "put(ing) students first" by "building on student strengths." It designs systems "that respond to student behavior well before triggers for the more intensive interventions are needed." It combines "whole school prevention" that includes targeted problem solving and supporting students when prevention does not work (Balfanz & Fox, 2011, p. 14).

c. Use school-wide data to identify at-risk students. The early warning indicators are data for each student that identifies those that have problem A (attendance), B (behavior), or C (course performance)—or a combination of them. Be certain that data is entered by appropriately trained staff and according to well-designed protocols (Balfanz & Fox , 2011, p. 16). Create a list of students who need support. Use teamwork to make decisions about actions and interventions. Create support interventions that fit your school and students. Involve the community in support interventions, including "students, parents, non-profits, and community organizations." Organize a "second shift" of adults from "non-profits and the community to insure all 'off-track' students can be supported" (Balfanx & Fox, 2011, p.19). Develop a network of relationships with service providers. To induce students to come to school, "create cognitively rich activities that combine teamwork with performance (e.g. robotics, debate, drama, chess, etc.)" (Balfanz & Fox, 2011, p. 21). Understand that "chronic absenteeism (missing a month or more of school) is much more widespread, particularly in high poverty communities, than is commonly recognized"—and "realize that it is driven by a combination of student choice, school factors driving students away, and out of school factors pulling them away" (Balfanz & Fox, 2011, p. 21). Model and teach students "staying out of trouble skills," as well as "resiliency and self-management/organization skills." "Build success scripts in students' heads (effort leads to success)" while "working to undermine failure scripts" (Balfanz, & Fox, 2011, p. 22). "Make sure tutoring efforts are linked tightly with needs and expectations of student courses, such as not working on fractions if Friday's test is on probability" (Balfanz & Fox, 2011, p. 23).

Balfanz (2011) contended that interventions begun in middle school should be expanded to high schools. He suggested that high schools should:

a. Build and provide transitional support from high school to college and career, since "a crack" exists between public schools and starting college and career training, which means that many students will need additional supports, both academically and socially to "successfully make this transition" (Balfanz & Fox, 2011, p. 25).

b. Help students have "a very strong 9th grade year (with) strong attendance, no behavior problems, B or better average—and (to) be on-age" because such students "have high odds of post-secondary attainment" (Balfanz & Fox, 2011, p. 26).

c. Recover dropouts by bringing them back into high schools so that they can eventually receive their diplomas; devise ways students can quickly make up credits in high school so that they can move through the natural sequence of high school courses in a timely manner.

Equality advocates need to identify web sites that provide empirical findings with respect to IUOPs that they develop, such as **The Campbell Collaboration** that provides a searchable list of reviews of social research, principally in the United States and Europe, that engage in meta-analysis to test whether findings from an array of studies demonstrate effectiveness of a specific intervention (www.campbellcollabation.org). Research can be found in government departments and research centers such as:

- Edutopia;
- National Center for Education Statistics;
- Urban Institute;
- U.S. Department of Education;
- EBSCO Information Services;
- Education Resources Information Center (ERIC);
- The Bill and Malinda Gates Foundation.

Identify and select rationing options. Limits have to be placed upon strategies devised by equality advocates because of the limited resources of governments, NGOs, foundations, and other funding mechanisms. Take the case of Senator Bernie Sanders, who during the 2016 Democratic presidential primaries proposed giving free tuition to all students who attend public universities. When considering the cost of this initiative, Hillary Clinton developed a counterproposal to restrict the subsidy to students from families whose income did not exceed $125,000 per year, at a savings of billions of dollars compared to Sanders' proposal. Had Hillary Clinton won the presidential election of 2016, she would have had to revisit this issue to see if she still wanted to ration student subsidies.

Rationing is achieved by restricting eligibility policies for specific programs, such as offering free services only to people who fall beneath specific income standards. The duration of services can be limited, such as providing no more than 10 counseling sessions for persons receiving mental health services. Agencies or services can be located in specific geographic areas so that a preponderance of their clientele comes from these areas, such as low-income areas. Use of sliding fee scales gives priority to low-income persons while obtaining resources from more affluent persons to help fund an IUOP.

Estimate the cost of the IUOP. In order the estimate the likely cost of an intervention, equality advocates need to answer some key questions (see below) described in Balfanz's (2009) initiative.

To what extent is additional staff needed? Schools in low-income districts are often under-staffed because budget allocation procedures favor affluent schools, staff is difficult to recruit because they encounter higher levels of absenteeism, and students have social problems caused by their families' poverty. Balfanz's intervention adds additional tasks to staff's workload, such as providing interventions for students with problems A, B, and/or C. Staff also needs to develop and oversee partnerships with community agencies and associations. More support staff needs to be hired including social workers, psychologists, and speech/language professionals. The costs of these new hires have to be estimated.

Does the innovation extend through middle school, as well as into to high school? Balfanz (2011 and 2014) suggests that his innovation needs to continue through middle school, into high school, and during the post-graduation transitional period. As it embraces these different levels of education, its cost will rise.

Can costs be shared with community partners, school districts, the Elementary and Education Act, foundations, and others? The cost of this innovation partly depends on what funding partners can be located. It depends on whether grant writers need to be hired to obtain resources from funding partners. Use of volunteers cuts the cost of an IUOP but may also have some drawbacks as compared to use of professional staff.

What will be the workload of school administrators, teachers, and support staff? The cost of Balfanz's IUOP will partly depend upon the severity of the A, B, and C problems that exist in low-income schools. "Severity" increases as (1) the number of students with these problems is relatively high; (2) the extent these problems can be solved relatively quickly; and (3) the extent these problems recur after students have receiving initial assistance. If they can be identified and resolved relatively quickly, the cost of this IUOP is lower than otherwise. "Severity" is likely to differ from school to school depending upon the characteristics of the student population.

How many schools are included? The cost of this IUOP will depend on its scope: does it target schools across the nation, schools of specific states, schools in specific school districts, or individual schools?

Developing a budget. Many legislators examine the budget of a policy proposal even before they read other materials. Go to a 16-minute webinar, dated September 10, 2015, developed by the Foundation Center @grantspace.org. It includes the Introduction (00.01), What Funders Want to See in Project Budgets (00:36), Components of a Project Budge (1:13), If You Know Your Project, You Can Plan Your Budget (2:44), How will I Know How Much My Project Costs (3:23), Estimating Personnel Costs (04:20), Estimating Non-Personnel Costs (5:45), Indirect Costs (6:58), Visible Costs (Direct Costs) versus Hidden Costs (Indirect Costs) (7:42), Calculating Your Indirect Cost Rate (8:29), Showing Your Income (10:18), Add In-Kind Contributions (12:11), Other Financial Information Often Requested (12:46), Budget Considerations After the Grant is Approved (13:46), Key Takeaways (14:54), and Where to Find Sample Documents (15:26).

Demonstrate that an IUOP produces positive outcomes. Public officials want to know whether an IUOP will produce a net positive outcome, calculated as an impact on its target population and on the broader society minus the cost of the program and the failure to help members of the target population. Balfanz's (2009) longitudinal research provided evidence that his innovation increased graduation rates of students—a notable accomplishment. He (and supporters of his initiative) argued persuasively that sufficient numbers of students benefited from the initiative to merit expenditures on it. Put differently, the "failures" of the program were exceeded by its successes, measured as increased graduation rates. Balfanz et al., (2014) and supporters of the initiative also persuasively argued that the program reduced so-called "negative externalities" such as cost of safety-net programs, welfare programs, unemployment benefits, and costs of health programs, because graduates of high school are considerably less likely to need these benefits and programs. The initiative, he and others persuasively contended, reduces poverty in the United States because researchers have discovered that students who do not graduate from high school and who have children are far more likely to experience familial poverty than persons who do not drop out.

Give a creative name to an IUOP. President Lyndon Johnson contended that it is easier to market policy innovations in the political marketplace if advocates give them names that are appealing to decision makers. Consider, for example the *Head Start*, preschool program for low-income children, named by the Johnson Administration in the mid 1960s. Professor Balfanz named his program "The Civic Marshall Plan to Build a Grad Nation" after the famous Marshall Plan developed by President Harry Truman to rebuild European nations in the wake of World War II (Balfanz et al., 2014).

Make the case that an IUOP will significantly reduce inequality. Balfanz and collaborators make a compelling case that this IUOP has sufficient overall merit to be prioritized by public officials (Balfanz et al., 2014). It receives high scores with respect to five criteria: (1) the ethical importance of reducing the core problem of failure to graduate from high school; (2) the extent the core problem creates economic and other hardships by the populations affected; (3) the extent the core problem, if unresolved, creates important negative externalities for the broader society; (4) the extent evidence-based solutions exist; and (5) the extent programs can find support from the American political system. These outcomes, singly and in tandem, increase the odds that public officials will prioritize and fund some variation of Professor Balfanz's initiative.

Position the IUOP in the American System of Governance. This IUOP could have been positioned in the federal government, in a specific state, or in a specific local jurisdiction. If it was positioned at the federal level, it would have to be approved by the Congress and president—and would likely be administered by the U.S. Department of Education. Or it could be positioned at the level of one or more states or local jurisdictions. Alternatively, it could be disseminated by one or more NGOs to specific school districts such as the Everyone Graduates Center at the School of Education at John Hopkins University (Balfanz et al., 2014).

Determine how an IUOP will be funded. An IUOP can be funded by one or more sources. It can seek funding from governmental funding from federal, state, or local levels—or a combination of these them. It can seek funding from foundations, corporations, and other private sources. It can include fees from users. I discuss in Chapter 8 why the federal government does not adequately fund many IUOPs even though it possesses tax revenues greater than tax revenues of all the states combined. This is a key challenge faced by equality advocates: they cannot move the Equality Roller Coaster downward unless they can obtain sufficient resources to fund an array of IUOPs.

Demonstrate political feasibility. While this proposal has overall merit, we must remember that even in 2017 many school districts, state boards of education, and federal agencies had not approved it, even though overall high school graduation rates had risen from 74% in 1990–1991 to 82% in 2012–2013. Equality advocates have to do the hard work of diagnosing who might support some form of this IUOP and the venue where it will be approved and funded, such as a specific school district, a state legislature, a federal agency, or the Congress. They have to decide what public officials possess the power to move it forward to deliberative bodies, such as high-level administrators, chairs of committees, influential persons with leadership skills, high-level politicians, advocacy groups, civil servants, and others. They have to decide which of these public officials might invest effort in promoting it. They have to find people who dislike a proposed IUOP, but who can be converted to it. Such converts may help to push a proposal over the top.

It is likely that more public officials can be convinced to prioritize Balfanz's IUOP. It enhances equality while decreasing negative externalities. It increases upward mobility. It is timely because strategies to reduce school dropouts receive considerable attention from the media, political leaders, and others. It is unknown to what extent President Trump and the Republican Congress will prioritize this issue because Trump's choice of Betsy DeVos to head the Department of Education favors charter schools and use of school vouchers at a time when 90% of American high school students attend public schools, and when most students do not receive school vouchers. Still, many governors, state departments of education, and local school districts have already supported programs to decrease school dropouts. Trade unions that represent teachers are a valuable ally.

Come up with data that demonstrates that elected officials will receive positive benefits if they support Balfanz's IUOP. School districts and schools exist in all of their constituencies. Trade unions that represent teachers make contributions to political campaigns. Effective schools contribute to economic growth. Effective schools diminish public spending for SNAP, Medicaid, and many other social programs.

Scaling up IUOPs from local to national ones and coupling them. Meritorious IUOPs are often developed at local and state levels, but more of them need to be scaled upward to the national level. Take the example of Balfanz's IUOP that was funded by local and state educational departments as they learned about it and were able to find resources to implement it—or by local schools that implemented it from their resources and their exiting staff. Why not have Congress enact a statute that funds Balfanz's IUOP in schools with particularly high levels of drop-outs at sufficient levels that schools can hire needed support staff to implement it?

Coupling Effective IUOPs. Why not federally fund Balfanz's IUOP along with other IUOPs that also have been found to be effective in reducing drop-out rates or in addressing any social problem. Bruce & Bridgeland

(2014) discovered, for example, that most low-income high school students lack mentors who provide them with support, direction, and guidance. Their graduation rates greatly increase when they are assigned mentors. Mentors might then be added to Balfanz's IUOP. These mentors might also be persons of the same race or ethnicity of students if data demonstrate that racial and ethnic congruity enhances students' academic success. *Coupling and funding multiple evidence-based strategies* may promise greater effectiveness than single initiatives.

Challenges Encountered With Other Kinds of IUOPs

Balfanz's initiative is a service-intensive one as well as one that seeks to transform institutions. Now I briefly discuss several other kinds of IUOPs to illustrate that each of them presents challenges and opportunities.

Regulations. Take, for example, regulatory reforms such as Senator Sanders' proposal to increase the federal minimum wage from $7.25 to $15 per hour by 2020. Twenty-nine states had minimum wages of their own that exceed $7.25 while remaining states either had no minimum wage or had wages that were less than the federal standard. Other regulations include civil rights regulations, voter-rights regulations, and environmental regulations.

A regulatory reform appears, at first glance, to be simpler to enact because it lacks the many "moving parts" of an IUOP that seeks to decrease dropout rates in high schools. Yet regulations have challenges of their own.

As Sanders' proposed regulation illustrates, regulations are often opposed by people with an anti-regulation ethos, such as conservatives who view them as excessive use of government power. Trump alternatively advocated raising the minimum wage only to $10 per hour or not at all during his presidential campaign. He advocated abolishing roughly one-half of all federal regulations. It is true: many regulations have negative externalities. If the minimum wage were raised to $15, for example, some employers would reduce the size of their workforce if they believed their businesses could not afford these additional costs, although economists differ widely in their estimates of the size of this externality. The policy might discourage some entrepreneurs from starting new businesses. It could lead some businesses to migrate to developing nations.

Equality advocates have to use empirical data to determine the size of negative externalities for specific regulations, including the proposed federal $15 minimum wage. They can ask to what extent negative externalities occurred when 29 states exceeded the federal minimum wage of $7.25 in recent years—and what negative externalities might occur when California and New York State raise their minimum wages to $15 in coming years. Equality advocates can also propose ways to remedy some negative externalities. They can offer training, moving expenses, and other benefits to displaced workers. They can offer subsidies to some employers who suffer particular economic harm. They can phase in the $15 wage more slowly for small employers than large ones.

Equality advocates can also contend that benefits to the low-wage workers outweigh some or all negative externalities. Realize, they might say, that the current federal minimum wage of $7.25 places many workers and their families in economic peril. Some of them have to work multiple jobs to meet their families' basic needs. The wage has stayed low because business interests have successfully lobbied the U.S. Congress not to raise the levels to keep up with inflation and productivity growth. According to David Cooper of the Economic Policy Institute, "If we had raised the federal minimum wage at the same pace as productivity growth since 1968 … it would be over $19 an hour today" ("What will Donald Trump Actually Do About the Federal Minimum Wage," attn: accessed at attn.com on 2/25/17). As discussed in Chapter 1, persons in poverty are prone to myriad physical and other problems. Raising the minimum wage would also decrease income inequality, which also has toxic effects on Americans, as illustrated by Figure 1.1.

Equality advocates can identify positive externalities that could flow from an increase in the minimum wage to $15. As the wages of low-wage workers rise, many of them will be catapulted above the eligibility levels of safety-net programs like the Supplemental Nutrition Assistance Program (SNAP), public housing, welfare, and other programs, and reduced benefits from the Earned Income Tax Credit. Senator Sanders estimates these savings could amount to $7.6 billion per year ("Bernie Sanders says minimum wage hike to $15 would reduce federal assistance by $7.6 billion a year," POLITIFACT, accessed at politifact.com on 2/25/17). Higher minimum wages will attract persons who currently are on the sidelines to the workforce, possibly increasing the nation's productivity.

Equality advocates have to identify what public agency will monitor a proposed regulation. They need to discuss the costs of monitoring the regulation, such as the hiring of additional staff. They need to discuss how to educate corporate officials or other entities about a proposed regulation. They need to predict who might seek to evade a proposed regulation and how they might be penalized. In the wake of Hurricane Katrina, for example, many immigrants entered the United States to help remove the debris. They received time-limited work visas from American immigration authorities. Federal work standards, working conditions, and the federal minimum wage applied to them but they were often not enforced by federal or state agencies (Jansson, 2015). Some of them were hardly reimbursed for their work and worked in unsafe settings including exposure to asbestos.

Many regulations protect residents' rights including scores of civil rights regulations. Most recently, conflict has arisen about regulations that protect the voting rights of all citizens. Repeated attempts have been made by some states to infringe on these rights by requiring personal identification at the polls, shortening the hours during which people can vote, and (in effect) creating long lines that discourage some people (often persons of color and senior citizens) from voting. Considerable litigation has taken place over these actions, and courts have declared many unconstitutional.

Place-based IUOPs. Equality advocates can provide "people-based" IUOPs in specific areas that are "distressed," as measured by availability of jobs, incidence of poverty, extent of safe and affordable housing, and whether residents are safe. Many distressed areas exist in the United States, whether in inner-city communities, rural areas, or small towns (Crane & Manville, 2008). Other IUOPs are place-based, such as those that provide economic enterprises with incentives to locate their facilities in distressed areas, training subsidies to companies in these areas, and tax breaks for people and employers who locate themselves in these areas. A mix of people-placed and place-based IUOPs can also be considered.

Place-based IUOPs encounter many challenges, as witnessed by the uneven performance of the Model Cities Program that was enacted during the presidency of Lyndon Johnson. That initiative provided many incentives and directives to coordinate programs of many federal agencies in specific distressed geographic areas. These federal agencies found it difficult to mesh their work. They also had to combat deep economic forces that were difficult to reverse, such as the aversion of many companies to remain in targeted communities despite incentives. Many of those companies chose to migrate to developing nations to cut their labor costs. The work of federal agencies had to be coordinated, as well, with local police, schools, and politicians. If residents don't feel safe, or if they think the police violate their rights, or they believe their neighborhoods lack good schools and medical care, they may be disinclined to remain in the targeted areas. Many relatively affluent persons chose to migrate from these areas despite tax incentives.

Many urban planning experts hoped to revitalize South Central Los Angeles in the wake of riots that occurred in the aftermath of the beating of Rodney

King. Many buildings were destroyed or damaged by riots in this area. Despite investing considerable capital, the economic restoration of the areas has been frustratingly slow.

Some place-based IUOPs have negative externalities, as illustrated by hundreds of urban renewal projects. Rather than helping low-income persons, they have often helped finance housing developments for relatively affluent people, leading to the exodus of low- and moderate-income persons of color.

Yet place-based IUOPs are necessary if distressed areas are to be improved. Programs that seek to move low-income persons to more affluent areas often fail for several reasons. Even with rent subsidies and vouchers, low-income people often cannot afford rents in more affluent areas. Zoning policies in affluent areas often make construction of low-income housing units impossible.

Place-based interventions can target decayed infrastructure in specific areas. Social policies can target low-income populations in those geographic areas. Concentrated efforts can be implemented to cut crime in areas with high crime rates, such as focusing law enforcement on the small group of people who commit homicides. (Recent research suggests that violence in communities causes companies to leave these areas.) Innovative programs can be developed in low income communities, such as developing community land trusts (CLTs) that hold title to land in these areas. The land trusts can then be used for affordable housing and other community projects (Davis & Jacobus, 2008). Many areas with low-income populations have dense social networks that include churches, small businesses, block clubs, and other amenities that can be retained while their infrastructure, schools, and housing are improved (Crane and Manville, 2008).

Garden City, a small town in Kansas, was on the verge of becoming a ghost town as many young people migrated to locations like Topeka and Kansas City, where economic growth was underway. Working with meat processing plants, members of the City Council decided to make their city a hub for this industry. They invited immigrants from many nations to augment the city's labor force over the objections of some White residents. Years later, Garden City has a vibrant economy, a diverse labor force, and a bright future. It is unclear, however, whether this innovation can be replicated in other small towns.

Equality advocates have revitalized some inner-city communities that were (and are) degraded by environmental pollution of toxic waste dumps, water pollution, or air pollution. Researchers at the University of Michigan discovered the toxic waste sites are disproportionately located in low income neighborhoods due to a consistent pattern pf placing hazardous waste facilities in neighborhoods where poor people and people of color live (Erickson,

2016; Massey, 2004). The classic example of pollution in low-income areas inhabited by people of color was Love Canal, whose residents pressured the federal government to subsidize their move to another area. Other examples include Panorama City in Los Angeles, where a coalition of health facilities, neighborhood groups, and public-interest attorneys engaged in an ongoing removal of toxic waste that still continues in 2017. Led by the community-based Environment Health Coalition, an environmental justice effort in San Diego succeeded in reducing pollution from toxic pesticides that caused persons of color in poor neighborhoods to have heightened rates of asthma, as well as vision and skin disorders (Massey, 2004).

Yet many experts believe place-based initiatives can bribe poor people to stay in poor places (Crane and Manville, 2008). They prefer people-based IUOPs that provide physical health, mental health, job training, and other programs that allow people to stay in their communities or migrate from them without losing eligibility to these programs.

In fact, people-based IUOPs, such as enhanced medical and mental health services, can be combined with place-based initiatives that improve housing, shopping, infrastructure, and educational facilities.

Population-based IUOPs. Chapter 1 discussed many populations that experience disproportionate poverty, including racial minority groups, women, and disabled persons. Single IUOPs can be developed that address their specific needs, as well as portfolios of IUOPs that address a number of populations' needs in tandem. In the case of persons of color, for example, increases in eligibility levels for safety-net programs, such as SNAP, can address their economic and nutritional needs; enhanced childcare programs can address their family needs; programs to reduce dropping out of high schools can address their education needs, job training programs can address employment needs, and improved monitoring of civil rights laws, such as with respect to police violence against unarmed persons of color, can address many more needs.

Donald Trump gained the presidency in 2016 partly because millions of White blue-collar workers voted for him. They contended that the Democratic Party, as well as the Republican Party, had abandoned them after thousands of manufacturing plants migrated from the places where they lived for other nations. Many workers were unemployed. A wave of opioid addiction swept through White working-class communities. Rates of suicide soared. Life expectancy shortened. Many of these men (and some of their wives) withdrew from their communities, spending each day watching TV. Yet neither President Trump nor leading Democrats had developed a multi-faceted strategy to address their needs, even well into 2017 (Chen, 2016). It was time for bold action, columnist Ross Douthat, a confessed conservative argued, such as a $2 trillion initiative spread over 5 years, to help roughly 22 million White working-class persons were scattered through the Midwest, Virginia, North and South Carolina, and the deep South (Douthat, 2017). Multiple IUOPs would be needed, he thought, to help this population enter the workforce, including job training, expanded counseling and medical programs for addiction, relocation (for some) from economically depressed areas to cities with more jobs, wage subsidies, large per-child tax credits, and hiring incentives to employers. Douthat contends that "sticks" are needed to complement these "carrots," including possible cuts in disability and unemployment benefits—a more controversial proposal because many low-income persons need these benefits and may not be able to find work. African American and Latino communities, segments of the Asian American community, Native Americans, disabled persons, and other populations with disproportionate levels of poverty, also need portfolios of IUOPs to address their needs.

References

Balfanz, R., Bridgeland, J., Fox, J., DePaoli, J, & Ingram, E. (2014). *Building a grad nation: Progress and challenge in ending the high school dropout epidemic.*

Balfanz, R. & Fox, J. (2011). Early warning systems—foundational research and lessons from the field, *presented at National Governors Association*, Philadelphia. Retrieved from https://nga.org

Balfanz R. (2009).*Putting middle grades students on the graduation path: A policy and practice brief.* Retrieved from https://www.amle.org

Bruce, M. & Bridgeland, J. The mentoring effect: Young people's perspectives on the outcomes and availability of mentoring. *Civic Enterprises with Peter D. Hart Research Associates.* Retrieved from http:/www.mentoring.org/images/uploads/Report_TheMentoringEffect.pdf.

Breslow, J. (2012, September 12). *By the numbers: Dropping out of high school.* Retrieved from http://www.pbs.org

Chen, V.T. (2016, January 16). All hollowed out: The lonely poverty of America's White working class. *The Atlantic,* accessed at htttps:/theatlantic.com/business/archive/2016/11/white-working-claa … /424341/

Crane, R. & Manville M. (2008) People or place? Revisiting the who versus the what of urban development. *Land Lines Magazine* , July, pp. 2–7.

Davis J. (2013, August 2–3) *Educational levels generally make a difference in earnings.* Retrieved from http://www.politifact.com/georgia/statements/2013/aug/02/don-lemon/educational-levels-generally-make-difference-earni/

Davis, J. & Jacobus, R. (2008) *The City-CLT partnership: Municipal support for community land trusts.* Cambridge, MA: Lincoln Institute of Land Policy.

Erickson J. (2016, January 16). *Targeting minority, low-income neighborhoods for hazardous waste sites*. Retrieved from http://ns.umich.edu/new/releases/23414-targeting-minority-low-income-neighborhoods-for-hazardous-waste-sites

Jansson, B. (2015). *The Reluctant Welfare State*. San Francisco: Cengage.

Massey R. *Environmental justice: Income, race, and health; A GDAE teaching module on social and environmental issues in economics*. Retrieved from www.ase.tufts.edu/gdae/education_materials/modules/Environmental_Justice.pdf

Rumberger R.W. (2013, May). Poverty and high school dropouts: The impact of family and community poverty on high school dropouts. *The SES Indicator,* Retrieved from http://www.apa.org/pi/ses/resources/indicator/2013/05/poverty-dropouts.aspx.

8 FINDING RESOURCES TO UPLIFT ORDINARY PEOPLE (RUOPs)

BY BRUCE JANSSON AND ANTHONY ORLANDO

Assume that a policy advocate has developed an extended policy paper and policy brief only to be asked, by a public official, "I like your policy proposal, but how do you expect us to fund it?" This question may be a polite way for a public official to reject a proposal that she or he believes has no merit, yet it often reflects budgetary realities confronted by public officials. They often confront a chronic lack of funds at local, state, and federal levels of government for new programs. This chapter discusses how equality advocates can develop Resources to Uplift Ordinary Persons (RUOPs) to fund specific IUOPs.

RUOPs are specific proposals that equality advocates can develop that they present to government committees that deal with budgets and taxes. They have many of the same features as working papers and policy briefs of IUOPs that I discussed in Chapter 7. Someone seeking to terminate a specific tax deduction, for example, would contend that this deduction serves no useful purpose (the core problem), analyzes why this tax deduction increases income inequality, identifies the size of revenues that could be raised if this deduction were stricken from the tax code, discusses why the deduction serves no ethical purpose, identifies empirical evidence that demonstrates that the deduction does not (for example) increase economic growth, estimates the monetary size of the RUOP that will emerge if this deduction is stricken from the federal tax code, and discusses the IUOP or IUOPs that could be funded by revenues gained if this deduction is stricken from the federal tax code. This RUOP can be attached to a specific IUOP in what I call a "Fair Exchange" where the RUOP funds the IUOP. The equality advocate can develop a working paper that discusses these RUOPs, as well as a two-page policy brief that succinctly explains why the tax deduction should be stricken—documents that can be submitted to policy officials on tax and budget committees of the Congress or their counterparts in local and state jurisdictions. I discuss subsequently how revenues from RUOPs can be stored in an Opportunity Trust Fund if they cannot be used immediately to fund an IUOP because they might otherwise be diverted to the military budget or other programs that do not reduce income inequality.

We propose four kinds of Resources to Uplift Ordinary Persons (RUOPs):

- Changes in the tax code to increase revenues available for IUOPs in the face of specific loopholes, tax expenditures, offshore accounts and other tax provisions that reduce revenues;
- Upward changes in tax rates, particularly for those people in the top economic echelons, such as raising marginal rates on the top 1% above the current 39.6% level for married joint filers who earn more than $466,950. Tax rate increases can also be developed for many other populations;
- Decreasing wasteful spending in the federal budget, particularly in health and military areas, but also in some agricultural subsidies, excessive earmarking of funds for ill-considered infrastructure, and elsewhere;
- Seeking resources in the regular budget process of federal, state, and local governments.

Why Changing Budget Priorities Is Necessary to Increase Equality

Recall Figures 3.2, 3.3, 3.4, 3.5, and 3.6 in Chapter 3, developed in 2001 by Jansson, that portrayed the miniscule levels of social and educational investments in federal budgets from 1945 through 2003. As can be seen in Figure 3.2 in Chapter 3, these investments were a major part of the federal budget only in the New Deal because Roosevelt initiated many work-relief programs. These relatively frugal work-relief programs consumed a considerable part of the federal budget only because it was so small in an era when the United States had scant revenues. It imposed its income tax on only the top 5% of the economic distribution because it funded virtually no military programs. So the relatively small expenditures on work relief programs *appeared* larger than they were because the federal budget was so small compared with contemporary federal budgets.

These figures in Chapter 3 reveal that so-called domestic discretionary spending (DDS) did not fare well in the annual budget battles of the U.S. Congress from 1943 to the present. (Discretionary spending is the part of the federal budget that is determined annually by appropriations and budget committees each year as contrasted with "entitlements" that are funded automatically to the level of claimed benefits each year.) It had to compete with military spending or military discretionary spending throughout the Cold War and to the present as well as interest payments on the national debt. DDS also fared poorly because the United States taxed itself at far smaller levels than many other industrialized nations after World War II to the present. With their higher taxes, these nations were able to spend a larger percentage of their Gross Domestic Product. If the nations of the European Union spent an average of roughly 48% of the GDP from 1987 to the present, the United States spent roughly an average of 36% of its GDP (Jansson, 2015, p. 530). Bear in mind, too, that nations of the European Union (EU) spend far less on military spending than the United States, so these European nations had far more disposable money for domestic spending than the United States. Also bear in mind that American medical spending was almost double the size of medical spending by EU nations, rising almost to 20% of its GDP by 2017 when many EU nations spent roughly half that level of their GDP's (Jansson, 2015, p. 530). The math is simple: the United States only had frugal DDS spending over many decades because it had smaller tax revenues than other nations—and those small tax revenues were depleted more severely by military and medical spending than in EU nations.

Also realize that the complex American budgetary process was, and is a cause of low DDS spending in the United States. Unlike parliamentary systems with only a single legislative chamber with its Prime Minister selected by the majority party, American politicians contend with annual full-court battles between members of the two major parties within each of the two legislative chambers and the incumbent president. American conservatives often cite budget deficits as a reason to slash DDS—often arguing they stem from runaway DDS spending rather than from military spending. So they seek cuts in DDS spending by falsely blaming its meager cost for the deficits rather than *also* blaming military spending or waste in the federal government in military and medical areas (Jansson, 2001).

Advocates of greater DDS spending often lack the political power of advocates of military spending (Jansson, 2002). The Department of Defense (DOD) places military contracts, as well as bases, throughout the nation in the districts of most federal politicians. They often oppose cuts in military spending. The Defense Department and the Joint Chiefs of Staff work together to muster support for military spending. By contrast, DDS funds hundreds of small social programs that often don't work in tandem to preserve DDS or to increase it. Nor can spending on funding interest payments that fund the national debt be easily reduced because it stems from spending deficits mostly created by Ronald Reagan and George W. Bush, as well as deficits caused by dwindling federal revenues during the Great Recession of 2007 through 2009. To make matters worse, Congress could have decided to terminate Bush's huge tax cuts when they were scheduled to expire in 2013, but chose to renew them so that almost all income earners other than families earning more than $400,000 did not return to their higher taxes in 2001 (Jansson, 2015). To make matters even worse, President Trump's tax bill that was enacted in late 2017 will raise the national debt by at least $1 trillion in ten years according to the Congressional Tax Committee.

Partisan gridlock from Ronald Reagan onward has also made it difficult to increase DDS. When the two chambers and the president cannot agree on a budget, "sequestration" takes place where DDS and military spending are frozen at current levels. A sequestration agreement in 2013 during Obama's presidency froze levels of military spending and domestic discretionary spending until 2023 leading to automatic cuts in discretionary spending of $1 trillion over ten years roughly split between domestic discretionary spending and military spending (Jansson, 2015). (President Trump promised in spring 2017 to break the terms of this sequestration by proposing spending increases in military spending of more than $50 billion but it was uncertain in September 2017 that he could achieve sufficient Congressional support for this proposal.)

As politicians squabbled over DDS and military discretionary spending in recent decades, overall entitlement spending eclipsed both kinds of discretionary spending including Social Security, Medicare, Medicaid, the Earned Income Tax Credit, SNAP or food stamps, and Unemployment Insurance. Recall that entitlement programs are *automatically funded to the level of claimed benefits each year.* This means that entitlements get a free pass in the annual budget battles of the Congress. Legislators *can* cut entitlements by revising the statutes that established each of them in the first place. President Trump has considered block-granting Medicaid, for example, which would give each state fixed amounts of money as compared to an entitlement that funds patients' medical costs by reimbursing providers. The fixed funds would likely cost less than existing Medicaid reimbursements of health providers (Pear, 2017).

Entitlement expenditures rose from only 13% of the federal budget in 1964 to roughly 60% in 2017 (Jansson, 2015; Jacobson, 2015). Entitlements have risen this rapidly because they have so many recipients who use their benefits and because they are so popular. Even Ronald Reagan concentrated on cutting DDS while mostly sparing entitlements from cuts (Jansson, 2015).

Equality advocates can mitigate income inequality not only by developing RUOPs, but through regulations. Regulations, such as the federal minimum wage, can be moved upward as was proposed by Senator Bernie Sanders in the 2016 presidential primaries when he sought increases in the federal minimum wage from $7.25 to $15 by 2020. Pensions for senior citizens can be increased by increasing the level of payroll taxes of affluent Americans into the Social Security Trust Fund. Trade treaties can be revised so they decrease the number of manufacturing plants that migrate to other nations. Splitting costs with the states can decrease the cost of some federal programs.

Prospects for enactment of social, housing, job training, and educational programs is not promising in the near term. Donald Trump had promised in his presidential campaign in 2016 to reform taxes to (primarily) increase resources of the middle class, but he enacted tax legislation and favored budget cuts that violated these promises. His tax legislation, signed in late 2017, primarily helped people in the top 1% by slashing their top marginal rate from 39.6% to 37% and by cutting other taxes that disproportionately helped them. These included cutting corporate taxes from 35% to 21% that many experts believed would lead corporations to raise dividends and fund stock buy-backs rather than raising wages or adding new jobs. Exemption of estate taxes was raised from $11 million to $22 million. The so-called carried interest loophole will enable wealthy investment managers to pay taxes on most of their income at lower capital gains rates. They enacted other taxes that helped people with real estate holdings and other business ventures including so-called "pass through" income earned by partnerships that is passed through to its owner and taxed at the individual rates, allowing it to be taxed at 29.6 % as compared to rates as high as 39.6% under existing rates. They allowed affluent Americans who send their children to private schools to establish tax-deferred savings plans currently only available for college. Other tax cuts help liquor businesses, architects and engineers, and tax accountants and lawyers (Drucker & Rappeport, 2017).

The tax legislation repealed the individual mandate in the Affordable Care Act that required younger people to get insurance—a repeal estimated by the CBO to cast 13 million people from health insurance and to raise premiums for millions of other people. The Joint Congressional Committee on Taxation estimated the tax legislation would add $1.5 trillion of the national debt over 10 years which would place downward pressure on social spending.

Respected analysts at the Urban-Brookings Tax Policy Center and the Joint Committee on Taxation view Trump's tax legislation as *increasing* inequality in the nation that already exceeds levels of 20 other industrialized nations. Republican leaders, such as Paul Ryan, vowed to cut Medicare, Medicaid, and Social Security in 2018—programs Trump had vowed not to cut during his campaign.

The tax legislation penalized persons living in states with relatively high income taxes by limiting the extent these taxes could be deducted from their income when computing their federal taxes, including residents of New York, New Jersey, Illinois, and California. This provision could increase income inequality in these states by placing pressure on these states to cut their social and educational expenditures.

The enactment of Trump's tax legislation reflected the power of persons in the top 1%—power that has grown as their resources have increased to control roughly 40% of the nation's resources compared to 27% for the bottom 90%. About 40% of campaign contributions in the 2016 elections came from 24,949 donors or 0.01 percent of the adult population—mostly from conservative persons (Editorial Board of New York Times, December 16, 2017).

The tax legislation gave small tax cuts to ordinary people, such as somewhat lowering their rates and doubling the standard deduction, but only until 2025 when they would be phased out *unlike* corporate tax cuts. The inclusion of a Child Tax Credit helped moderate income persons.

Public opinion polls in late December, 2017 revealed low public support for the Republicans' tax legislation. Only 23% of voters liked it. Roughly two-thirds of voters believed the Trump family benefited from the legislation.

States should become major players in the quest to increase income equality in the United States, but many of them lack sufficient tax revenues to be major players. Revenues of the federal government are roughly double the revenues of all the states put together. Many states levy relatively low taxes. Budgets of red states in the South, Midwest and mountain states deemphasize social and educational investments (Hacker & Pierson, 2016). Even blue states, such as New York and California with relatively high income taxes, struggle to fund social and educational investments, because their budgets are overwhelmingly devoted to prisons, Medicaid expenses, infrastructure, and public education. Some states still lack an income tax, forcing them to rely on sales and property taxes. States raise only 28% of the nation's tax revenues as compared to 61% for the federal government and 11% for local governments (Urban Institute & Brookings Institution, 2015).

A strong case can be made that the United States cannot decisively move toward greater equality unless it (1) greatly increases its tax revenues, (2) greatly decreases its military spending, and (3) greatly cuts the waste of its medical system.

What's needed is a shift in budget and tax priorities to develop more revenues for IUOPs. IUOPs can only be funded in sufficient numbers and at sufficient levels to move the Equality Roller Coaster downward if the federal government increases its revenues by raising taxes and decreases government waste. A *combination* of these Resources to Uplift Ordinary Persons (RUOPs) could provide trillions of dollars to fund meritorious IUOPs.

The federal government must emulate Robin Hood if it seeks dramatic decreases in income inequality. It must take resources from affluent Americans to help fund programs for persons in the bottom 50% of the income distribution. The combined outcomes of the two strategies reduces income inequality more rapidly than either of them alone. Income inequality derives, afterall, from a high ratio of resources of affluent persons to the resources of persons in the lower economic distribution as illustrated in Figure 1.1 when Wilkinson and Pickett (2009) measured the ratio of income of the top 20% to the bottom 20%. It is simple math: if the income of the top 20% is reduced with RUOPs *and* the income of the bottom 20% is increased with IUOPs, the ratio of the top 20% to the bottom 20% is likely to decrease *if* these IUOPs and RUOPs have sufficient monetary magnitude, in tandem, to move the Equality Roller Coaster lower.

Kleinbard (2015, p. xxiv, 364–366) makes an excellent case that the United States should not rely exclusively on tax increases of the most affluent Americans. It should consider raising taxes of working and middle classes, albeit at much lower levels than affluent Americans. It should consider a tax on goods that many other industrialized nations use. He documents that European nations tax these classes at higher levels than the United States yet their relatively non-progressive tax systems are offset by their very progressive fiscal or spending systems that place huge resources in the hands of persons in the lower economic echelon (Kleinbard, 364–366). In other words, they collect far more taxes than the United States, but use these resources to provide amenities to their citizens. He discusses how the paying of taxes by (mostly) everyone increases their sense of ownership of the nation's social and educational programs. He hypothesizes that funding of these many programs makes citizens of many other industrialized nations more happy than Americans (Kleinbard, 2015, pp. 367–368).

Submission of IUOPs to public officials will itself place pressure on them to open space for even more IUOPs. We discuss in the concluding chapter how a social movement is needed not only to develop and fund IUOPs, but also to change taxing and spending priorities of states and the federal government to create RUOPs.

Equality advocates should consider three tactics for developing RUOPs that can fund IUOPs: funding them in the budget process, funding "Fair Exchanges" that couple IUOPs with RUOPs; and funding them by developing an Opportunity Trust Fund that receives money from specific RUOPS until IUOPs are developed that can be funded by them.

Funding IUOPs in the Budget Process

Equality advocates can initiate an IUOP and ask for appropriate funding for it during the budget processes of federal and state governments. This strategy requires the concurrence of legislators, appropriators, and heads of government for each IUOP.

Equality advocates usually fund IUOPs through the regular budget process (Wildavsky, 2003). A single legislative committee approves the IUOP if it falls exclusively in its jurisdiction in each chamber of the federal or state government. These committees have responsibility for human services, education, labor, health, entitlements, and other areas. If the IUOP falls within the jurisdiction of several committees, such as one that has health and education provisions, it must be approved by each of them, with one of them issuing a statute that combines contributions of both of them. Legislative committees usually assign a bill to subcommittees that mark up the proposed legislation rather than let the bill die. They vote whether to send it to the full committee, which can decide to accept their marked-up version or to make changes of its own. The full committee decides whether to approve it or to reject it.

Equality advocates get them approved by legislative committees in state and federal jurisdictions with estimated budgets called *authorizations*. These budgets often identify when the budget must be re-authorized, such as after five years.

If committees in both houses enact the IUOP with the same provisions, it is submitted to the head of government in federal or state governments who make it an official statute if she or he approves it. If it is enacted but with different provisions in the two chambers, it goes to a conference committee and members from each chamber see if they can agree on a final version. If not, the IUOP is defeated.

If a compromise is reached, the legislation is returned to each chamber. It dies if both chambers do not enact it. If both chambers approve it, it is forwarded to the head of government, whether a president or a governor. If the head of government approves it, it becomes a statute. If the head of government vetoes it, the two chambers can override the veto with a required margin of votes, such as two-thirds of each chamber in the federal government.

The statute is then forwarded to appropriation committees charged with deciding how much money to allocate to the enacted statute in each legislative chamber (Wildavsky, 2003). It is assigned to the appropriation subcommittee charged with allocating funds in specific areas, such as education, social services, and health services. The appropriate subcommittee may decide to hew to the authorization level established in the statute or it may decide to authorize it for lower or higher amounts. The full appropriation committee in each chamber decides whether to ratify the decisions of the appropriation subcommittee or can recommend lesser or greater resources. If the appropriation committees of each chamber authorize the legislation for different amounts, a conference committee of appropriators selects the final amount.

Even this cursory overview underscores the challenges faced by equality advocates. They have to deal with at least two legislative committees and their subcommittees; interact with additional committees if their IUOP falls within multiple jurisdictions; follow it to a conference committee if the two chambers do not agree; follow it to the head of state, whether the president or a governor; and then get support from the head of state. At the federal level, presidents can veto statutes, but their vetoes can be overridden if each chamber approves the measure with a two-thirds majority. Lastly, the advocates have to follow the statute through the appropriations process once it is enacted.

Equality advocates need assistance from legislators, committee staff, and lobbyists to select a legislative trajectory that increases the odds that their legislation is enacted and funded in a timely manner and with adequate resources. They need "patron saints" that support the IUOP, monitor its progress, and give helpful tactical advice.

In the best of circumstances, this process takes one or two years. In other cases, it may take many years of "hand-offs" advocacy during which the equality advocates who began the process turn to other equality advocates to monitor its progress and to develop ongoing strategy. That's why equality advocates often need the help of professional lobbyists employed by ongoing advocacy organizations. This process of developing statutes and authorizing them varies across states, requiring that equality advocates get expert consultation in each of them.

The annual budget process presents yet another complexity. Every president and governor follows a budgetary process that establishes overall spending goals for specific years. These goals often include specifying the size of deficits in specific years. When legislators and the head of government want to reduce deficits in a specific year or over the course of many years, they may establish budget rules that freeze spending on specific kinds of programs, such as discretionary programs, for a year or for many years in a process known as "sequestration," which employs automatic, across-the-board spending cuts (or freezing of budgets of programs) to reduce annual budget deficits (Wildavsky, 2003). A budget deal approved by President Obama and the Congress in 2011 that took effect in 2013 required that most discretionary programs, whose funding is determined annually in the budget process, would be frozen at their levels of 2013 through 2023, including both military and domestic discretionary spending. (President Donald Trump wants Congress to waive the limits on military spending in this sequestration so that he can raise its allocation by roughly $70 billion.) These discretionary programs are distinguished from "entitlements" whose funding is automatically determined by the annual levels of claimed benefits in those programs (e.g., Social Security, Medicare, Medicaid, SNAP, the Earned Income Tax Credit).

Each state has its own distinctive budget procedures. In California, for example, the Governor has the power to veto legislation at the end of the year with no recourse given to the legislature to override his decision.

Minimizing Budgetary Attacks on IUOPs

Equality advocates can build into their IUOPs money-saving and money-generating options to demonstrate their frugality and decrease the likelihood that they will be caricatured as "big spending liberals." They can save money by rationing their IUOP to persons most likely to benefit from them, such as persons in the lower 50% or some other fraction of the population with particular needs for additional services, benefits, or opportunities. They can identify specific ways that consumers can share in the expense, such as fees, as long as they do not harm persons who cannot afford them or deter people from using them. They can establish reasonable limits on the services, benefits, and opportunities in their IUOP, such as limits on their duration or amount. They can split costs of some IUOPs between the federal government and states so that neither bears the full cost. They can develop partnerships between public programs and local governments. By demonstrating frugality, they may prevent attacks on their proposals.

Funding IUOPs with Fair Exchanges

Equality advocates can fund an IUOP by attaching an RUOP to it. Take the case of President Obama, who partially funded the ACA by placing tax increases on persons in the top 1% in the legislation. This strategy meant that tax increases that averaged $33,000 per year on these affluent Americans became a major funding source for the ACA (Nitti, 2016). We have already noted that advocates of mental health programs used a similar strategy with respect to Proposition 63 in 2004 in California when they attached revenues from tax hikes on the top 1% to it. Senator Bernie Sanders proposed funding some IUOPs with a financial transactions tax on banks. Democratic contender Hillary Clinton promised to fund free tuition in colleges for students from families with less than $125,000 with tax increases on the top 10% in the Presidential election of 2016. We call this strategy a "Fair Exchange" because it funds the costs of an IUOP with tax revenues from a specific tax loophole, revenues obtained by raising tax rates, and revenue by cutting specific waste. The concept of Fair Exchanges is simple: costs of [IUOP]—revenues of [RUOP]= zero. It reduces inequality because it simultaneously takes from the rich and gives to the poor, copying Robin Hood albeit through a legal strategy rather than thievery.

There is no shortage of RUOPs that can be coupled with IUOPs such as those itemized by think tanks and advocates that include tax *loopholes*, reforms of military procurement policies, closing of corporate tax breaks, closing investors' tax breaks, and ending tax subsidies for fossil fuels (see Table 8.1). Further research is needed to identify negative externalities of each of these proposed reforms, as well as to determine the extent to which they decrease income inequality. Equality advocates can try to undo some of the tax cuts approved by the Congress and President Trump in late 2017 if Democrats win majorities in both chamber and the presidency in 2020.

Many tax breaks fall under the rubric of "tax expenditures" that allow taxpayers to get tax concessions for specific expenditures. Most notable is the mortgage interest deduction where homeowners can write off their mortgage interest against their earned income. This is a huge tax break. Homeowners, who are wealthier on average than renters, will get roughly $75 billion with this write-off per year. Renters, by contrast, cannot deduct their rental fees from their earned income so they do not receive this gift from the government. The Earned Income Tax Credit gives single and married low- and moderate-income persons tax credits if they are employed and meet eligibility requirements.

RUOPs include changes in tax policies to provide more resources to fund IUOPs such as ones in Table 8.1. RUOPs also include cuts in government waste such as excessive numbers of specific kinds of weaponry such as missiles, military aircraft, aircraft carriers, and military bases. It does not include excessive prices for medications and medical devices that are purchased through Medicare and Medicaid. Existing statutes do not allow authorities to bargain with pharmaceutical companies about prices of their products or to encourage consumers of service to purchase medications in other nations such as Canada and Mexico. It does not include the extraordinary cost of using private health insurance companies to manage health plans for roughly 85% of Americans. The CBO predicted the private insurance equivalent of Medicare would cost almost 40% more in 2022 for a typical 65-year old, due to its higher administrative costs, profits, and marketing costs. While administrative costs of Medicare are only about 2% of operating expenditures, administrative costs of private insurance are roughly 17% of their revenues (Archer, 2011). The National Academy for Social Insurance calculated that Medicare spending would have cost an additional $114 billion between 1997 and 2009 had its services been provided by private insurance companies (Ibid). Table 8.1 does not cover many other deductions that benefit affluent people and corporations. They don't have to pay taxes on retirement savings—they only pay taxes on these funds when they receive them as retirement benefits. Corporations don't have to pay taxes on monies they use to fund their employees' health insurance. Oil companies receive lucrative oil depletion allowances that allow them to deduct a large share of the income they receive from oil wells. Investors pay lower tax rates on capital gains (profits) and dividends than on their regular income. Owners of real estate lower their taxes by depreciating it over time. Business expenses can be deducted from business profits. Corporations get tax credits when they purchase equipment. And the list goes on of tax policies that mostly benefit affluent persons.

We need to remember that income taxes are the largest single source of funding of the federal government, far exceeding corporate taxes. Payroll taxes are a close second. Taken together, income taxes and payroll taxes constitute roughly 80% of government revenues. Equality advocates need to focus, then, on corporate and payroll taxes to develop Fair Exchanges or to find revenues to place in the Opportunity Trust Fund that we discuss subsequently.

Remarkable resources could be obtained by raising the top marginal tax rates of affluent Americans as contrasted with Trump's cutting of top marginal rates. Almost $1.4 *trillion* could be obtained by raising some of these rates, as illustrated by Hungerford (2015) in Table 8.1, by reverting to 36% and 39.5% top marginal rates for persons earning between $200,000 and $250,000. Even this tax reform would produce revenues roughly twice the total cost of the Stimulus Program in the Obama Administration that was spread over roughly 4 years—or roughly $750 billion. We should remember that the relatively low top marginal rates enjoyed by the top 5% are a recent invention: Presidents Roosevelt (in the New Deal and in World War II), Truman, Eisenhower, Kennedy, Johnson, Nixon, Ford, and Clinton had top marginal rates for the top 5% that equaled or exceeded 70%. Also realize that the top marginal rates in most of the 20 industrialized nations depicted in Figure 1.1 **far** exceed 40%. Estate taxes are far higher in many industrialized nations than the United States. Many industrialized nations do not fund homeowners' deductions of mortgage interest payments. Many industrialized nations also tax their middle class at considerably higher rates than the United States. Most other industrialized nations possess a "consumption or value-added tax" that is levied at various stages in the production of many consumer items and that produces huge revenues.

Extraordinary tax revenues are obtained from payroll taxes that primarily fund Social Security Medicare Unemployment Insurance. They are relatively regressive taxes because of ceilings that cut levels of taxes paid by affluent people. Were these ceilings to be lifted or eliminated, major resources could be used to fund higher pension levels particularly for low- and moderate-income persons. Or revenues achieved in this way could be used to fund specific IUOPs or placed in the Opportunity Trust Fund to be discussed later.

It is no surprise, then, that many other industrialized nations have more resources for social and educational investments than the United States that the United States does not possess. Simply add the following revenue sources they possess: consumption or value-added tax + higher income taxes on upper class as compared to the U.S. + higher taxes on middle class as compared to the U.S. + savings on military spending as compared to the U.S.

Table 8.1: *A New Equality*: Revenue Options for Fair Exchanges (*Over 10 Years*) Tax Reforms (Citizens for Tax Justice 2014)

• Repeal "deferral" for multinational corporations	759 billion
• Repeal accelerated depreciation	714
• Repeal capital gains break	613
• Limit benefits of deductions and exclusions for high-income	498
• Repeal stock dividends break	231
• Repeal domestic manufacturing deduction	145
• Enact 30% minimum tax for millionaires ("Buffett Rule")	70
• Calculate foreign tax credit on "pooling" basis	59
• Repeal fossil fuels tax subsidies	51
• Bar interest deductions related to untaxed offshore profits	51
• Restrict excess interest used for earnings stripping	41
• Close payroll tax loophole for S corporation owners	25
• Repeal stock options loophole	23
• Prevent corporate "inversions" for tax purposes	19
• Scale back carried interest loophole	17
• Reform like-kind exchange rules	11
• *Limit total savings in tax subsidized retirement plans*	4
TOTAL	**3,331 billion**
Additional Revenue in the "People's Budget" (Hungerford 2015)	
• Revert to 36% and 39.6% rates for those above $250K/$200K; enact Fairness in Taxation Act and Obama tax credits	1,443
• Price carbon at $25 (refunding 25%)	1,242
• Financial transactions tax	921
• Repeal the step-up basis for capital gains at death	352
• Comprehensive immigration reform	241
• Eliminate Highway Fund shortfall with 15 cent fuel charge	206
• Progressive estate tax reform	178
• Excise tax on systemically important financial institutions	112
• Reduce the deductibility of corporate meals and entertainment	70
• Limit deductibility of executive bonus pay	51
• Unemployment Insurance Solvency Act	45
• Increase the excise tax on cigarettes by 50 cents per pack	38
• Curb corporate deductions for stock options	26
• Reinstate superfund taxes	21

Continued

• End direct advertising of certain foods	15
• Deny the home mortgage interest deduction for yachts and vacation homes	14
• *Eliminate corporate jet provisions*	*3*
TOTAL	**4,978 billion**
Cost Savings and Revenue Enhancements (U.S. GAO 2015)	
• Improve process for Medicaid demonstration waivers	42
• Direct procurement spending to strategically sourced contracts	40
• Limit premium subsidy for crop insurance	20
• Consolidate federal data centers	15
• Rescind Advanced Technology Vehicles Manufacturing Loans	4
• *Improve management of federal oil and gas resources*	*2*
TOTAL	**123 billion**
DOD Business Process Improvements (Defense Business Board 2015)	
• Contract spend optimization	92 billion
• Labor optimization (retirement & attrition)	46
• *IT modernization + business process re-engineering*	*12*
TOTAL	**150 billion**
TOTAL REVENUES AVAILABLE FOR FAIR EXCHANGES	**$8.58 trillion**

Sources: Citizens for Tax Justice. (2014). "Addressing the Need for More Federal Revenue," http://ctj.org/ctjreports/2014/07/addressing_the_need_for_more_federal_revenue.php.Defense Business Board. (2015). "Transforming DoD's Core Business Processes for Revolutionary Change," http://dbb.defense.gov/Portals/35/Documents/Meetings/2015/2015–01/CBP%20Task%20Group%20Out-brief%20Slides_FINAL.pdf.

Hungerford, Thomas L. (2015). "The 'People's Budget': Analysis of the Congressional Progressive Caucus Budget for Fiscal Year 2016," Economic Policy Institute Research Center, http://s1.epi.org/files/pdf/81480.pdf.

United States Government Accountability Office. (2015). "Report to Congressional Addresses: Additional Opportunities to Reduce Fragmentation, Overlap, and Duplication and Achieve Other Financial Benefits," http://www.gao.gov/assets/670/669613.pdf

+ savings on health spending as compared to the U.S. + resources obtained by not allowing homeowners to deduct mortgage interest from their income. The cumulative additional income from these various items, which amounts to more than $1 trillion in a relatively short period, provides many other nations with more spendable resources on domestic and social programs than the United States. It is no wonder that many of them spend more on teachers, pensions, unemployment insurance, childcare, vocational training, full scholarships for college and graduate students, educational programs in prisons, retirement homes, safety-net programs, and housing programs than the United States.

Nor is it surprising that many industrialized nations have lower levels of income inequality than the United States as depicted in Figure 1.1 in Chapter 1. They tax affluent persons at higher levels than the United State and invest more heavily in an array of programs that redistribute resources to persons in the lower economic echelons. Thus, it isn't surprising that the industrialized nations listed in Figure 1.1 have lower income inequality than the United States, as measured by the ratio of income of the top 20% to the bottom 20%. Nor are the discrepancies trivial: if the ratio of income of the top 20% to the bottom 20% is roughly 9 for the United States, it is 6 or less in many other industrialized nations. Wilkinson & Pickett (2009) contend that extreme-income inequality in the United States causes it to have a heavier burden of social problems than other industrialized nations, such as incarceration rates, homicides, teen births, adults who have not graduated from high schools, emergency-room healthcare, chronic diseases such as obesity, and rates of juvenile offenders.

Equality advocates confront logistical challenges when constructing Fair Exchanges. They need to obtain approval from legislative committees as well as tax committees. They need to coordinate the Internal Revenue Service with operating programs to be certain that income that comes from cutting tax loopholes and increases in tax rates in an RUOP are correctly targeted to an IUOP.

Equality advocates confront political opposition not just to their IUOPs but also to their RUOPs. Affluent people and special interests will not want to fund IUOPs by and raising their tax rates as with respect to the ACA. Pharmaceutical companies will not want the fund them by cuts in the costs of their products to Medicare.

Creating "Opportunity Trust Funds"

Recall that President Clinton had returned the annual federal budget to surplus after President Ronald Reagan had caused historic budget deficits from the combination of massive tax cuts and large increases in military spending. David Stockman, his budget director, had correctly predicted that Reagan would cause these massive deficits as I discussed in Chapter 3. Fearing that public officials would use these emerging surpluses to cut taxes even further or to fund wasteful programs, Gore proposed developing a "lockbox" that would hold the surplus funds of the budget so they would not be "raided" by other programs until they could be transferred to the Social Security Trust Fund and to Medicare's Trust Fund. Budget surpluses would be placed in this lockbox to protect the solvency of Social Security and Medicare for years to come. This strategy failed when George W. Bush defeated Gore in the presidential election of 2000 and proceeded to replicate Reagan's policies, creating massive deficits due to huge tax cuts and increased military spending. Senate Democrats sought to revive Gore's lockbox in 2011 only to have it succumb, as well, to mounting deficits and debt in the wake of the Great Recession.

Why not create our own "lockbox" called an Opportunity Trust Fund that becomes a repository for revenues generated by RUOPs? It would protect resources obtained by tax reforms, tax-rate increases, and cuts in wasteful spending—resources that could not be raided by public officials for other purposes. A Board of Trustees would approve IUOPs that decrease income inequality. They would submit them to the Congress for approval.

Let's take an example drawn from proposals to revise how homeowners obtain tax deductions for home mortgages developed by staff at the Tax Policy Center (Lu & Toder, 2016). Homeowners currently deduct interest payments from their income, yielding total annual reductions of $77 billion in tax revenues in FY 2016, which will increase to $96 billion in FY 2019. The Tax Policy Center discusses the option of both replacing this deduction over time with a 15% non-refundable credit and imposing a $500,000 cap on eligible debt. These reforms would raise about $241 billion over 10 years. If these reforms were enacted, homeowners with mortgages would still receive tax benefits, but (1) affluent homeowners' benefits would be reduced and (2) the size of lost tax revenues to the Internal Revenue Service would be sufficiently reduced and raise about $241 billion over 10 years. Were these reforms enacted without the Opportunity Trust Fund in place, these $242 billion could be used to cut taxes of affluent Americans, reduce deficits, increase military spending, or improve American airports rather than decreasing income inequality. With the Opportunity Trust Fund, resources could fund a portfolio of IUOPs without raising the nation's taxes or increasing federal deficits and debt, a portfolio hopefully sufficiently large that it would edge the Equality Roller Coaster somewhat lower. Now imagine that revenues from other tax reforms were added to the $241 million, such as raising top marginal tax rates to 45%, lowering the size of estates that are taxable, setting a lower limit on charitable gifts that can be deducted from taxable income, and raising the current ceiling on income that is taxed for Social Security payroll taxes. In light of the sheer size of income inequality in the United States and given the toxic effects of inequality, a good case can be made that tax modifications like these would not place highly affluent people in economic jeopardy, particularly those in the top 1%, the top .5%, and the top .1%. Here, too, enhanced tax revenues produced by one or more of these reforms could be placed in the Opportunity Trust Fund.

Evaluating RUOPs

Potential RUOPs need to be evaluated just like IUOPs. Let's start with RUOPs that are related to the tax code of the federal government. Equality advocates must engage in research to determine whether specific changes in the tax code would reduce income inequality by decreasing resources of persons in the upper economic strata and/or increasing resources of persons in the lower economic strata. Take the example of inheritance taxes that Trump and the Republican Congress restricted *only* to estates exceeding $22 million in their tax legislation in 2017. Assume that we wanted to lower this level to $3 million. We would have to estimate the extent this revision would increase estate taxes. We would need to identify negative externalities that might come from lowering estate taxes, such as the degree it would force owners of small businesses and farms to pay the estate taxes. We would have to identify different levels of estate taxes for persons with estates valued at more than $3 million. We would need to analyze the impact of increases of this tax on people in different economic strata. We would need to analyze what revenues might be produced by specific modifications of this tax. We would need to ask what negative externalities might be produced by different upward revisions of the estate tax, including impacts on work incentives. Some experts contend, for example, that taxes on estates have minimal impact on work decisions prior to death (Gale & Slemrod, 2000). We would need to estimate the extent to which persons would seek to evade upward revisions by gifting relatives and others prior to their deaths or by other tactics. We would also need to evaluate the likely politics of revising inheritance taxes.

We would need to consider normative considerations. Only 0.2% of estates pay any estate taxes because few individuals have estates exceeding $5.49 million. Proponents of relatively high taxes on large estates contend that the needs of the public should trump the needs of heirs. They contend that, absent estate taxes, a large class of "idle rich" might develop that would also exacerbate income inequality. Estate taxes are far higher in many industrialized nations where citizens and public officials prefer conveying large portions of large estates to government. A vigorous debate has taken place in the United States. While President George W. Bush succeeded in passing legislation that phased out the estate tax in 2010 over arguments against this policy by Bill Gates, Sr. and Warren Buffet who favored relatively high taxes on their own estates, it was renewed in 2011 with legislation that developed a 35% tax on estates in excess of $5 million, that was raised to 40% in 2014.

Some tax decisions could lead to outcomes that are difficult to predict. Take the case of placing taxes on imports of American companies that choose to move their operations to developing countries to cut labor costs and evade regulations over work conditions and environmental protections. Its proponents would need to ponder whether this proposal would lead to trade wars with those nations where the companies had relocated. These nations might place tariffs on imports from the United States, possibly leading to loss of jobs in the United States. Tariffs of other nations might also raise the cost of imported products to American consumers that might disproportionately be borne by Americans in the American lower and middle classes. Many other variables would influence whether penalties on imported goods of these companies would induce them to return to the United States, including currency values, cost of labor, and cost of work regulations. Yet penalties for companies that exit the United States, including taxes on products they export to the United States, may deter many of them from leaving the nation in the first place.

Equality advocates also have to evaluate expenditures to see if they deserve the title "wasteful expenditures." Some of them are relatively small expenditures that can easily be evaluated like "the bridge to nowhere" that was eliminated once legislatures realized it would go from the Alaska mainland to an unpopulated island. Others are funded programs that have been evaluated negatively like educational programs in schools that sought to convince high school students that they should be abstinent to avoid venereal disease and teenage pregnancies. Others are excess spending on military weapons that have limited use in the modern world of missiles and submarines, such as aircraft carriers (Jansson, 2001). Others involve institutions with mixed outcomes, such as many for-profit prisons, for-profit detention centers, and for-profit colleges. Still others are institutions, like for-profit health insurance companies, that deliver services at a cost far higher than Medicare.

Equality advocates have to make the case that wasted expenditures do not produce positive outcomes commensurate with their cost. They have to develop alternative programs or institutions that are less expensive. Even more difficult, they have to persuade public officials to substitute these alternative programs or institutions for the existing ones even as adherents of these wasteful programs and institutions often powerfully defend them.

Not Sugarcoating the Challenges of Obtaining Funds For IUOPs

We can't sugarcoat the challenges of getting funds for an IUOP in light of these funding challenges. No magic bullets exist. Zillions of IUOPs are proposed but go nowhere because their advocates cannot get public officials to fund them. Sometimes IUOPs become phantom programs because legislative committees approve them but they receive little or no funds from appropriation committees.

We suggest that equality advocates go into their work with full understanding of funding challenges they will likely confront. Sometimes they will succeed in enacting and funding IUOPs as many successes suggest. When they get an IUOP enacted but with no or inadequate funding, they (at least) place pressure on government funding systems to find new revenues. If no one attempts to fund meritorious IUOPs despite these many barriers, then no one questions the insufficiency of public resources.

This chapter is just as important to equality advocates' work as the preceding chapters. Chapters 2 and 3 provided proof that public servants often found their hands tied by the chronic shortage of resources in a nation where tax revenues are far more Spartan than most of the 20 other industrialized nations depicted in Figure 1.1.

Data in this chapter support the thesis that inadequate revenues, as well as wasteful spending in military, medical, and other areas, are the major cause of extreme income inequality in the United States. Minus higher taxes and minus cuts in waste, the United States remains on a trajectory that greatly degrades the lives of tens of millions of Americans who barely scrape by and who have low odds of achieving upward mobility. As Kleinbard (2015) says in the title of his book, *We are Better than This*.

References

Archer, D. & Marmor, T. (2012: February 15). Medicare and commercial health insurance: The fundamental difference. [Health Affairs Blog]. Retrieved from healthaffairs.org. on September 25, 2017.

Drucker, J & Rappeport, A. (2017: December 16). The tax bill's winners and losers. *New York Times*.

Editorial Board of the New York Times, "The tax bill that inequality created," *New York Times*, December 16, 2017.

Gale, W.G. & Slemrod, J. (2000). Resurrecting the estate tax. Brookings Policy Brief Series, Policy Brief, No. 62. Retrieved from https://www.brookings.edu.

Hacker, J.S. & Pierson, P. (2016, July 30). The path to prosperity is blue. *New York Times*, https://www.nytimes.com .

Jacobson, L. (2015; August 17). Chart of 'federal spending' circulating on the Internet is misleading. Politifact accessed at politifact.com on September 24, 2017.

Jansson, B. (2002). Empowering domestic discretionary spending in federal budget deliberations. *Social Policy Journal*. Vol. 1, pp. 5–18.

Jansson, B. (2015). *The reluctant welfare state*. Boston: Cengage.

Jansson, B. (2001). *The sixteen-trillion-dollar mistake: How the U.S. bungled its national priorities from the New Deal to the present*. New York: Columbia University Press.

Kane, J. (2012; October 22). Health costs: How the U.S. compares with other countries. PBS Newshour. Retrieved from Leonhardt, D (2017 September 11), 5 questions about single-payer health care. *New York Times*.

Kleinbard, E. D. (2015). *We are better than this: How government should spend our money*. Oxford University Press.

Lu, C. & Toder, E. (2016, December 6) Effects of reforms of the home mortgage interest deduction by income group and by state. Retrieved from http://www.taxpolicycenter.org. @ www,taxpolicycenter,org/ … /options-reforms-home-mortgage-interest-deduction-inco on September 25, 201

Nitti, T. (2016; December 15). Obamacare repeal results in tax cuts for the rich, *Forbes*. Retrieved from https://www.forbes.com/sites/anthonynitti/2016/12/15/obamacare-repeal-results-in-tax-cuts-for-the-rich-tax-increases-and-lost-insurance-for-the-rest/#77dff0b74cdf

Pear, R. (2017; January 22). Trump's health plan would convert Medicaid to block grants, aide says. *New York Times*. Accessed at https://mobile.nytimes.com/2017/01/22/us/politics/donald-trump-health-plan/

Wildavsky, A. (2003). *The new politics of the budgetary process, Revised Edition*. Boston, Mass: Pearson.

Wilkinson R.G. & Pickett, K.E. (2009). Income inequality and social dysfunction. *Annual Review of Sociology, 35* 493–511.

9

MOVING TOWARD GREATER INCOME EQUALITY IN THE POLITICAL ARENA

I discussed in chapters 2 and 3 how the United States has swung between periods of income equality and income inequality during its history. I identified the following 4 periods in these chapters:

- Period 1: Relative equality in the colonial period from roughly 1751 to 1825
- Period 2: Relative inequality from roughly 1866 to 1930
- Period 3: Relative equality from roughly 1933 to 1980
- Period 4: Relative inequality from roughly 1981 to (at least) 2017

I discussed in chapter 4 periods of transition that preceded each of these four periods might shed light on why the Equality Roller Coaster moved upward and downward including 1730 to 1776 (preceding and in the early phase of Period 1), 1825 to 1865 (preceding Period 2), the 1920s (preceding Period 3), and the 1970s (preceding Period 4). I wondered if commonalities existed in these periods of transition, while recognizing the complex and multi-faceted nature of historical developments.

I now briefly describe the transition to the last period of relative equality from 1933 through the 1970s—the 1920s and early 1930s. I then ask whether events in the 1920s and early *1930s could* suggest the possibility of a new period of income equality that *might* emerge in the wake of the presidential election of 2020 *if* a new period of equality *did* emerge. I place the three words in italics because we can't predict the future with precision with respect to elections.

Period of Transition Before the Last Equality Era.

The 1920s *appears* to have reverted to the Gilded Age in its politics as compared to the so-called Progressive Era from roughly 1900 to 1917. Conservative presidents including presidents Warren Harding, Calvin Coolidge, and Herbert Hoover, ruled it. Harding summarized their mindsets: "What we want in America is less government in business and more business in government" (Jansson, 2015). It was marked by extreme income inequality with highly affluent Americans at the top of the economic distribution as compared with very poor first and second-generation immigrants and their descendants. The nation had virtually no welfare state even as many residents were impoverished. These presidents subscribed to a trickle-down economic approach at a time when tens of millions of Americans were impoverished even *before* the Great Depression began in 1929. These presidents reduced federal taxes to one-quarter of the taxes that sought to pay off debt from World War I and relaxed or did not enforce many regulations enacted in the Progressive Era. In other words, the nation was unprepared for the Great Depression. This saga describes a tinder box ready to burn if the nation had an economic downturn—and the Great Depression was the worst economic conflagration in American history even to the present. President Herbert Hoover's small policy initiatives were no match for the economic hurricane that had struck the nation. The nation also lacked banking institutions that could survive a catastrophic economic downturn. The federal government did not insure them. The federal government poorly regulated them. Many affluent persons had speculative investments. Politicians in the federal government were out of touch with these dangers. Neither major political party was attuned to these risks. Conditions were ripe, then, for a sharp downward movement of the Equality Roller Coaster if a sustained economic downturn took place—and if voters decided to elect a relatively progressive president. Franklin Roosevelt's landslide victory over Herbert Hoover in 1932 when coupled with the ongoing Great Depression initiated a period of relative income equality that would last through the 1970s.

Could the U.S. Be In Another Transition to a Period of Equality?

The 1920s had *some* of the attributes of the contemporary period. Its extreme income inequality was roughly similar to contemporary extreme income inequality as measured by economists (Piketty, 2014; Saez, 2013) If Americans were disenchanted with their relatively ineffective presidents of the 1920s, contemporary polls show widespread dissatisfaction with the Congress and President Trump with 66% of Americans strongly or somewhat disapproving of the Congress and with 55% of Americans strongly or somewhat disapproving of the president (Bedard, 2017, June 18). The president and the Congress were unable to enact any of Trump's campaign promises by September 2017. They could not agree on a replacement for the ACA after months of trying. Trump could not obtain a ban on immigrants due to adverse court rulings. Congress could not agree to build a wall on the Southern border of the United States. Trump's decision to withdraw from the Paris Climate Accord was relatively unpopular among voters with 46% somewhat or strongly opposing it and 29% supporting withdrawal (Delk, 2017).

President Trump finally secured his first major legislative victory with Congressional approval of this tax policies on December 20, 2017. While it contained some redistributive measures, such as a refundable child tax credit, it was widely seen by citizens as favoring affluent people and corporations as reflected in polls. A considerable majority of the population believed the president and his family had greatly benefited from the tax package. Nancy Pelosi, the Democratic Minority Leader in the House, contended that 86% of the tax bill's benefits would benefit the top 1%.

Moreover, polls showed that the president's popularity was lower than any modern president at this point of his presidency with approval ratings ranging between 30% and 35% in them. Other polls indicated that 56% of voters said they would vote for Democratic candidates in the Congressional races of 2018. Democrats had achieved striking victories in November and December, moreover, in New Jersey, Virginia, and Alabama.

Taken together, these events and polls suggested Democrats *might* control the presidency and both houses of Congress by 2020.

Were these events to happen, the issue of extreme income inequality *might* be positioned to take center stage in the legislative priorities of the federal government. While Republicans and the president achieved a noteworthy victory with enactment of their tax legislation, the tax legislation brought economic inequality to the fore in the nation. Only 33% of the public approved the tax legislation primarily because they viewed it as unfairly favoring affluent people and corporations. It is likely that the Congressional elections of 2018 and the presidential and Congressional elections of 2020 would be referendums on the tax legislation.

We should remember, too, that President Trump was the most divisive president possibly in the nation's history. While he attacked members of his own party and his cabinet, his vitriol and slights were often directed at members of marginalized populations, whether persons of color, women, disabled people, immigrants, Native Americans, and others. Moreover, he repeatedly supported measures that harmed his base of support, blue-collar Whites in rural and semi-rural areas, including attempts to repeal and replace Obamacare, cut Medicaid, and cut the Supplemental Nutritional Assistance Program (SNAP). All of these programs are widely used by White blue-collar people.

When Trump supported Republican Roy Moore for the race for the Senate seat in Alabama in November 2017, he chose a candidate that had opposed civil rights and was charged with pedophilia by many women. Democrat Doug Jones defeated Moore by a narrow margin that he obtained only because of the remarkable turnout of tens of thousands of African Americans across Alabama's so-called "black belt." If this mobilization of African Americans continued into 2018 and 2020 and was replicated by women, Latinos, millennial persons, and members of other marginalized populations, the chances for a Democratic sweep in 2020 will markedly increase.

If we step back and place events of the first year of the Trump presidency in a broader perspective, we see that issues of inequality and marginalized populations came into public consciousness long before Trump took office. Recall that the Great Recession of 2007 to 2009 was widely discussed as the worst economic downturn since the Great Depression. It spawned radical movements such as the Occupy Wall Street Movement. It gave African Americans an unprecedented representation in the federal government with the election and two terms of the presidency of Barack Obama.

Many people on the liberal side of the equation were lulled into complacency during the presidential campaign of 2016 when most pundits—and both Hillary Clinton and Donald Trump—were convinced Clinton would win up to the eve of the presidential election. It became apparent in the year after they had digested the surprise victory of Trump, many Democrats and Independents came to see that they would have to become energized if they wanted to avoid even further legislative set-backs and repeals of regulations that they had witnessed in the first year of Trump's presidency.

Other events in the lead-up to Congressional and presidential elections in 2018 and 2020 suggested that issues related to extreme income equality might surface during these elections. Recall that almost no discussion took place in the Congress or presidency about poverty, lack of upward mobility, and other causes of extreme income inequality from the mid 1970s to 2016. Presidents Ford, Carter, Reagan, George H.W. Bush, Bill Clinton, and George W. Bush did not discuss these issues much or at all. Even Barack Obama acknowledged that he had not addressed these issues very much during his presidency, even lamenting his failure to introduce an infrastructure bill during the Great Recession. French economist Thomas Piketty startled intellectuals with his book on income inequality in the United States in 2014 as I discussed in Chapter 3. Then Bernie Sanders made it the centerpiece of his presidential campaign in 2016. Then Congressional Democrats, including Sanders, brought the issue before the nation in their televised debates with leading Republicans during the first year of Trump's presidency.

Unlike the 1920s, then, when a single event—the onset of the Great Depression—catalyzed the election of Franklin Roosevelt and Democratic candidates for the Congress—a series of events radicalized marginalized groups and liberals. They knew they had to re-take the House in 2018 and re-take the Senate and Presidency in 2020 or they would face a nation with even greater income inequality that had existed for decades prior to the election of Trump. They learned during the first year of Trump's presidency that they had to use marches by women, immigrants, supporters of climate control measures, African Americans, and others to redress regressive policies by Congressional Republicans and the president. They helped prevent the repeal of Obamacare by attending and disrupting Town Hall Meetings of Republican legislators.

Like the 1920s, huge numbers of the population were in dire economic straits, including virtually everyone in the bottom 50%. Poverty spread across all of the 16 populations we discussed in Chapter 1. While the economy improved greatly in the wake of the Great Recession of 2007 to 2009, wages continued to stagnate as during the prior three decades.

Republicans hoped in the aftermath of enactment of Trump's tax measures that economic angst among persons in the middle class would dissipate as they observed augmentation of their income stemming from Trump's tax legislation as early as February 2018 when the Internal Revenue Service would change their withholding rates as they moved into lower tax brackets. This augmentation, many experts believed, would be modest at best, ranging from $700 to several thousand dollars for most middle class persons. Persons receiving benefits from the Child Tax Credit would likely receive the highest benefits. Were they to view their tax reductions in the context of tax concessions of affluent people, however, they might view the tax benefits as paltry—many of whom will receive tax benefits into the millions of dollars after receiving benefits from stock buybacks, dividends, and benefits accruing from deductions and write-offs linked to real estate and business enterprises—not to mention reduction of the top marginal tax from 39.6% to 37% and the near-termination of inheritance taxes.

Trump also accentuated the economic divide between affluent Americans and persons in the lower economic echelons by recruiting billionaires and multi-millionaires for his cabinet. By not placing his businesses in a Trust headed by a non-family member or by selling his businesses, he publicized his wealth, as well as charges that he sought to enrich himself yet further by his presidential policies and actions.

Trump's popularity descended, as well, due to the corrosive effects of multiple investigations by House and Senate Committees, as well as the Directors of the Federal Bureau of Investigation including James Comey (who he fired) and Robert Mueller. These investigations examined whether the president, his aides, and his family members had engaged in obstruction of justice, collusion with the Russians when they meddled in the presidential election, and violation of the emoluments clause of the U.S. Constitution that forbids presidents from obtaining funds from heads of other nations.

These policy failures of Trump were partly due to his own actions and partly due to a deeply divided Republican Party. Trump repeatedly stepped on his message in his first nine months in office by diverting attention from his policies with Tweets and extemporaneous statements on other subjects. He engaged in disputes seemingly unrelated to his policy agenda, such as arguing that players in the National Football League should not kneel during the national anthem despite their first amendment rights to free speech. He could not keep order among his staff, who often leaked information to the press, were fired, or resigned from the White House. His Republican Party was deeply divided between hard-right persons and moderate persons—divisions so deep that Trump could not obtain sufficient votes to enact the repeal and replacement of Obamacare (Jansson, 2018, in press).

I hypothesize, then, that Trump and the Republican Congress are creating conditions that *might* lead to a Democratic president and Congress by 2020. Just like the late 1920s and early 1930s, the nation has presidents and Congresses that are out of touch with the nation. Just like the 1920s, the nation has millions of residents that are impoverished. Following the lead of many of its current leaders, the Democrats might launch a series of policies that would redistribute resources to persons in the lower economic strata if they regain the presidency and the Congress. They might replicate Roosevelt's New Deal. They might seek to increase taxes of affluent Americans and others to fund these programs. While this scenario might not take place in 2021 or even in ensuing years, parallels between the current period and the late 1920s and early 1930s do exist.

Inadvertently Building Support for Greater Equality.

Trump made clear from his campaign's outset that he wanted to address the pressing needs of White Americans, particularly blue-collar persons scattered across the nation. Many of them lived in or near poverty. Many of them had chronic health problems like diabetes. Many of them were chronically unemployed in small cities where manufacturing firms had departed for other nations. Many of them had alcohol and opioid addictions.

To his credit, he proposed an array of policies to help them. He proposed revising trade treaties like the North American Free Trade Agreement (NAFTA), as well as bilateral trade agreements with Japan, China, and other nations. He proposed large infrastructure projects to provide them with jobs. He proposed retaining Social Security, Medicare, and Medicaid in their existing form (Jansson, 2018).

His fixation on a single group—one with serious problems—hardly speaks to the needs of fifteen other vulnerable populations that I discussed in Chapter 1. He seemed to be implementing affirmative action in reverse. If Whites were asked to leave jobs to give preference to women and persons of color under affirmative action, Trump appeared to favor White persons *only*. He stated on a number of occasions during his campaign that African Americans had many of the same problems as White blue-collar Americans, but was unable to articulate reforms he might consider in their communities (Jansson, 2018).

Trump was unable to champion reforms that extended beyond White Americans to the broader population of persons in the lower economic distribution because he engaged in culture wars through his presidential campaigns and his first nine months in office. He *divided* the nation rather than uniting it. He knew that considerable numbers of White blue-collar persons blamed other vulnerable persons for their plight, whether because they believed immigrants took their jobs or because persons of color received preferential treatment from employers. Many of his attacks on other vulnerable populations stemmed from his own prejudices that were deeply ingrained in him whether it was animus against a Latino judge, arguments that immigrants from Mexico often rape and kill White people, and disparaging comments about women. He attacked *black* professional football players for kneeling during the National Anthem while comparing them unfavorably to *white* professional race-car drivers who did not engage in this behavior—while forgetting that the black football players' actions stemmed from their belief that they experienced discrimination from white police officers rather than from dislike of the American flag (Jansson, 2018). By engaging in culture wars, which many of his White base liked, Trump risked becoming irrelevant to the needs of other vulnerable populations.

Trump seemed unaware of startling findings of economists that the United States had transformed itself from a period of relative income equality in the 1970s to a nation of extreme income inequality in 2017 (Ashkenaz, 2016). Nor was he aware of deep and legitimate discontents of members of vulnerable populations that disproportionately lived in the bottom 50% of the economic distribution. He did not seem to know that five research studies demonstrated that the United States had lower levels of upward mobility than many European nations and Canada.

The Great Betrayal?

Trump *seemed* committed to helping blue-collar Whites at his many campaign rallies as he roared out to them how he would achieve so many victories for them that they would grow tired of hearing about them. Yet proof is in the pudding. When examining his work product in the first nine months of his presidency, the evidence is overwhelming that he did not seek to better their condition (Jansson, 2018). He heartily approved a House version of the replacement of Obamacare that proposed to take away medical insurance for 23 million Americans—many in the White blue-collar population. He agreed to deep cuts in SNAP (food stamps) during an early draft of his budget—a program that was widely used by the White blue-collar population. He agreed to deep cuts in Medicaid that was the major source of medical care for opioid poisoning that killed 50,000 people in 2016 in the House replacement of Obamacare—many from the White blue-collar population (Jansson, 2018). He claimed to have brought many jobs to the United States when many of them had already been in the works by American corporations (McCaskill, 2017). He knew that coal production was waning due to competition with cheaper forms of energy like natural gas, but acted as if he could revive it by rescinding anti-pollution regulations that had been put in place by President Obama. As I discuss subsequently, he supported deep cuts in tax revenues in late September, 2017 that would dry up revenues needed to fund initiatives to help his base.

Why didn't Trump fulfill his promises to his base of support? Trump had long had an uneasy relationship with the truth as evidenced by hundreds of lies that he told during his campaign and the first nine months of his presidency—1,000 lies identified by the *Washington Post* (Kelly, Kestler & Lee, 2017). We can rightly ask whether Trump is a con man that traffics in false information and hyperbole—in this case to his base of support. Trump may have seen his White blue-collar base primarily as a ticket to the White House if he could get them to vote in record numbers in states that possess high number of electoral votes, like Ohio, Pennsylvania, and Michigan. He may have sensed their vulnerability because they so desperately wanted an advocate after leaders of both political parties had shunned them for decades. They liked his in-your-face style of interacting with others (Vance, 2016). Some of them liked his attacks on members of other vulnerable populations.

Trump doomed his chances to help White blue-collar persons, by refusing to work across the aisle with Democrats during his first twelve months in office. He soon learned that the powerful conservative wing of the Republican Party—descendants of the far-right Tea Party—would not tolerate social reforms. They sabotaged his effort to repeal and replace Obamacare by insisting on draconian cuts in insurance among ACA beneficiaries (Jansson, 2018, in press). Had Trump *really* cared about blue-collar Whites, he would have worked across the aisle to obtain support from Democrats to develop social programs that would increase medical care, food, and drug treatments for White blue-collar persons.

Launching a True Campaign for Greater Income Equality

Identifying Evidence-Based IUOPs. Equality advocates need to initiate a major campaign to place income inequality on the agendas of public officials at local, state, and federal levels. They need to put forward Initiatives to Uplift Ordinary People (IUOPs) such as some of the ones discussed in Chapters 5 and 6—or other ones. They need to identify possible sources of revenues by developing Resources to Uplift Ordinary Persons (RUOPs).

Identifying Possible Causes of Income Inequality. IUOPs can address our hypothesized causes of income inequality that are identified in Chapters 1 through 6 such as poverty, lack of upward mobility, lack of hope by members of at-risk populations, discrimination, and inadequate funding of social and educational investments. Income inequality marginalizes people in the lower economic strata. They live in a nation where roughly 45 million people live in extensive poverty, and individuals in the bottom 50% earn an average pretax income of roughly $16,000, (or just over $20,000 when safety net and other social benefits are counted). Poverty is the flip side of extreme economic inequality because it juxtaposes roughly 45 million people in the bottom 50% who own 13% of the nation's income, as compared to the top 1% that owns 20 % of the nation's wealth (Ashkenas, 2016). Lack of upward mobility has created a stratified society that decreases the odds that persons in the lower economic strata can move higher. Many people in at-risk populations encounter discrimination despite the enactment of many civil rights laws during the past 50-plus years. The nation spends a far smaller percentage of its national income on social and educational investments than most other industrialized nations as I discussed in Chapter 8. These possible causes of income inequality interact with one another. As persons in poverty don't have opportunities to climb up the economic ladder, the negative impacts of extreme economic inequality increase and cause further harm to low-income people. I hypothesize that African American males subjected to police discrimination are less able to focus on moving up the economic ladder than ones who do not bear this burden.

Resist Efforts to Deplete Tax Revenues—and Enact Resources to Uplift Ordinary People (RUOPs). Presidents Reagan and George W. Bush invented a strategy for depleting resources necessary to fund a robust set of social programs—albeit with considerable support from some Democrats (Jansson, 2001, 2015). They secured huge tax cuts from the Congress that disproportionately helped affluent Americans even as they also cut taxes of Americans in lower economic echelons. They greatly increased military spending—indeed, Reagan's military increases were roughly the size of expenditures for the Vietnam War at a time when the nation was *not* at war (Jansson, 2001). This one-two punch produced massive deficits—deficits that led many Congressional leaders to demand spending cuts. These tactics taken together were highly effective. Reagan and Republicans mostly rejected requests for new spending in social programs due to deficits. Some moderate Democrats also voted for large tax cuts, such as for George W. Bush's $1.35 trillion cut in 2001 (Barnes, Baumann & Cohen, 2001).

I return to the argument in Chapter 8: equality advocates need to place as much emphasis on developed RUOPs as developing IUOPs. The lack of tax revenues is a leading cause of extreme income inequality because it impedes social, educational, and other investments that uplift ordinary people.

Equality advocates need to persuade affluent persons to "Share the Wealth," a slogan developing in the 1930s by followers of Senator Huey Long of Louisiana. They benefit from the nation's infrastructure, financial system, educational institutions, and law enforcement—not to mention the nation's commercial system and foreign trade. We need to talk to them and seek their involvement, while not being reticent about increasing their taxes. We need to encourage them to follow the generous tradition established by wealthy people who want and do share their wealth such as Warren Buffet and Bill Gates.

Opening Up the Political System to Equality Advocates

One route to greater equality is through partisan politics because Democrats usually held the presidency and one or both chambers of Congress during Period 3 of relative equality from 1933 to 1981—whereas Republicans had similar levels of power during Period 4 of relative inequality from the early 1980s to the present. Yet two provisos exist. A relatively small group of moderate Republicans exists and sometimes opposes conservative Republicans as illustrated by their role in opposing the repealing and replacing of the ACA in 2017. Moreover, a large group of relatively moderate Democrats, including Hillary Clinton and Barack Obama, were reluctant to use the word "poverty" in recent years. (Obama labeled economic inequality as one of the nation's four top problems, however, in his final speech as president (Transcript of Obama's Farewell Speech, 2017). Equality advocates will need, then, to stitch together coalitions of moderate and ultra-liberal Democrats with moderate Republicans to get key measures enacted. Their odds of success will increase when they obtain significant Democratic majorities in both chambers and the Presidency as took place in the New Deal of the 1930s and the Great Society of the 1960s—or majorities in both chambers of the Congress and a Republican president as occurred during President Nixon's first term. Equality advocates will also need grassroots support from "ordinary people" who demand IUOPs and RUOPs before, during, and after elections. They need to join forces with Reverend William Barber's populist interracial coalition against poverty (Cobb, 2018) and other efforts to cut across the 16 marginalized populations discussed in Chapter 1.

Equality advocates need to consider how to describe their work with different audiences. The words, "increasing income equality" may resonate with relatively liberal persons, but may appear radical to moderate voters who may equate it with socialism. Words used in this book may demystify this complex topic with persons not familiar with economics, including Initiatives to Uplift Ordinary Persons (IUOPs), Resources to Uplift Ordinary Persons (RUOPs), Fair Exchanges, and the Equality Roller Coaster. We may need, too, to identify portfolios of IUOPs, RUOPs, and Fair Exchanges that might, in tandem, move the Equality Roller Coaster lower. The use of the term, Opportunity Trust Fund, to describe an entity that can contain surplus revenues and budget allocations that can later be used to fund IUOPs, will appeal to Americans who favor upward mobility in a nation whose rate of upward mobility has been eclipsed by most industrialized nations (see Chapter 8 for a discussion of it). It may also be useful to use the term, Share the Wealth, to persuade some voters and legislators to increase taxes on persons in the upper economic echelons and to celebrate those wealthy people who agree that they have an ethical obligation to pay higher taxes like Warren Buffett.

Looking Forward: Not Backward

Equality advocates should push back at Trump's signature slogan, "Make America Great Again" and replace it with "Make America Greater." It is true: the Equality Roller Coaster was at a much lower level in Period 3 from 1933 to the late 1970s. It is also true that the United States enacted myriad social policies in the New Deal, the Great Society, and the Nixon Presidency that greatly improved the United States. I suspect, however, that Trump did not view Period 3 as the golden era of the United States, but rather chose the Gilded Age as its golden era like Ronald Reagan. Reagan believed that the Gilded Age was the zenith of American economic growth. He liked its near absence of social policies. He liked the weakness of the federal government (Canon, 1982). He was unaware—or chose to ignore—the grinding poverty of millions of immigrants who were the laborers in the emerging industrial system. He ignored widespread lynching of African Americans in this era. And the list goes on as I discuss in Chapter 2.

Equality advocates realize that Period 2 should not be glorified. Nor should Period 3 from 1933 through the 1970s be glorified despite its relative equality. Even with enactment of civil rights laws, discrimination persisted against persons of color, the LGBT population, women, and many other vulnerable populations. Much of the federal budget was devoted to military spending—and relatively little federal funds were devoted to social and educational investments as Figures 3.3 through 3.5 illustrate in Chapter 3 (Jansson, 2001). Indeed, federal social and educational investments by the federal government were so low in the 1960s that the War on Poverty and many other domestic programs were severely underfunded (Jansson, 2001).

Equality advocates should look forward by rallying behind the slogan, "Make America Greater." The United States has extraordinary income and wealth, if only it taps it at higher levels to fund a domestic agenda on a par with other industrialized nations. It has technological and scientific expertise to "Make America Greater." It can use its great diversity to its own advantage by tapping its talents and perspectives. It has a relatively youthful population as compared to most European and Asian nations that can fuel its economy, partly because it has millions of hard-working and youthful immigrants from around the world.

Equality advocates can help develop these potentials by moving the Equality Coaster downward to lessen the toxic effects of extreme income inequality that residents of the United States endure. It can move it downward by addressing the ten hypothesized causes of extreme income inequality.

Political support for IUOPs and RUOPs may be enhanced if equality advocates identify specific vulnerable populations that can help to lower economic echelons of the American economy. Why not ground the quest for greater equality by improving the lives of (at least) the 16 vulnerable populations identified in Chapter 1?

Making Connections Between Periods 3 and 4

It seems not possible that the United States is at a level of inequality that is virtually identical to the so-called Gilded Age of the decades following the American Civil War—even *after* the nation developed many social and economic programs during the New Deal, the Great Society, and the Nixon presidency. I've often thought back to Jane Addams, one of the founders of the profession of social work during the Gilded Age and its immediate aftermath, as, I worked on this book. I wondered what she might think were she alive. She became an advocate for African Americans, women, immigrants, and youth in the wake of the Gilded Age of the late 19th century, when the United States had virtually no social programs other than harsh poorhouses and a sprinkling of institutions for mentally ill people, abandoned children, and deaf and blind people. She surmounted the many prejudices of her era, including scientists who contended that the brains of persons of color were smaller than the brains of Caucasians, that rich people had risen to their station due to selective advantages from evolution, that Native Americans could be made whole only by purging them of their native languages and customs in segregated boarding schools, and that women could not engage in many professions due to their emotions and hysteria. She even championed African Americans as gentle and caring people who might mitigate the greed and prejudices of the United States.

Were she alive today, she would see the same level of economic inequality that she observed in her era. She would see the same poverty among millions of contemporary immigrants that she saw among the millions of immigrants of her era. She would see the same impulse to close the nation's borders that existed in the early 20th century, which led to enactment of an exclusionary immigration law in 1924 that favored Northern Europeans over other groups.

She would be impressed by the current American welfare state that has a myriad of social programs that did not exist in her era. She would likely have been amazed, however, that they attract such hostility, mostly from White and conservative directions. She might have thought that these opponents of social programs might have reconsidered their opposition had they seen the paucity of social programs in her era, including people in breadlines outside police stations, poor people required to enter poorhouses to meet their survival needs, and persons warehoused in mental institutions.

The challenge of our times is to retain the spirit of Jane Addams. We now have a welfare state, but a poorly funded one with many gaps and omissions. We now have a federal system of taxation, but one filled with inequities. We now have economic inequality that rivals her era. We still possess many of the problems she saw, but we now live in an affluent nation that has the capability to do much better.

After a slow and arduous trip through time, the United States has become a more civil place with the advent of the New Deal, the Great Society, and social programs enacted during Richard Nixon's presidency. The nation finally has a major welfare state, albeit one with many flaws.

The nation engaged, however, in a downward trajectory of mind boggling speed from 1974 to the present, as the top 1% and the bottom 50% changed positions in the U.S. economy. Whereas the top 1% owned 11% of the nation's income in 1974, it now owns 20% of its income. While the bottom 50% owned 21% of the nation's income in 1974, it now owns only 13% of it (Ashkenaz, 2016). Some civil rights issues have been partly redressed by civil rights legislation of the 1960s, but the slaying of many African American males coupled with widespread discrimination in employment against pre-seniors and seniors, disabled persons, persons of color, women, immigrants, low-income people, LGBT persons, and others puts to rest the myth that discrimination is not still a problem in the United States. The nation has two segregated school systems: one for inner city persons of color, and one for affluent suburban Whites who increasingly attend private schools, charter schools, or public schools with better facilities. Suburban schools reimburse their teachers at higher rates than school systems in low-income areas as I discussed in Chapter 7.

We live in an era with extreme economic inequality, a disappearing middle class, and extensive poverty. Staggering numbers of Americans rely on safety-net programs (Jansson, 2016). Mitt Romney, the Republican presidential candidate in 2012, blamed people using safety-net programs when he was secretly taped praising the "makers" (about 53% of the population) and criticized the "takers" (about 47% of the population) (Corn, 2013). If "makers," he argued, do not need support from social programs because they work so hard, "takers" use government programs at numerous points in their lives, he contended, including Food Stamps, Medicaid, Medicare, Unemployment Insurance, housing programs, mental health and substance abuse services, and Social Security (Corn, 2013). Romney was incorrect, however, because many people need government resources for reasons not related to their character. Members of the various vulnerable populations need resources and services, such as the 46.5 million persons who received Food Stamps in January 2012; 56 million Americans in 2011 (or 18% of the population) who used retirement benefits or who were surviving spouses, disabled people, and dependents; 5 million disabled persons who used the Supplemental Security Income benefits (SSI) in 2011; 6.5 million persons who used the Earned Income Tax Credit in 2009; 20 million Americans who received health insurance from the Affordable Care Act in 2016; 54 million Americans who were Medicare beneficiaries in 2014; and 74 million persons (or 1 in 5 Americans) who used Medicaid and the Children's Health Insurance Program (CHIP) in November 2016.

Inequities are piled on top of one another as discussed in Chapter 8. While well-educated and affluent people receive pensions from their corporate or professional jobs, low-income people mostly don't receive private pensions, or the tax advantages they bring. While White people often inherit considerable resources that are not taxed or only lightly taxed, people in the bottom 50% inherit nothing or not very much. While affluent people receive their healthcare from corporate or institutional health plans that are heavily subsidized by federal tax concessions to their employers, poor people rely on means-tested programs like Medicaid or do without. Even after the ACA removed roughly 20 million persons from the ranks of the medically uninsured, more than 30 million persons still lack health insurance (Collins, Gunja & Beutel, 2015). While affluent White people can write off their mortgage interest payments against income when they pay taxes, renters can't write their rent payments off against their taxes as discussed in Chapter 8.

Addams, too, faced political challenges. She encountered millionaires and billionaires who dominated the political process and often resorted to bribing public officials. She came to realize that the Democratic and Republican parties of that era did not represent the needs of immigrants, and workers, so she teamed with Teddy Roosevelt to form the Progressive Party only to be defeated by Democrat Woodrow Wilson in 1912 (Jansson, 2015).

We, too, encounter political challenges. Neither of the major parties has been highly responsive to the ten hypothesized causes of income inequality. Barack Obama rarely uttered the word poverty during his presidency even though he ranked income inequality as one of the four most important problems in the United States in his final speech before he left office. (Transcript of Obama's Farewell Speech, 2017). Hillary Clinton may never have uttered it during her campaign for the presidency in 2016 (Appelbaum, 2016; August 11). Republicans have sought to cut the already poorly funded social programs of the United States—and even to end the Affordable Care Act with a replacement version that would have removed 23 million people from coverage.

Many blue-collar Whites switched from the Democratic to the Republican Party in the presidential election of 2016 because they believed Democrats took them for granted. It was Bernie Sanders, alone, who said to an African American audience in Maryland in the final weeks of his 2016 campaign for the Democratic presidential nomination:

> Poverty is a death sentence. They say, 'Well, you're poor, that's not good because you don't have a fancy TV or go out to eat. That's not the issue. If you are born in Baltimore's poorest neighborhood, your life expectancy is almost 20 years shorter than if you were born in its wealthiest neighborhood (Atwood, 2016).

He added that 15 neighborhoods in Baltimore have lower life expectancies than North Korea, and two of them have a higher infant mortality rate than the West Bank (Atwood, 2016).

This indifference took place despite the omnipresence of poverty in the United States, reported to affect 43.1 million people in 2015 (Jansson, 2016). It infiltrates all of the vulnerable populations we have discussed to this point, including children, young adults, seniors, disabled persons, persons of color, Whites in rural areas and distressed towns and cities, former felons, women, and single mothers. It is spread across the nation: nine states have poverty rates exceeding 17% and 11 states have poverty rates between 15% and 17% (The State of Poverty, Poverty Map accessed at povertyusa.org on 2/6/17). Poverty profoundly interacts with longevity and incidence of many diseases. It impacts mental health. It is linked to various disabilities. Its economic toll on the United States is so huge as to not be measurable, including excess health costs, cost of criminal justice, family violence, disunited families, substance abuse, mental health problems, and many other problems.

It would be historically inaccurate, however, to argue that important differences don't exist between the two major political parties from the New Deal onward. Chapters 3 and 4 documented that Democrats dominated presidencies and congresses during the period of relative economic equality from the early 1930s through the 1970s, when most social programs of the American welfare state and most of the nation's civil rights were enacted. Sometimes, bipartisan agreements were fashioned, but Democrats often had little support from Republicans. Republicans dominated presidencies and the Congress during period 4 from the early 1980s to the present time when far less social and civil rights legislation was enacted, and when an anti-spending and anti-regulatory ethos prevailed. Even Democratic presidents Bill Clinton and Barack Obama had little legislative success when confronted by large Republican majorities in the Congress.

Just when the nation seemed ready to move back toward greater equality, it encountered the maverick presidency of Donald Trump. I've argued that, when his histrionics are removed, he is a conservative person who ended up in the Republican Party after belonging to the Democratic and then the Reform Party. He gained the remarkable allegiance of blue-collar Whites, only to betray them with repeated policy decisions. He endorsed a version of the Republican's proposed alternative to the ACA that would particularly harm White working-class people many of whom voted for him (Levey, 2017). He proposed a tax plan on September 27, 2017 that disproportionately benefited the wealthy class only to propose a similar tax plan in November that was enacted by the Congress on December 20, 2017.

Developing a Coherent Structure for Combating Extreme Income Inequality

If Barack Obama's assessment was correct in his valedictorian presidential address in January 2017, income inequality is one of the top four problems encountered by the United States. It requires a coherent structure that includes at least five levels: a cadre of public officials who place the issue on their agendas; policy entrepreneurs who take leadership roles in legislatures at local; state; and federal levels; proposal designers; and community advocates.

This book innovates a broad approach to redressing inequality. It identifies 16 marginalized populations. It discusses the need for a coherent structure for combating extreme income inequality. It identifies 16 professions whose members can work to redress income inequality. It contends that most Grand Challenges cannot be adequately addressed without linking them to extreme income inequality because they are linked to poverty and other hypothesized causes of extreme income inequality.

A Cadre of Enlightened Public Officials

A cadre of public officials needs to be developed that prioritize redressing extreme income inequality. They need to understand the magnitude of income inequality in the United States not just in general, but as it impacts disproportionately at least 16 populations discussed in Chapter 1. They need to find ways to publicize the issue, educate fellow legislators about it, and secure media coverage of it.

Policy Entrepreneurs

Policy entrepreneurs need to be identified who assume leadership in moving promising IUOPs and RUOPs through the legislative process. Presidential candidates need to be identified who know about and prioritize extreme income inequality. Senator Bernie Sanders placed income inequality on the policy agenda during the presidential campaign of 2016. Barack Obama declared income inequality to be one of the nation's four most-serious problems in his valedictory speech.

Proposal Designers from Multiple Professions and Disciplines

Income inequality can be addressed by policies in at least eight policy sectors that, taken together, constitute the American welfare state. They include:

- Safety-net programs redistribute resources to marginalized populations
- Mental health services help persons with mental conditions join the workforce
- Health professionals increase longevity and address chronic health conditions that impede involvement in the work force
- Educational innovations help low-income persons obtain credentials and knowledge that allow them to be upwardly mobile
- Gerontologists devise strategies that allow seniors to remain in the workforce
- Child and family policies help youth become productive members of society, such as foster children who "emancipate" at age 18

- Criminal and juvenile justice systems develop policies that allow incarcerated persons to integrate into society
- Immigration policies, such as DACA, help immigrants obtain education and a path to citizenship

Income inequality falls within the province of (at least) 16 professions and disciplines that are listed in this book's preface. Leaders and researchers in these 16 professions and disciplines should be designers of IUOPs, RUOPs, and Fair Exchanges. Many existing research centers should also be integrated into this coherent structure, including think tanks like the Center on Budget and Policy Priorities and the Urban-Brookings Tax Policy Center. Many universities have research centers including the Center on Poverty and Inequality at Stanford, the Multidisciplinary Program in Inequality and Social Policy at Harvard, the Center for Equitable Growth at UC Berkeley, the Institute on Inequality and Democracy at UCLA Luskin, the Blum Center for Poverty Alleviation at UC Irvine, the Center for the Study of Wealth and Inequality and the Center for Social Inequalities and Health at Columbia University, the UC Davis Center for Poverty Research, the Stone Center on Socio-Economic Inequality of the Graduate Center of the City University of New York and the West Coast Poverty Center at the University of Washington.

Community Advocates

A network of community advocates is needed to put pressure on public officials to prioritize enacting, funding and monitoring policies and programs that can decrease income inequality. Community advocates need to educate the public about the sheer extent of income inequality in the United States and why this is a serious social problem. This network only minimally exists in the United States.

Community advocates should include outreach to those affluent people, evangelicals, and others who have traditionally opposed greater economic equality.

Grassroots movements need to be developed such as "Share Our Wealth" that was organized by Senator Huey Long in 1934. At least five social movements arose during the first year of the Trump Presidency including the Sanctuary Campus Movement, the Defend Science Movement, the Feminist Pro-Choice Movement, the Anti-Islamophobia Movement, and the LGBTQ Movement. The mobilization of African Americans to defeat Roy Moore and elect Doug Jones can be considered as a movement in defense of civil rights in Alabama in November and December 2017 just as Black Lives Matter protested the unwarranted killing of persons of color from the slaying of Travon Martin in 2012 to the present.

Integrating Mechanisms

Methods of linking the different levels of this coherent structure need to be invented and funded. These disparate movements, intellectual products, organized centers, and social movements need to find ways to identify legislation that they can prioritize and pressure legislators to enact. Equality advocates have to make common cause with Reverend William Barber's populist interracial coalition against poverty that revives Martin Luther Kings' battle against poverty and militarism (Cobb, 2018)—as well as other efforts to cut across the 16 subpopulations that experience extreme inequality. They also need to block legislation that increases extreme income inequality as witnessed by regressive taxes enacted by Republicans in late 2017.

A Web Site

This book will have a companion web site that will initially discuss new developments and research findings that supplement content of this book. The web site is: **uplifting ordinary people.org**. Please submit abstracts of IUOPs, RUOPs, and Fair Exchanges to be added to the web site.

Linking Income Inequality with Other Social Problems

We need to understand with more precision not only the genesis of extreme income inequality, but its links with other major social problems such as the other 12 Grand Challenges identified by the American Academy of Social Policy & Social Welfare. They are:

1. Ensure healthy development for all youth
2. Close the health gap

3. Stop family violence
4. Advance long and productive lives
5. Eradicate social isolation
6. End homelessness
7. Create social responses to changing environments
8. Harness technology for social good
9. Promote smart decarceration
10. Reduce extreme economic inequality
11. Build financial capability for all
12. Achieve equal opportunity and justice

We have already implicated inequality and poverty as contributing to the development of poorer health for persons in the lower economic strata, including insuring health development for all youth (#1), closing the health gap (#2), and advancing long and productive lives (#4). It contributes to inability to build financial capability for all (#11) to the extent that extreme inequality, poverty, and lack of upward mobility make it difficult for many people in the lower strata to increase their resources. Banks and same-day lenders discriminate against many persons of color. We can hypothesize that extreme inequality and poverty increase the odds that people in the lower economic strata will not be able to achieve equality opportunity and justice (#12), as they cannot move upward in the economic order.

The nexus between homelessness (#6) and extreme income inequality is clear. Both homelessness and economic inequality are exacerbated by favors given to economic elites such as in the housing industry. Developers and landlords are rarely subject to rent controls or requirements that they include significant numbers of affordable housing units in their new construction. They receive tax concessions when they replace older units with more expensive units. They often evict tenants when they modernize units. They build and market mansions in neighborhoods, demolishing affordable housing with impunity. They flip houses with substantial write-offs. Vast swaths of American cities lack affordable housing. Low- and moderate-income families commute hours each day to work due to lack of affordable housing near their workplaces. Many municipalities and counties engage in a losing battle against homelessness. They build affordable units only to find several years later that private markets have placed more units out of the reach of tenants than governmental entities have constructed. Minus preemption of land by cities and governments for rental housing *plus* rent control *plus* greatly increased resources for new construction targeted to affordable units *plus* enhanced job training, placement, and job mentoring services for persons with mental and substance abuse problems *plus* higher levels of income for persons in the bottom economic strata, homelessness is likely to remain high among persons who cannot find affordable units in many urban areas. The nation's inequality is increased, as well, by excessive spending on housing by low-paid workers—even as much as 90% of their earnings (Desmond, 2016).

Extreme income inequality may increase family violence (#3) to the extent that it induces hopelessness and desperation among low-income males who fear they cannot improve their unequal condition in a society with maldistribution of income. Their poverty may rob them of self-respect. Their hopelessness may increase the likelihood that they will make excessive use of alcohol and drugs that, in turn, often lead to violent behaviors in their families. Extreme income inequality may enhance isolation (#5) among specific subgroups of the American population as Eberstadt (2017) believes takes place with blue-collar White males who often withdraw from the community when they have lost their jobs.

This discussion suggests that extreme income inequality is linked in complex ways to many other major social problems. Persons who analyze these 11 social problems in addition to extreme, economic inequality might benefit from using this book as an overview of the policy landscape of the United States. They, too, will need to identify an array of possible solutions. They, too, will need to write policy briefs. They, too, will need to find ways to finance their policy proposals. They will also have to navigate them through legislative systems.

Members of the 16 at-risk populations share extreme income inequality, as well as many of the other Grand Challenges. They possibly share the hypothesized ten causes of extreme income inequality including toxic effects of extreme income inequality itself, poverty, lack of upward mobility, lack of hope, discrimination, and lack of access to social and economic opportunities and resources. Members of these at-risk populations have been sufficiently preoccupied with their own problems that they often haven't worked with members and leaders of other at-risk populations. They are all in the same boat, even with many of the White blue-collar persons who helped Donald Trump gain the White House.

Returning to Politics

Equality advocates will need to participate in the electoral process to elect public officials who will seek ways to decrease extreme income inequality. The challenge is to place their IUOPs and RUOPs, on the policy agendas of the general public and public officials. They have to hear constituents, advocates, and advocacy groups—over and over again. They need to see drafts of IUOPs and RUOPs. They need to see op-ed pieces and letters to editors. They need to meet advocates in person rather than just on social media. That's how advocates gained traction on many other issues. That's how advocates defeated Republicans' efforts to repeal and replace the ACA with versions that would have increased economic inequality (Jansson, 2018).

Push comes to shove when public officials make equality a campaign issue. Recall that when conservatives wanted to repeal the ACA, they incessantly told supporters that, if they were elected, they would repeal Obamacare. Conversely, Barack Obama frequently promised his supporters that he would reform healthcare when he ran for the presidency in 2008. Equality advocates have to aim for the same goal: to make equality not an esoteric concept but a vital part of the political process by participating in campaigns and electoral politics by participating in grassroots campaigns that cut across the 16 populations discussed in Chapter 1, lobbying, and political campaigns (Cobb, 2016). They might also invite others to accompany them as they ride the Equality Roller Coaster downward.

References

Appelbaum, B. (2016; August 11). "The millions of Americans Donald Trump and Hillary Clinton barely mention: The Poor." *New York Times*. Accessed at https://www.nytimes.com/2016/08/12/us/politics/trump-clinton-poverty.html?mcubz …

Appelbaum, B. (2017; September 27). Trump tax plan benefits wealthy, including Trump. *New York Times*. Accessed @ https://nyti.ms/2yu2M6i

Ashkenaz, J. (2016; December 16). Nine new findings about inequality in the United States. *New York Times*. Accessed at https://www.nytimes.com/ … /2016/ … /16/ … /nine-new-findings-about-income-inequality-p …

Atwood, K. (2016: May 3). *Why is Bernie Sanders suddenly talking more about poverty?* Retrieved from http://www.cbsnews.com/news/why-is-bernie-sanders-suddenly-talking-about-poverty/.

Barnes, J., Baumann, D. & Cohen, R. "Surplus politics," *National Journal* (March 3, 2001), pp. 624–627.

Bedard, P. (2017, June 18). "Poll: Trump's approval higher than Congress." *Washington Examiner*. Accessed on September 28, 2017 @ washingtonexaminer.com

Cobb, J. (2018; May 14). "The Southern strategist: The Reverend William Barber's effort to build a populist interracial coalition against poverty." *The New Yorker*, pp. 68-75).

Collins, S.R., Gunja M.Z., & Beutel, S. (2015; September 16). New census data show the number of uninsured Americans dropped by 8.8 million [Blog post]. Retrieved from www.commonwealthfund.org.

Canon, L. (1991). *President Reagan: The role of a lifetime*. New York: Simon & Schuster.

Committee for a Responsible Federal Budget (2017; September 27). "Big 6 tax framework could cost $2.2 trillion. Accessed at www.crfb.org/blogs/big-6-tax-framework-could-cost-22-trillion

Corn, D. (2013; March 4). "Mitt Romney's 'twisted' defense of his 47 percent rant." *Mother Jones*. Accessed @https://www.google.com/search?source=h ... 22/29/30k1j33i 160k1j33i21k1.0.fjkDH_n7UR4

Delk, J. (2017; June 20). Poll: Few Americans approve withdrawal from Paris agreement. *The Hill*. Accessed @ thehill.com/ ... /338550-poll-few-americans-support-us-withdrawal-from-paris-climate

DeParle, J. (2012, January 4). Harder for Americans to rise from lower rungs. *New York Times*. Accessed @newyorktimes.com/2012/01

Desmond, M. (2016). *Evicted: Poverty and Profit in the American City* (Random House).

Eberstadt, N.N. (2017, February 21). Our miserable 21st century, *Commentary*. Retrieved from https://aei.org/publication/oour-miserable-21st-century

Jansson, B. (2015). *The Reluctant Welfare State, 8th Edition*. Boston: Cengage.

Jansson, B. (2018). *The Reluctant Welfare State*, 9th Edition. Boston: Cengage

Jansson, B. (2016). *Social welfare policy and advocacy: Advancing social justice through 8 policy sectors*. Sage: Thousand Oaks, CA, pp. 245–289.

Kelly, M., Kessler G., & Lee, M. (2017; August 22). President Trump's list of false and misleading claims tops 1,000. *Washington Post*. Accessed at https://www.washingtonpost.com/ ... /president-trumps-list-of-false-and-misleading-claims ...

Levey, N. (2017: March 12). Obamacare replacement hits Trump voters hard. *Los Angeles Times*, A1, A10.

McCaskill, N. (2017; April 11). Trump overstates job creation in his administration. *Politico*. Accessed at www.politico.com/story/2017/04/trump-overstates-job-creation-237110

Piketty T. (2014). *Capital in the Twenty-first Century (A. Golhammer, Trans.)*. Cambridge, MA: Harvard University Press.

Reich, R. (2017; September 27). Robert Reich's comments on Anderson Cooper panel.

Saez, E. (2009). Striking it richer: The evolution of top incomes in the United States (update with 2007 estimates). http://elsas.berkeley.edu/~saez/saez-UStopincomes-2010.pdf.

Tax Policy Center of the Urban Institute and Brookings Institution (2015). Tax Policy Center Briefing Book.

Transcript of Obama's Farewell Speech (2017; January 10). *Los Angeles Times*. Accessed at www.latimes.com/ ... ?la-pol-obama-farewell-speech-transcript-20170110-story.html

Trump, D. (2017; September 27). Donald Trump's press conference on CNN at 12:30 PM.

Vance, J. D. (2016). *Hillbilly Elegy*. New York: Harper.

Wilkinson R. & Pickett, K (2009). Income inequality and social dysfunction. *Annual Review of Sociology*, 35, 493–511.

INDEX

A

ACA. *See* Affordable Care Act (ACA)
Addams, Jane, 67, 259–261
affluent people
  and income inequality, 7
  FDR and, 88–91
  Great Depression and, 84
  tax paid by, 12
Affordable Care Act (ACA), 34, 126, 150, 231
  described, 131
  enactment of, 138
  Trump on, 128, 158–159, 254–255
African Americans, 19, 97, 99, 104, 121
  civil rights, 104–105
  discrimination against, 60
  Roy Moore and, 160–161, 250, 265
  sharecropping system and, 60
  trade unions and, 86
Age Discrimination Act of 1967, 105
agrarian economy, 53
Agricultural Adjustment Agency, 80
Aid to Families with Dependent Children (AFDC) program, 102, 109, 115–116, 140
American Revolution, 45–46
American squatters, 43
Americans with Disabilities Act, 112, 130, 138, 198
Asian Americans, 20–21
  immigration to United States, 59
  prejudice against, 154

B

Balfanz, Robert, 206–207, 212, 216–217
Boomers, 27
Brown v. Board of Education, 104, 179

Buckley, William, 107
Bush, George H. W., 102
  Civil Rights Act of 1964 and, 142
  political miscue of, 112–113
  tax cuts and, 149–150
Bush, George W., 102, 229
  Equality Roller Coaster and, 117–121
  tax cuts and, 118, 142
  war on global terrorism and, 119–120

C

California Gold Rush, 56
The Campbell Collaboration, 214
Capitalism and Freedom (Friedman), 107
Carter, Jimmy, 103, 106–107, 250
CCC. *See* Civilian Conservation Corps (CCC)
Cheney, Dick, 113
children, in poverty-stricken families, 25
Chinese Exclusion Act of 1882, 59
Chrysler Corporation, 91
cities
  as industrial centers, 61
  growth of, 53–55
"Civic Marshall Plan to Build a Grad(uation) Nation", 206–207, 217
Civilian Conservation Corps (CCC), 79
Civilian Works Administration (CWA), 79
Civil Rights Acts of 1964, 97, 104
Civil Rights Acts of 1965, 97, 104
Civil War, 46
  discrimination and, 57–58
  Native Americans and, 58
  slave emancipation, 60

Clinton, Bill
  Equality Roller Coaster and, 113–114
  staying power of the ten causes of inequality from Reagan through, 128–132
Clinton, Hillary, 214
Cold War, 90–91, 91–95, 97–98, 113, 139, 148
colonial mercantilism, 62–63
colonial period
  Equality Roller Coaster and, 48, 50–52
  income inequality in, 41–52
community advocates, 265–266
community-based public health, 202
Comprehensive Employment and Training Act (CETA), 101
Comprehensive Employment Training Act (CETA), 101, 109
Conrad, Paul, 108
Cooper, David, 220
cumulative toxic effects, 8–10
CWA. *See* Civilian Works Administration (CWA)

D

Darwin, Charles, 65
DDS. *See* domestic discretionary spending (DDS)
deaths of despair, 9
Declaration of Independence, 45
Department of Housing and Urban Development (HUD), 97
Dewey, John, 67
Dickens, Charles, 55
discrimination, 9
  against African Americans, 60
  against Native Americans, 41, 51
  and income inequality, 4–5
  Civil War and, 57–58
  New Deal and, 85–86
  women, 20
Dix, Dorothea, 47
domestic discretionary spending (DDS), 228–229
Douthat, Ross, 224
dropout rates, school, 208–209

E

early warning systems (EWSs), 207
Earned Income Tax Credit, 96, 103, 106, 108, 125, 139–140, 163, 171–172
economic uplifting
  of the lower 50% during the 1950s, 91–96
  of the lower 50% during World War II, 91–96
Education for All Handicapped Children Act of 1975, 101
education level, and income inequality, 23
Eisenhower, Dwight
  Equality Roller Coaster remaining low during, 93–96
  Interstate Highway System and, 181
  unpaid debt, inherited by, 90–91
Elementary and Secondary Education Act (ESEA), 97, 212
employment
  IUOPs, 181
  long-term unemployed people and, 181
  low-income youth and, 181
enclosures, 41
English Enlightenment, 42
entitlement expenditures, 230
equality
  factors causing transitions between periods of inequality and, 143–146
  sustaining periods of, 146–155
equality advocates
  and political system, 257–258
  criteria for selecting IUOPs, 164–168
  future role of, 258–259
Equality Roller Coaster
  ascended from 1982 to the present, 106–108
  Barack Obama and, 121–127
  Bush, 117–121
  causes of movements from period 3 to period 4, 137–140
  Clinton and, 113–114
  colonial period and, 48, 50–52
  Donald Trump and, 127–128
  during 1920s, 69–70
  from Pearl Harbor to 1960, 88–91
  history revealing about the trajectory

of, 132
new policies for a new era, 160
Obama and, 121–127
period 5, beginning of, 155–160
rapid ascent from 1865 to 1929, 60–69
Reagan and, 108–109
rise of, 52–56
ten causes from 1865 to 1932, 70–73
Trump and, 127–128
ESEA. *See* Elementary and Secondary Education Act (ESEA)
European Union (EU), 228
evidence-Based IUOPs, 255
EWSs. *See* early warning systems (EWSs)
Executive Order 9066, 86

F

Fair Exchanges, funding IUOPs with, 236–241
Fair Labor Standards Act of 1938, 80
Falwell, Jerry, 107
Faubus, Orval, 113
FDIC. *See* Federal Deposit Insurance Corporation (FDIC)
Federal Deposit Insurance Corporation (FDIC), 79
Federal Emergency Relief Administration (FERA), 78–79
Federal Home Administration Act (FHA), 79
Federal Housing Administration, 94
FERA. *See* Federal Emergency Relief Administration (FERA)
FHA. *See* Federal Home Administration Act (FHA)
Firing Line, 107
Folks, Homer, 68
Food Stamps Program, 101–103, 108–110, 116, 125, 140, 170
Ford, Gerald, 103, 141
Fourteenth Amendment, 61
French Revolution, 46
Friedman, Milton, 107, 169

G

Gentlemen's Agreement of 1907, 59
Gen Xers, 27

G.I. Bill, 93. *See also* Servicemen's Readjustment Act of 1944
Gilded Age, 40, 60, 62–63, 91, 109, 126, 128, 145, 155, 248, 259
Gingrich, Newt, 115
Gini coefficient, 57
Goldwater, Barry, 97
government job training and placement programs, 184–185
government resources
low levels of, 7
scarcity, 18–19
Gramm-Rudman-Hollings measure, 110
Great Depression, 39–40, 69, 76–78, 91, 94, 96, 122–125, 137–139, 142–143, 145, 155–159, 181, 248, 251
affluent Americans and, 84
income inequality and, 84–88
Great Recession of 2007, 229
Great Society, 97–98, 100–101, 105, 140
Griswold v. Connecticut, 105

H

Hamilton, Alexander, 47
Harding, Warren, 69–70
hard right
emergence in 1994, 114–117
Republican Party and, 159, 252
Head Start Program, 97, 167, 201, 216–217
heath system. *See also* Affordable Care Act (ACA)
lack of, 59
public hospitals system, 73
Hispanics, 19–20
historical evolution, of income inequality, 39–40
homelessness, 23–24
Hoover, Herbert, 248
Housing and Community Development Act of 1974, 101
Humphrey, Hubert, 100
Hyde Amendment, 105

I

immigrants, 22
immigration

to the United States, 61
unions and, 64
income equality, campaign for, 255–256
Income Equality Roller Coaster, 39–40
income inequality
   affluent people and, 7
   causes/hypotheses, 1–8, 255–256
   coherent structure for combating, 263
   discrimination and, 4–5
   extreme, in United States, 10–18
   government resources and, low levels of, 7
   in 1920s, 248–252
   in 1930s, 84–88
   in colonial period, 41–52
   Index of Social Problems score and, 14–15
   IUOPs and, 168–170
   low levels of upward mobility, 3
   person's level of hope, 4
   political system and, 8
   politics and, 140–143
   poor health and, 6–7
   poverty and, 3
   rivals levels in social classes, 2–3
   school dropout rate and, 208
   social problems and, 266–268
   sustaining periods of, 146–155
   ten causes, from 1950 to 1979, 103–106
   ten causes from Reagan through Clinton, 128–132
   transitions between periods of equality and, 143–146
Income Tax Credit of 1975, 101
Indentured servants, 50
Index of Social Problems score, 14–15
industries, growth of, 53–55
Initiatives to Uplift Ordinary Persons (IUOPs), 10
   addressing access to opportunities, 200–202
   addressing barriers to graduation from colleges, 186–187
   addressing barriers to graduation from secondary schools, 186–187
   causes of high dropout rate and, 209–210
   challenges of, 219–224
   civil rights legislation for disabled people and, 198–199
   conceptualizing, 206–224
   cost estimation, 215–216
   criteria for evaluating, 164
   criteria for selecting, 164–168
   decreasing loss of jobs to other nations, 195–196
   diminishing use of part-time workers, 180–181
   discrimination and, 198–200
   diverting juveniles from institutions and camps, 188–189
   dropout rates and, 208
   empirical evidence for, 210–214
   enforcing rights of LGBT persons in military, 199–200
   facilitating "smart decarceration", 189–190
   funding of, 217, 233–235
   funding of community-based public health and, 202
   funding steps toward universal healthcare, 202
   giving option to move to new places, 178–179
   helping people avoid dead-end trajectories, 188–189
   identifying core problem, 208
   improving access to healthcare in rural areas, 201–202
   income inequality and, 168–170
   increasing job and wage growth, 194–195
   inequality and, 208
   lack of upward mobility and, 176–197
   linking NGOs and public agencies with government programs, 184–185
   low levels of hope and, 197–198
   menu of, 168–175
   overview of, 163–168
   persons with disabilities in jobs and, 190–192
   place-based, 192–194, 221–223
   placing on paper, 203
   political feasibility of, 217–218
   population-based, 223–224
   position in American system of governance, 217

positive outcomes, 216
poverty and near-poverty, decreasing, 170–175
preparing to succeed in economy, 185–186
providing construction jobs, 181
providing employment to long-term unemployed people, 181
providing employment to low-income youth, 181
providing geographic access to quality jobs, 187
rationing options and, 214–215
regulations, 219–221
removing barriers to trade unions, 196
removing disincentives to work, 186
rescuing people from downward trajectories, 187–188
restoring funding of Head Start, 201
revising trade treaties, 177–178
Stimulus Program and, 182
technology and, 183–184
training younger workers to replace aging workers, 184
unemployment and, 182–183
upgrading and integrating schools, 179–180
upgrading professions, 190
Interstate Commerce Commission, 62
Interstate Highway Act of 1956, 94
IUOPs. *See* Initiatives to Uplift Ordinary Persons (IUOPs)

J

Japanese Americans, 86
Jefferson, Thomas, 46–47
Jim Crow laws, 71–72, 86
Johnson, Lyndon, 216
  Equality Roller Coaster remaining low during, 96–99
  Great Society program, 97–98, 100–101, 105, 140
  market policy innovations and, 216–217
  tax cuts and, 98–99
  welfare state and, 106, 142
Jones, Doug, 250

K

Kennedy, John, 96–99
Knights of Labor, 64
Koch, Charles, 95
Koch, David, 95
Koch, Fred, 95
Korean War, 90–91, 91–95, 139, 148
Ku Klux Klan, 86

L

labor income, 33
Laffer, Arthur, 107–108
LGBT population, 24–25, 199–200
Lincoln, Abraham, 58, 99, 126
Los Angeles Times, 108
low income persons, 25–26

M

Madison, James, 46
McGovern, George, 100
McKinley, William, 66
Meals on Wheels, 97
Medicaid, 96–98, 101–106, 115–116, 125, 131, 138–140, 158–160, 167, 172, 201–202, 250, 261
Medicare, 96–98, 101–106, 115–116, 125, 131, 138–140, 158–160, 167, 172, 201–202, 218
Medicare-for-All, 202
Mexican Revolution of 1910, 72
Millennials, 27
Model Cities Program, 221
Moore, Roy, 160–161, 250, 265
Morris, Dick, 113
Mothers Pension, 72–73

N

NAFTA. *See* North American Free Trade Agreement (NAFTA)
National Recovery Act of 1933 (NRA), 79
National War Labor Board, 92
Native Americans, 20
  Civil War and, 58
  death from diseases, 49–50
  discrimination against, 41, 51

negative externalities
   defined, 216
   IUOP and, 217–220
   place-based IUOPs and, 222
New Deal, 78, 81, 92
   discrimination and, 85–86
NGOs. *See* non-government agencies (NGOs)
Nineteenth Amendment, 72
Nixon, Richard, 100–103
non-government agencies (NGOs), 184–185, 188, 212, 214, 217
North American Free Trade Agreement (NAFTA), 253
Northern Securities Company, 66
Northwest Ordinance of 1787, 49
NRA. *See* National Recovery Act of 1933 (NRA)

O

Obama, Barack, 261–262
   Equality Roller Coaster and, 121–127
   on income inequality, 11
Obamacare. *See* Affordable Care Act (ACA)
Occupational Safety and Health Administration (OSHA), 101
Occupy Wall Street Movement, 250
O'Connor v. Donaldson, 105
OECD. *See* Organization for Economic Co-operation and Development (OECD)
Older Americans Act, 97
Omnibus Budget Reconciliation Act, 109
Opportunity Trust Fund, 241–243
Organization for Economic Co-operation and Development (OECD), 4, 16
OSHA. *See* Occupational Safety and Health Administration (OSHA)

P

Panic of 1819, 53–54
part-time workers, 180–181
Perot, Ross, 113–114
Personal Responsibility and Work Opportunities Act, 115
persons with disability, 23

place-based IUOPs, 192–194, 221–223
policy entrepreneurs, 264
Political Strategies to Uplift Ordinary Persons (PSUOPs), 10
political system, and income inequality, 8
politics
   inequality and, 140–143
   Roosevelt and, 148–149
population-based IUOPs, 223–224
poverty
   and colonial America, 50–51
   and income inequality, 3
   and recessions, 71
   as personal failure, 64
   Great Depression and, 137
   increase in, 57
   initiatives to uplift ordinary people (IUOPs) and, 170–175
   Native Americans, 20
Professional Air Traffic Controllers Organization, 111
proposal designers, 264–265
prostitution, 55
PSUOPs. *See* Political Strategies to Uplift Ordinary Persons (PSUOPs)
public agencies, 184–185
public officials, 264
Pullman strike of 1894, 66

R

Reagan, Ronald, 229, 241
   cutting resources of the bottom 50%, 109–112
   Equality Roller Coaster and, 108–109
   ten causes of inequality, 128–132
Red Scare, 95
refugees, 41
Regents of the University of California v. Bakke, 101
Rehabilitation Act of 1973, 101, 105
Reich, Robert, 114
Republican Party, 159, 252
Resources to Uplift Ordinary People (RUOPs), 10
   budget priorities and, 227–233
   creation of Opportunity Trust Fund and, 241–243

defined, 226
efforts to enact, 256
evaluating, 243–244
funding IUOPs with Fair Exchanges and, 236–241
IUOPs funding and, 233–235
minimizing budgetary attacks on IUOPs, 235–236
types of, 227
Roe v. Wade, 105
Roosevelt, Eleanor, 87
Roosevelt, Franklin Delano (FDR), 88
   African Americans and, 86
   economic elites and, 88–91
   emergency assistance during Great Depression, 76–84
   Great Depression and, 251
   New Deal, 78, 81
   on corporate profit taxes, 83
   welfare programs, 81
Roosevelt, Theodore, 66
Ruggles, William, 94
RUOPs. *See* Resources to Uplift Ordinary People (RUOPs)

S

Sanders, Bernie, 214, 219, 230, 251
schools
   dropout rate, 208–209
   IUOPs, 186–187
   upgrading and integrating, 179–180
sequestration, 235
Servicemen's Readjustment Act of 1944, 93. *See also* G.I. Bill
sharecropping system, 60
Sherman Antitrust Act, 62
slavery, 51
   legitimization of, 49
   Northerners on, 49
   Southerners on, 49
SNAP. *See* Supplemental Nutrition Assistance Program (SNAP)
social capital, 6
social classes, rivals levels of income inequality, 2–3
social policy, 41
social problems

and income inequality, 266–268
growth of, 55–56
social programs, 52
Social Progress Index of 2016, 16
Social Security, 92, 100–108, 115, 118–120, 139, 160
Social Security Act, 79, 86–87, 106, 152, 167
   Title XX of, 101
Social Security Trust Fund, 230
Spencer, Herbert, 65
"Square Deal", 66
SSI. *See* Supplementary Security Income Program (SSI)
stagflation, 107
Stimulus Program, 182
Stockman, David, 110, 241
strikes, 63–64
   Pullman strike of 1894, 66
subpopulations, and risk of extreme income inequality, 19–28
Supplemental Nutrition Assistance Program (SNAP), 220, 250
Supplementary Security Income Program (SSI), 100

T

Taft-Hartley Act, 95
tax expenditures, 237
technology, and IUOPs, 183–184
The National Review, 107
Title XX of the Social Security Act, 101
total income, inequality of, 33–34
trade treaties, 177–178
trade unions
   blue-collar wages and, 111
   decline in, 129
   IUOPs and, 175
   IUOPs removing barriers to, 196
Transitional Living (TL) Program, 176–177. *See also* YVLifeSet Program
Treaty of Guadalupe Hidalgo, 58
Truman, Harry, 93
   Equality Roller Coaster remaining low during, 93–96
Trump, Donald, 223, 229–231, 249–250
   affluent cabinet members, 251–252

Equality Roller Coaster and, 127–128
first year of presidency of, 127–128
on Obamacare, 254–255
policy failures of, 252
presidential campaign promises, 253–254

U

unemployment
   IUOPs developing entrepreneurial strategies to increase, 182–183
   physical or mental disabilities and, 190–191
unions, 63
   immigration and, 64
   trade. *See* trade unions
upward mobility, 26
   levels, and income inequality, 3
U.S. Constitution, 46

V

Vietnam War, 92, 97, 99–100, 107, 110, 113, 148
voting, 67

W

Wagner Act, 80–81, 86, 92, 95, 152
Wagner-Steagall Housing Act of 1937, 79
War on Poverty, 97, 106, 149
Washington, George, 47
wasteful expenditures, 244
wealth income, 33
White blue-collar persons, 22–23
women
   discrimination among, 20, 51–52
   Eleanor Roosevelt and, 87
   suffrage and, 72
Wood, Gordon, 45
World War II
   economic uplifting of the lower 50% during, 91–96
   Marshall Plan and, 217
   trade unions and, 94

Y

youth, in poverty-stricken families, 25

YVLifeSet Program, 176–177. *See also* Transitional Living (TL) Program